Series Editors:
Vincent Hoffmann-Martinot (Sciences Po Bordeaux)
Dario Castiglione (University of Exeter)

---

masters of political science

Edited by Donatella Campus and
Gianfranco Pasquino

© Campus and Pasquino 2009

First published by ECPR Press in 2009

ECPR Press is the publishing imprint of the European Consortium for Political Research (ECPR), a scholarly association, which supports and encourages the training, research and cross-national cooperation of political scientists in institutions throughout Europe and beyond. The ECPR's Central Services are located at Harbour House, 6-8 Hythe Quay, Colchester, CO2 8JF, UK

All rights reserved. No part of this book may be reprinted or reproduced or utilised in any form or by any electronic, mechanical, or other means, now known or hereafter invented, including photocopying and recording, or in any information storage or retrieval system, without permission in writing from the publishers.

Typeset by ECPR Press
Printed and bound by Lightning Source

British Library Cataloguing in Publication Data
A catalogue record for this book is available from the British Library

Paperback ISBN: 978-0-9558203-3-5

Also available in the Masters of Political Science series:

Maestri of Political Science, Volume 2
Edited by Martin Bull, Donatella Campus, Gianfranco Pasquino

Paperback ISBN: 978-1-9073011-9-3
Ebook ISBN: 978-1-910259-02-3

Maestri of Political Science, Volume 3
Edited by Martin Bull and Gianfranco Pasquino

Hardback ISBN: 978-1-9102592-3-8
Paperback ISBN: 978-1-910259-66-5

Please visit ecpr.eu/shop to browse the complete publications catalogue.

The Contributors

IAN BUDGE is Professor in the Department of Government at the University of Essex, where he founded the Essex Summer School in Social Science Data Analysis in 1968. He has been President of the European Consortium in Political Research between 1979–83. Among his recent publications, (with Klingemann et al.), *Mapping Policy Preferences: Estimates for Parties, Electorates and Governments 1945–1998* (2001), *Elections, Parties, Democracy: Conferring the Median Mandate* (with Michael D. McDonald) (2005); *The New British Politics* (Ian Budge, David McKay, Kenneth Newton and John Bartle) (2007).

DONATELLA CAMPUS is Associate Professor of Political Science at the University of Bologna. She is the author of *L'elettore pigro. Informazione politica e scelte di voto* (Mulino, 2000); *L'antipolitica al governo* (Mulino, 2006); *Comunicazione Politica: Le nuove Frontiere* (2008).

HANS DAALDER is Professor Emeritus at the University of Leiden. He has been one of the founders of the European Consortium of Political Research, of which he has been President between 1976 to 1979. Recently he edited *Comparative European Politics. The Story of a Profession* (1997; new paperback edition 1999).

DOMENICO FISICHELLA is a former Professor of Political Science at the University La Sapienza of Rome. He served in the Italian Senate (1994–2008) where has been Deputy Speaker for ten years. He was Minister of Cultural Affairs. Among his publications, *Istituzioni politiche. Struttura e pensiero* (1999); *Denaro e democrazia. Dall'antica Grecia all'economia globale* (2000); *Politica e mutamento sociale* (2002); *Elezioni e democrazia. Un'analisi comparata* (2003).

GIORGIO FREDDI is Professor Emeritus of Political Science at the University of Bologna. He has been President of the European Consortium of Political Research. Among his publications, *L'analisi comparata di sistemi burocratici pubblici* (1968); *Tensioni e conflitto nella magistratura* (1978); *Controlling Medical Professionals. The Comparative Politics of Health Governance* (1989); *Scienza dell'amministrazione e politiche pubbliche* (1989).

DIETER FUCHS is Professor of Political Science at the University of Stuttgart. Among his recent publications, *Citizens and the State* (con Hans-Dieter Klingemann) (1995); *The Democratic Culture of Unified Germany*, in Pippa Norris (ed.), *Critical Citizens: Global Support for Democratic Government* (1999); *Participatory Democracy and Political Participation. Can participatory engineering bring citizens back in?* (with Thomas Zittel) (2006). *Eurosceptisism. Images of Europe among Mass Publics and Political Elites* (with Raul Magni-Berton and Antoine Roger) (2008).

HANS-DIETER KLINGEMANN is Professor Emeritus, Social Science Research Center, Berlin. Among his recent publications: *Public Information Campaigns* (con A. Roemmele) (Sage Publications, 2001); *Mapping Policy Preferences* (con I. Budge et al) (Oxford University Press, 2001); Russell J. Dalton and Hans-Dieter Klingemann, eds. 2007. *The Oxford Handbook of Political Behavior* (2009); *The comparative Study of Electoral Systems* (2009).

URSULA HOFFMANN-LANGE is Professor of Political Science at the University of Bamberg. Among her publications *Social and Political Structures in West Germany. From Authoritarianism to Postindustrial Democracy* (Westview Press, 1991); *Eliten, Macht und Konflikt in der Bundesrepublik.* (Leske & Budrich, 1992); *Jugend und Demokratie in Deutschland* (Opladen: Leske & Budrich 1995).

KEIKO ONO (Ph.D. in political science from Georgetown University) is Assistant Professor in the Department of Political Science of Millikin University. Before returning to graduate school to pursue her degrees in political science, Ono worked as a journalist in Washington, D.C. She has published book chapters and articles on U.S. elections and public opinion.

ANGELO PANEBIANCO is Professor of International Relations at the University of Bologna. He also teaches Political Theory at S. Raffaele University of Milan. Among his recent publications, *Guerrieri democratici. Le democrazie e la politica di potenza* (1997), *Il potere, lo stato e la libertà* (2004); *L'automa e lo spirito* (2009).

GIANFRANCO PASQUINO is Professor of Political Science at the University of Bologna. He also teaches at the Bologna Center of the Johns Hopkins. Since 2005 he has been a member of the Accademia Nazionale dei Lincei. His most recent book is *Le istituzioni di Arlecchino* (2008, 5th ed.). He has also edited *L'Elezione del segretario, Organizzazione e potere* (2009).

PHILIPPE C. SCHMITTER is Professor Emeritus at the European University Institute. Department of Political and Social Sciences. He founded and directed the Center for European Studies at the University of Stanford. Among his publications: *Transitions from Authoritarian Rule: Prospects for Democracy* (with Guillermo O'Donnell) (4 vols.) (1986); *Governance in the European Union* (with Gary Marks, Fritz Scharpf and Wolfgang Streeck) (1996), *How to Democratize the European Union.... And Why Bother?* (2000).

CLYDE WILCOX is Professor in the Government Department at Georgetown, Washington. His research interests center on public opinion and electoral behavior, religion and politics, gender politics. His latest books include *Religion and Politics in Comparative Perspective* (2002); *The Financiers of Congressional Elections: Investors, Ideologues, and Intimates* (2003); *The Values Campaign: The Christian Right in the 2004 Elections*, coedited with John Green and Mark Rozell. (2006); *The Interest Group Society* (with M. Berry and Clyde Wilcox) (2008).

contents

Introduction
Donatella Campus and Gianfranco Pasquino   1

Chapter 1 – Robert Dahl: The Democratic Polyarchy
Domenico Fisichella   11

Chapter 2 – Anthony Downs: Master of Many Models
Ian Budge   37

Chapter 3 – David Easton: The Theory of the Political System
Dieter Fuchs and Hans-Dieter Klingemann   63

Chapter 4: S. E. Finer: The Erudite Individualist
Hans Daalder   85

Chapter 5 – Samuel P. Huntington: Political Order and the Clash of Civilizations
Gianfranco Pasquino   99

Chapter 6 – Juan J. Linz: An Intellectual and Personal Biography of the 'Maestro-Compositore'
Philippe C. Schmitter   121

Chapter 7 – Seymour Martin Lipset: Modernisation, Social Structure and Political Culture as Factors in Democratic Thought
Ursula Hoffmann-Lange   141

Chapter 8 – Giovanni Sartori: Democracy, Parties, Institutions
Gianfranco Pasquino   167

Chapter 9 – Sidney Verba: His Voice
Keiko Ono and Clyde Wilcox   179

Chapter 10 – Aaron Wildavsky: Civic Passion and Scientific Commitment
Giorgio Freddi   205

Chapter 11 – Morgenthau: Political Theory and Practical Philosophy
Angelo Panebianco   223

Index   239

Introduction
Donatella Campus and Gianfranco Pasquino

THE SELECTION

For a while now, political science as a discipline has been big enough (in terms of the number of academics) and analytically mature enough to justify reflections on and reviews of its achievements. In fact, there is no lack of general handbooks, dictionaries and 'state of the art' assessments (as well as 'reflective' journals such as the ECPR's own *European Political Science*), which are useful in helping us to understand and evaluate where we currently are and where we might still need to go. The focus of these texts, however, is on particular concepts, themes, research areas, institutions or behaviour (see, for example, Panebianco 1989; Goodin and Klingemann 1996; Pasquino 2001; *Comparative Political Studies*, Special Issue, 2000). What they rarely do is indulge in a critical reflection on the political scientists themselves, especially those who are commonly accepted as having made the most significant contributions to the growth of their discipline. Two exceptions to this are Daalder (1997) and Munck and Snyder (2007). The first consists of a series of accounts by key comparative political scientists concerning their professional development and the research they have undertaken. The second is a series of interviews by the Editors with key political scientists concerning their experiences. This book, in its focus, differs from both of these and therefore, in our view, fills an important gap in the growing reflective literature on the political science discipline: it consists of a series of 'objective' profiles of the 'Masters of Political Science', written by political scientists who have read and studied their work and who are therefore in a position to evaluate the nature of their contributions.

Of course, this immediately begs the question, what makes a 'Master'. For Norberto Bobbio (1981: 215–16) a 'classic author' is one to whom three specific achievements may be attributed:

a) he is considered as the one and only authentic interpreter of his times and his works are used as an indispensable tool for understanding them;
b) he is always contemporary, so that each age and generation feels the need to read and re-read his works and to give them fresh interpretation;
c) he has constructed model theories which are used over and over again

to understand reality, even when this differs from the reality in which his theories were derived and applied and with time these models have become actual mind-sets.

Bobbio's definition was formulated with a classic political scientist in mind about whom there can be no doubts: Max Weber. In this sense, a classic political scientist is different from a classic political science text, even if the production of the latter is normally essential to being considered the former. Inevitably, Bobbio's definition should be treated with caution, at least in relation to the authors chosen in this volume, simply because, for many, it may be too early to tell whether they are or will become 'classics' – even though Downs, at least, whose path-breaking book was published in 1957, could aspire to this title.

Yet, whether or not 'classics', we would be bold enough to assert that they are 'Masters'. The eleven political scientists whose contributions are presented and analysed in this volume offer an overall vision of what contemporary political science has been and is today, and it is a vision that is broad, articulated and pluralistic with regard to both their approach and analytical fields. Whether or not they are classics, the great thinkers whose analyses and contributions are discussed in the various chapters that follow have been chosen to represent the discipline as a whole, with its various themes and its variations through geographical location, national schools and perspectives. In addition, our selection is designed to represent both American scholars and different European nations.

Introducing these criteria suggests a less scientific approach to our final choice than might be expected, but our defence would be that many could be considered as potentially crossing the Masters' threshold, and that a representative sample of the discipline is therefore important. Indeed, we should, at this point, refer to the origins of this project, which are, for the most part, papers presented at a conference held in the Faculty of Political Science at Bologna University on 5–6 June 2003, a selection of which were subsequently published in a special issue of the journal *Rivista italiana di scienza politica* (3/2003), with the original choice being partly influenced by whether or not authors' works were easily accessible to Italian readers (hence the special issue containing only those papers about non-Italians). Understandably, therefore, in that collection there were good reasons (besides those of space) not to include some authors who might nevertheless stake a claim to Masters' status, for example: Gabriel Almond, Raymond Aron, Norberto Bobbio, Philip Converse, Karl Deutsch, Maurice Duverger, Carl Friedrich, Stanley Hoffman, Harold Lasswell, Paul Lazarsfeld, Theodore J. Lowi, Elinor Ostrom, William Riker, Stein Rokkan, Giovanni Sartori, Susan Strange, and so on.

For these reasons, at the same time as expanding the selection in this volume by including a chapter on Giovanni Sartori (whose exclusion from the original Italian project was due to the wide availability of his works in Italian and critical reflections on that work e.g. Pasquino 2005a), we have already embarked on a second volume of Masters to emphasise that the choices in the first volume are not exhaustive (and we have not, as yet, excluded the possibility of a third). However, it is important to convey the ECPR Press' gratitude and acknowledgement to the Italian political scientists and the *Rivista italiana di scienza politica* for the originality of the idea, its completion in Italian and for permitting the production of revised versions of the original chapters (since most were produced in English) as well as revised versions of translated chapters.[1]

For the ECPR Press, converting this project into English and expanding its scope was an attractive proposition because it dovetailed closely both with its existing 'Classics' book series (which aims to republish political science classic texts which have gone out of print), and with the mission of one of its journals, *European Political Science*. Indeed, the highest downloaded article by far in the history of that journal is Pasquino (2005b), which the author has updated and revised to include in this volume.

The ECPR Academic Director Martin Bull thoroughly checked and edited the English translation. We take the opportunity to express our grateful acknowledgement of his indispensable and extremely generous advice and support. We also want warmly to thank Maria Bucalo for her precious secretarial assistance.

THE CONTRIBUTIONS

This introduction is not intended to summarise or reproduce what the authors of the various chapters argue concerning their 'Masters'. Rather, it aims to locate the great thinkers within the broader framework of 20th century political science, viewing their contributions through the prism of a more general evaluation of the development of our discipline. To do so, it is useful to start from a particularly polarised debate that occurred in the world's largest political science association, the American Political Science Association (APSA, with 16,000 members) in 2001–02, although to some extent it was simply a resurgence of an old debate in a new form. The debate focused on APSA's *American Political Science Review* (APSR), and the quality, representativeness and importance of the articles published in the journal. A number of leading American political scientists sent an open letter to the journal, denouncing the alleged bias in the selection of the articles for publication towards those characterised by mathematical formalism and which were frequently obscure and of limited interest and usually made use of a single 'theory' of political science. The Editor's reply was defensive, arguing that no selection bias existed in relation to any particular theory, perspective, approach or method, and that the problem lay in the lack of supply of other articles: respected scholars preferred either to publish books or send their articles to other journals. This identification of the problem in terms of supply highlighted the limited perspective, relevance and importance of many, if not most, articles in the APSR, and the consequence was the birth of a new journal, *Perspectives*, which, since 2003, has come out three times a year and which offers space to articles which are not highly formalised but are usually more broadly conceived and give greater importance to significant political phenomena. This book is published in the same spirit, identifying precisely those authors whose careers have been characterised by efforts to go beyond the narrow confines of single areas of the discipline and grasp the 'big picture'.

As a consequence, the chapters in this book give a highly diversified, pluralistic and articulated image of political science in the twentieth century. Indeed, the plurality of analytical, methodological, and theoretical perspectives has been one of the strong points of research, knowledge acquisition, development and reflection in political science (see Panebianco 1989). The Masters presented in this book are certainly representative of this pluralism. Some have drawn up original theories themselves, such as David Easton on the political system and Anthony Downs on rational choice. Others have provided high-level interpretations of existing theories, refining and decisively systematising them, such as Robert Dahl on polyarchal democracy and Hans Morgenthau on realism in international relations. Highly original too was the broad spectrum of research carried out by Sidney Verba on comparative political participation. The other scholars share, to a greater (e.g. Samuel Finer) or lesser (e.g. Juan Linz) extent an important characteristic: they have studied a plurality of political phenomena while keeping their eye on one phenomenon in particular. Linz is above all interested in understanding and explaining the dynamics of political regimes (authoritarian, totalitarian, democratic, sultanistic) and institutions, with a clear cut distinction between presidential and parliamentary governments, and there is no doubt that his work has left an analytical mark that cannot be ignored. Lipset's core concerns are the requirements or needs of democracy and the functioning of democracies in practice, first and foremost that of the US. Huntington's most important contributions regard the role of the military, modes of development, the downfall of democracies (even 'consolidated' democracies), and systems of religious beliefs and the part they play at an international level (with the potential for a 'clash of civilisations'). Finally, Wildavsky is an eclectic political scientist *par excellence*, focusing on a plurality of themes ranging from the American presidential elections to the role of political culture and, in possibly his most valuable and long-lasting contribution, public policy analysis.

If these Masters represent, above all else, the defining characteristic of the development of political science (a pluralism of analytical, methodological and theoretical perspectives) the question arises as to whether this plurality has been a positive feature, enriching our knowledge, or whether, by contrast, it has wasted human resources and hindered the growth of our knowledge. Have we, in fact, learned a little about lots of things when we would have been in the position (and are today, some critics would argue) of focusing our resources on developing a single theory, that of rational choice. Evidently, the corollary of that argument (which is especially strong in contemporary American political science but not only there), is that it would be better to rationalise, constrain or simply put aside a pluralism of perspectives, with the goal of providing real scientific value to the discipline through the theory of rational choice (the variations of which will not be dealt with here).[2]

Leaving aside any judgment on the actual quality, originality and importance of the works of rational choice theories, it is surely the case that any attempt to rationalise political science through the elimination of other analytical perspectives is destined to fail. Furthermore, even if it were achievable it would result in a hefty reduction in the breadth and depth of themes analysed, leaving the discipline all the poorer. Indeed, rational choice theory has yet to demonstrate that it is capable of making up for the shortcomings in political science or interacting better with other disciplinary or sub-disciplinary fields, and many critics believe it never will. It could be argued that in some areas it still seems unable to offer an original or convincing contribution to the field.

One of the basic methods, if not objectives, of scientific research, is to exploit and build on the cumulative effect of previous findings. This, of course, is one of the principal means through which knowledge grows. Research is carried out starting from what we already know, and we then attempt to test and verify the generalisations and theories that exist with the aim of refining and revising hypotheses and using data in order either to confirm or undermine theories found in the existing literature. Giorgio Freddi, in his analysis of Wildavsky's work, is right, therefore, to emphasise the importance of the accumulation of knowledge, but it can equally be applied to the other Masters discussed in this volume, all of whom could be said to have followed a similar path and one which eventually led them into formulating original 'non-conformist' hypotheses, generalisations and theories which are still worthy of attention today. Yet, it might be questioned to what extent this tradition or approach is any longer accepted as valid in political science. Indeed, with regard to both research and theorisation it could be argued that a dangerous break in this tradition has occurred. Almond (1999b), in raising the problem, spoke of the existence of 'separate tables' within American political science, with dinner guests not speaking to each other. Worse, he suggested that there existed 'sects' of disciples who, rather than comparing their ideas amongst themselves, made reference only to rational choice theory and to those authors bent on sweeping away the past without a sufficient knowledge or understanding of what went before (this being perhaps the very reason why they wish to do so). Without going into the merits of Almond's specific criticism of group analysis (Almond 1990c), it should be noted that not only does the problem still exist but has probably got worse in the period since Almond's first observations. Two examples will suffice.

The first concerns themes dear to both Huntington and Lipset: the conditions of democracy and political development (for the necessary references see the chapters on the two authors in this volume). Does it not seem strange (and is surely open to criticism) that the mass of studies on democratisation make little or no reference to political development? Naturally, Huntington retains a central position in both fields and his analysis proceeds accordingly. Too many authors, however, and the 'democratisers' especially, seem to have little idea of the research that went before nor of the construction of concepts in political development – or at least they appear to be unable to use and integrate them into their theoretical models (if indeed there are any). The distance between two collections of studies (Bunce 2000; Hagopian 2000) is emblematic. Taken on their own, each is enlightening and comprehensive, but the lack of any inter-connection between the two is indicative of something fundamentally wrong in political science regarding the accumulation of knowledge.

The second example concerns one of the longstanding unresolved problems of rational choice theory (referring to the founding premises of the theory itself): the paradox of the vote. Why should individuals vote if, on the basis of a rational calculation, voting is costly as regards time, energy and even money, and offers no certainty of obtaining the desired ends? Most rational choice theoreticians do not attempt to explain this paradox, or, if they do, it is through 'bending' the premises of their theory. Gary Cox (1997), by contrast, not only gives a convincing explanation of the paradox of the vote, but does it by specific reference to three great scholars (Maurice Duverger, Colin Leys and Giovanni Sartori) in order to obtain 'a fertile combination of traditions' (Cox 1997: 12). The analysis he produces is not only much richer and more convincing than those of other exponents of rational choice, but also offers an admirable example of the accumulative impact of research, assumptions and theories.

In all likelihood it is only through reference to the accumulative process of knowledge that it becomes possible to apply the fundamental principle of control of different assumptions and theories in order to verify or refute them. Indeed, how could it be possible to test, revise, improve or even refute a theory without referring explicitly to those that already exist? Moreover, how could we claim originality and greater explicative power for our own assumptions and theories without an awareness of the research of authors preceding us and the ability to draw close comparisons? As Karl Popper (1969: 248) wrote, 'we look for theories which, however fallible, progress beyond their predecessors'. In short, in order to move on from existing theories it is necessary to know those theories well in the first place.

Obviously, the challenging or refuting of existing theories is not a sufficient condition for progress in knowledge to occur. Existing theories which have been undermined may not yet be ready to be replaced by new theories, which must, in any case, undergo a similar process of testing. It may even be that the search to exploit the accumulative quality of knowledge, which is indispensable to challenging existing theories, may create conditions that, in fact, limit progress, acting as a form of strait-jacket. The risk is that we may be left with theories that are weakened but not yet replaced on the one hand, but with only small, unsatisfactory steps made in terms of their revision, on the other. Thomas Kuhn (1970), while masterfully codifying what was already generally known, at the same time made an important contribution to our understanding of the process of accumulation of knowledge, explaining how progress may be triggered by 'paradigm shifts':

> Discovery commences with the awareness of anomaly, i.e., with the recognition that nature has somehow violated the paradigm-induced

expectations that govern normal science. It then continues with a more or less extended exploration of the area of anomaly. And it closes only when the paradigm theory has been adjusted so that the anomalous has become the expected. Assimilating a new sort of fact demands a more than additive adjustment of theory. (1970: 52–3).

Some of the Masters examined in this book have produced paradigm shifts, and we will cite here only three examples which are of particular importance. The first (chronologically speaking) was that of Juan Linz when in 1964 he formulated his famous (and as yet unsurpassed), definition of an authoritarian regime, which clearly separated it from that of its totalitarian counterpart. The second was that of Samuel Huntington whose 1965 work tackled the concept of political decadence in the analysis of changes in 'developing' countries, which until then had been one-sided, teleological and overly optimistic. The third concerns the redirection of research on and theorisation of political participation by Sidney Verba in 1995, who revealed the inadequacy of socio-economic status to explain levels of participation in the political process and proposed a convincing replacement in the form of 'civic voluntarism'.

'ON THE SHOULDERS OF GIANTS'

The temptation to conclude this Introduction by using an expression that has become axiomatic, if not proverbial (as well as being the title of a book by the well-known sociologist, Robert Merton 1991) is too strong: to produce good science (of which political science is no exception), one needs to climb 'on the shoulders of giants', those scholars who have produced studies that have notably advanced our knowledge of substance, methodology and theory. For a better view of the nature of democracy, its workings and transformation, it is necessary to climb onto the shoulders of Dahl and Lipset, but also onto those of Downs (who provides us with a good view of the potential of rational choice theory). From Easton's shoulders we observe the systemic theory of politics, from Finer's the notion of government in all its forms. To capture the differences between authoritarian and totalitarian regimes it is essential to jump onto Linz's shoulders. Without standing on Verba's shoulders, we would be unable to understand what motivates political participation. And the vistas from the shoulders of Morgenthau on the one hand and Wildavsky on the other are essential to anyone embarking on the study of either realism in international relations or public policy.

Yet, the task of climbing onto the shoulders of these giants should not be underestimated. It requires reading, studying, assimilating, mastering and evaluating their writings. The alternative, however, is stark: staying on the ground, unable to see the bigger picture (or pictures) of political science, and basing one's vision only on the exchange of ideas with members of one's own narrow tribe or sect. The consequences of completing that task are clear for the scholars who manage it and for the growth of the discipline. In addition, those who manage the struggle and are afforded the view realise not only how poorer political science would have been without their contributions, but also that, while we might not be able to define a 'Master' in a scientifically rigorous manner, we know when we're standing on one's shoulders.

Notes
1 Thanks are also due to the Fondazione della Cassa di Risparmio in Bologna (and especially its president, Fabio Roversi Monaco), for the generous funding which made it possible to produce the original Italian version.
2 For a comprehensive outline of the variations in rational choice see Giannetti (2003). The most up-to-date and sophisticated contribution is probably Tsebelis (2002). For early and astute critical observations argued in reference to Down's seminal text see Almond (1990a).

REFERENCES

AA.VV (various authors) (2000) 'Comparative Politics in the Year 2000: Unity Within Diversity', *Comparative Political Studies*, 33: 699–991.

Almond, G.A. (1990a) 'Rational Choice Theory and the Social Sciences', in G. A. Almond, *A Discipline Divided*, Newbury Park, Calif: Sage.

(1990b) 'Separate Tables; Schools and Sects in Political Science', in G. A. Almond, *A Discipline Divided*, Newbury Park, Calif: Sage.

(1990c) 'Pluralism, Corporatism, and Professional Memory', in G.A. Almond, *A Discipline Divided*, Newbury Park, Calif: Sage.

Almond, G.A. and Powell, G.B. Jnr. (1966) *Comparative Politics; A Developmental Approach*, Boston: Little, Brown and Co.

(1978) *Comparative Politics; System, Process, and Policy*, Boston: Little, Brown, and Co.

Bobbio, N. (1981) 'La teoria dello stato e del potere', in P. Rossi (ed.), *Max Weber e l'analisi del mondo moderno*, Torino: Einaudi.

Boudon, R. (2002) *A lezione dai classici*, Bologna: il Mulino.

Bunce, V. (2000) 'Comparative Democratisation; Big and Bounded Generalisations', *Comparative Political Studies*, 33: 703–34.

Campus, D. (2001) 'L'eredità di Herbert Simon: tra psicologia cognitiva e scienza politica', *Rivista Italiana di Scienza Politica*, 31: 291–311.

Cox, G.W. (1997) *Making Votes Count; Strategic Coordination in the World's Electoral Systems*, Cambridge: Cambridge University Press.

Daalder, H. (1997) (ed.) *Comparative European Politics; The Story of a Profession*, London/New York: Pinter.

Eulau, H., Pye, L.W. and Verba, S. (2003) 'Gabriel A. Almond', in *PS. Political Science & Politics*, 36 (3): 467–70.

Friedrich, C. J. (2002) (S. Ventura ed.) *L'uomo, la comunità, l'ordine politico*, Bologna: il Mulino.

Giannetti, D. (2003) *La teoria politica positiva*, Bologna: il Mulino.

Goodin, R. and Klingemann, H. D. (1996) *New Handbook of Political Science*, Oxford: Oxford University Press.

Hagopian, F. (2000) 'Political Development Revisited', *Comparative Political Studies,* 33: 880–911.

Kuhn, T. S. (1970) *The Structure of Scientific Revolutions*, 2nd ed., Chicago: University of Chicago Press.

Lasswell, H. D. (1975) (M. Stoppino ed.) *Potere, politica e personalità*, Torino: Utet.

Lowi, T. J. (1999) (M. Calise ed.) *La scienza delle politiche*, Bologna: il Mulino.

Merton, R. K. (1965) *On the Shoulders of Giants*, New York: The Free Press.

Munck, G. L. and Snyder, R. (2007) (eds.) *Passion, Craft and Method in Comparative Politics*, Baltimore-London: The Johns Hopkins University Press.

Panebianco, A. (1989) (ed.) *L'analisi della politica; Tradizioni di ricerca, modelli e teorie*, Bologna: il Mulino.

Pasquino, G. (2001) 'Trent'anni di scienza politica: temi e libri', *Rivista Italiana di Scienza Politica,* 31: 5–29.

(2005a) *La Scienza politica di Giovanni Sartori*, Bologna: il Mulino.

(2005b) 'The Political Science of Giovanni Sartori', *European Political Science*, 4 (1): 33–55.

Popper, K. (1969) *Conjectures and Refutations; The Growth of Scientific Knowledge*, London: Routledge and Kegan.

Rokkan, S. (1970) *Citizens; Elections, Parties*, Oslo: Universitetsforlaget.

(1999) *State Formation, Nation-Building, and Mass Politics in Europe*, Oxford: Oxford University Press.

Sartori, G. (1976) *Parties and Party Systems; A Framework for Analysis*, Cambridge: Cambridge University Press.

Tsebelis, G. (2002) *Veto Players; How Political Institutions Work*, Princeton: Princeton University Press.

chapter one | Robert Dahl: The Democratic Polyarchy
Domenico Fisichella

ANALYSIS OF THE CONDITIONS

Anyone looking back over the intellectual itinerary of Robert A. Dahl is struck by the constant reappearance of two themes that are present throughout the entire production of this American political scientist. The first theme inspires much of his subject matter. 'The First Problem of Politics – how citizens can keep their rulers from becoming tyrants' is pronounced by Dahl in *Politics, Economics and Welfare*, which was written with Charles E. Lindblom (Dahl and Lindblom 1953: 273). This statement, thanks to the lofty tone imparted by the use of capitals and the syntactical rhythm reminiscent of that of ancient pronouncements, would seem even from a stylistic point of view, to descend directly from the problems as posed in classical political thinking. The second theme is found in his intention to place the theories he develops within the context of a scientific investigation of advanced hypotheses. In fact, at the methodological level, Dahl wishes rigidly to interpret the requirements of analysis in modern methodological criticism. The weaving together of the two themes – the classical inspiration and the attempt at an advanced method – gives rise to a singular combination, of which we will try to examine certain fundamental elements.

The volume produced by Dahl and Lindblom is one of the first systematic attempts of the two disciplines of political science and economics to work together (an approach repeated many times in Dahl's later production) and of the reciprocal use of interpretive models created within the two sectors. Published in 1953, this book appeared after *Capitalism, Socialism and Democracy* by Schumpeter, which came out in 1942, but preceded Anthony Downs' *The Economic Theory of Democracy*, by four years.

The subject of the book is the development of a new concept of 'plan', assuming the definition of plan to be 'a rationally calculated action to achieve a goal', (1953: xx) and therefore taking for granted that an economic policy based on a plan can be enacted not only in a collective logic but also within a market economy. What is important is to verify the prerequisites for rational social action, on the one hand postulating a group of social ends, and on the other examining a group of social processes, which are instrumental (or *means*) for the furtherance of the ends advanced. The rationality of the action is dependent on the suitability of the means to the ends (the *rational calculation of the means*), and the more the ends can be 'maximized' the more the means will be able to ensure the achievement of the ends themselves.

There are essentially two problems that emerge from such a stance. First, there is a problem of incompatibility – beyond empirically ascertainable limits – between the ends of social action. Let us look at the political systems of the Western area. The two authors list seven fundamental ends as being typical of the area: freedom, rationality, democracy, subjective equality, security, progress, appropriate inclusion (1953: 25). Each of these represents a 'value' for western political culture, which aspires towards their increase. Now, the observation is that the achievement of all these goals simultaneously gives rise to problems that are irresolvable both as regards structural balances and also the availability of the means themselves. Beyond certain limits for example, the maximization of rationality becomes contradictory to the goal of maximizing equality. The same is true for freedom and security, and so on.

The second problem arises from the consideration that not all the social processes hypothesised as means for the achievement of the ends are available and can be used to the same extent for all the ends. The social processes appropriate to the maximization of the value of rationality are not necessarily 'good' as instruments for the fulfilment of the values of freedom or equality. Not only this. Given that the existence of each social process requires certain essential conditions, this entails that not all the means are available and present at the same time (and even less so in high concentrations) as in no social context do the conditions exist for the simultaneous flourishing of a large number of means. From this assumption it follows that – compared to the variety of ends – in each given situation there would tend to be a scarcity of means.

To summarize: a) the ends of social action are manifold, and beyond certain levels of increase, contradictory; b) the means, on the other hand, are scarce and not all appropriate to all of the ends. This being the *status quaestionis*, how is the scientific discussion on politics defined within the perspective of the two authors? It is defined as *the analysis of the conditions*. More precisely, this is the analysis of the conditions for the selection of the values or the ends, which do not become 'maximized' only on the basis of the criteria of which is preferable, but rather on the basis of the criteria of availability of the means. And, it is also the analysis of the conditions that favour certain means rather than others.

But what are the means of social action? Dahl and Lindblom distinguish between four fundamental social processes. The first is the price system. The second is the control by leaders, or the hierarchy. The third is the control among leaders, which takes the form of negotiating or bargaining. The fourth, lastly, is the control of the leaders from above, which is termed 'polyarchy'. At this point the problem that was initially considered in terms of economic policy becomes a subject matter for political scientists. In fact, if preventing rulers from becoming tyrants is the fundamental problem of politics, it is the polyarchy which represents the concrete solution (1953: 275).

The concept of polyarchy is essential for an understanding of the intellectual history of Robert Dahl, and I will discuss the word itself later on. The word crops up in all the works of the American scholar, though not always with exactly the same connotations, and there is no doubt that in the work co-authored with Lindblom – who was above all an economist – the chapters dedicated to the expansion of the concept can be traced back to Dahl. The first definition that Dahl gives us of the notion of a polyarchy, which is to a certain extent surprising, is a definition of what it is not, and which is gleaned from the statement that 'Polyarchy, not democracy, is the actual solution to the First Problem of Politics' (1953: 275). To start with, therefore, polyarchy is not democracy. Moreover, and this is an equally significant aspect, democracy does not represent an adequate solution to the problem of preventing rulers from becoming tyrants, given that the control of the leaders is a specific function of the polyarchal process.

The relationship between democracy and polyarchy will be one of the main themes in a later book by Dahl, *A Preface to Democratic Theory* (published in 1956), in which not only is the subject considered in greater depth but certain ideas are further defined and a number of themes are corrected. Meanwhile, I will attempt to reconstruct the analysis of the conditions that make the existence of a polyarchy possible, as developed in the book *Politics, Economics and Welfare*.

Nowadays, as Dahl states, in both small groups and complex organisations two fundamental tendencies are at work. The first is the push towards inequality of control, or towards unilateral control: a trend that Michels evoked in relation to socialist parties, when he talked about 'the iron law of oligarchy.' However, there is also a second tendency in which organisms do not operate in an exclusive form through the unilateral use of command and the manipulation of the base, but create certain relationships of reciprocity. The formula that Dahl proposes in this latter case is a 'law that counterbalances reciprocity'. In other words, while the law of oligarchy emphasises the push towards inequality, the law of reciprocity emphasises the trend towards the counterbalancing of inequalities.[1] When this latter trend becomes strong and empowering enough, then according to Dahl, an organisation takes on the characteristics of a polyarchy.

Naturally, in order for the trend to reciprocity to be able to contrast and rebalance the trend towards inequality[2] certain conditions are necessary. Dahl sums them up in two points: 1) the leaders must win power by competing for the support of non-leaders: 2) the non-leaders must be able to transfer their support from the leaders in power to their rivals. 'Given these two conditions, leaders will be highly responsive to the preferences of non-leaders or lose their control', (Dahl and Lindblom (1953: 283)). In other words, these two conditions help to consolidate the reciprocity of controls and to weaken unilateral control. Returning to the law of oligarchy, 'the presence of these conditions means that two or more hierarchical organisations can actually contribute to the operation of a polyarchal organization.' Political parties, as Michels observed, tend to be oligarchic or, as we would say, hierarchical. 'But two or more political parties which are competing with one another for the votes of citizens can make a polyarchy' (1953: 283). It is true, however, that the two key conditions do not arise within an historical vacuum, nor are they merely accidental. Rather, they presuppose a whole series of other preconditions whose interdependence and interaction create the terrain in which a process of polyarchy can exist and grow.

For a start, 'a polyarchy requires social indoctrination and habituation in the process and the desirability of democracy' (1953: 287). While polyarchy is not the same as democracy, for it to operate it is nevertheless necessary that both leaders and common citizens perceive democracy as a value. This is, then, a peculiarity of the relationship between polyarchy and democracy: while it is true that democracy as a goal of social action is conditioned by the availability of the means or the social processes, it is also true that democracy, as a value in itself, conditions the actual working of the polyarchal social process. Effectively, in the complex game of political partners, means and ends would appear to be mutually conditioning and conditioned.

The second precondition emphasises the need for a basic consensus as regards the 'rules of the game', concerning the fundamental issues and the methods that facilitate peaceful competition and allow citizens freely to transfer their votes from the governing leaders to the opposition (1953: 294). The logic of this second condition is that the models of citizen orientation as regards the political process (the 'political culture' as Gabriel Almond and his followers would put it) must have an area, or a level, of generalised homogeneity, without which dissent will involve not only those in power and their actions, but would also risk involving the foundations of the political regime itself, thus endangering the very institutions that could resolve conflicts peacefully.

The other four preconditions set out by Dahl can be quickly summarised: a considerable degree of social pluralism, that is to say a variety of social organisations each of which has a wide measure of independence; a relatively high degree of political activity and popular participation; the inability to win elections as the main obstacle to the access of positions to political power; and the presupposition of a society that has an appreciable level of psychological security, resulting from limited differences in wealth and income, and perhaps from widespread education (1953: 302–19).

This rapid summary is because – apart from the aspects of substantial theory – I am interested at this point in outlining Dahl's argumentative procedure and the logical syntax as they take form in this early work. Two essential problems, however, remain open: the issue of the relationship between democracy and polyarchy, which has certain ambivalent aspects; and the question of measuring techniques, which are of utmost importance in a discussion that is rich in expressions such as 'considerable degree', 'appreciable level', relatively high rate', and which in general is set out in terms of maximization and of appropriateness/adequacy of the means to the ends.

THREE CONCEPTIONS

As mentioned earlier, Dahl deals in depth with the relationship between democracy and polyarchy, and sets out his point of view in the book *A Preface to Democratic Theory*. The author distances himself from the idea of a single theory of democracy, but talks rather of 'democratic theories' (Dahl 1967: 1). One could make a long list of possible democratic theories, and Dahl himself puts forward some proposals. However, his analysis is limited to a few representative types of democratic theory: in particular to Madisonian democracy[3], populist democracy and polyarchal democracy. It should be noted that Dahl thus abandons the, albeit ambiguous, contraposition between democracy and polyarchy that had been outlined in the book co-authored with Lindblom. In this volume the idea of polyarchy is clearly a theory of democracy.

One of the central preoccupations of the Madisonian concept of democracy[4] is the establishment and conservation of a 'non-tyrannical republic'. But what is tyranny? Dahl's interpretation of Madison's vision paints tyranny as any serious violation of a natural right, and this is engendered when all powers – legislative, executive and judiciary – are concentrated in the same hands, and, as such, an aggregation involves the elimination of those external controls that alone guarantee full respect of individual rights. As Alexander Hamilton said so succinctly, 'give all power to many and they will oppress the few: give all the power to few and they will oppress the many' (Dahl 1967: 7). From such a perspective, at least two conditions are necessary to guarantee the existence of a republic that is not tyrannical: that the concentration of all the power in the same hands is avoided at all costs[5]; and that those factions are controlled so that they are unable to operate successfully against the rights of citizens or the interests of the community.[6]

According to Dahl, the means which Madisonian democracy foresees for the fulfilment of such conditions are the organisation and the functioning of a system of constitutional checks and balances, and the division of powers. However, this is the point of the doctrine most open to criticism. Actually, the Madisonian concept boils down to a fundamental political mechanism, that of reciprocal control among leaders (1967: 21). The reason is easy to explain: in its essence, Madisonian democracy does not forget its origins as a political system aimed at protecting the 'natural rights of the well-born and the few' (1967: 83). In this sense, the accent is placed above all on the rules of the constitutional game, since in a republic of 'the well-born and the few', what counts is the action of these minorities and of the mutual checks, which come down to – as *Politics, Economics and Welfare* shows us – a process of bargaining. Once the process of bargaining and the mutual control between minorities has been sorted out, one is more than half way there.

Dahl puts forward three reservations about this concept. First, it does not state that the mutual control between leaders, considered sufficient to avoid tyranny, requires that a separation of powers be written into the constitution. Second, it does not fully weigh the significance of the psychological reality that comes into play with checks on behaviour. Third, and most importantly, the Madisonian theory overestimates the importance of constitutional checks and underestimates the mechanisms of social checks and balances that exist in any pluralistic community. 'Without these social checks and balances it is doubtful that all of the intragovernmental checks on officials prevent tyranny; with them it is doubtful that all of the intragovernmental checks of the Madisonian system as it operates in the US are necessary to prevent tyranny' (1967: 21–22). While these are the main criticisms made of Madisonian democracy, the populist theory of democracy provokes another type of criticism.

In the democratic tradition there are two main lines of thinking, one that prizes 'freedom' and the other that prizes 'equality'. In Dahl's opinion the first line of thinking is linked to the Madisonian doctrine, whereas the essence of the latter is to be found in the populist conception of democracy (1967: 37n). The fundamental difference between Madisonianism and populism lies in the different importance given to the principle of majority rule. While in the Madisonian approach majority rule is no more than a single step in a complex mechanism of constitutional balances (and indeed a step that foresees the presence of minority checks and 'blocks'), according to the populist view there is an essential link between democracy and the principle of majority rule, as this latter embodies the supreme values of popular sovereignty and political equality. According to the populist view, writes Dahl,

> an organization is democratic if and only if the process of arriving at governmental policy is compatible with the condition of popular sovereignty and the condition of political equality. The condition of popular sovereignty is satisfied if and only if policy choices are perceived to exist, the alternative selected and enforced as governmental policy is the alternative most preferred by the members. The condition of political equality is satisfied if and only if control over governmental decisions is so shared that, whenever policy alternatives are perceived to exist, in the choice of the alternative to be enforced as governmental policy, the preference of each member is assigned an equal value. (1967: 37)

From these three preconditions comes the principle of majority rule: 'The principle of majority rule prescribes that in choosing among alternatives, the alternative preferred by the greater number is selected' (1967: 37).

Turning now to the criticisms, in Dahl's opinion the populist theory of democracy is a theory that is 'formal and axiomatic' (1967: 83). In particular, this theory is not an empirical system but is made up solely of logical relations between ethical postulations (1967: 51). This is, then, the essential core around which the critique of populist democracy is built.

Looking at some of the details – and ignoring some of the more minor points or those which are self-evident[7] – it is worth noting four main lines of observation. First, the populist theory proposes only two goals to be maximized – popular sovereignty and political equality – but it fails to explain *why* only these two goals should be maximized to the detriment of all other ends of social action. Second, even bearing this in mind, it does not explain *how* these two goals should be maximized in practice. The third problem is that no guarantees are foreseen (such as the right to veto of minorities on particularly important issues) in order to avoid a majority exploiting majority rule to carry out actions that would destroy the democratic system itself. Lastly, giving equal weight *a priori* to the preferences of all the members of the community, the populist theory ignores the differences that actually exist in the intensity of individual preferences and, in doing so, excludes itself from any analysis of the conditions that would enhance the stability of the democratic system, and the search for the best means to ensure this stability.

This last point is developed by Dahl even beyond his reflections on democratic populism, and it is worth considering at greater length. Taking the basic definition of intensity to be 'the degree to which an individual prefers or desires an alternative', the truth is that this degree varies from individual to individual and between one alternative and another. Whatever the reasons, there are individuals who desire more than others a given alternative, and this is equally true for political alternatives. Of course, it is difficult to devise techniques and instruments suitable for measuring to a reliable extent the degree of intensity, but this does not mean that these differences do not exist or that we should be unaware of them.

As regards the political system, various models for the distribution of the intensity of preferences of the members between political alternatives can be hypothesized. Given an alternative, it is possible, for example, to predict a model of broad-based and intense consensus (the 'yes' sector greatly exceeds the 'no' sector both as regards size and intensity). Alternatively, there could be a model where the consensus is broad but of weak intensity of preference; or again, a model of moderate dissent with a symmetrical distribution of the intensities of preference, i.e. with groups that are strongly, moderately or weakly intense, that percentage-wise balance each other out on the two sides. Finally, the model of moderate disagreement could show an asymmetric trend.

Clearly, for each model there could be a different system of political decision-making. Different conditions tend to give rise to different results. The majority rule of populist democracy, therefore, even from this brief outline is seen to be inadequate in describing the variety and complexity of decision-making processes within democratic systems. Moreover, the importance of the intensity of preferences becomes particularly significant – to the point of affecting the stability and even the survival of a political regime – when a model of distribution of intensity arises in which not only the yes sector and the no sector are equally broad, but in which each of the two sides sees the victory of the other as a 'fundamental threat to some very highly rated values' (1967: 98). In this last case, which would be the expression of a deeply rooted social conflict, the recourse to majority rule is useless, as are – Dahl adds – all the constitutional solutions of Madisonian thinking.

DESCRIPTION AND MAXIMIZATION

This last observation leads directly to the heart of the discussion on polyarchal democracy. In fact – Dahl writes

> whether we are concerned with tyranny by a minority or tyranny by a majority, the theory of polyarchy suggests that the first and crucial variables to which political scientists must direct their attention are social and not constitutional. (1967: 83)

Once this has been established, how can we proceed with the analysis? Broadly speaking, two methods exist to construct a theory of democracy. The first is the method of maximization: a group of ends to be maximized are specified and democracy is defined on the basis of the specific processes of legal enforcement necessary to maximize these ends, or a certain number of them. The second is the method of description. That is to say, all those organisations – national, state or social – which are commonly called democratic by political scientists, are considered together as a single class of phenomena. An attempt is made first, to recognize what they have in common and second, to distinguish the necessary and adequate conditions for these organisations to have the characteristics identified previously.

In Dahl's view maximization and description are not mutually exclusive, but are different stages of a process that develops in successive steps. The term 'maximizing democracy' is meant to indicate a logical status that denotes a 'limit' and all the actions that help to draw nearer to that limit should be considered 'maximizing actions' (1967: 64). This means, among other things, that the democratic process should be seen as developing in a number of successive stages; the methodological warning that results from this is that many ambiguities may be avoided if there is awareness of the particular stage that is being dealt with each time.

In order to be clear about the notion of polyarchal democracy, according to Dahl, it is necessary to distinguish at least two phases in the democratic process: an electoral phase and an inter-election phase. The former should then be divided into three further periods: pre-voting, voting and post-voting. Thus, the polyarchy can be defined as the political system in which such conditions are present to a relatively high degree through all of these periods and phases. On the basis of earlier discussion, the content of these conditions, totalling eight in all, will be intuitively evident.[8] However, it would be useful to go back over the process that Dahl followed to reach his method for measuring the degree and frequency of such conditions.

Each of the eight conditions can be interpreted as a limit, i.e. as the last and normative stage of a continuum, or of scale (1967: 75). In this series of steps there are several levels, each one corresponding to a certain degree of intensity in the existence of the condition under consideration. In other words, given the continuum whose lowest possible limit is the minimum degree of intensity a, while the uppermost limit will be z, a political system can be characterised, on the basis of the intensity of any given condition, by a degree b, degree c, or d etc. Naturally, not all eight conditions are necessarily present in each political system with the same intensity. In a given political system, for instance, condition number one may have a degree of intensity n, while condition number three has a value of f, and condition number six a level of h, and so on.

At this point, let us hypothesise that each condition determines certain actions whose frequency can, in principle, be calculated. If the frequency can be calculated it is possible to translate the conditions into propositions about past frequencies – on a scale from 0 to 100 – or in assertions regarding future frequencies as probabilities along a scale from 0 to 1. By means of a series of mathematical calculations Dahl thus manages operationally to define a polyarchy as an organisation in which all eight of the conditions reach a value of 0.5 or higher. For there to be a polyarchy, therefore, it is both necessary and sufficient that each of the conditions judged to be absolutely indispensable be present at least with a degree of intensity of 0.5. If one or more of these conditions are absent, or are present but with a degree below 0.5, then the organisation cannot be said to be polyarchal.

The special feature of this proposal of metric analysis of political conditions is that it would seem to provide political scientists, among others, with an instrument for comparing political systems. On the basis of the degrees of intensity of the various conditions, different political systems could be rated in a numerical classification. This idea is roughly set out by Dahl in an outline that is brief but not without appeal. Hence, hierarchies are defined as all those organisations that are scaled at less than 0.5 for all eight conditions; oligarchies are hierarchical systems in which the same conditions are scaled at values of 0.25 or less; dictatorships are the hierarchical systems in which all eight conditions fall below 0.25; mixed polities are those organisations in which at least one condition scores at 0.5 or more, and at least one has a value lower than 0.5. Moreover, within the polyarchies themselves it is possible to distinguish between egalitarian polyarchies (in which all eight conditions reach scores of 0.75 or more, thus coming close to the upper limit) and non-egalitarian polyarchies, which are defined as 'all other polyarchies' (1967: 87).

I will not repeat here the misgivings I have about a comparison between political systems based on criteria of intensity alone. I discussed these when considering the multifunctional approach of Gabriel Almond[9], and the same is true for Dahl, given that both authors present quite similar concepts on this point. I will merely add one consideration. While it may be true that the presence of these eight conditions at varying levels of intensity leads to operational differences, and it is therefore right to distinguish between different kinds of polyarchal systems according to levels of intensity, in my opinion it is not possible to define systems as non-polyarchal on the basis of the intensity of conditions that apply specifically to polyarchies. In other words, if these eight specific conditions exist at levels below those necessary to define them as polyarchies, or do not exist at all, we can at most say that these systems are not polyarchies, or even better, that they are non-polyarchies. What we cannot do is use the conditions necessary to define a polyarchy to define in positive terms those systems that are non-polyarchal. Thus, oligarchies and dictatorships should not really be identified and defined using these eight conditions, but on the basis of the existence and intensity of other, different, conditions which are not set out by Dahl and cannot therefore be included in the 'calculations'. To sum up, I believe it to be incorrect to distinguish, for example, between an authoritarian hierarchical system and a totalitarian hierarchical system merely on the basis of intensity of conditions that relate to a polyarchy. Rather, a set of different conditions should be sought and developed that would enable us, once the non-polyarchal nature of a given regime were to be established, to specify what type of non-polyarchal system it was.

CONSTITUTIONAL STRUCTURES AND OPPOSITION

As an analyst of possible democracy, Dahl has always been motivated by a fundamental source of inspiration: the search for conditions that would keep rulers from becoming tyrants. Within this framework of interest, the editing of the large volume on *Political Oppositions in Western Democracies* (Dahl 1966b) was a natural succession to his earlier work. For this publication Dahl wrote the preface, the chapter devoted to the United States and three substantial concluding chapters.

The opening words of the book confirm, as if it were necessary, Dahl's loyalty to the theme that first inspired him and which was central to his previous work:

> Somewhere in the world, at this moment, a political group is probably engaged in the antique art of imprisoning, mailing, torturing and killing its opponents. Somewhere, as you read these words, a government and its opponents are no doubt trying to coerce one another by violent means. For without much question the most commonplace way for a government to deal with its opponents is to employ violence. (1966b: xiii)

In contrast to the use of violence as an instrument to resolve controversy, democracy proposes the logic of a peaceful resolution to conflicts.[10]

> Because some conflict of views seems to be unavoidable in human affairs political societies have always had to deal somehow with the fact of opposition. Nevertheless, that there might legitimately exist an organized group within the political system to oppose, criticize, and if possible oust the leading officials of government was until recently an unfamiliar and generally unacceptable notion [...] The system of managing the major political conflicts of a society by allowing one or more opposition parties to compete with the governing parties for votes in elections and in parliament is, then, not only modern; surely it is also one of the greatest and most important social

discoveries that man has ever stumbled onto. Up until two centuries ago, no one had accurately foreseen it. Today one is inclined to regard the existence of an opposition party as very nearly the most distinctive characteristic of a democracy itself; and we take the absence of an opposition party as evidence, if not always conclusive proof, for the absence of democracy. (1966b: xvi, xvii, xviii)

While this is the general framework within which Dahl's observations on political oppositions lie, as the analysis gradually unfolds by examining the various democratic experiences, it becomes clearer what place this work has in the development of Dahl's thinking. In fact, in this volume we can find, in addition to the usual themes and methods, a new feature which it seems to me partly modifies and corrects previous arguments.

This new feature emerges with Dahl's considerations on the role of constitutional structures in the dynamics of the democratic political system. It will be remembered that in previous works Dahl had repeatedly emphasised that the first and crucial variables that political scientists must consider are social and not constitutional variables. Hence, the emphasis has now changed. Indeed, to those who argue that the constitutional framework and the electoral system are in no way connected with the characteristics of the opposition, and that what is important are social, economic, cultural and psychological factors, Dahl answers that

> This kind of objection reflects a 'reductionism' that seeks to reduce political factors to something more 'basic', just as biophysicists seek to explain biology by evoking the 'more basic' laws of physics. Yet just as biophysicists have encountered severe difficulties in reducing biology to physics, to ignore the effects of constitutional and electoral institutions leaves one in serious difficulties. (1966b: 349)

This is certainly not a complete reversal of what Dahl said before. In fact, previously in his comparison between Madisonian and polyarchal democracy he had not denied that constitutional factors could also have a part in the polyarchal project, just as he recognised that Madisonism was not indifferent to social conditions (Dahl 1967: 82). The principal difference is, however, that the latter were clearly dominant and 'crucial' in polyarchal theory, while they were only considered secondary in Madisonian theory. Therefore, even though this not a u-turn, it can be considered a precise limit or *caveat*, and perhaps one that is not lacking in self-criticism. In any case this can be seen as an important stage in Dahl's scientific development.

By this last statement, I mean that Dahl, in my opinion, only reached full comprehension of the role of constitutional structures when he came to accept fully a comparative approach.[11] The book on political oppositions is actually Dahl's first *sortie* out of the parochial analysis of the United States to expand into the study of an entire political and cultural arena. Now, whether or not the conclusions on this specific issue of constitutional structures are valid, the methods by which he reached them are undoubtedly important. It is abundantly clear that the need for comparative analysis was increasingly recognised as important in Dahl's work from the debate in which he was involved with another American political scientist, Jack L. Walker, regarding the relationship between élites and democracies. In the course of this discussion, which took place in 1966 – the same year as the publication of the book on oppositions – Dahl states in black and white that it is necessary to 'call attention to a methodological matter that until recently has generally been ignored: the need to examine the problem in a comparative framework and not exclusively in the American setting' (Dahl 1966a: 304).

The comparative approach does not conflict with the analysis of the conditions. Rather, the latter complements the former. This then shows the continuity of approach that underlies the innovation. What, then, are the conditions of opposition? Just as earlier Dahl had emphasised the possibility of having different types of polyarchy and later hypothesised various types of democratic power in *Who Governs?*, a study on the distribution of influence and political resources in the American town of New Haven (Dahl 1961), so here he concludes that 'there is no single prevailing pattern of opposition in Western Democracies' (Dahl 1966b: 332). On the contrary, there are many different models of opposition. Dahl proposes six indicators of these differences. In fact, he writes that oppositions differ from each other according to at least six fundamental factors:

1) The organizational cohesion or concentration of the opponents;
2) the competitiveness of the opposition;
3) the site or setting for the encounter between opposition and those who control the government;
4) the distinctiveness or identifiability of the opposition;
5) the goals of the opposition;
6) the strategies of the opposition. (1966b: 332)

It is, then, necessary to understand whether these differences correspond to variations in a certain specific factor alone which becomes the 'cause'. Once again, the answer is negative. There is not a single cause, but at least seven conditions exist that can be attributed to differences in the opposition models. They are as follows:

a) constitutional structure and electoral system;
b) widely shared cultural premises;
c) specific subcultures;
d) the record of grievances against the government;
e) social and economic differences;
f) the specific patterns of cleavage, conflict and agreement in attitudes and opinions;
g) the extent of polarization. (1966b: 348–9)

Of these conditions, the first five are judged to be the main ones, while the last two are linked to and, to a certain extent, dependent on the previous five.

THE METHOD OF INCREMENTS

At this stage, an initial, brief assessment of Dahl's contribution to the development of modern political science may be made by reflecting on the theme of incrementalism. When discussing – in the book on oppositions – the relationship between consensus, disagreement and rationality, Dahl observes that in consensual communities social and political changes are largely the result of what he calls the method of increments, whose procedures are described as follows:

> Changes are likely to come about by paying attention to a relatively small number of marginally different alternatives to existing policies, examining a limited set of possible consequences, comparing the results of whatever changes are made, and making whatever further modifications are suggested by subsequent experience: in short, by incremental action. (Dahl 1966b: 391–2)

The theme of *incrementalism* is to be found right from the start in Dahl's works. It had been discussed already in the book, *Politics, Economics and Welfare* (Dahl and Lindblom 1953: 82), and this is hardly surprising as then (and as was true later on) the problem was one of rational political action. However, the main point of interest here is the judgement that is made of the method of increases, after fifteen years of scientific work.

> Although incrementalism evidently seems to a great many people a less rational process than comprehensive and deductive approaches, in fact it offers great advantages as a process for relatively rational change. The characteristics and effects of existing policies and institutions are more easily, more accurately, and more confidently known than for hypothetical policies and institutions. The effects of small changes are much easier to predict than the effects of larger changes. Current processes generate information about effects [...] changes can be reversed, accelerated or altered. In practice, moreover, peaceful change is usually highly incremental. (Dahl 1966b: 391)

Briefly, the consideration is that in Dahl's writings rationality of method should lead to rationality in political action (without there necessarily being a contradiction between the method of reasoning and *incrementalism*, between deduction and 'normal science')[12]. In other words, the discussion about method corresponds to the discussion about theory. Not that in the method of increments risks are altogether absent, just as they are still present even in democracies whose widespread consent would seem to make them relatively insensitive to problems. In both cases, the other hypothesis is an excess of caution that borders on immobility, a fact of which Dahl is completely aware. However, this said, both the analysis of conditions and the method of successive approximations from the existing reality to the limit on the one hand, and the method of increments in political action on the other, give an idea of a coherent adhesion to a programme of procedural rationality, to a plan of political realism and to an empirically informed attitude.

POLITICAL REPRESENTATION AND PLURALISM

Until now we have discussed Dahl's theoretical contribution to the construction of a broad and complex democratic theory. In order to approach the second part of the development followed by Dahl, we can start by examining the term 'polyarchy' itself, which for many years Dahl held to be a term of his own creation (together with Lindblom). Even in the essay *On Democracy*, written in 1998, Dahl writes that he introduced the concept and invented the term in 1953, explaining why, even at that early stage, it was important in the author's thinking: 'because the institutions of modern representative democratic government, taken in their entirety, are historically unique, it is convenient to give them their own name' (Dahl 1998: 90). This is only true in part, as may be easily determined from what has already been said here. However, Dahl's paternity of the word has been given weight by many scholars of the American author's work. Thus, for example, Sergio Fabbrini writes that Dahl (together with Lindblom) coined the term 'polyarchy' (Fabbrini 2001: x). In fact, not until 2002, that is to say relatively recently, did Dahl specify that the 'new term' which he and Lindblom had put together had been 'with the help of a colleague from the classics department' and that 'what we did not know at that time was that the term had already been used by a Dutch author in the nineteenth century, Johannes Althusius, whereas we believed we were the first to use it' (Dahl 2002: 18).

However, I would remind readers that back in 1980 I had drawn attention to the fact that the word 'polyarchy' was not an 'invention' of Dahl's, and that it had already been used by two Italian authors writing in the nineteenth century. In fact, in the *Saggio teoretico di diritto natural appoggiato sul fatto* (1840–1843), the philosopher Luigi Taparelli d'Azeglio made an early distinction between the political forms of monarchy and polyarchy. Some years later, in his book *Il Re*, published in 1899, the scholar of constitutions, Alberto Morelli, defined 'governments where more than one person commands' as polyarchies, adding that 'thus both democracies and aristocracies are polyarchal forms'[13].

Having made this clear, let us get to the point. As we know, in the early stages for Dahl, polyarchy did not signify democracy. Later on, the polyarchal concept became a democratic theory, though not the only democratic theory. Now, lastly, as we have just seen, the term polyarchy refers to modern representative democracy with universal suffrage. It is this identification of the term with this latest meaning that leads to the second part of our considerations on Dahl.

On the subject of the 'democracy of modern man' Dahl does not add many new elements in a lengthy illustration on that theme inspired at least, in part, by the speech given by Benjamin Constant in 1819 on the freedom of the ancients, compared to that of modern man. The subject is developed with reflections from the political science literature on the relationship between demographic spaces, territorial spaces, the complexity and division of social labour in industrial societies, and the necessity for political representation, where elections are the dominant form of participation of the *demos* in public and institutional life, while the function of political control over the government by representative institutions becomes a central and unavoidable issue in the democratic political process. Within this framework, on the one hand Dahl emphasises that the nation, considered as the nation state, is the largest democratic unit possible (Dahl 1982), so much so that it is essential to have 'democracy within the government of the state' (Dahl 2002: 116), and on the other hand emphasises not only a radical scepticism as to the possibility of a 'world state' (2002: 69), but goes as far as to state that it is impossible to conceive of a 'world state with a democratic constitution' (2002: 70). To be sure, the planet already has a large number of transnational organisations, some of which are decidedly not inefficient and which have considerable effects on the lives of ordinary people (NATO, Comecon, the U.N., not to mention the ubiquitous multinational corporations). However, none of these organizations is very democratic. (Dahl 1982: 15).

On the subject of pluralism (which occurs frequently in the author's work) Dahl develops a number of variations on the theme that are of interest, even if they appear within a broader discussion on political doctrine that adds little that is new. When dealing with the issue of pluralism Dahl begins by specifying that he directs his attention more to organisations than to individuals. From the start then, the influence of the American tradition (indeed, of the Anglo-Saxon tradition) is evident as this vision of democracy gives greater importance to the relationship between three actors (the state, intermediate groups and citizens), rather than the relationship between two actors (citizens and the state) which has influenced political thinking in continental Europe and is markedly French in origin. Having said this, and emphasising that the polyarchy is the social order that tends to make large governments more democratic, Dahl adds that:

4. In the expressions democratic pluralism or pluralist democracy, the terms pluralism and pluralist refer to organizational pluralism, that is, to the existence of a plurality of relatively autonomous (independent) organizations (subsystems) within the domain of a state. 5. In all democratic countries, some important organizations are relatively autonomous. 6. A country is a pluralist democracy if (a) it is a democracy in the sense of a polyarchy and (b) important organizations are relatively autonomous' (Dahl 1982: 5)

In short, he viewed the plurality and autonomy of the subsystems, especially of the intermediate organisations of many different kinds, religious, economic, geographical, cultural (the associations identified with Toqueville) as a condition (essentially social) of democracy, even while being aware that if the lack of pluralism may lead to the risk of a concentration of power, an excess of pluralism tends to make governing difficult. Moreover, closely linked to social conditions (and I will return to this point shortly) we have institutional guarantees, which in the book *Polyarchy: Participation and Opposition* (1971) Dahl sets out in eight points: freedom to form and join organisations; freedom of expression; right to vote (and from this it is clear that the democratic character is 'perfected' in a logic of 'inclusion' of the masses in the political system also and above all through the extension of the franchise to that of universal suffrage); eligibility for public office; rights of political leaders to compete for support and for votes; alternative sources of information; free and fair elections; and institutions for making the government dependent on votes and other expressions of preference (Dahl 1971: 3).

It is clear that, while in the first phase of the development of Dahl's thinking he attempted to distinguish between social and institutional conditions, giving more weight first to one and then the other, and hence sometimes giving the impression of wavering between the two, in the mature stage of his development the synergy of the social and institutional dimensions appears. At the same time, the importance of the comparative element of Dahl's scientific work becomes clear and a balance emerges in the reasoning on the relationship between politics and that particular area of society represented by the economic situation.

As regards the first point, we should recall an example of the reception given to a consideration formulated earlier in his thinking, and which Dahl sums up as follows: 'To avoid misunderstanding, let me point out that not all pluralist systems are democratic: relatively autonomous organizations also exist under some nondemocratic regimes' (Dahl 1982: 29), a statement which clearly echoes Gabriel Almond's thesis, when in 1956 he listed structural pluralism as one of the characteristics that is typical of authoritarian regimes:

> If we take a system such as Spain it is evident that the religious bodies, organized interest groups, social groups and bureaucratic agencies are elements that are 'recognised', at the same level as the Falangist party, in the pluralistic political structure.[14]

Regarding the second point, a reconstruction of Dahl's thinking could be inspired by Alexis de Toqueville's writings on American democracy.

EQUALITY AND FREEDOM: THE PROBLEM

The first point to note about Toqueville's work, and that of those who followed in his intellectual footsteps, is that much weight is given to the risk facing freedom in mass democracy because of equality, but the inverse situation is neglected. Of course, not all equality is desirable; and, of course, inequality has a factual consistence that influences equality as a value, producing a continual tension between reality and the ideal which undoubtedly enriches both public and individual life, but that at the same time brings us back to a sense of proportion which stops us from falling into the trap of utopia. That said, if we consider the idea of the public good and the pursuit of the general interest not in objective terms but rather in terms of a process;[15] if we consider that the politics of civic virtue, intended abstractedly, is impossible to put into practice; if, on the other hand, we assume that the politics of hyper-egoism is morally repugnant and potentially self-destructive; then, to join civic duty and realism there remains a further prospective which Dahl sums up in the phrase the 'politics of robust civilisation'. This concept does not mean resignation and abandoning ideals, but rather expresses values that are less extreme than those of intransigent civic virtue, yet more demanding than the logic of hyper-egoism.

Within this framework, the reference to the idea and to the procedures of political equality is fundamental (an argument dealt with in the context of populist democracy and now taken up again and reformulated). In fact, if in a community – whose characteristics 'are not the sum of their individual characteristics' (Dahl 1989: 230) in that a community is not merely a group of individuals but also (and above all?) a system of interactions between individuals, between these and subsystems, between the subsystems themselves and lastly between the subsystems and the system itself – a relatively high rate of political equality becomes reality and it becomes possible to decide peacefully what forms of inequality are tolerable, how much inequality is fair and how far it is desirable, in relation to merit, social balance, to the relevant gains and losses, to the enterprise of single individuals and of groups, to their ability to work and to save, and to the quality and quantity of resources dedicated to its continuation. However, Dahl introduces an important objection, which involves an important general issue: that of the relationship between politics and economics and which brings us back to Toqueville and the necessity of reconsidering and taking account of his concerns about the interaction between equality and freedom. Is it possible to exclude the hypothesis that social inequalities, varied as they are, may interfere with political equality, progressively robbing it of power? Can we exclude the idea that this may continue to the point that it may destroy the very foundations of democracy, and therefore of both individual and group freedom too? To both questions, Dahl's response is that we cannot exclude these possibilities. Furthermore, this is true because 'maintaining the type of basic political equality that is necessary for democracy goes against certain human instincts' (Dahl 2002: 127), starting from the instinct that has the most significant effect on politics i.e. the desire to dominate others and to have power. This fact makes it necessary, in order to resist these instincts, to institutionalise political equality and keep it alive with a series of rules and regulations and to root it within the culture. In addition, there is the problem of the economy, which we will now address.

THE DILEMMA OF THE MARKET ECONOMY

Dahl's initial interest in socialism soon waned, given that he recognised the role of the market as the arena that provides a comparatively high potential for economic development compared to all other forms seen in history for the organisation of production, distribution and consumption, and also because of the close link between democracy and a market economy. Of course, Dahl realistically reminds us that 'a market economy alone is not a sufficient condition for democracy', to the extent that 'capitalistic economies have existed in many countries governed by authoritarian regimes'[16]. Having said that, in *On Democracy*, quoted earlier, the author emphasises that historically, the emergence of a democratic culture is closely bound up with what could roughly be termed market-capitalism and that 'in the long run market-capitalism has typically led to economic growth; and economic growth is favourable to democracy' (Dahl 1998: 167).

There is also a paradox that must not be overlooked. A capitalist market economy inevitably engenders inequalities regarding the resources to which individual citizens have access. Hence, a capitalist market economy seriously endangers political equality: 'the inequalities in resources that market-capitalism churns out produce serious political inequalities among citizens' (1998: 178). It is this knowledge that has led to the birth of two different lines of action both in the intervention of the 'public hand' in economic processes (with welfare policies for example) aimed at reducing pressure towards inequality, and in the regulation that policies have imposed on the market to the same end, as well as to protect freedom. Indiscriminate market freedom, which constantly risks the domination of the weak by those stronger, could lead in turn to the danger of reducing the freedom and the liberties of democracy itself, that is to say of political freedom.

Furthermore, as Dahl so lucidly sums up, the theory of democracy rests on the concept of individuals as citizens; the idea of capitalism is that of individuals as consumers of goods and services. The citizen exists within a limited and confined political space, the city-state or the nation state in the modern era. The state, it is believed has clear confines: the liberties, the equalities and the duties of the citizens depend on their position within or outside the system. Producers and consumers, on the other hand, operate within the framework of an economic system that has no confines and that, generally speaking, coincides with the entire world.[17] The feelings of belonging and loyalty of citizens towards the nation state are no doubt a consequence of these factors. However, the same is not typically true of the producer/consumer, who is part of a logic in which the aim is to obtain the greatest possible economic advantage, to the exclusion of other considerations.

This distinction has become even more evident in the current era of globalisation.[18] It is also clear that in the arena of a global economy, the theme of a technocracy, of a 'government of experts' able to cope with the public issues that emerge from the extraordinarily complex reality of the contemporary world, may come back into play. After all, democracy, despite its efforts at modernisation, has its cultural roots in the small and much simpler Greek *polis*.

TECHNOCRACY, MEANS AND ENDS

As far as technocracy is concerned, the contribution of Dahl, which has been repeated on several occasions and which has been put together in *Controlling Nuclear Weapons; Democracy versus Guardianship* (1985b), is not particularly innovative. It is useful in that it repeats certain warnings which are conceptually correct, but which do not add any original considerations on the subject. His reflections go back to Plato, as is quite normal in the literature, even though the knowledge of this ancient philosopher is very different to the technical knowledge of a technocrat. He does not display any awareness of the works of the first, real theoreticians of technocracy, the French writers of the nineteenth century, Claude Henri de Saint-Simon and Auguste Comte[19], or of the problems they raised with reference to an industrial society, which is the period in time and space from which it is correct to start a debate on the risks of technocracy. While it is true that, directly, Dahl's work on guardianship aims to criticise a conception which according to him appears in ancient philosophy, it is nevertheless true that by applying this criticism to the debate on the control of nuclear weapons his thinking is transferred undoubtedly to a contemporary context. From here we must consider the problem of technocracy.

Where is the matrix to which the 'government of guardians', and its modern version i.e. technocracy, should refer in order to legitimise their right to the exercise of power? It lies in the claim that they interpret the general interest, on the basis of their superior scientific and technical expertise: at the basis of the idea of the 'government of the guardians' there is an idea that the realm of politics is one of incompetence, special interests and corruption. Indeed, these special interests make it impossible to comprehend the sense of common interest, whereas expertise makes it possible to recognise it objectively and thus work towards the common good in managing public affairs, to the extent that expertise becomes the basis of civic virtue.

It is clear that this general illustration of power in a technocracy is in no way new to the thinking expressed in the literature of over a century and a half. The responses to the 'ideology of the technocracy' – as this is indeed what it is – are by now well consolidated,[20] and the writings of Dahl are little more than variations on a theme, interesting enough but not decisive.

It is worth looking at the relationship between 'moral competence' and 'technical or instrumental competence'. The first relates to the understanding of the 'ends, the goals or objectives that a government should try to achieve'; while the latter refers to the 'best, most efficient or most appropriate to achieve desirable ends' (Dahl 1985b: 25). Thus, the first question is whether competence, in the sense of an understanding of the goals which it states it will attempt to achieve, is enough morally to legitimise governing in the best general interest? Undoubtedly, knowledge of the ends is important when leading a community. However, there are many ends which may often be in contradiction, and they are the result of value choices, choices of civilisation and even metaphysical considerations.

Competence alone is not sufficient, and especially a competence claimed by a group of people (appointed how and by whom?), successfully and legitimately to cross the tricky terrain of the pursuit of the general interest. As far as technical competence is concerned and its relationship with 'virtue', Vilfredo Pareto has highlighted in a few words the limits of the technocracy argument: 'you may sin through ignorance, but you may also sin for interest. Technical competence may avoid the former, but can do nothing to avoid the latter' (Pareto 1951: 180). This is paraphrased by Dahl as 'Technocrats are no more qualified than others to make essential moral judgements and may even be less so' (Dahl 1985b: 45). He later writes that it is necessary to see 'whether our putative guardians deserve our faith because they pursue the common good instead of just their own interests, that is to say whether they do or do not have a sufficient supply of that quality defined as virtue' (1985b: 47–8).

Undoubtedly, the lesson of Dahl and Lindblom on the 'calculation of the means' suggests that in politics, and not just in politics alone, the means are of the utmost importance. You may have the most worthy goal in the world, but if you do not have the means to reach it and you use the means wrongly, then all is in vain. This also poses the problem of whether technocrats are necessarily free from technical errors, and experience shows that this is practically impossible to guarantee. Moreover, if the courses of action to choose from are more than one, and if the 'availability of means is such as to equally permit more than one end, then the choice between these ends is a purely political choice' (Fisichella 2002b: 116).

Yet, this is not everything, as there is a dilemma much emphasised by Dahl, which is expressed as follows. As we already know, Dahl does not believe that the properties of a system will always be the same as the properties (or the desires, or interests) of the units (firstly individuals, but also groups) that make it up. Moreover, we are aware that the systems are not only formed of parts, but depend also on the relationships between the parts. Thus, it follows that while the instrumental élite, i.e. the technocracy, does not have (or may not have – this is unimportant for the logic of speculation) 'the special moral competence that might entitle them to make decisions on matters of public policy, ordinary people often lack the instrumental knowledge to judge which policies would be in their best interests' (and even more so of the system's interests). Hence, when it comes to complex issues 'neither instrumental elites nor ordinary citizens are politically competent to rule' (Dahl 1985b: 64). In the attempt to find a possible solution to escape this impasse, the essay on democracy and technocracy, published in 1985, can still permit itself the luxury of playing with the 'semi-utopian' idea of using technology for an 'urgent democratic goal: fostering politically competent citizens',[21] which would create a sort of *minipopulus* who would be active at national, state and local levels, and each of whom would be able to deal with and perhaps decide on issues of greater or lesser importance. Now we are in the third millennium, and given the more recent developments in mass communication and internet, it is unlikely that such a solution could be considered, even if there were no other objections to it. Moreover, all of Dahl's most recent works focus on representative, pluralistic and competitive democracy. It is within this framework that the possibility of achieving a greater or lesser balance between criteria of expertise and of elective criteria, which would be compatible with the greater or lesser extent of democracy possible in today's world or that of the future, should be sought. In fact, more than thirty years ago in an essay on the risk of technocracy, I underlined that the checks on political responsibility, typically performed by the representative institutions in our current day democracy, guarantee (may guarantee – but there are no plausible alternatives) two advantages. Typically, at least, they are a guarantee against the danger that the resources of science, technology and production are used by the powers-that-be as a source of pressure, rather than a possibility of freeing man and society from evil and need. Furthermore, at least typically, a system of political control centred on representative institutions (and therefore also, and primarily, on the institutionalised presence of an opposition)[22] guarantees independence to the experts in the work of technical control of public policies and in the calculation of means. Indeed, what sense would a check on technical validity carried out by an expert (or team of experts) on any programme of action by the governing power have, if that control could be ignored without the obligation of giving any plausible technical justification and without the possibility of the governing power being forced to answer politically for its actions? Undoubtedly, the governing power (the government) is not tied by a technical consultancy; it is at its discretion to ignore it wholly or in part. However, the government must answer for this decision. Hence, in a representative democracy the choice is subject to political responsibility. This ensures both freedom and a reasoned political evaluation of expert competence.[23]

DEMOCRACY AS A METAPARADIGM

Throughout history democracy has been rare. It was rare in the ancient world where only a few *poleis* were governed according to democratic standards and even then only for periods that at most stretched to a couple of centuries. As far as the future is concerned, a world state is very difficult to imagine, and indeed it is impossible for it to be organised along democratic lines. International and supranational organisations already exist and they are likely to become more common, but they do not appear democratic even if it is true that 'democracy can take on different institutional forms' (Dahl 2001b: 37). Having said this, if we for example imagine that federalism, as practised in the United States, could be a solution for the European Union, then we should, Dahl reminds us, note that in 1790 when the federal constitution was adopted, the US had a population of less than four million. Moreover, the white population had rapidly constructed a national identity, partly because of the push west. Despite this, the consensus on institutions was not sufficient to avoid a particularly cruel civil war.[24]

And what can be said about the current situation? The situation is thus, Dahl states in his *How Democratic is the American Constitution?* published in 2001:

'including the United States, there are 22 countries in the world [...] in which basic democratic political institutions have functioned without interruption for a fairly long time, let's say at least half a century, that is, since 1950'.[25] It is worth noting that the starting date would not have to be moved more than ten years for the list to be greatly reduced. To name but a few, Japan, Germany and Italy would not figure, as a long world war was necessary to convince these nations to 'convert' to democracy. One of these 22 on the list is the United States. If we consider as one of the characteristics of a democracy, inclusiveness (that is the inclusion of most of the white, male population in political citizenship, including the right to vote), then the US is practically the only country which can boast (almost) two centuries of experience with modern democratic institutions (Dahl 2001c). However, in this essay Dahl poses a rather worrying question: how democratic is the American constitution? The essay thus entitled is an exercise in style that, it should be noted, is abstract and an end in itself. Everything gets harsh treatment in the essay and practically no part of the constitutional structure of the American nation, or of the beliefs that surround it, is spared:

> Many Americans appear to believe that our constitution has been a model for the rest of the democratic world. Yet among the countries most comparable to the United States and where democratic institutions have long existed without breakdown, not one has adopted our American constitutional system. It would be fair to say that without a single exception they have all rejected it. (Dahl 2001c: 41)

Moreover, from the constitutional principles of American democracy there derives 'a political system so opaque and so at odds with general conceptions of public virtue that it weakens both civic understanding and citizens' confidence in our political institutions' (2001c: 146). And therein lies a basic problem.

It is clear that in his ruthless criticism of his country's constitutional framework Dahl has used rigid parameters, even though when it comes to listing how much and what may be changed, there is substantially only one response: despite all its democratic deficiencies, it would be unrealistic to consider changing federalism, presidentialism, inequalities linked to representation as determined by the make-up of the Senate, the electoral college, or even a system that swings between majority and consensual criteria ('the Framers of 1787 appear to have limited today's framers to a system that is neither consensual nor majoritarian but is a hybrid that possesses the vices of both and the virtues of neither', 2001c: 148–9). It thus seems reasonable to ask, given that any attempts at reform of the many things that are wrong are judged to be impossible, what sense does this essay have apart from highlighting the dissatisfaction of a scholar who has remained constantly faithful to the theme of democracy? Or should we conclude that a democracy can function even when the constitutional structure is so bad and so undemocratic? But had Dahl not reached the point where he recognised the importance of constitutional structures in the dynamics of the democratic political system? And to what extent and for how long can a constitution contradict a (the) democracy without removing the very foundations of its credibility?

It does not, however, finish here. If it is not possible to change the constitution, a move destined to failure, 'we need a second strategy, one designed to achieve greater *political* equality within the limits of the present American Constitution. A major objective of such strategy would be to reduce the vast inequalities in the existing distribution of *political resources*' (2001c: 156). Is this strategy destined to produce meaningful results? It may be considered doubtful, if we consider the critical comments Dahl made of Tocqueville with reference to the relationship between freedom and inequality, if we consider the effect of economic and social inequality on political equality, if we consider the characteristics of the process of globalisation, the temptations of globalism and the pressures that arise from it towards ever increasing social and economic inequalities, and the problems it produces for democratic legitimacy, which Dahl rightly holds to be a decisive factor in the stability of these political regimes. If we bear in mind all these points then the problem is clearly not one of the collapse of democracies under assault from anti-democratic movements, as occurred in the twentieth century. The problem is rather a sort of shrivelling up of democracy, which will progressively dry up from inside, and increasingly take on oligarchic features.[26]

Dahl is realistic when analysing possible democracies, obstinately clever when pruning this form of public regime of conceptual branches that are considered superfluous or inessential and bringing our attention back to the central importance of political equality (even though it is described as 'democracy of the ancients' or 'democracy of modern man') and for him democracy is more than a mere phenomenon to be observed. If it were no more than this it would be an object of study that would be limited over time and space. The point is a different one. To use the language of epistemology, for Dahl democracy is the great metaparadigm of his research,[27] as a categorical paradigm that is taken with a certain measure of dogmatism. His research consists of contrasting and disproving criticism and eliminating weaknesses and irregularities in the theory. Basically his aim is to solve a 'puzzle' in order to strengthen the cognitive and explicative reach of the theoretical system and ultimately to make it more scientific. Dahl's work, undoubtedly so rich in arguments, reproduces what he sees as the continual uphill struggle of democracy: to bring reality closer to an ideal which will never be reached but to which no alternative hypotheses exist. What type of government is the best, or the least imperfect? Dahl's answer remains unchanged. The question remains as to why man, a creature not lacking in rationality, or reasonableness (in fact I know of no theory of democracy that does not assume a human being capable of reason or reasonableness) has exercised this gift so little throughout the course of history.

Notes

1. As we will see more clearly later on, inequality in fact is, for Dahl, a 'limit' to social action in democracy, more than a given result of historical experience, and therefore the real problem ends up being the counterbalancing of the inequalities rather than achievement of equality.
2. If the two trends had the same weight there would be a state of paralysis or a break up of the system.
3. Which Dahl presents within the framework of the historical-cultural context of the United States, but which in many ways goes back to the nineteenth century models of constitutional bourgeois democracy.
4. For Dahl, the adjective 'Madisonian' does not mean that this type of democratic system exactly coincides with the descriptions present in Madison's works (Dahl 1967: 4–5). The reference is more to a particular era and a particular atmosphere.
5. Be it the hands of a single person, of a small or large group and whether by legitimate accumulation, through inheritance or election or whatever else.
6. A faction is 'a group of citizens, be they a majority or minority, united and moved by a common impulse or passion, or interest, contrary to the rights of other citizens or the permanent or shared interests of the community'. See The Federalist 10.
7. Such as the page dealing with the empirical problem posed by Mosca's analysis and by its political category which, obviously, conflicts with the postulates of populism, see Dahl (1967: 54). On the relationship between élites and democracy, however, Dahl returned later and at greater length. See Dahl (1958; 1966a). Both articles are examples of applications of polyarchal theory to research into the notions about dominant élites.
8. For the enumeration of the points see Dahl (1967: 84).
9. See Fisichella (2002b: 36–49).
10. On the relationship between political conflict and popular government, see Dahl (1963).
11. The rating along a scale attempted by Dahl (1967) was in fact only a theoretical exercise, which did not begin from a real comparative approach, nor was rooted in one.
12. On this subject see Fisichella (1994, especially 26–42).
13. See my essay (Fisichella, 1980), now part of the collection Fisichella (2002b chap. III, p.80).
14. See Almond (1956: 40). See also my 'Opinione sul pluralismo' (Fisichella, 1976: 151–2). 'The concept of pluralism merits specifying and completing: on its own, it can refer both to democratic and non-democratic experiences [...] Not only, then, a plurality of partners, but a plurality of rival partners in direct competition'. To sum up, pluralism in democracy is competitive pluralism. See also Fisichella (2002a: 103–7) for further details.
15. See Dahl, 'Is Civic Virtue a Relevant Ideal in a Pluralist Democracy?' (1996) now in Dahl (2001a: 103). The consideration on Toquevillian thinking is greatly developed in Dahl (1985a, Italian translation 1989, esp. 13–50).
16. See Dahl 'Why all Democratic Countries have Mixed Economies' (1993), now in (Dahl 2001a: 26).
17. See Dahl 'Equality versus Inequality' (1996), now in (Dahl 2001a).
18. On the dichotomy between *polis/apolis*, citizen/stateless person, see Fisichella (2000 chapter VII).
19. See Fisichella (1965).
20. See for example, in addition to previously cited Fisichella (1965), my essay 'Il rischio tecnocratico' (1972), now in Fisichella (2002b: 105–124), as well as Fisichella (1997).
21. Dahl (1985b: 76), where he continues as follows: 'What I am going to suggest is a set of organizations and processes to accomplish three objectives: 1) To ensure that information about the political agenda, appropriate in level and form, and accurately reflecting the best knowledge available, is easily and universally accessible to all citizens. 2) To create easily available and universally accessible opportunities for all citizens to influence the informa-

tional agenda and to participate in a relevant way. 3) To provide a highly informed body of public opinion that (except for being highly informed) is representative of the entire citizen body.'
22 See Fisichella (1996, passim).
23 See Fisichella (2002b: 121), as well as Fisichella (1997: 64–5), where I conclude thus: 'a mechanism of political control is a necessary, though insufficient, condition for the free stating of proposals of technical control'.
24 I developed another argument in Fisichella (2001: 225–8), when considering the quite clear differences between the history and culture of the US and Europe. I nevertheless observed that in the American experience it was also necessary to deal with some tricky constitutional issues (such as questions of quotas, veto rights, unanimity) which have now come up in the European context.
25 See Dahl (2001c: 43). I may add here that on page 166, Italy is mentioned among those countries that have a multi-preference, proportional electoral system. This has not been the case for some years.
26 On this subject see Fisichella (2000, esp. chapter XI).
27 On the notion of 'metaphysical paradigm' or 'metaparadigm' see Fisichella (1994, esp. 26–36) where the theories of T. S. Kuhn are discussed on the subject of 'normal science'.

REFERENCES

Almond, G. A. (1956) 'Comparative Political Systems', in H. Eulau (ed.), *Political Behavior*, Glencoe, Free Press, pp. 36–42.

Dahl, R. A. (1958) 'A Critique of the Ruling Elite Model', *American Political Science Review* LII: 463–9.

(1961) *Who Governs? Democracy and Power in an American City*, New Haven-London: Yale University Press.

(1963) *Modern Political Analysis*, Englewood Cliffs, NJ: Prentice Hall.

(1966a) 'Further Reflections on "The Elitist Theory of Democracy"', *American Political Science Review,* LX (2): 296–305.

(1966b) (ed.) *Political Oppositions in Western Democracies*, New Haven and London: Yale University Press.

(1967 [1956]) *A Preface to Democratic Theory*, Chicago: University of Chicago Press.

(1971) *Polyarchy: Participation and Opposition,* New Haven-London: Yale University Press.

(1982) *Dilemmas of Pluralist Democracy*, New Haven-London: Yale University Press.

(1985a) *A Preface to Economic Democracy*, Berkeley: University of California Press.

(1985b) *Controlling Nuclear Weapons: Democracy versus Guardianship*, Syracuse: Syracuse University Press.

(1989) *Democracy and its Critics*, New Haven-London: Yale University Press.

(1998) *On Democracy*, New Haven-London: Yale University Press.

(2001a) *Politica e virtù: La teoria democratica nel nuovo secolo*, Roma-Bari: Laterza.
(2001b) 'Is Post-National Democracy Possible?', in S. Fabbrini (ed.), *Nation, Federalism and Democracy. The EU, Italy and the American Federal Experience*, Bologna, Editrice Compositori.
(2001c) *How Democratic is the American Constitution?*, New Haven-London: Yale University Press.
(2002) *Intervista sul pluralismo*, edited by G. Bosetti, Roma-Bari: Laterza.

Dahl, R. A. and Lindblom, C. E. (1953) *Politics, Economics, and Welfare*, New York: Harper & Row.

Fabbrini, S. (2001) 'Robert A. Dahl: un viaggiatore «liberal» della democrazia', in R.A. Dahl, *Politica e virtù. La teoria democratica nel nuovo secolo*, Roma-Bari: Laterza.

Fisichella, D. (1965) *Il potere nella società industriale*, Napoli: Morano, new ed. (1995) Roma-Bari: Laterza.
(1976) 'Opinione sul pluralismo', in D. Basili (ed.), *Pluralismo: appunti*, Roma, Rai.
(1980) 'Gruppi di interesse e gruppi di pressione nella democrazia moderna', *Rivista Italiana di Scienza Politica*, X (1): 53–71.
(1994) *Epistemologia e scienza politica*, Roma: La Nuova Italia Scientifica.
(1996) *La rappresentanza politica*, Roma-Bari: Laterza.
(1997) *L'altro potere: Tecnocrazia e gruppi di pressione*, Roma-Bari: Laterza.
(2000) *Denaro e democrazia: Dall'antica Grecia all'economia globale*, Bologna: il Mulino.
(2001) 'Una visione realistica del costituzionalismo dell'Unione europea', in S. Fabbrini (ed.), *Nation, Federalism and Democracy: The EU, Italy and the American Federal Experience*, Bologna: Editrice Compositori.
(2002a) *Totalitarismo: Un regime del nostro tempo*, Roma: Carocci.
(2002b) *Politica e mutamento sociale*, Lungro di Cosenza: Marco Editore.
(2003) *Elezioni e democrazia: Un'analisi comparata*, Bologna: il Mulino.

Michels, R. (1915) *Political Parties: A Sociological Study of the Oligarchical Tendencies of Modern Democracy*. Translated into English by E. and C. Paul. New York: The Free Press.

Pareto, V. (1951 [1902]) *I sistemi socialisti*, Torino: Utet.

chapter two | Anthony Downs: Master of Many Models
Ian Budge

INTRODUCTION

Anthony Downs is unusual in having been active in economic and political research during the 1950s and 1960s, and then turning to real estate and urban planning for the rest of his career. He left political economy in spite of the great and enduring success of his first book, *An Economic Theory of Democracy* (1957). A new manuscript on the *Theory of Democracy* is currently circulating. This chapter concentrates on the *Economic Theory*, starting from the fact that the book presents not one but many theories of democracy even if they are all generally couched in economic terms. Some of these theories (or models) of party competition and voting have mutually contradictory predictions, such as parties sticking to the same policies to demonstrate reliability and responsibility, while in terms of the two-party spatial model they will converge in policy terms. The confusion is heightened when assumptions and conclusions from one model are grafted on to another in the text.

This chapter expounds the argument of the *Economic Theory* systematically and sequentially covering:

a) the general non-spatial model of party competition;
b) effects of information shortage;
c) party reliability and responsibility;
d) the two-party spatial model;
e) the multi-party spatial model;
f) further consequences of information shortage;
g) problems of voting turnout.

Evidence from quantified election programmes is used to show that the models leading to limited party policy movement and non-convergence are the more realistic ones. The Appendix provides the full set of 22 assumptions necessary to derive Downs' propositions at the end of the *Economic Theory*. In spite of its defects, the book has laid down the agenda for mathematical political theory and empirical research over the last 50 years and has a fair claim to being the most influential single book written on politics in that period.

THE ENDURING INFLUENCE OF 'AN ECONOMIC THEORY OF DEMOCRACY'

Asked to nominate the most important professional book of the last 50 years, many political scientists – perhaps a plurality or even a majority – would opt for *An Economic Theory of Democracy*. This work is almost unique in being cited more often 50 years on than when it was first published, although it attracted attention even then. It has been seminal in the development of the rational choice approach, now hegemonic in the discipline. Its influence has extended far beyond mathematical modellers however, to shape the outlook of mainstream political scientists across the globe – not bad for an only slightly modified Ph.D. thesis!

The book's attractions lie in its relevant simplifications of central democratic processes, its accessibility, readability and to some extent in its ambiguities. Clarity of exposition and directness of argument are in many cases bought at the price of ignoring difficulties which have preoccupied theorists ever since. The most famous is the question of whether party leapfrogging is allowed or not in the two-party spatial model (Downs 1957: 111–17; Barry 1970: 112–15). But there is ambiguity even in the title. Far from Downs giving us one economic theory of elections and party competition, he gives us many. There are non-spatial and spatial models; there are models with two parties and models with many parties; there are policy-flexible and ideologically-rooted parties. Sometimes parties seem to be concerned with vote maximisation and sometimes with office-seeking.

The *Economic Theory* tends to be identified with only one of these variants – the spatial model of two-party competition under certainty, with totally flexible office-seeking parties which converge in policy terms to maximize votes. The popularity of this model rests partly on what seemed (initially at any rate), to be a good approximation to US electoral politics. Thus it has been Americans above all who have been interested in Downs, particularly in the early days. We should note however that the relevant model for practically all party systems outside the US is Downs' multi-party one, predicting policy rigidity (Downs 1957: 122–3) – a point explored further below.

The ambiguities in Downs' arguments and models have by and large rendered the *Economic Model* more, rather than less, appealing. The initial simplification of electoral processes to parties and electors[1], characterized by their policy positions, has been highly fruitful, leaving room for infinite modifications on the theme of convergent or divergent policy equilibria. Again most such analyses have concentrated on two-party or two-candidate competition, ignoring the fact that a) this is a rare case; b) that Downs has other models – even for the two-party situation – which produce different results quite parsimoniously. The great scope which exists for modifying the spatial model in various ways has made it a happy hunting ground for ambitious young scholars, and resulted in continual citation and use.

Examples of its continuing influence are to be found in many fields. The most important are:

a) (Mathematical) democratic theory

In Barry's *Sociologists, Economists and Democracy* (1970) Downs' arguments were extensively analysed as exemplary of rational choice approaches. Riker and Ordeshook's *Positive Political Theory* (1973) was concerned with formally modifying assumptions of the two-party spatial models and following them through to their consequences. Many subsequent writers have been concerned doing with this both verbally (Aldrich 1983) and mathematically (Calvert 1986; Coughlin 1992; McKelvey and Ordeshook 1985) – to name but a few.

b) Party competition and voting

David Robertson in *A Theory of Party Competition* (1976) proposed a modified two-party Downsian model where parties sought votes and converged only if the election was competitive. He tested this on statistical evidence from British party manifestos, followed by Budge and Farlie (1977); Budge (1994); Adams (2001). The checking of Downsian convergence ideas is still going on, as evidenced below in this chapter and e.g. Dalton and Wattenberg (2000).

c) The Left-Right dimension

Downs' claim that this has to be the main context for communication between party leaders and electors in an information-starved environment has been discussed, analysed, and disputed ever since by survey-based and political analysts. There is an emerging consensus that it is indeed the context for electoral discussion as evidenced in Miller *et al.* (1999) and Budge *et al.* (2001) on the basis of comparative survey and textual data.

One could go on, but enough has been said to illustrate Downs' influence both on rational choice thinking and on general democratic theory, to which parties, elections and voting must be central. The success of the *Economic Theory*'s initial move in focussing on the barest and most basic aspects of the electoral process should never be underestimated. Appearing in 1957 the book cut through the welter of detailed findings beginning to be produced by election studies, concentrating on the key players and their motivations at every time and place – electors' concern to get their preferences accepted as public policy and parties' desire to attain public office. The idea of arranging parties and electors along the Left-Right dimension so commonly used in practical political discussion, brought it at one stroke closer to party strategic concerns and eliminated the newly rediscovered problem of cyclical preferences without a stable majority (Arrow 1951).

Both moves had of course been anticipated by Hotelling (1929), Smithies (1941), and paralleled by Black (1958). The fact that they were taken up from the *Economic Theory* while being largely ignored previously, rests in part on its engaging axiomatic and quasi logical style. But it was also fortunate in appearing at just the right time, when aspirations for a genuinely scientific study of politics seemed to be met by it and a growing appreciation of mathematical approaches to politics was spreading among the profession. Not that the *Economic Theory* was mathematical – that was part of its appeal. Everything was argued in clear English prose with easy to read spatial diagrams, so non-mathematicians could readily understand its arguments. However, it was also clear that the book offered both a basis for and a push towards greater mathematisation. So it appealed both to those with and those without mathematical skills within political science.

The crucial effects of timing are illustrated by the fate of Downs' other book, *Inside Bureaucracy*. Applying the same kind of analysis to bureaux as the *Economic Theory* did to elections – even to the extent of having axioms generating specific hypotheses (Downs 1967: 262–80) – it simply failed to attract much attention. Possibly this was because of a more complex argument which could not be represented spatially – bureaucracy is harder to reduce to simple key processes than elections. Basing himself on the bureau or department as the basic unit of bureaucracy, Downs posits three 'central hypotheses':

a) bureaucratic officials act rationally
b) bureaucratic officials are self interested
c) the bureau's social functions strongly influence its internal structure.

The rational choice and self interest postulates are familiar from the parties and electors of the *Economic Theory*. The third is already more complex (there was no need to state this for political parties!). The general argument deploys concepts already familiar from the *Economic Theory*, such as information shortage and ideology. However, they have to be located in a more complicated argument, with no simple spatial diagrams of dynamic movement available to hit the reader between the eyes.

To some extent Downs' argument goes against the mainstream of the rational choice literature. For example, he argues trenchantly that the 'coalition of minorities' supporting the bureaux which benefit them is stronger than any potential majority for cutting government activity. This is shown by the continuing failure to mobilize such a majority. Thus the current size and activities of bureaucracy cannot be regarded as excessive (Downs 1967: 258). Among free market theorists using rational choice ideas to demonstrate that bureaucracies must *always* be excessive, this argument exerted no appeal and was not one they wished to put either to students or disciples.

Downs' argument about budgets normally basing themselves on last year's expenditure owing to information shortages (1967: 248–9) interestingly anticipated theories of incrementalism, but was put in the shade by Davis *et al.* (1966) actual demonstration of this process at work in their article of the previous year. This coincidence demonstrates a weakness of the book which explains its failure to repeat the success of the *Economic Theory*. Too much of the ground it covers had already been explored by others (e.g. Simon 1947). Where it was original (e.g. in arguing against theories of excessive bureaucratic growth) it was anathema to most of its potential audience. Thus it never caught general attention in the way its sister book did. Its lack of impact must have been an influence on Downs' withdrawal from political research. But it was amply compensated by the enduring success of *An Economic Theory of Democracy*, on which we shall concentrate below.

AN OVERVIEW OF THE 'ECONOMIC THEORY' (OR THEORIES!)

Even in terms of this one book, professional attention has been selective, focussing for the most part on the spatial models of Chapter 8 and discussion of coalition governments in Chapter 9 – just 50 pages in all. 'Rational abstention' in Part III probably attracted more attention initially than now. Some idea of how these high points of the argument fit into the general themes of the book is necessary for their full appreciation however, as well as bringing out neglected aspects of the analysis which turn out to have a considerable contemporary relevance.

Political scientists have naturally tended to take the title *An Economic Theory of Democracy* as signalling a sustained attempt to apply economic models of reasoning to politics. While this is true, Downs initially conceived it as explaining how a central economic player, the government, would act within the context of capitalist democracy. Hence, his interest in government budgeting (1957: 52–3, 67–73) and in the policy consequences of party competition – leading to such propositions (4, 6, 7 on p. 297) as action on social problems, redistribution of income from rich to poor, and privileging of producers rather than consumers. The last substantive chapter on 'Economic Theories of Government Behaviour' explicitly enjoins economists to apply self-interest axioms to governments as well as to firms and consumers. However, the effect of analysing political actors such as parties and electors is to shift attention from economics to politics, as is perhaps generally true in the study of 'political economy'. Certainly Downs from the start attracted more attention from political scientists than economists, even though he drew heavily on the latters' work.

This helped, in a way election studies could not, in stripping down the elements of the democratic process to a set of procedural devices for ensuring the fairness of elections and their determining role in choosing governments (1957: 23–4) on the one hand, and interactions between parties and electors on the other. Following Schumpeter (1950: 269, 282) democracy is defined as a competitive struggle for votes between parties, which consist of leadership teams united by their desire for office – their sole concern. Electors on the other hand gain only from the implementation of policies they prefer, and will therefore vote for the party which holds out most prospect of advancing them within government. In maximising votes so as to form a government – even though their sole concern is to be in it – parties therefore have to concern themselves with policy.

As the winning party (or coalition of parties) will have endorsed the policies supported by the electoral majority, Downs is in effect proposing a government mandate theory of democracy. Individual preferences are aggregated by parties in such a way that the position(s) endorsed by a majority become public policy, as is required for fully democratic decision-making.

The technical attraction of democracy for Downs (again stemming from the initial economic concerns of his analysis) is that it avoids interpersonal comparisons of utilities between citizens by endowing them with an equal vote. As a normative principle each counts as one and no more than one. The way citizens actually cast their votes is determined by their party differential, i.e. the difference in personal utility they expect from one party being elected rather than another. Calculating this is made more difficult by having many parties in competition rather than only two, and by uncertainty.

Where there is only a government and opposition, under certainty, the opposition party is advantaged because it can wait until the governing party commits itself, as it has to in making public decisions. The opposition can then take advantage of varying intensities of feeling among electors to build a 'coalition of minorities' where each minority feels more intensely about one issue than about the others where its members form part of the majority. Or it can wait until a voting cycle emerges as illustrated in Table 1.

Preference Orderings Over Policy Alternatives or Candidates A, B and C	Extreme Case	Less Extreme Case
A→B→C	33.3	22.2
A→C→B	0	11.1
B→C→A	33.3	22.2
B→A→C	0	11.1
C→A→B	33.3	22.2
C→B→A	0	11.1
Voting to choose A over B	66.6	56.5
Voting to choose B over C	66.6	56.5
Voting to choose C over A	66.5	56.5

A B and C represent three policy alternatives or candidates. The arrow → represents preferences as between alternatives. Thus A → B → C stands for 'A is preferred to B and B is preferred to C'.

Table 1: Individually consistent preference orderings give rise to cyclical and unstable majorities

As any alternative the government chooses can always be defeated in a paired election by some other alternative, the opposition party has only to bide its time until some issue provokes such a cycle and then choose the alternative that will defeat the government (1957: 61). This interestingly anticipates Riker's (1982, 1993) argument that the art of politics consists in searching out new issues which introduce cycling into previously stable situations, undermining previously dominant coalitions and creating new opportunities for the astute political entrepreneur.

Where electors rank issues the same way, and cycling does not arise (perhaps avoided by presenting only two alternatives on each issue) 'both parties nearly always adopt any policy that a majority of electors strongly prefer' (1957: 64). ('Strongly' in this context simply means that they prefer the majority position on this issue to the minority position on any other issues under consideration).

This conclusion deserves underlining because from it derives the (in)famous convergence result, usually associated with the spatial two-party model of party competition (1957: 118 and Figure 2, page 53), from strictly non-spatial assumptions. These are summarized in Table A1 of the Appendix. This non-spatial, general, model of party competition is the first of the several distinct models presented by the *Economic Theory*. While its assumptions underlie the two-party spatial model they are not implied by it: the reverse in fact, as the spatial model needs these assumptions to work as well as the additional ones in Table A3. As Barry (1970: 102) remarks, if the spatial assumptions turned out to be ill-founded one could go back to the general model and try again.

Rather than following through directly to the spatial model from the general model of which it is a specialized development, Downs inserts a discussion of uncertainty and of an entirely different model (party responsibility and reliability) between the two. For many readers this has perhaps obscured their connection.

The existence of uncertainty does however support the development of the spatial model, based on a Left-Right continuum, by suggesting why electors might use such broad ideological characterisations of parties. Basically this is because the costs of gathering and processing information about detailed policies far outweighs its value for voters, so to calculate their party differential they rely on various economising devices – advice from intermediaries, the general Left-Right stance rather than specific policies adopted by parties, and so on.

Having adopted a particular ideological position as a means to attract voters, parties cannot simply abandon it. Parties must be reliable, in the sense of effecting their ideology when in office, and responsible, in the sense of maintaining ideological consistency over time. Both are necessary for maintaining the trust of voters that the parties will do what they say they will. Otherwise there is no point in voting for them.

It is important to note that Downs is here proposing a quite distinct model of two-party behaviour from the ones he is generally associated with, of unrestricted policy mobility for parties. Reliability and responsibility imply that parties will stick to much the same policy positions over time, thus completely undermining either spatial or non-spatial policy convergence. Recognising this, Downs suggests that where ideological consistency and strategic adjustment conflict, the latter will always prevail, though he stresses that this assumption is subject to empirical testing (1957: 111–13).

This 'opinion' clears the way for the spatial representation of two-party competition, based on Hotelling's (1929) and Smithies' (1941) spatial markets which they applied to politics as a Left-Right scale. Electors place themselves at different points on the scale in terms of their (information economising) general policy preference. They must all agree on the position each party takes on the scale, thus introducing certainty back into the argument. Their preference for a party decreases the further it lies from them on the scale: hence they will always vote for the nearest party.

Downs innovates on earlier models by allowing distributions to vary along the continuum in different party systems. As voter preferences are fixed extraneously to the model, at any rate for the short-term, their distribution can explain both the number and strategic behaviour of the political parties – unlike Lipset and Rokkans' (1967) classical account of party system development where parties played a major part in developing their own support and might carry some electors with them when they moved position. Unimodal distributions of voters (Figure 2 below) and bimodal ones produce two parties: multi modal ones many parties. In the latter two cases this is because each party sits on its own 'part' of the distribution from which it has no incentive to move.[2] In a unimodal situation both parties can increase votes by moving towards the denser parts of the distribution – at the extreme, up to the median voter, though Downs suggests that abstention by voters on the wings as a result of the party moving from them in policy terms could slow convergence (cf Aldrich 1983). Strictly this would require additional assumptions in the model (cf. Hinich and Ordeshook 1969).

At one stroke, therefore, a unimodal policy distribution explains why two parties only are in competition (any others get squeezed out in the move to the centre) and introduces a dynamic (convergence on the median) as compared to the static nature of other situations. Most US political scientists were happy until about 1980 to accept this as a theoretical explanation of the perceived moderation, pragmatism and policy compromises of US parties. As Republicans and Democrats have been increasingly perceived as more ideological and less compromising, unhappiness has grown with the 'unrealistic' convergence result and many theoretical attempts have been made to modify it by changing specific assumptions.[3] This has proved difficult within Downs' overall set of assumptions – non-spatial as well as spatial (Appendix A), since the former also produce policy convergence.

In their search for more votes Downs also suggests that two parties use ambiguity about their exact location on the Left-Right space as a tactic, as compared to the more exact demarcation of positions by the many parties under a multi-modal distribution of opinion. Ambiguity makes calculations of how to vote more difficult, though calculating is also difficult in a multi-party situation where the nature of the government to emerge after an election is obscure. This is a point which anticipates and may have prompted later contrasts between these two 'visions' of democracy (Powell 2000).

The spatial models are certainly the best-known part of the *Economic Theory* and possibly the only part most people read. This may be explained by the fact that they are followed by an economics-orientated discussion of how one may expect a government dominated by vote-seeking to act in the economy. Certainly not by aiming at a pareto optimum by benefiting some while making no-one worse off! On the whole it will favour the more numerous poor against the rich and intervene more in the market.

Downs returns to an election-linked topic in his next three chapters, on information. The basic point is that the costs of acquiring any really detailed information about policies are large compared to any gains one could expect from voting for the party. The rational elector will therefore not bother to acquire detailed information himself but will rely on broad characterisations of the party (by Left-Right position, for example, as we have seen) or on judgements by intermediaries (interest groups or press) which will, as a result, have some scope for manipulation for their own purposes.

The reasoning about information costs leads into Downs' best known discussion after the spatial models – of non-voting. The discussion runs along the same lines as the one on information, since the costs of actually going to vote are high compared to the average party differential – especially when this is multiplied as it realistically should be by the vanishingly small probability that one's vote will crucially determine the election outcome. On strictly rational 'objective' grounds hardly any one should vote at all.

Downs is, of course, well aware of the sharp contrast between this prediction and the reality of turnout in national elections of between 50% and 90%. He fills the gap with a notorious *ad hoc* argument that citizens have a vested interest in strengthening democracy which outweighs costs and stimulates them to vote (1957: 269–70). Why short-term selfish maximisers should take this view is not made clear, nor – even if it were – are problems of free riding considered (Olson 1965). We are again on the verge of a totally different model of behaviour being proposed – and hardly an 'economic' one at all, relying on duty and internal motivation (Barry 1970: 13–19).

Downs skips over these problems to turn to the 'Comment on Economic Theories of Government Behaviour' (Chapter 15) already cited as an example of the *Economic Theory* being originally directed at economists. The argument is basically that government motivations should be viewed on a par with those of other self-interested economic actors and not invoked as a *deus ex machina* to set optimal social welfare functions. Given the sustained analysis of this point in the book the caution is entirely convincing.

It is followed in Chapter 16 by a bold attempt to state the full argument (verbally) as an axiomatic theory, with 25 'testable propositions' at varying levels of generality and interest, purporting to derive from either the 'office-seeking hypothesis' about politicians or the 'rationality hypothesis' about citizens voting for parties nearest them; or the two combined.

In fact the propositions need to be derived using many more assumptions than these two, most of which are specified at some point in the text. An attempt is made at presenting the non-spatial ones (adding up to what we have called Downs' General Model) in Table A1 below, with linked propositions in Table A2. The same is done for the Spatial Model in Tables A3 and A4. Taken together the Tables serve as a propositional analysis of Downs' full argument, from which we select the high-points below.

SPATIAL MODELS OF 'THE ECONOMIC THEORY'

We concentrate here on Downs' spatial models of voting and party competition (1957: 96–163) not because they are the only models in the book (cf the General Model in Table A1 and the analysis of non-voting) but because they are still at the focus of current discussions. With them Downs introduced an early version of the power of the median argument, so popular today.

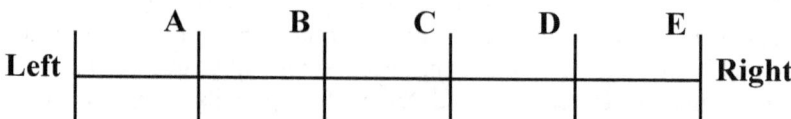

Figure 1: The dominant position of the median actor, C, in a one-dimensional policy space

The power of the median is simply illustrated in Figure 1. With a one-dimensional policy continuum assuring easy identification of the median position, one can see that C crucially determines what majority forms, and also what policy will be adopted. If, say, the majority ABC refuses to locate its agreed policy very close to C, the latter can always join up with D & E to get an alternative majority which will do this, though on the Right side rather than the Left side of the spectrum. C can thus always play off A & B against D & E to get what she wants. Even a grand coalition of the other players would have to adopt a compromise policy close to C's position. (However there is no justification for any coalition leapfrogging C under one-dimensional policy assumptions).

Downs was among the first to recognize the importance of the median position to securing majorities. His famous unimodal model of two-party competition, shown in Figure 2, underlines the conclusion that the party which gets the median elector to vote for it will have an electoral majority and form the government.

Office-seeking parties will therefore adapt their policies so as to get as close as possible to the policy position of the median elector. They will either both end up at the median, if leapfrogging is allowed; or, if it is prohibited, as Downs seems to insist, they will take up the same position to Left or Right of the median.[4]

In any case the tendency towards policy convergence, with both competitors adopting the same position, is very strong in this spatial model – not unnaturally since Downs' supporting assumptions of the General Model (Table A1) lead to the same conclusion on their own (Section 2)! This has been accepted as a natural result by American party analysts particularly in regard to Congressional contexts. General discussions of the US parties up to 1980 (APSA 1950; Wright 1971) also tended to stress their pragmatism and lack of ideological differentiation.

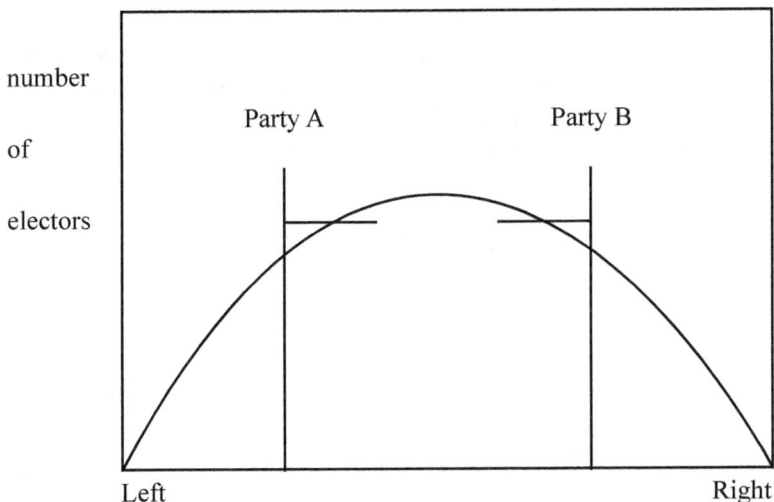

Figure 2: Downs' model of two-party competition: vote-seeking parties converge on the median policy position under certainty about policy positions

With increasing ideological differences emerging between Republicans and Democrats, and new evidence showing that they have always been well differentiated in policy terms (Budge *et al.* 2001: 25) this convergence result has come to be regarded as unrealistic. It has continued to emerge analytically however even under modifications of the Downsian conditions, such as introducing uncertainty about party locations (McKelvey and Ordeshook 1985). Within the context of his model Downs himself suggests that electors on the wings might experience a diminution of their party differential as their preferred party moved away from them. It is not clear that this strong additional assumption really works however in terms of keeping parties apart since a party would still gain votes by moving to the centre. (Other complications are discussed in Barry 1970: 113–14). Aldrich (1983) suggests that party activists might pressure the party leaderships to stay apart. They exert pressure internally through withholding resources or influencing decision-making.

This suggestion does, however, drive a coach and horses through the unitary actor conception of parties as just the leadership team, which is crucial to much of Downs' discussion. Introducing such an assumption creates an entirely different election model and even a different *Economic Theory*. Unfortunately, many analysts seem to think they can slip in quite substantial modifications to Downs' models without producing other modifications to the general conclusions. Sadly this is not so and simply muddles clear thinking. The tendency to slip in or modify assumptions is however certainly encouraged by Downs himself – as when he starts talking about extremist abstention as a drag on convergence (1957: 118–20) without considering the other aspects of the argument.

Within the context of the pure spatial model there is, however, already a built-in factor which militates against party policy identity – a multi-modal distribution of preferences giving rise, Downs postulates, to a multi-party system in which parties emerge at each mode.[5] This is illustrated in Figure 3. Not only do these clusters of electors generally generate a separate party, but the party remains at the same policy position.

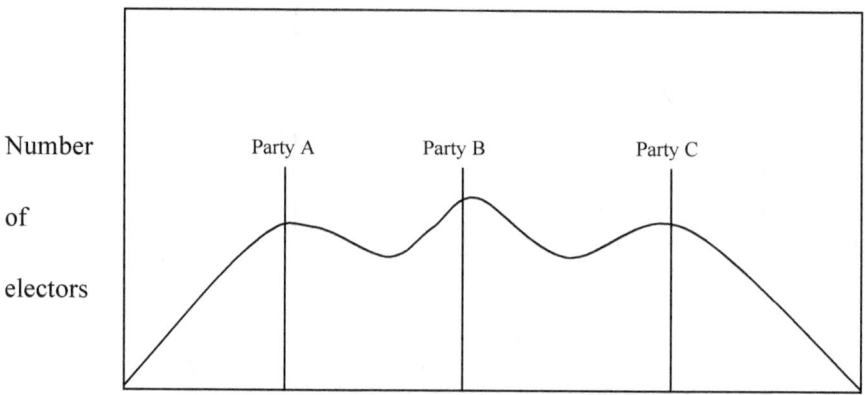

Figure 3: Downs' model of multi-party competition: immobility of parties at each mode of the distribution of preferences under certainty about policy

Why it does so is a little obscure. Downs invokes previous arguments about ideology, reliability and responsibility (1957: 122–3) which, however, belong to a different model of party competition (see Section 2 above). Strategic arguments are also adduced along the lines that movements to Left or Right in a multi-modal distribution lose as many votes as they gain in the short-run (1957: 123). In any case, for participation in coalition governments – inevitable in a multi-party situation – it is more important to keep existing votes than to gain new ones (1957: 124). This has the consequence that parties remain ideologically more consistent ('responsible' in Downs' terms) than parties under two-party competition. However this does not help voter rationality or aid the translation of individual preferences into public policy, as electors do not know which government will emerge as a result of the vote they cast (1957: 143 ff).

The contrasts Downs draws between clarity of choice and accountability under a majoritarian two-party system, and their blurring under a multi-party one, anticipate a lively contemporary debate over the relative merits of the two in promoting democracy (cf. Powell and Whitten 1993). We should note, however, that the only case of relatively strict two-party competition in the developed world are the United States. This renders it surprising, in the abstract, that so much attention has been devoted to the two-party situation at the expense of the model which covers 90 per cent of the cases! The explanation is probably two-fold: most spatial or mathematical analysts are American or work in the US, hence the two-party case is the one which interests them. And a dynamic model is more interesting than a static one, since it permits more mathematical development.

What is more interesting is not necessarily more true however. Textual analyses of authoritative party policy documents (platforms, manifestos and election programmes for 25 countries over the last 50 years (Budge *et al.* 2001[6]) give us a unique opportunity to see whether policy convergence occurs at elections or whether parties remain at a relatively fixed position. If Downs' argument is correct we should expect the latter result in all cases except the mostly two-party United States, where the parties should converge instead.

Figures 4, 5 and 6 show actual Left-Right movements over the post-war period for the extreme multi-party system of The Netherlands, the moderately multi-party system of Germany and the contrasting case of the Democrats and Republicans in the United States.

There is limited policy movement in all these cases which may well be strategic. However, the overall impression is that parties maintain their position – especially their relative position – along the Left-Right continuum. In particular 'leap-frogging' of other parties is severely limited (Budge 1994: 460). All this confirms Downs' theoretical expectations from the multi-party spatial model (Figure 3 above). Parties in multi-party systems are predominantly static.

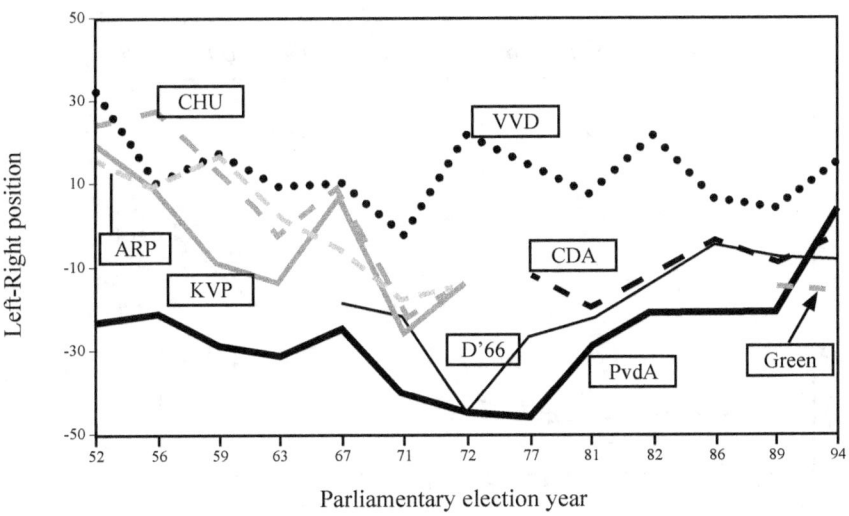

Figure 4: Left-Right movements of Dutch Parties 1952 – 1994

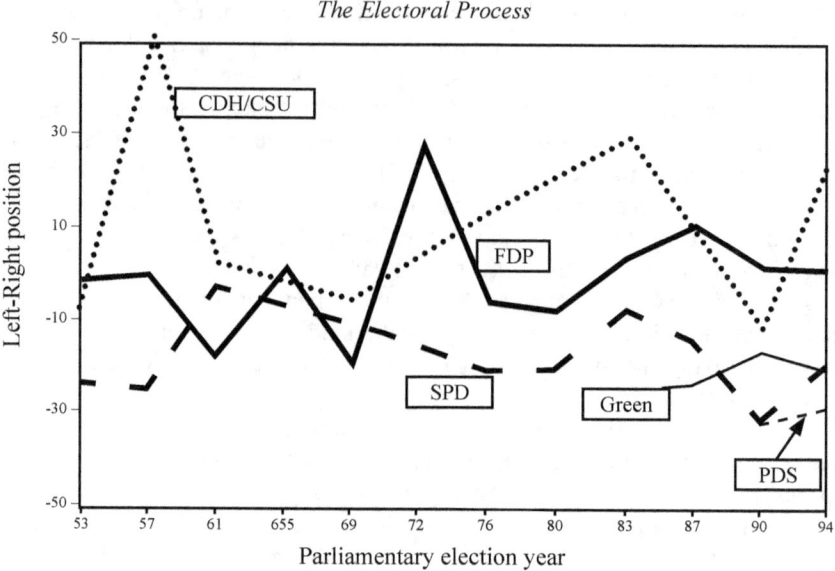

Figure 5: Left-Right movements of German Parties 1949–1994

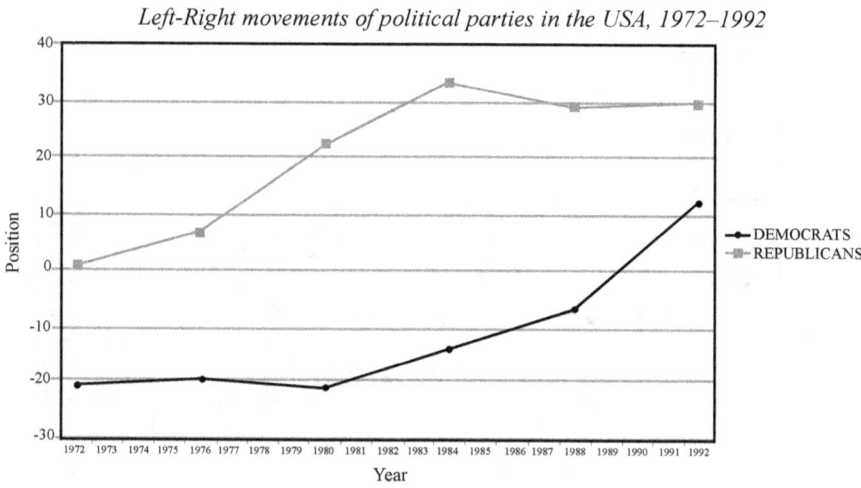

Figure 6: Left-Right movements of US Parties 1948–1992

In contrast, the two-party Downs' model (Figure 2 above) giving rise to policy convergence is empirically refuted by the mapping of American parties in Figure 6. The Republicans and Democrats in the United States behave very like the Christians and Socialists in multi-party Germany. They never leapfrog[7] and show tendencies to converge only occasionally – balanced by strong ideological divergence as at the last Presidential election. On the basis of Figures 4, 5 and 6 indeed we would be justified in saying that Downs' neglected multi-party model of Figure 3 is the one that generally applies, rather than the more cited two-party one which has become almost synonymous with the 'Economic Theory'.

THE NEGLECTED STATIC MODEL: RESPONSIBILITY AND RELIABILITY

Both spatial models do however rest on assumptions about electors' preferences being produced exogenously, and the shape of their distribution determining the party system. These are quite strong and controversial assumptions (Lipset and Rokkan 1967; Barry 1970: 122–3). Downs himself however had already introduced a simpler and more parsimonious explanation of why parties should stay in roughly the same place ideologically, moving only slightly for strategic reasons and certainly not leap-frogging.

This is the need for parties to be reliable and responsible in order to maintain the confidence of electors that they will do what they say they will if elected (1957: 103–13). Reliability is the extent to which a party's promises predict its actions in office. Responsibility is maintaining consistency between present policies and its statements and actions of the past. As Downs notes (1957: 109), 'If a party frequently adopts new policies inconsistent with its old ones, voters will suspect that it cannot be trusted to carry out any long-range policies at all'.

If all party leaders, no matter how office-seeking, share this basic assumption, we can explain ideological rigidity and the dominance of statics over dynamics in party competition quite simply and directly. Perhaps these very qualities account for its neglect by spatial modellers, since there is little to elaborate on here. However that may be, this 'policy consistency model' does seem to fit the actual evidence on party policy records more closely than any other, reversing Downs' 'mere opinion' (1957: 112) that strategic considerations would win out over consistency in most cases. In real life the reverse seems to be true.

Though Downs distinguishes between the consistency and strategic models unusually clearly, this does not stop him invoking ideological consistency as a constraint on strategic movement within the spatial models (e.g. 1957: 122–3). To some extent this is a case, familiar throughout the argument of the *Economic Theory*, of Downs having his cake and then eating it: that is, introducing previously rejected assumptions in an *ad hoc* way when they support the conclusions the author wants to reach. However, one can come to a more generous interpretation: Downs feels that both factors may be at work in party competition but has no way of quantifying their effects so as to combine them empirically rather than *ad hoc* within the model. Doing so would bring his approach to voting much closer to the general consensus in election studies that both long term predispositions (ideology) and short-term issues (policy) influence the vote and hence leaders' calculations (Budge and Farlie 1977: 120).

It is a testimony to the continuing stimulus provided by Downs' open-ended discussion that forty years after the publication of the *Economic Theory*, Adams (2001) took up the idea that a voters' ideological bias combines with the attractions of current policy to produce the characteristic zig-zag pattern of (restricted) policy movement that one sees over time in Figures 4–6 (and in almost all other countries too). Electors, especially those stationed closest to them, support parties on other grounds than current policy, though on that too. This makes it tempting for other parties to move up on rivals, but the extent of movements is limited by the non policy commitments of core voters to the threatened party. In any case, at the next election the latter heads back closer in policy terms to its vulnerable marginal electors, while the aggressor in turn has to move back to avert policy challenges from *its* neighbour on the other side. The zig-zag party movements calculated with survey estimates on these assumptions provide a good overall match with the reported Left-Right paths of post-war British parties (Budge *et al.* 2001: 25).

By putting Downs' two models together in an explicit, consistent and above all quantified form, one can thus go a long way to explaining parties' competitive behaviour within a general spatial framework on the basis of *a priori* theory. This forms a valuable corrective to the tendency inherited from Downs by many rational choice theorists, of elaborating abstract models without any real attempt to test them, other than quoting highly selective and tendentious examples. This is a pity when we now have rich comparative data collections explicitly designed to test Downsian propositions (Robertson 1976; Budge *et al.* 1987; Budge *et al.* 2001). Fitting actual data is not simply an optional extra for rational choice models but their *raison d'être*. Otherwise, as Downs' discussion also illustrates, we are left swimming in a sea of plausible but unknown possibilities, not clearly distinguished from each other.

DOWNS' CONCEPTUAL LEGACY: MEDIANS AND MANDATES

Despite the continuing usefulness of specific models as a springboard for further research, the 'Economic Theory's' main contribution to contemporary political science perhaps lies in the higher level assumptions it makes about the political world. The broadest of these is the 'economic approach' itself: the building of simplified models of reality peopled either by real or collective individuals motivated by self-interest, more or less narrowly defined. Unrestrained by considerations such as mathematical tractability (since he rarely puts arguments in mathematical form) Downs has been broader than many of his successors in giving factors such as uncertainty and ideology a central place in his reasoning. Of course this has resulted in the many ambiguities spelled out above. The reaction to this by many successors however has often been to set neo Downsian models in a world of narrowly self-interested, omniscient individuals one hardly recognises as real.

Leaving aside the way it presents their motivations and interactions, the focus of the book on a stripped down confrontation between parties and electors has also had great influence, effectively posing the central question of representative democracy: how do individual preferences get aggregated into public policy?

In answering this question Downs starts from a standard government mandate position. The party which gets a majority of votes in a competitive election is authorized to run the next government. In this way one knows that the government which is formed is the one desired by a majority – that is what makes the system democratic. To be really sure of this, however, one needs more than one party competing, a point which Downs builds explicitly into his conditions for democracy (1957: 23–4).

While in theory one could rationally choose between governments on any grounds, in practice Downs quickly focuses on policy as the main element in voters' calculations of the party differential (1957: 39–42) – it is of course the *only* element in the spatial models. So the mandate is extended beyond simply forming a government to effecting the policies the majority party has been elected on. Hence the importance of reliability and responsibility (1957: 103–13): it is essential both that the party carries out the policies it was elected on and maintains some consistency with them over time, otherwise electors do not know what they are getting when they vote for the party.

This development of Downs' argument thus brings us to a full blown government mandate position, as enunciated for example by Aldrich (1995: 10). According to this, parties:

1) make policy commitments to the electorate;
2) are willing to carry them out when in office;
3) develop alternatives to government parties when out of office;
4) differ sufficiently between themselves to 'provide the electorate with a proper range of choice between alternative actions'.

The problem is that the other expectations developed from Downs' non-spatial reasoning about convergence on any policy strongly preferred by the electorate, and in particular the spatial convergence on the median predicted by the unimodal two-party model (Figure 2), quite subvert the electoral policy choice so central to mandate theory. The idea of two parties differing in at least some respects is also one of Downs' conditions for democracy itself (1957: 24). The logic of convergence ultimately undermines its own conceptual foundation. Some realisation of this surely underpins Downs attempt to use abstention by extremists to inhibit convergence (1957: 118–20).

Of course in the multi-modal, multi-party situation envisaged in Figure 3 there are clear choices to be made between ideologically rooted parties. Mandate doctrine is still undermined however because it is not clear what coalition government will emerge from post-election negotiations between non-majoritarian parties. Hence electors do not really know which public policy they are going to get when they vote for a given party. Nor will they be able to enforce accountability since the next coalition government will always be bound to include some parties from the last one.

There are two ways out of this dilemma, one suggested directly by Downs himself and one indirectly through his emphasis on the determining role of the median:

a) By introducing party responsibility, i.e. policy consistency and reliability, into the spatial models – not in an ambiguous and *ad hoc* way as the *Economic Theory* sometimes does, but transparently. Ideally this involves building a quantitative model which assigns specified values to ideology and strategy – somewhat as Adams (2001) does. Ideological consistency would then effectively prevent even two parties moving much beyond their normal policy confines (cf. Figure 6 above).

b) However, this still leaves in place Downs' enormously influential critique of multi-party systems based on PR (perhaps three-quarters of all democracies!). How indeed can majority preferences be transmitted into public policy when the government formed after an election may bear little relation to the parties which gained or lost in that election?

One problem with the *Economic Theory* is that it abandons the discussion at this point, leaving this crucial question hanging in the air, rather than going on to the next question, which might provide an answer. That is, how *do* coalitions form and is there any element in the process which links the majority electoral preference to eventual public policy?

There is in fact a link. We can base this on the strand in Downs' discussion which emphasises the power and influence of the median. The strategic influence of that policy position applies not just to the electorate but to any group, including parties involved in coalition negotiations. The party at the median position in Parliament is crucial to any majority government that forms. This is attested empirically by the major finding to come out of comparative research on governments – over 80 per cent of coalitions contain the legislative median party (van Roozendaal 1990, 1992; Laver and Budge 1992: 415–20; Müller and Strøm 2000: 563–9). Those that do not are often minority governments dependent on median support in legislative coalition-building.

Even a primarily office-seeking median party will seek to promote its declared programme in order to retain the support of electors – reliability and responsibility again. Such self-interested action could serve a representational function, however, *provided* that the election system makes the median legislative party the one for which the median elector voted. In that sense, the median party, whether in a majoritarian system (Figure 2) or multi-party system (Figure 3) can act as a carrier for the majority will (which must settle at or near the position of the median elector to form a majority at all).

This argument is more fully developed in McDonald *et al.* (2004), who point out:

a) depending on a majority-supported party to carry the popular will over into public policy is unreliable because in practice only about eleven per cent of all governments are formed by a single party with an electoral majority. Single member district electoral systems do often manufacture a legislative majority on the basis of a popular plurality (Powell 2000). However, this is without regard to whether their position would be supported or opposed by a popular majority. It seems therefore that the idea of the popular will being transmitted by a party winning a popular majority based on the median (Figure 2) is strictly limited in its application, even in the US.

b) a popular majority, however, is only a special case of the median mandate where there *is* a cohesive party majority. By definition the median elector must be part of this. But the reverse does not hold. In other words there can be a median without a majority – there is always a median even in the case of the multi-modal distribution in Figure 3. As the median preference is the one a popular majority would necessarily endorse if it ever emerged, all that is required for effective representation is that the median party in the elected legislature is the one the median voter supported in policy terms. PR systems generally allow this equivalence to be made. SMD is less reliable in this respect.

Arriving at this result does not require any effort of calculation by the voters. Each simply votes for the party they are closest to in policy space and the median party is identified from the aggregate results (knowing how the parties are distributed on the policy continuum). Downs' critique of multi-party systems as subverting rationality of choice by the voter is irrelevant from this perspective. Voting is as easy, and as rational, under the conditions of Figure 3 as under those of Figure 2.

Acceptance of these median mandate ideas requires us to abandon the idea that elections are all about winning – the conception Downs took over from Schumpeter (1950: 269). Rather, elections are about first identifying the median voter preference and then empowering it by making it that of the median legislative party (in a Parliamentary system). This idea is foreshadowed by Downs' emphasis on the median. But it is not developed in his book as he did not follow through from the functions of elections to the functions of governments. Both need to be considered in a fully-fledged theory of democracy.

CONCLUSIONS

The preceding discussion illustrates how Downs' formulation, through its very tensions and ambiguities, powerfully stimulates further research questions and possible answers to them. While some masters of political science seek to bind their followers within an iron framework of concepts and definitions, Downs' strength is that he remains open-ended but also stimulating. He may not have settled any question definitively but he certainly raised most of the ones important to democracy in a way which pushes them forward for resolution. He did not have the last word on anything. But perhaps it is more important to say the first word with force and elegance. Certainly that seems the secret of the *Economic Theory's* immense and enduring appeal.

APPENDIX A

In Chapter 16 of the *Economic Theory* Downs makes a bold and commendable attempt, remarkable for the time at which it was written, to propositionalise (verbally) the whole argument of his book. This results in 25 'testable propositions' which he claims to derive from only two basic hypotheses – the 'party-motivation' hypothesis (political parties in a democracy plan their policies so as to maximise votes) and the 'citizen-rationality hypothesis' (every citizen rationally attempts to maximise his utility income, including that portion of it derived from government activity).

It is no discredit to Downs' pioneering attempt to maximize the transparency of his argument, to say that these assumptions by themselves are insufficient to derive the propositions in even a loose way. Budge and Farlie (1977: 104–11, 132–43) tried to provide a more adequate inferential base for the propositions, even though this involved making almost as many assumptions as Downs' derivations! As a summary of the full *Economic Theory,* it seems of interest to present this reworking of its argument here. Exposition is divided into two parts: the General Downs Model incorporating non-spatial assumptions and 'testable propositions' – roughly the first and last 100 pages of the book. Table A1 gives the assumptions which seem necessary to derive Downs' propositions in Table A2. Some assumptions are rather *ad hoc* but needed to derive a particular proposition. These are bracketed in Table A1. The numbers given to derived 'Testable Propositions' in Table A2 are taken from the book. Proposition A predicting non-voting is not listed by Downs but so clearly indicated by his argument that it is included.

The additional assumptions (building on the non-spatial ones) required to generate the Spatial Model are listed in Table A3 and the derived 'testable propositions' in Table A4.

Of course, these attempts at propositionalising the *Economic Theory* and stating its full assumptions are themselves just that – attempts. Given ambiguities in the text itself they could be disputed and cannot claim to be definitive. It is in any case more useful to build on the spatial models of the *Economic Theory* and develop them in a way which is more coherent, more logical and increasingly more mathematical. However the tables do supplement the text of this article for readers who wish to review more specific arguments and connections.

Table A1: Full assumptions of the general Downs' model

1.	The polity is democratic in the sense that the single party or coalition of parties which receives most votes in the previous election controls government, voters are fully enfranchised and count equally, results of elections and freedom of political activity are respected, elections are regular and contested by at least two parties.
2.	Electors' preferences remain the same whatever the movement of parties.
3.	Electors vote independently for the party whose declared programme/record on balance will most advance their own preferences.
4.	Electors judge parties' ability to advance their preferences either through direct similarity between their preferences and party programmes/records, or through indicators of policy-similarity such as ideology, judgement of trusted associates etc.
5.	The party programme/record on which similarity is estimated is the programme/record of the party leadership team.
6.	If voting is not likely to advance their policy-preferences significantly in comparison with the costs entailed, voters do not vote.
7.	The poor form a majority of electors.
8.	A majority of electors do not feel intensely on all issues.
9.	The party leadership team is always united.
10.	Leaders' chief goal is to attain/keep office, hence by Assumption 1 they must gain/retain votes, and by Assumptions 3 and 4 they must to gain votes seek to alter the party programme/governmental actions so as to resemble the preferences of most electors.
11.	All parties are equally effective in presenting their declared programme/records.
12.	Leaders know what electors' preferences are and also their incidence.
	Electors know which party programme/record has a greater probable resemblance to their own preference.
14.	The information required to decide the direction of a vote is costly, hence electors try to economise on its collection except in areas where they feel intensely.
15.	The information required by leaders to decide on policy in relation to electors' preferences is costly, hence leaders try to economise on its collection except in areas where they feel intensely.

Table A2: Propositions implied by the assumptions of the general Downs model

Proposition 2	Both parties in a democratic two-party system agree on any issues that a majority of citizens strongly favour (Assumptions 1–5, 9–13).
Proposition 6	Democratic governments tend to redistribute income from the rich to the poor (Assumptions 1–5, 7, 9–13).
Proposition 7	Democratic governments tend to favour producers more than consumers in their action (Assumptions 1–5, 9–13, 15, given that government is short of information and producers are more likely to supply it).
Proposition 11	Many citizens who vote and consider voting important are nevertheless not well-informed on the issues involved in the election (Assumptions 1, 4, 8, 14).
Proposition 12	Because nearly every citizen realises his vote is not decisive in each election, the incentive of most citizens to acquire information before voting is small (Assumption 1, 8, 14).
Proposition 13	A large percentage of citizens – including voters – do not become informed to any significant degree on the issues involved in elections, even if they believe the outcomes to be important (Assumptions 1, 14).
Proposition 14	The citizens who are best informed on any specific issue are those whose income is directly affected by it, i.e. who earn their incomes in the policy areas it concerns (Assumptions 1, 14).
Proposition 15	Citizens who are well-informed on issues that affect them as income-earners are probably not equally well-informed on issues that affect them as consumers (Assumptions 1, 8, 14, given that electors feel more intensely about wages than prices).
Proposition 16	Citizens who have definite party-preferences are more likely to vote than those who cannot see such differences between parties (Assumptions 1, 4, 6).
Proposition 17	Many citizens delegate even the evaluative steps in voting to others and follow the advice of those others in casting their ballots (Assumptions 1, 4, 14).
Proposition 19	The percentage of low-income citizens who abstain in elections is higher than the percentage of high-income citizens who abstain, ceteris paribus (Assumptions 1, 3–6, 14, given that poor electors are less able to bear information – and voting-costs).
Proposition 22	Citizens who are exposed to information chosen by means of non-homogeneous selection principles tend to abstain from voting more than those whose information comes from sources with homogeneous principles (Assumptions 1, 4, 6, 14, given that cross-pressures from non-homogeneous information increase costs of information-processing, hence of voting and thus swing the cost-benefit ratio against voting).
Proposition A	Most citizens will not vote (Assumptions 1, 3–6, 14, given that the probability of an individual vote changing the election outcome is low).
Proposition 23	Political parties tend to carry out as many of their promises as they can whenever they are elected (Assumptions 1, 3, 4, 10, 13).
Proposition 24	Political parties tend to maintain ideological positions that are constant over time unless they suffer drastic defeats, in which case they change their ideologies to resemble that of the party which defeated them (Assumptions 1, 2–5, 9–13, 15).

Note: The numbers given to propositions are the original ones given by Downs (296–300). The propositions omitted are in three cases (1, 8, 20) simple specifications of assumptions and in all other cases require assumptions additional to those in Table 31 before they can be discussed. Proposition A is inserted from Downs' textual discussion (265–73).

Table A3: Additional assumptions required for the spatial Downs' model

1.	Policy preferences can be adequately represented by a line, i.e. representation in any higher number of dimensions can always be reduced by devices such as weighting and without excessive distortion to a line (unidimensionality).
2.	Such a line is bounded by two points (a) and (b) (boundedness).
3.	Policy preferences can be ordered in a continuous distribution between (a) and (b) (continuity).
4.	All individual preferences can be located at a point (x), which is either at (a) or (b) or any point between such that a policy located at a point closer to (x) in any possible direction is preferred to a policy located further from (x) in any possible direction (single-peakedness and quasi-symmetry of preferences).
5.	Party leadership teams can be located on the line at a particular point which represents either (a) a unique ideological placement or (b) the weighted mean of the different points occupied by the different party policies (party placement).
6.	Where party policies have a variance as well as a mean position, the party differential is calculated in terms of both variance and mean (modified differential).
7.	Parties cannot pass each other on the line (no leap-frogging).

Table A4: Propositions derived from the assumptions of the general Downs' model (Table 3.1) and the additional assumptions of the spatial model

Proposition 3	In a two-party system (with unimodal distribution of electoral preferences) party policies are (a) more vague, (b) more similar to those of other parties, (c) less directly linked to an ideology than in a multi-party system (Assumptions 1, 2–5, 9–13, 16–22).
Proposition 4	In a multi-party system governed by a coalition, the government takes less effective action to solve basic social problems, and its politics are less integrated and consistent than in a two-party system (Assumptions 1, 2–5, 9–13, 16–22).
Additional Proposition B	In a two-party system based on a unimodal distribution of electors' preferences party policies are (a) more vague, (b) more similar to those of other parties, (c) less directly linked to an ideology, (d) more consistent in spite of changes in party control and (e) less likely to provoke public disorder than in a two-party system based on a bimodal distribution of electors' preferences (Downs 120: Assumptions 1, 3–5, 9–13, 16–20, 22).
Additional Proposition C	A two-party system is produced by either a unimodal or bimodal distribution of electors along the political scale, whereas a multi-party system is produced by a multi-modal distribution along the political scale (Downs 117–22: Assumptions 1–5, 9–13, 16–20, 22).

Proposition 5	New parties arise when either (a) a change in suffrage laws sharply alters the distribution of citizens along the political scale, (b) there is a sudden change in the electorate's social outlook because of some upheaval such as war, revolution, inflation or depression, or (c) in a two-party system, one of the parties takes a moderate stand on an issue and its radical members organise a splinter-party to force it back towards an extreme position (Assumptions 1–5, 9–13, 16–20: Propositions 5(a) and 5(b) only follow from these assumptions however if there has been a temporary breakdown previously in Assumptions 10, 12 which would otherwise ensure that existing parties adapted to the new electoral situation).
Proposition 25	In systems usually governed by coalitions, most citizens do not vote as though elections were government selection mechanisms (Assumptions 1–5, 9–14, 16–20 are all involved, but Proposition 25 mostly follows from Assumption 4).
Note: The numbers given to propositions are the original ones given by Downs 296–300 All other propositions are either simple specifications of assumptions or derived from the general model and listed in Table 32, with the exception of Propositions 9 and 10 These two propositions, on strategic voting for hopeless parties or parties other than those primarily preferred, are linked with Proposition 5(c) in our text, and discussed generally in regard to the possibility of extremist abstention The concept of extremism depends on relative location in a space: hence though Propositions 9 and 10 are not strictly dependent on spatial assumptions they are discussed in the spatial context Proposition B is not explicitly listed by Downs among the other propositions but is a clear and important derivation from his discussion at 117–22; Proposition C likewise is derived from Downs 120 The wording of the numbered propositions is Downs' own except that words within brackets have been interpolated by us to clarify Downs' meaning	
Sources: Downs 1957; Budge and Farlie 1977	

Notes

1. The only two actors in the two-party model though governments also enter as distinct entities in the multi-party one. Although Downs mentions interest groups and other intermediaries in Chapter 6 he does not develop their role very much.
2. This could be queried in terms of the direct assumptions of the model. Only when ideology or inertia also operate or when coalition bargaining is brought directly to the model and puts a premium on retaining rather than increasing support, can party immobility be fully explained. We shall discuss this below.
3. These have included activist commitments (Aldrich, 1983) uncertainty (Calvert 1986; McKelvey and Ordeshook 1985) and non-policy commitments of voters to parties (Adams 2001).
4. If even this limited overlap is prohibited in the model then the first party to station itself between its rival and the median will win – not a consequence considered in the Economic Theory.
5. It is a little unclear from the discussion in the Economic Theory whether each mode will generate a party. But there will be several parties and they will spread along the spectrum and be static in any case.
6. The sentences of these documents were counted into a broad range of detailed policy categories, some of which were combined to form a Left-Right scale. Both data and supporting descriptions and tests are provided in Budge *et al.* 2001.
7. Downs assumes that parties never leapfrog because of ideological constraints. This is borne out by our evidence but is at odds with other assumptions and expectations of the two-party model.

REFERENCES

APSA (American Political Science Association) (1950), *Toward a More Responsible Two-Party System*, New York: Rinehart.
Adams, J. (2001) 'A Theory of Spatial Competition with Biased Voters', *British Journal of Political Science*, 31: 121–58.
Aldrich, J. H. (1983) 'A Downsian Spatial Model With Party Activism', *American Political Science Review*, Vol.77: 974–90.
(1995) *Why Parties: The Origins and Transformation of Political Parties in America*, Chicago: Chicago University Press.
Arrow, K. (1951) *Social Choice and Individual Values*, New York: Wiley.
Barry, B. (1970) *Sociologists, Economists and Democracy*, London: Collier Macmillan.
Black, D. (1958) *The Theory of Committees and Elections*, Cambridge: Cambridge University Press.
Budge, I. (1994) 'A New Spatial Theory of Party Competition', *British Journal of Political Science* 25: 443–467.
Budge, I. and Farlie, D. J. (1977) *Voting and Party Competition*, London: Wiley.
Budge, I., Klingemann, H.-D., Vokens, A., Bara, J. and Tannenbaum, E. (2001) *Mapping Policy Preferences: Estimates for Parties, Electors and Governments 1945–1998*, Oxford: Oxford University Press.
Budge, I., Robertson, D. and Hearl, D. J. (1987) *Ideology, Strategy and Party Change*, Cambridge, Cambridge University Press.
Calvert, R. (1986) *Models of Imperfect Information in Politics*, Boston: Harwood.
Coughlin, P. J. (1992) *Probabilistic Voting Theory*, Cambridge: Cambridge University Press.
Dalton, R. and Wattenberg, M. (eds.) (2000) *Parties Without Partisans,* Oxford: Oxford University Press.
Davis, O. A., Dempster, M. A. H. and Wildavsky, A. (1966) 'A Theory of the Budgetary Process', *American Political Science Review*, Vol LX: 549–547.
Downs, A. (1957) *An Economic Theory of Democracy*, New York: Harper.
(1967) *Inside Bureaucracy*, Boston: Little Brown.
Hinich, M. J., and Ordeshook, P. C. (1969) 'Abstentions and Equilibrium in the Electoral Process', *Public Choice*, 7: 81–100.
Hotelling, H. (1929) 'Stability in Competition', *The Economic Journal* Vol.39: 41–57.
Laver, M. J. and Budge, I. (eds.) (1992) *Party Policy and Government Coalitions*, London: MacMillan.
Lipset, S. M. and Rokkan, S. (1967) *Party Systems and Voter Alignments*, New York: Free Press.
McDonald M., Mendes, S. and Budge, I. (2004) 'What are Elections For? Conferring the Median Mandate', *British Journal of Political Science* 34: 1–26.

McKelvey, R. and Ordeshook, P. C. (1985) 'Elections with Limited Information', *Journal of Economic Theory*, 35: 55–85.
Miller, W., Pierce, R., Thomassen, J., Herrera, R. *et al.* (1999), *Policy Representation in Western Democracies,* Oxford: Oxford University Press.
Müller, W. C. and Strøm, K. (eds.) (2000) *Coalition Governments in Western Europe*, Oxford: Oxford University Press.
Olson, M. (1965) *The Logic of Collective Action*, Cambridge, MA: Harvard.
Powell, J. B. (2000) *Elections as Instruments of Democracy: Majoritarian and Proportional Visions,* New Haven: Yale.
Powell, J. B. and Whitten, G. D. (1993) 'A Cross-National Analysis of Economic Voting: Taking Account of the Political Context', *American Journal of Political Science,* 37: 391–414.
Riker, W. H. (1993) *Agenda Formation*, Ann Arbor: Michigan.
Riker, W. H. and Ordeshook, P. C. (1973) *Positive Political Theory,* Englewood Cliffs: Prentice Hall.
Robertson, D. (1976) *A Theory of Party Competition,* London: Wiley.
Schumpeter J. A. (1950) *Capitalism, Socialism and Democracy*, New York: Harper.
Simon, H. A. (1947) *Administrative Behaviour,* New York, MacMillan.
Smithies A. (1941) 'Optimum Location in Spatial Competition', *Journal of Political Economy,* 59: 423–439.
Van Roozendaal, P. (1990) 'Centre Parties and Coalition Formation', *European Journal of Political Research* 18 (3): 325–48.
(1992) 'The Effect of Dominant and Central Parties on Cabinet Composition and Duration', *Legislative Studies Quarterly* 17: 5–36.
Wright, W. (1971) 'Comparative Party Models: Rational Efficient and Party Democracy', in W. Wright (ed.), *A Comparative Study of Party Organisation*, Columbas, Ohio: Merrill.

chapter three	David Easton: The Theory of the Political System
Dieter Fuchs and Hans-Dieter Klingemann

INTRODUCTION

Born on June 24, 1917 and raised in Canada, David Easton finished his undergraduate education at the University of Toronto (1939: B.A.; 1943: MA). Subsequently Easton's academic career is linked to three of the most distinguished US American Universities: Harvard, Chicago and the University of California. In 1947 he received his Ph.D. at Harvard University where he had been a Teaching Fellow since 1944. For almost a quarter of a century David Easton served as one of the most prominent political scientists at the University of Chicago (1947–1982) where he became full professor in 1955 and was appointed Andrew MacLeish Distinguished Service Professor in 1969.

In 1981 David Easton joined the Department of Politics and Society, University of California, Irvine, where he is still teaching today. It would go beyond the scope of this article to do justice to all his academic positions, membership of boards of editors, or his functions as a political consultant. Suffice to say that he has been President of the American Political Science Association (1968–89) and a Fellow (since 1962) as well as a Vice-President of the American Academy of Arts and Sciences (1985–88). He has also received three honorary degrees (McMaster University; Kalamazoo College; Free University of Berlin).

Easton's professional reputation has a solid base. The selected bibliography of David Easton cites 13 books and about 70 articles some of which have been translated in foreign languages and a great number which have been reprinted many times. For example, *A Framework for Political Analysis* (1965) has been translated into Japanese, Portuguese, Spanish, Greek, Korean, and Italian. And the 1957 World Politics article on 'An Approach to the Analysis of Political Systems' (1957) has been reprinted more than 25 times. This is a clear and simple indicator of his impact on the development of political theory, in particular, and political science in general. Most of what follows in this chapter attempts to describe his role as a pioneer of modern political science.

THE HISTORICAL CONTEXT OF THE SYSTEM ANALYSIS OF POLITICS

David Easton has proposed what can be regarded the most important non-normative general theory of politics in modern times. He developed his ideas above all in three monographs, which he himself regards as a related trilogy: *The Political System* was published in 1953, followed in 1965 by *A Framework for Political Analysis* and – in the same year – by *A Systems Analysis of Political Life*.

The Political System proposes a general programme of theory development and propositions of specific theory formation. These ideas are influenced by a specific historical context (Falter 2001). From David Easton's point of view – as described above all in *The Political System* (1953) and mentioned already somewhat earlier in 'The Decline of Modern Political Theory' (1951) – political science in the early 1950s was dominated by 'historicism' and 'hyper factualism' which he criticised for various reasons.

'Historicism', he contends, regards political theory primarily as the history of political ideas which are interpreted in the context of a particular historical period by various authors. This assessment involves a double qualification: first, political theory is not autonomous, and, second, it cannot offer answers to important societal problems with any measure of commitment. This non-committal stance of political theory is important for Easton primarily because he believes that Western civilisation is undergoing fundamental change (1951: 40).

'Hyper factualism' – a second dimension of criticism – denotes an a-theoretical accumulation of empirical data. Whereas in his earlier writings Easton addresses this critique in principle to historical positivism (Falter 2001), in *A Framework for Political Analysis* (1965a) he extends it to empiricism in a broader sense. This critique is mainly targeted at the electoral and opinion research of the late 1940s and early 1950s, which experienced a major rise in popularity in social science, a consequence of development of representative surveys and statistical methods of analysis. Easton (1965a: 17) concisely summarises his critique: '[...] bad habits of crude empiricism, the accumulation of data for the sake of the data themselves, with relatively little consideration to matters of the relevance and broader significance of the findings'.

Easton's criticism of the practice of political science at the beginning of the 1950s was not just the isolated opinion of an individual academic. It was raised in the context of a broader movement in political science which later initiated and carried through the 'behavioural revolution'. The behavioural revolution comprises a whole range of different types of approaches, scientists and their investigations. However, a constitutive core of general assumptions can be identified (Falter 2001). Behaviouralism can be described as theoretically guided empiricism which ultimately aims at the establishment of general laws. Its goal is the description, explanation and prediction of political processes based on quantitative data. David Easton has been – without any doubt – the most influential protagonist of behaviourialism in political science.

His critical assessment of the state of political science led Easton to the conclusion that an independent and *general theory of politics* was needed. A theory of this type should also specify relevance criteria. These criteria of a prospective general theory were later elaborated in *A Framework for Political Analysis* (1965a) and in *A Systems Analysis of Political Life* (1965b). It turned out to be an empirically oriented political theory that differed from low- and medium-range empirical theories in two respects. Its subject matter is more comprehensive and generalised, and its conceptual coherence is much greater (Easton 1965b: 7). A general theory of politics should, according to Easton, consist of *logically integrated* sets of concepts of *extended range* with a *strong empirical reference*.

DESCRIPTION OF THE SYSTEMS ANALYSIS OF POLITICS

The Concept of the Political System
There are various yardsticks for the quality of a theory. For David Easton, the most important is 'the adequacy of explanation and understanding offered by the theory' (1965b: 473).[1] The mention of 'understanding' is somewhat surprising, since this is not an important category in the empirical-analytical paradigm embraced by Easton. With regard to the explanation criterion, his claims tend to be understated. His general theory of politics is accordingly 'a framework for the analysis of political life' (1965a: ix). This frame of reference is also described at this point as a *form* in which substantive theories can be placed and integrated. According to Easton, this form can best be described as 'systems analysis' (1965a: ix). The systems analysis concept is used in various theoretical approaches, 'such as game theory, functional research, or equilibrium theory' (1965a: 24). But Easton gives this term a quite specific meaning, as will become clear from the following account of his theory.

In elaborating his general theory of politics, Easton makes several fundamental decisions that determine the further course of theory-building. The following account and discussion is primarily systematic, deviating in some respects from the sequence followed in Easton's two central works.

Objectively the first and most important decision is specifying the fundamental unit of analysis, the *political system*: 'Its major and gross unit of analysis will be the political system' (1965a: 23). The political system is understood as '*a system of behaviour*' (1965a: 23). Somewhat ambiguous is a definition that follows some pages later in the same book: '[...] I shall be arguing that all social systems are composed of the interactions among persons and that social interactions form the basic units of these systems' (1965a: 36). But this does not adventitiously introduce the interaction as the basic unit of analysis – as postulated, for example, by the early Niklas Luhmann (1970). The system remains the unit, but can in turn be divided into subunits, namely interactions. In taking the political system as the fundamental unit of analysis, Easton differs particularly from Talcott Parsons (1951), who, in the tradition of Max Weber, regards actions as the basic units (1965a: 15). David Easton stresses that actions are always interrelated and systematically networked, and thus constitute a social system. Every social system is formed by interactions between people, with society as the most comprehensive and inclusive social system (1965a: 38).

Against this conceptual background, the theoretical problem is to identify political interactions among the totality of interactions taking place in a society: 'How shall we distinguish those interactions in society that we shall characterize as the components of a political system?' (1965a: 48). The second fundamental decision was made at this critical point in theory-building: political interactions are to be distinguished from other social interactions in that they are oriented on the binding allocation of values to society. Political interactions form the interaction system '[...] through which [...] *binding or authoritative allocations* are made and implemented' (1965a). This allows the political system to be specified as follows: 'A political system [...] will be identified as a set of interactions, abstracted from the totality of social behaviour, through which values are authoritatively allocated for a society' (1965a: 57). People who are involved in such interactions, i.e., people performing political roles, become members of the system through their actions. They do not belong to the system as human beings but as role players. In the theory of systems analysis of politics, the political system is thus not a 'natural system' but an 'analytic system' (1965a: 37ff), which nevertheless has empirical reference.

Although Easton disassociates himself from functional analyses like those of Talcott Parsons, and therefore seeks to avoid the concept of function, his definition of the political is in fact a functional one. And this subsequently gained broad acceptance, not only in almost all systems theories of politics (including Luhmann, 1970 as well as Almond and Powell, 1988), but also in political science as a whole.

The function of the political system in a society is thus the authoritative allocation of values for society. In another, now more usual formulation, this function is described as the production and imposition of generally binding decisions. Only with reference to this function can political interactions be analytically distinguished from other social interactions, and the political system from other social systems. From an empirical point of view, political interactions are thus embedded in the totality of social interactions, which they influence and which are influenced by them. This entails a third basic theoretical decision. The political system is understood as an open and adaptive system, having a dynamic exchange relationship with society, which constitutes the most important *environment* of the political system (1965a: 25; 1965b: 18). The environment of the political system is further differentiated. David Easton postulates an 'intra-societal environment', comprising the other social systems in society, for example, the economic system and non-social systems (e.g., the ecological system). Another environment of the political system is the 'extra-societal environment', comprising the political systems of other societies and supranational organisations like NATO, UNO, etc. (1965a: 59ff).

Like every social system, the political system is a boundary maintenance system that is differentiated from society, establishing and stabilizing a *boundary* against the societal environment. The degree to which a political system is differentiated from society and the clarity of the boundary drawn between it and the societal environment can, according to Easton's theory, be determined by the following criteria: first, the extent to which political roles are distinguished from other social roles; second, the extent to which the players of political roles form a group of their own in society; third, the extent to which political roles are internally hierarchical; and, fourth, the extent to which the selective mechanisms for 'casting' political roles differ from those for other social roles (1965a: 69). If a political system is differentiated and there is a boundary with the societal environment, the political system faces the permanent problem of maintaining this boundary and thus safeguarding its function for society. The problem of boundary *maintenance* is one of the subjects dealt with in the following section.

THE PERSISTENCE OF THE POLITICAL SYSTEM

Influence exerted on the political system by the societal environment is inevitable but also necessary if the political system is to fulfil its function for society. The political *authorities* need informational *feedback* about the conditions under which they make their decisions, what problems need solving, what goals are to be set, and what impact their *decisions and actions* have on the societal environment. This impact includes acceptance by the citizens and the relevant actors in other social systems affected by the decisions made and the measures taken. This informational feedback is a prerequisite for an adequate *response* to shifting environmental constellations.

A special category of influence is relevant to the further development of the theory, namely 'disturbances'. Disturbances are influences on the political system that have the effect of changing in a marked way: '*Disturbances* is a concept that may be used to identify those influences from the total environment of a system that act upon it so that it is different after the stimulus from what it was before' (1965b: 22). Easton takes specification of the environmental influences on the political system still further, introducing a category he calls '*stress*': 'Stress will be said to occur when there is a danger that the essential variables will be pushed beyond what we may designate as their critical range' (1965b: 24). What is meant by 'essential variables' and 'critical range'?

'Essential variables' are distinctive features of the political system: '[...] these two distinctive features – the allocation of values for a society and the relative frequency of compliance with them – are the *essential variables* of political life' (1965b: 24). Underlying the concept of a *'critical range'* of a political system for these essential variables is the notion of a 'normal pattern of operation' (1965a: 92). If these operations – and this means particularly the activities of political actors – deviate from normality and exceed a critical point, the existence of the system is at risk. This critical point differs widely from political system to political system, and is very difficult to identify empirically. But, in keeping with his claim to generality, Easton is concerned with a theoretical definition not of specific political systems but of all political systems or the political system as such. Political systems are first and foremost concerned with self-preservation and thus with performing their function. And this means that the essential variables must not be allowed to exceed a critical range:

What this means is that something may be happening in the environment – the system suffers total defeat at the hands of an enemy, or widespread disorganisation in and disaffection from the system is aroused by a severe economic crisis. Let us say that as a result, the authorities are consistently unable to make decisions, or if they strive to do so, the decisions are no longer regularly accepted as binding. Under these conditions, authoritative allocations of values are no longer possible, and the society would collapse for want of a system of behaviour to fulfil one of its vital functions. (1965b: 24)

This brings us to another basic theoretical decision with very far-reaching consequences. It is concerned with the central issue in Easton's systems analysis of politics, which he calls 'persistence' and which follows on from aspects mentioned in connection with stress: 'In its ultimate returns this mode of analysis will enable the investigator to understand more fully the way in which some kinds of political system in a society manage *to persist in the face of stresses*, that might well have been expected to lead to its destruction' (1965a: 25). This definition, which is strategic for Easton's general theory, is expressed elsewhere as follows: 'The perspectives of a systems analysis of political life impel us to address ourselves to the following kind of question. How can any political system ever persist whether the world be one of stability or of change?' (1965b: 14ff). The persistence of the political system is thus about keeping the 'essential variables' within a 'critical range.'

Easton deliberately uses the concept of persistence and not that of stability or 'system maintenance' to obviate any notion of static orientation and to emphasize the dynamic nature of the systems analysis of politics. The persistence of a political system, i.e., the stabilisation of interaction structures to perform its function is generally realised through change: ' [P]ersistence and change of systems or rather, *persistence through change*, as it is more often the case, has seemed to be the most inclusive kind of question that one might ask about a political system' (1965b: 475).

The issue of persistence is thus the most inclusive and fundamental for a political system. It can integrate all other issues and related theories. Among those Easton mentions are theories of electoral behaviour, interest groups, party politics, policy making and implementation, coalition behaviour, etc., for which he postulates common ground: 'But all of the ways of looking at political life implicit in these questions do have one thing in common. They impinge directly on the allocative consequences of political interaction. To the extent that they lead to theoretical inquiry, we may classify them generally as theories of allocation'

(1965b: 474). However, these *partial theories* of the authoritative allocation of values for society presuppose the existence of a political system and that this system is persistent, and this is precisely the issue addressed by the general theory of politics: 'But what these allocative theories take for granted – the actual and continued existence of some kind of political system – I have here questioned and subjected to theoretical examination. How is it that a political system as such is able to persist through time?' (1965b: 475).

The persistence of a political system thus consists in the maintenance of interaction patterns to produce and impose generally binding decisions (authoritative allocation of values for society). It is primarily this aspect and this issue that lend the theory generality and a capacity to integrate partial theories. The persistence of a political system in the face of disturbing and onerous influences from the environment of 'stress' is secured by adapting the system to the environment. The nature of this adaptation is discussed particularly in *A Systems Analysis of Political Life*. The focus is on the concepts *demands* and *support*.

THE CONCEPTS 'DEMANDS' AND 'SUPPORT' AND THE OBJECTS OF THE POLITICAL SYSTEM

In Easton's general theory, the political system is understood as an open and adaptive system, having a dynamic exchange relationship with its environment. It seeks to persist in the face of disturbing and stressful environmental influences. But influences from the environment do not impact the political system directly; they have to be transformed to render them compatible with the rationality and procedures of the political system. The theoretical task is therefore to specify 'linkage variables between system and environment' (1965a: 108). These are basically referred to as '*inputs*' and '*outputs*'. Outputs are specified as 'decisions and actions' that are generally binding, and inputs are divided into 'demands' and 'support.' The two input categories are the more important with regard to persistence. Figure 1 shows a simplified model of the political process found in Easton's early study (1957: 384). This simplified model was then elaborated into a more complex model (1965a: 110; 1965b: 30). The contents of the simplified model will now be discussed in detail.

In the environment of the political system, there is a multitude of expectations, interests, preferences and the like directed at the political system. Collectively they are termed '*wants*.' But wants become relevant for the political system and provoke reaction only when they are addressed to the authorities as requests for binding decisions. They are therefore termed 'demands': 'A *demand* may be defined as an expression of opinion that an authoritative allocation with regard to a particular subject matter should or should not be made by those responsible for doing so' (1965b: 38). Elsewhere Easton draws a clear distinction between demands and interests: '[T]he expression of an interest in a matter is not identical with the input of a demand. To become a demand, there needs to be voiced a proposal that authoritative action be taken with regard to it' (1965b: 47). Conflicts about demands are 'the flesh and blood of all political systems' (1965b: 48), but they are also a source of stress.

Every political system has only a limited capacity for processing demands by means of the political decision-making process, which results first from structurally scarce resources (e.g., money), and second, from the structurally scarce time available to the authorities. If too many demands are thrown at the political system in relation to the resources and time budget available, 'demand input overload' occurs (1965b: 58). If overload exceeds the capacity of the authorities to convert demands into decisions, the fundamental function of the authoritative allocation of values is threatened, producing 'volume stress' (1965b: 59). Over and above this, Easton postulates a 'content stress' (1965b: 59) that arises when specific demands cannot be processed by political procedures owing to their content.

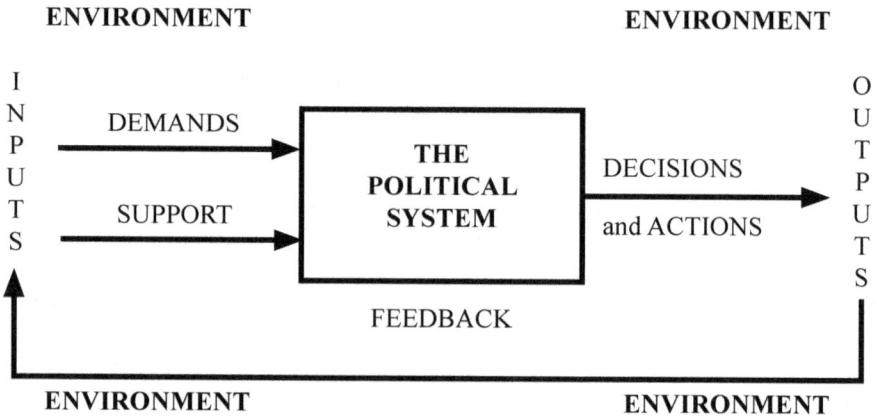

Source: based on Easton 1957: 384.

Figure 1: A simplified model of the political process

The second input category is 'support.' It is concerned with citizens' positive or negative attitudes and behaviours towards the political system: '[W]e can describe *support* as an attitude by which a person orients himself to an object either favourably or unfavourably, positively or negatively' (Easton 1975: 436). Without adequate support, a political system cannot persist indefinitely. A decline in support is therefore also a source of stress – ultimately the decisive one. However, not every form of support is equally important for the persistence issue. Easton distinguishes between forms of support with respect to the objects of the political system and the modes of orientation towards these objects. To begin with, we shall now discuss the objects of support.

In defining the objects of the political system, Easton is guided by the following question: 'What elements of a system are most relevant to its capacity to persist in the face of a threatened loss of support?' (1965b: 171). In answering the question he identifies three objects that can be ordered in terms of their relevance to the persistence issue: first, the political community, then the regime, and finally the authorities.

The *'political community'* is the most fundamental object of the political system. What exactly is meant by this, however, is not very clear, and the distinction between the object and the attitude towards the object is relatively vague. The 'political community' refers to the fact that the members of a political system are linked by a political division of labour and perform political functions for a society through this division of labour:

> This concept [...] will refer to that aspect of its political system that consists of its members seen as a group of persons bound together by a political division of labour. The existence of a political system must include a plurality of political relationships through which the individual members are linked to each other and through which the political objectives of the system are pursued, however limited this may be. (1965b: 177)

In this analytical perspective the institutional form is irrelevant; the important thing is *that* it happens. As an example of the status of the political community, Easton cites, among others, the United Kingdom. Although the regime in Britain has changed considerably over the past centuries, the political community has remained intact (1965b: 190). The concept thus includes the notion that – for whatever reason and in whatever form – a group of people are joined in a common political undertaking and that some sort of cooperation takes place among them. Such political cooperation between groups of different cultures and traditions, and even entirely separate nationalities, can in fact occur.

Easton emphasises the analytical difference between political community as an object of attachment and the attachment itself (1965b: 182ff). He describes this type of attachment as a *sense of community*:

> The we-feeling or sense of community which indicates political cohesion of a group of persons, regardless of the kind of regimes they have [...] consists of the feeling of belonging together as a group which, because it shares a political structure, also shares a political fate. (1965b: 185)

The second object of the political system is the *regime*. The regime constitutes the framework that guides and constrains political interactions. It is defined as a set of 'constraints on political interaction' comprising three elements: 'values (goals and principles), norms, and structure of authority' (1965b: 193).

In comparison with the theory of Talcott Parsons (1969; 1971), in which values are the point of departure for an informational control hierarchy of different levels of social systems, they have a more limited status in Easton's theory: 'The *values* serve as broad limits with regard to what can be taken for granted in the guidance of day-to-day policy without violating deep feelings of important segments of the community' (1965b: 193).

Norms constitute the second component of the regime: 'The *norms* specify the kinds of procedures that are expected and acceptable in the processing and implementation of demands' (1965b: 193). They are also referred to as 'operating rules' and 'rules of the game' (1965b: 200). In 'mainstream' political science, the 'rules of the game' are understood to be structural elements of the political system (cf. Fuchs 1999). Easton's concept of structure differs. He reserves the term in the first place for the pattern of power distribution among 'authority roles': '[T]he *structure of authority* designates the formal and informal patterns in which power is distributed and organised with regard to the authoritative making and implementing of decisions – the roles and relationships through which authority is distributed and exercised' (1965b: 193). The distinctive aspect of the structure concept in Easton's theory, however, is that it is primarily concerned with empirical interaction patterns, which can be identified only empirically.

Easton admits that the concept of political structure was to a certain extent, neglected in his most important writings of the 1960s. To do justice to this gap in his earlier theoretical considerations he published, in 1990, a monograph on *The Analysis of Political Structure*. In line with his attempt to develop a general theory of politics Easton does not focus on specific political structures. Rather, he tries to suggest concepts in order to meaningfully analyse political structures. At the core of this study he proposes a typology of political structures which differentiates between basic analytical concepts. The most general distinction is between higher and lower order political structures. Lower order structures are the object of observable political structures. The observable political structures, in turn, are divided into formal and informal structures. As compared to formal structures, informal structures are characterised by a lower degree of 'explicitness' as well as a lower degree of clear-cut consequences. Easton (1990: 81, 86) uses the terms customs or norms or habitual rules of behaviour. In modern society, formal structures are defined as the rule of law. In pre-modern society, the functional equivalent is the ritual or ceremonial legitimation of binding expectations of behaviour (1990: 60, 81). Easton tries to develop the concept of higher order structures to reconstruct critically the post-Marxist structuralism of Nicos Poulantzas. He tries to demonstrate that systems theory and structuralism are, in principle, compatible (1990: 188ff). The higher-order structures cannot be observed. They are, however, constraints for the lower-order structures which can be observed (1990: 260ff.). Thus, the decisive structures for the political system are latent. They cannot be theoretically reconstructed.

After this short excursus we shall continue to discuss the objects of the political system as developed in the 1960s in Easton's general political theory.

The third object of the political system is the '*authorities*'. They are the 'occupants of the authority roles' (1965b: 212) and are thus explicitly distinguished from the roles themselves. Ultimately, however, it is these authorities that make the generally binding decisions. By this definition the political parties are not per se 'authorities' and are accordingly assigned to the political system not necessarily perforce but only in so far as they are the holders of decision-making roles or provide such holders. For a European observer in whose country political parties are the most important actors in politics, this definition is certainly not immediately evident. But in view of the problem formulation of Easton's theory, which is concerned with the authoritative allocation of values, it is logically consistent.

The differentiation of the political system into these three objects is of central importance for persistence – but above all in connection with support for these objects. Without sufficient support, the persistence of the political system is in danger. Support is therefore a possible source of stress – 'Stress through the erosion of support' (1965b: 200) – and support is therefore one of the two input categories of his dynamic systems analysis. Easton (1975: 436) understands support in general as 'as an attitude by which a person orients himself to an object either favorably or unfavorably, positively or negatively'.

Going into greater detail in explaining the status and meaning of support in his theory, he distinguishes two subcategories: 'Within the context of systems analysis, it has been important to discriminate between two kinds of support: specific and diffuse' (Easton 1975: 436).

'*Specific support*' means that citizens examine 'in a rough and ready way' whether the demands they articulate are realised by the perceived outputs. If this is the case, the output-generating authorities are evaluated favourably: 'The authorities will be evaluated according to the extent to which these demands are perceived to have been met' (Easton 1975: 438). Specific support thus relates to the authorities, and does so in two respects: 'Specific support [...] is directed to the perceived decisions, policies, actions, utterances or the general style of these authorities' (Easton 1975: 437). If one relates specific support to fundamental differentiations made in attitude research then specific support rests upon instrumental considerations or benefit calculations.

If specific support erodes, the probability that the citizens will accept and approve the decisions of the political system declines, and stress develops for the political system. In view of the structural scarcity of resources and time, a political system would always face stress and would not be able to survive in the long term if it were not for another form of support, which Easton calls *diffuse support*.

The essential characteristic of 'diffuse support' is its relative independence of outputs: '[...] the level of *diffuse support* will normally be independent of outputs and performance in the short run' (Easton 1975: 444). Accordingly:

> [...] diffuse support [...] forms a reservoir of favorable attitudes or good will that helps members to accept or tolerate outputs to which they are opposed or the effect of which they see as damaging to their wants ... Except in the long run, diffuse support is independent of the effects of daily outputs. It consists of a reservoir of support that enables a system to weather the many storms when outputs cannot be balanced off against inputs of demands. (1965b: 273)

Apart from its independence of outputs and its 'reservoir' function, diffuse support differs from specific support in the objects towards which it is directed:

> Whereas specific support is extended only to the incumbent authorities, diffuse support is directed towards offices themselves as well as towards their individual occupants. More than that, diffuse support is support that underlies the regime as a whole and the political community. (Easton 1975: 445)

Diffuse support is thus concerned with all three objects of the political system, and is of strategic, graduated importance for its persistence. The first and least fundamental stage is diffuse support for the authorities. Without a modicum of such support, approval of the decisions made by the authorities is at the very least problematic. The second and more important stage is diffuse support of the regime. If the regime and thus the structural framework in which the production and imposition of generally binding decisions takes place, and which makes this decision-making activity possible in the first place, finds no diffuse support among the citizenry, the political system will be subject to corresponding stress. This leads to the paralysis of political processes and, in the longer run, to the collapse of the existing regime and its replacement by another.

In view of the outstanding importance of diffuse support for the persistence of a political system, it must be asked how it is generated and what sources it has. Easton identifies two: '[…] diffuse support […] arises from two sources: from childhood and continuing adult socialisation, and from direct experience' (Easton 1975: 445). Socialisation generates diffuse support in two ways. First, through psychological transfer processes from the primary socialisation agents – especially fathers – (literally) diffuse affective attachments to the objects of the political system are produced (Easton and Dennis 1969). Second, an attachment to certain values is generated, which will subsequently serve as a yardstick for assessing the authorities and the regime. Easton calls this diffuse support based on value attachments 'legitimacy'. *Legitimacy* 'reflects the fact that in some vague or explicit way […] [a person] sees these objects as conforming to his own moral principles, his own sense of what is right and proper in the political sphere' (Easton 1975: 451). With reference to the fundamental differentiations made in attitude research, legitimacy is a normative type of consideration.

Diffuse support stemming from direct experience is termed '*trust.*' It is based on lasting positive experiences with the outputs of the authorities: '[…] that trust will be stimulated by the experiences that members have of the authorities over time […] In time, such sentiments may become detached from the authorities themselves and take the form of an autonomous or generalised sentiment towards all incumbent authorities and perhaps the regime as well' (Easton 1975: 448). In the same way as specific support rests upon instrumental or benefit calculations so trust does as one dimension of diffuse support. The difference to specific support lies in a generalisation of satisfaction with the everyday outputs and a detachment of authorities and an attribution to the regime.

Replacing one regime by another is one way a political system can adjust to changing environmental conditions that place the system under massive stress. Britain has been cited as an example of this type of adaptation. Since the 16th century it has changed its regime several times, sometimes quite radically. But these changes can be understood as modes of adaptation *by* the political system only if there has been a certain continuity in the system. This continuity is provided by the 'political community' and by the support for it.

As we have seen, a political community comprises a number of people who are linked by a political division of labour. But this definition poses a conceptual problem. A political division of labour is generally determined by the roles and procedures of a regime, but the political community as an object is to be defined independently of a specific regime because it is more fundamental than any regime. An alternative would be to consider the political community, in the tradition of Max Weber, merely as the subjective sentiment of belonging to a definable group with certain characteristics. In a certain fashion, Easton does indeed proceed in this manner: 'The *we-feeling* or *sense of community* which indicates political cohesion of a group of persons, regardless of the kind of regime they have or may develop, consists of the feeling of belonging together [...]' (1965b: 185). But the problem is that this 'we-feeling' or 'sense of community' is the attitude of that community which Easton wishes to see defined independently of this attitude.

		Objects of support		
		Political community	*Regime*	*Authorities*
Modi of support	*Diffuse support* [a]	Sense of community (expressive orientation)	Legitimacy (normative orientation) Trust (instrumental orientation / generalised)	Legitimacy (normative orientation) Trust (instrumental orientation / generalised)
	Specific support [b]			Performance (instrumental orientation / specific)

[a] independent of output and performance in the short run respectively, reservoir of favourable attitudes or good will.

[b] directed to the perceived decisions, policies, actions or the general style of the authorities

Source: based on Easton 1965b: 30.

Figure 2: Types of political support

Disregarding the problem of analytically distinguishing the object of the political community from the diffuse support for this object, it is essential for the persistence of a political system that a group of people recognize the necessity of there being common matters that have to be regulated by generally binding decisions, and that this implies some form of political cooperation. Without a political community in this sense, the 'essential variables' of a political system would no longer exist even minimally, and this political system would cease to exist.

The concept of political support is one of the core elements of Easton's theory and to this day has a major influence on empirical research. We shall now schematically summarise this concept (cf. Figure 2).

ORIGINS OF DIFFUSE SUPPORT

One major hypothesis of Easton's theory is that the persistence of any kind of political system at all depends on the input of diffuse support to the objects of the political system. This significance inevitably raises questions about the origins of diffuse support. Within the range of his speculation Easton makes a basic assumption: 'It is our theoretical interest with origins of support as a major mechanism in the persistence of political systems that leads directly to children' (Easton and Dennis 1969: 5). If this diffuse support has its origins in childhood, then this statement might be proven empirically. Easton makes exactly this statement, mainly in cooperation with Jack Dennis (1969). Besides the empirical clarification of a question with an important content, this study is exemplary of how to meet the standards of theory-led empiricism. In the preface *Children in the Political System* (1969: viii) Easton and Dennis substantiate their claims as follows: 'This book is one effort to bring theory and research into closer accord. We seek to stretch a slender footbridge between systems (or persistence) theory, as it has been developing within the terms of its own logic, and behavior in the political systems'. Their study belongs to the tradition of political socialisation research. The authors define 'political socialisation' as 'those developmental processes through which persons acquire political orientations and patterns of behavior' (Easton and Dennis 1969: 7). They stress again, that the 'origins of diffuse support' are due to childhood: 'Diffuse rather than specific support is likely to be particularly relevant in the study of childhood socialisation' (Easton and Dennis 1969: 67).

Using ingenious methods, samples of more than five thousand school children from second to eight grade in eight cities from different regions of the United States were asked to fill in elaborated questionnaires and draw pictures of various authority figures. The children were interviewed at relatively close age intervals in order to observe the year-by-year shifts in political orientations.

Contrary to the preconceptions of socialisation research, Easton and his collaborators were able to demonstrate that, by the time they leave elementary school young children have assembled a formidable array of basic political orientations. The child is likely to absorb, if only in latent form, some of the most profound feelings human beings are capable of developing toward political systems: diffuse political support. How do new members, who are born into a political system, typically learn their basic lessons? Easton demonstrates that these first membership roles are shaped by politicisation, personalisation, idealisation, and institutionalisation. The authors theoretically assume that diffuse political support is mainly acquired in childhood. Their empirical investigation shows convincingly that this is indeed the case – at least under the societal and political conditions pertaining at the time of the data collection.

A CRITICAL DISCUSSION OF A SYSTEMS ANALYSIS OF POLITICS

As already noted, Easton elaborated his general theory of politics primarily through the two monographs, *A Framework for Political Analysis* and *A Systems Analysis of Political Life*. In later publications he took up some aspects of the theory again, which he differentiated and partly modified. This was particularly the case in 'A Re-Assessment of the Concept of Political Support' (1975) and *The Analysis of Political Structure* (1990). The theory developed in these works, which the author himself calls a systems analysis of politics, is an outstanding intellectual achievement, which has been appropriately recognised in the various honours awarded to Easton. In the early years after publication of his two important works in 1965, his general theory met with an extraordinarily wide response, which, however, for reasons intrinsic and extrinsic to his theory, subsequently declined.

The extrinsic reasons included, first, the consequences of the protest movements in the 1960s and, second, the dynamics of the scientific system itself. In his publications, Easton has repeatedly emphasised the empirical relevance of his theory, and for many he thus helped pave the way for the so-called 'behavioural revolution.' However, in the context of the protest movements, behaviouralism was strongly criticised from a neo-Marxist perspective. Elements of such criticism were the detachment of techniques and methods from content and the inevitably conservative nature of a scientific approach based on empirical data which – by definition – reflect a reality that is 'bad' and therefore in need of change. In his 'presidential address' to the 1969 annual meeting of the American Political Science Association, Easton described this development as a 'post-behavioral revolution,' and tried to bring its criteria of relevance in line with his own notions (Easton 1969). Today there is no doubt that neo-Marxism has lost ground and with it many of the arguments previously posed against behaviouralism (Almond 1997).

What played a bigger role in the declining attention paid to Easton's general theory was, paradoxically, the success story of the rational choice paradigm. As in Easton's theory, the point of departure is empirically observable actions by individuals. Although this point of departure is taken intuitively, political action is deduced and explained in the framework of a general theory of rational action. The perspective of the rational choice paradigm gave rise to a critical assessment of constructing a general theory like that of Easton: 'Empirical general theory was viewed as the pre-scientific construction of frameworks, which the hard science, deductive-inductive approach of rational choice theory would somehow replace' (Almond 1997: 220). Rational choice theory also claims to be a general theory, but it is an action theory whereas David Easton's general theory is a systems theory. In the paradigm dispute between systems theory and action theory, American political science, at least, has so far given a clear preference to action theory couched in the form of the rational choice paradigm.[2]

However, a notable change has taken place since the beginning of the 1980s within the rational choice paradigm. Originally, political structures were seen merely as a product of rationally acting individuals without independent theoretical status. James Buchanan summarises it as follows: '[T]he political structure is conceived as something that emerges from the choice processes of individual participants' (quoted by Almond 1997: 220). In the context of the 'new institutionalism,' however, political structures were rediscovered as constraints on individual action, and it was conceded that these structures cannot be completely reduced to the concepts of rational decisions taken by utility-calculating individuals. Structural constraints, i.e., predetermined rule structures, are a prerequisite to rational action. Without this 'prescription,' interrelated – and thus social – action would be impossible. 'New institutionalism' systematically includes these structural constraints in its explanatory strategy.[3] But structural constraints themselves cannot be specifically defined by rational choice concepts; recourse must be taken to other approaches – and this offers a potential interface with David Easton's systems theory. If this has not and perhaps cannot be exploited, it is due not least of all to reasons intrinsic to the theory, to which we now turn.

The last and most important reference point in Easton's theory is the persistence of political systems as such, and not that of specific political systems with specific political structures. From this point of view, structures are primarily means to an end, namely system persistence. Structures therefore have no special status in the context of the theory and are therefore defined abstractly. They are therefore not instructive for determining the structural constraints on the rational action of individuals in empirical analysis contexts. For this reason, the 'new institutionalism' also follows the notions of 'classical institutionalism,' reformulating them in its own categorical apparatus.

The abstractness of the theory and the consequent neglect of concrete structures, and thus concrete regimes, has another implication. Relevant aspects for theories and analyses are also, or perhaps even primarily, decided by public discourse. And regarding the question of the political system of government, the normative model of democracy has gained almost worldwide acceptance. The resulting research questions address, for example, the conditions for the coming into being and maintenance of democracies, and which form of democracy is to be preferred. Easton's theory is not very instructive with regard to these research questions either, because the price of its generality is, among other things, an indifference towards differences in the system of government. A political system is persistent if the authoritative allocation of values for society is still ensured in some manner.

Easton accordingly regards, for instance, the political system in Germany as persistent or persisting even in the transition from the democracy of the Weimar Republic to the totalitarianism of National Socialism. From the persistence point of view, both types of regime are thus treated as functionally equivalent. Ralf Dahrendorf has reacted sharply – and certainly somewhat excessively – to this indifference: 'But what a miserable, indeed almost inhuman, way to describe the most dramatic changes in the composition and substance of Germany's political order!' (quoted by Miller 1971: 232)

Another intrinsic reason for the decline in interest in Easton's theory is its limited capacity for integrating substantial theories of low and medium range. This limited integrative capacity has been indicated as one of the reasons why a general theory is required. But such integration can succeed only if low- and medium-range theories are in fact understood as partial theories of the authoritative allocation of values for society and can systematically relate to this perspective. For many theories, however, this is not the case. And even if it were basically possible, the cognitive gain would often be of little value. If, for example, an attempt were to be made to explain the political participation of citizens in a democracy, the findings of the analysis would have an immediately evident cognitive value for the functioning and quality of that democracy. For the researcher involved, there would presumably be little incentive to go further and relate these findings to the persistence issue.

CONCLUSION

The Systems Analysis of Politics to and Contemporary Approaches
The theory developed by David Easton in his two fundamental monographs (1965a; 1965b) has constituted an important contribution to the political science debate through significant influence on other systems theories. Without the works of Easton, systems theories such as those of Gabriel A. Almond and G. Bingham Powell Jr. (1988) and Niklas Luhmann (1984; 1995) would have been inconceivable. However, systems theory as a whole has lost ground to competing theoretical approaches over the past two decades. We have mentioned a number of extraneous and intrinsic grounds. In short, it could perhaps be said that Easton's theory, with the persistence of political systems as its pivotal reference point, is so general that it has become somewhat divorced from current political science controversies.

The lasting effect of his theory is probably threefold: first, as a general theory of politics or the political system it still has no competitors; second, diverse categories and aspects have long become commonplace in the profession – such as the concept of persistence, the functional definition of the political system, the conceptualisation of the political system as a dynamic feedback model, etc.; and, third, some of his concepts have had and still have a decisive influence on empirical research. To conclude, we will discuss some of these in brief.

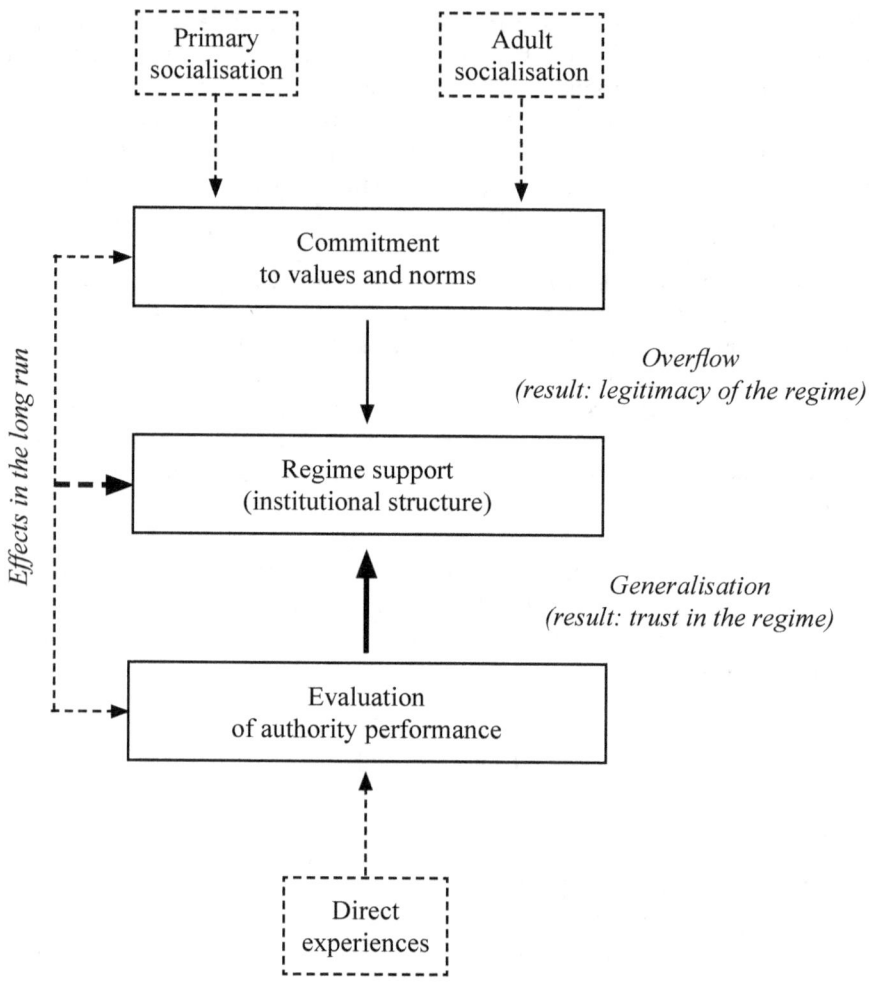

Figure 3: Reformulation of the Concept of Political Support

The concept of 'demand-input overload' directly influenced the debate over the governability crisis in the mid 1970s (Crozier *et al.* 1975; King 1976; Rose 1979). The idea of a potential overload of the democratic regime through the demands of citizens has become commonplace in political science. For several decades now, the concept of political support has been a key factor in empirical research on democratic systems. It has now been integrated into the paradigm of political culture (Almond 1980; Fuchs 2007) and research into the consolidation of new democracies (Rose *et al.* 1998; Klingemann 1999; Rohrschneider 1999; Fuchs and Roller 2006).

A systematic connection of the concept of political support to the paradigm of political culture can be made via a simple analytical differentiation. The term regime, used by Easton, contains values as well as norms as well as the structure of authority (1965b: 193). The significance of culture in contrast to structure is disregarded. By detaching values and norms from the regime concept and by restricting the concept to institutional structure, a reformulation of the concept of political support can be made (Fuchs 2007):

This reformulation (Figure 3) is conceptually beneficial for two reasons. First, a core assumption of the paradigm of political culture can be considered, i.e. the congruence between culture (values and norms) and structure (regime defined as the institutional arrangement). Second, a theoretically meaningful causal relationship between the different levels can be specified and tested empirically.

The conceptualisations Easton elaborated for the political conversion process have also had far-reaching consequences for empirical research and for the concepts that guide research. Many policy process models relate directly to Easton's theory (incl. Brewer and de Leon 1983; Windhoff-Héritier 1987).

For a systematic integration of multifaceted partial theories within a consistent frame of reference, Easton's comprehensive theory remains necessary and fruitful. In order to connect it with the contemporary discussion of democratic theory, a specification of that general theory for *democratic systems* would make much sense. The focus of this theory would then no longer be some authoritative value allocation in general but the production and imposition of generally binding decisions by means of democratic structures and processes.

This theory of a lower range could – and should – take up problems which belong to democratic institutions which are indispensable to democratic government and its structures (Dahl 1989). On the one hand, this theory would violate the principle of value neutrality of behaviouralism. Yet, on the other hand, this strategy could further common discussion and development with modern normative democratic theory.

This line of development of a general theory of democratic political systems would not replace Easton's more comprehensive theory. Rather, the many hints he provided in his writings would help a great deal to achieve the more modest goal outlined above.

Notes
1 To enhance the legibility of the text, reference to the author will be omitted, i.e., all further dates without mention of author refer to publications by David Easton.
2 Green and Shapiro (1994:3) demonstrate empirically that almost 40% of all contributions published in the American Political Science Review in the 1990s were articles on rational choice.
3 The key difference with rational choice theory is that between choices and constraints: choices refer to the selection/action options available to or taken up by a rationally acting agent. Not all conceivable options for action are available to a rational actor in a given situation; they are limited. These limitations are referred to collectively as constraints; the literature differentiates between such subcategories as situative constraints, constitutional constraints, etc., which cannot be dealt with here.

REFERENCES

Almond, G. A. (1980) 'The Intellectual History of the Civic Culture Concept', in G. A. Almond and S. Verba (eds.) *The Civic Culture Revisited*, Boston: Little, Brown and Company.
(1997) 'The Political System and Comparative Politics. The Contribution of David Easton', in K. R. Monroe (ed.) *Contemporary Empirical Political Theory*, Berkeley: University of California Press.
Almond, G. A. and Powell, G. B. Jr. (eds.) (1988) *Comparative Politics Today: A World View*, Glenview, Ill./Boston/London: Little, Brown and Company.
Brewer, G. D. and de Leon, P. (1983) *The Foundations of Policy-Analysis*, Homewood, Ill: Dorsey Press.
Crozier, M., Huntington, S. P. and Watanuki, J. (1975) *The Crisis of Democracy*, New York: New York University Press.
Dahl, R. (1989) *Democracy and its Critics*, New Haven and London: Yale University Press.
Easton, D. (1951) 'The Decline of Modern Political Theory', Journal of Politics, 13: 36–58. Reprinted in J. A. Gould and V. Thursby (eds.) *Contemporary Political Thought*, Holt, Rinehart and Winston, 1969.
(1953) [2nd ed. 1971, re-issued 1981], *The Political System: An Inquiry into the State of Political Science*, New York: Alfred A. Knopf.
(1957) 'An Approach to the Analysis of Political Systems', World Politics, 9: 383–400.
(1965a) *A Framework for Political Analysis*, Englewood Cliffs: Prentice Hall.
(1965b) [re-issued 1979] *A Systems Analysis of Political Life*, New York: John Wiley.
(1969) 'The New Revolution in Political Science', *The American Political Science Review*, 63: 1051–1061.
(1975) 'A Re-Assessment of the Concept of Political Support', *British Journal of Political Science*, 5: 453–457.
(1990) *The Analysis of Political Structure*, New York: Routledge.
Easton, D. and Dennis, J. (1969) *Children in the Political System: Origins of Political Legitimacy*, New York: McGraw-Hill.
Falter, J. (2001) 'Behaviorism: Political', in N. J. Smelser and P.B. Baltes (ed.), *International Encyclopedia of the Social and Behavioral Sciences*, Vol. 24 plus 2 index Vol. Amsterdam, pp. 1125–28.
Fuchs, D. (1999) 'The Democratic Culture of Germany', in P. Norris (ed.) *Critical Citizens: Global Support for Democratic Government*, Oxford: Oxford University Press.
(2007) 'The Political Culture Paradigm', in: R. J. Dalton and H.-D. Klingemann (ed.), *Political Behaviour*, Oxford: Oxford University Press.
Fuchs, D. and Roller, E. (2006) 'Learned Democracy? Support of Democracy in

Central and Eastern Europe', *International Journal of Sociology*, 36: 70–96.

Green, D. P. and Shapiro, I. (1994) *Pathologies of Rational Choice Theory: A Critique of Applications in Political Science*, New Haven/London: Yale University Press.

King, A. (1976) *Why is Britain Becoming Harder to Govern?*, London: British Broadcasting Corporation.

Klingemann, H-D (1999) 'Mapping Political Support in the 1990s: A Global Analysis', in P. Norris (ed.) *Critical Citizens: Global Support for Democratic Government*, Oxford: Oxford University Press.

Luhmann, N. (1970) 'Soziologie des politischen Systems', in N. Luhmann, *Soziologische Aufklärung*, Vol. 1, Opladen: Westdeutscher Verlag.

(1984) *Soziale Systeme: Grundriss einer allgemeinen Theorie*, Frankfurt am Main: Suhrkamp.

(1995) *Social Systems*, Stanford, CA: Stanford University Press.

Miller, E. F. (1971) 'David Easton's Political Theory', *The Political Science Review*, 1: 184–235.

Parsons, T. (1951) *Toward a General Theory of Action*, Cambridge: Harvard University Press.

(1969) *Politics and Social Structure*, New York: Free Press.

(1971) *The System of Modern Societies*, Englewood Cliffs, New Jersey: Prentice Hall.

Rohrschneider, R. (1999) *Learning Democracy: Democratic and Economic Values in Unified Germany*, Oxford: University Press.

Rose, R. (1979) 'Pervasive Problems of Governing: An Analytic Framework', in J. Matthes (ed.) *Sozialer Wandel in West-Europa*, Frankfurt-New York: Campus.

Rose, R., Mishler, W. and Haerpfer, C. (1998) *Democracy and its Alternatives*, Oxford: Polity Press.

Windhoff-Héritier, A. (1987) *Policy-Analyse: Eine Einführung*, Frankfurt am Main: Campus.

chapter four | S. E. Finer: The Erudite Individualist
Hans Daalder

THE FINER SIBLINGS

A portrait of Samuel E. Finer (endearingly known in the profession as 'Sammy') inevitably starts with two unusual features: his was a case of rare upward intellectual mobility, and of a unique sibling relationship. Samuel Finer was born in 1915 as the youngest child of a Jewish couple, who had immigrated to England from Romania in 1900 and per force settled in one of the poorer London districts. His elder brother by 18 years was Herman Finer, shortly to become a highly successful junior lecturer at the London School of Economics, who would move later to the University of Chicago. The young Sammy is alleged to have pronounced early on: 'I want to be like my brother' (Finer 1980b: 346). At the age of about 15 he must have witnessed Herman renting a horse and buggy to bring a manuscript of several feet high to his London publisher. It contained the draft for the book *The Theory and Practice of Modern Government*. Tradition has it that the publisher insisted on a 50 percent cut, before it appeared in 1932 in a two-volume edition, containing over 1500 pages of densely printed texts plus appendices. The book was a landmark in the comparative government literature, replacing the traditional country-by-country treatment with lengthy institutional analyses of Parliament, the Executive and the Civil Service, comparing data from Britain, the US, France and Germany. In 1934 an abridged one volume edition was published, which did much to widen the appeal of the book (my own copy of the new 1949 edition still contains 954 two-column pages plus!). Together, Herman Finer's opus and Carl Friedrich's book, *Constitutional Government and Democracy; Theory and Practice in Europe and America* (1937; various later editions under somewhat different names) became for long the leading text on comparative government replacing the seminal volumes by J. Bryce, A. L. Lowell, and others. It set an example in the thoroughness of its coverage, the strong historical element in the subjects treated, and its general erudition. It also betrayed the perennial problem of such texts, in that a comparative treatment presupposes knowledge of the political systems to be compared. No wonder therefore that Herman Finer found it necessary later to publish a new volume entitled *Governments of Greater European Powers* (1956), which returned towards a country-by-country format covering the same four countries. This book, less successful than the earlier volume although equally learned, also counts some 951 two-column pages, with another 94 pages in appendices, comments, index, etc.

It was Herman who persuaded their parents to allow Sammy not to go to medical school as they had wanted, but to compete for an open Oxford Scholarship at Trinity College, which he won. He obtained a (rare) first class Oxford degree in Modern Greats (PPE, i.e., Politics, Philosophy and Economics) in 1937, and was then persuaded by his tutors to attempt the Modern History School in one year, which he also ended with a first class degree. 'I bless the day I decided to take their advice', Sammy was to write later, getting from the Modern History School 'an historical breadth and perspective without which the study of politics is either a barren *a priorism* or an empty set of mechanical computations' (Finer 1980b: 347). It was Herman again who suggested the topic for his younger brother's dissertation, a biography of a leading 19th century civil servant, *The Life and Times of Sir Edwin Chadwick* (London 1952). The two brothers remained close throughout their life. For all his self-confidence and seeming intellectual arrogance, Sammy continued to regard his brother as his true mentor. I remember him telling me that he had again been to Chicago, where he had talked intensively with Herman. 'I work hard to catch-up with him,' he exclaimed, 'but he is still 18 years ahead of me in his reading.' At age 47, Sammy published *The Man on Horseback* (1962) with the dedication: 'In recognition, gratitude and love to my great teacher and constant guide my brother Herman.'

MILITARY SERVICE DURING WORLD WAR II

For six years Finer's academic career was interrupted by military service. He served as Captain in the Royal Signals in the Middle East. Life in the military left definite traces. I remember him already in the 1950s talking on the importance of the military as an object of study. After a special trip to South America he spoke about the different forms of military take-over in that part of the world, institutionalised to such an extent that he quoted with gusto the special Spanish vocabulary developed to characterise them. More importantly, I remember his seemingly obvious, yet eye-opening, remark which was at the foundation of his work on *The Man on Horseback*:

Instead of asking why the military engage in politics, we ought surely ask why they ever do otherwise. For at first sight the political advantages of the military *vis-à-vis* other and civilian groupings are overwhelming. The military possess vastly superior organisation. And they possess *arms*.[1]

He published his exploratory volume on the role of the military in politics in 1962, the first of his works not specifically concerned with British politics. He was to emphasise the eminent importance of war and military preparation in European state-building in the seminal essay he contributed to the volume, edited by Charles Tilly, *The Formation of National States in Western Europe* (Finer 1975a). The armed forces remained together with the bureaucracy a powerful variable in his classification of states in *The History of Government from the Earliest Times*.[2]

THE FORMATION OF THE SCHOLAR

We are fortunate in having ample material for Finer's intellectual biography. He provided us with at least two major sources written by himself, e.g. the chapter he contributed to 'A generation of political thought', a seminal special issue of *Government and Opposition* (Finer 1980b); and the important address he delivered in the 1983 *Government and Opposition* lecture at the London School of Economics entitled 'Perspectives in the World History of Government – a Prolegomenon' (Finer 1983). In the latter he discussed his plan for the most ambitious project of an already full intellectual life, i.e., the writing of *The History of Government from the Earliest Times*. And this is not all.

Those who knew him, remember the vivid statements which, inveterate and entertaining talker as he was, he gave to work which preoccupied him at any particular moment. And more durably: he was wont to spell out both the contours and the working methods used in his books in prefaces, introductions, let alone longer introductory sections, such as Part One of his *Comparative Government* (1970), or the editorial notes he put down for *The History of Government,* the basis of the important *The Conceptual Prologue* which introduces that three-volume work (Finer 1997, vol. 1: 1–94). Then, Dennis Kavanagh has contributed two important chapters on Finer's life and writings (Kavanagh 1984 and 1997). He also edited with Gillian Peele a *Festschrift* published in 1984 to which a number of Finer's colleagues at different times and locations contributed essays on subjects which had concerned Finer at earlier moments (Kavanagh and Peele 1984). And there is the special commemorative issue of *Government and Opposition* of 1994, written mainly by his close associates on the editorial board of that journal.[3] That volume also contains an original contribution by his widow Catherine Jones Finer (1994) on his working methods, observed from nearby, and analysing Finer's particular influence on the development of one younger scholar in a neighbouring discipline, i.e., herself.

From his student days, Finer has singled out as particular influences, apart from his general work for the PPE and Modern History degrees, some great economists, notably Keynes's *General Theory* ('I mastered it and felt that economic theory had at least broken its silken fetters and joined the living world.'), Marxism ('I became one. With Marxism everything seemed clear. History became manageable, politics explicable. Everything was in its place') and, somewhat rarer, Pareto ('I got myself a copy of the *Manuel d'Economie Politique* [...] and made a *précis* of the entire volume during the summer vacation') (Finer, 1980b: 348). Pareto was important to him for his realism, debunking the claims of prevailing normative moral and political theory. These he had read extensively but they bored him at the time. He was later to issue a volume with selected texts from Pareto, entitled *Pareto: Sociological Writings* (1966), with an important introduction of his own.

His work on Chadwick was interrupted by World War II. It was lastingly important to him for being a clear example of the complexities of public policy-making, and the key role that an important civil servant exercises. Ever after he was immune to the idea that bureaucrats were purely instrumental actors, and policy-making a mere neutral process. Finer was himself to remark with some astonishment that there was no trace left of his youthful Marxism in the *Chadwick* book itself.

His earliest writings remained within the field of (British) public administration. His first book was *A Primer of Public Administration* (1950), followed by *Chadwick* (1952), and the book *Local Government in England and Wales* (1953), co-authored with J. M. R. Maud. One might note, in passing, that here too Sammy followed his older brother Herman, who had published early in his career, *The British Civil Service; An Introductory Essay* (1927) and *English Local Government* (1933), but had tackled much earlier also non-British subjects such as *Representative Government and a Parliament of Industry; A Study of the German Federal Economic Council* (1923), and of course his *Theory and Practice of Modern Government*.

Two new challenges were greatly to influence Sammy Finer in the early 1950s, moving him in different directions: first, the need to develop a political science syllabus for the new Department he was to set up in a new university, and second, his closer acquaintance with new developments in American political science. As for the first, his appointment at Keele was originally as Professor of Local Government and Administration, but it was soon changed to a Chair of Political Institutions. The new job forced him to seek much wider ground, to round off a department with complimentary specialisations. Secondly, two American studies were to influence his own future work: Sidney Bailey's *Congress Makes a Law* (1950) and David Truman's *The Governmental Process* (1951). Both studies prompted him to engage in the study of pressure groups in Britain. He worked for some years on a large-scale study of group interests in the nationalisation and denationalisation of public transport which never saw the light of day. Instead, he wrote the much smaller, but highly influential *Anonymous Empire; A Study of the Lobby in Great Britain* (1958) as well as *Private Industry and Political Power* published in the same year. Whether he had advance knowledge of David Truman's work on *The Congressional Party; A Case Study* (New York 1959) is not clear. But there is little doubt that this type of study was to direct him towards an attempt to get closer into power relations of the different parliamentary parties in Britain. Undertaken with his Keele colleagues Hugh Berrington, David Bartholomew and others, which resulted in the book *Backbench Opinion in the House of Commons* (1961), it was for Finer an unusual 'behaviourally oriented', collaborative study based on an analysis of so-called early day motions introduced in Parliament.

However, a third element was to have a greater impact on Finer's later work: his contact, interaction and running debate with representatives of the 'new comparative politics'. In 1952 a group of younger scholars met at North-Western University (Evanston) and then published a manifesto-type programme in the *American Political Science Review* calling for a drastic overhaul of traditional studies of comparative government (see Macridis and Cox 1953). The International Political Science Association organised a Round Table Conference in Florence in 1954 where a number of major figures of more traditional inclination faced a small delegation of the new Young Turks.[4] Less traditional than older stalwarts such as C. J. Friedrich, W. A. Robson, Norman Chester, Max Beloff, Dolf Sternberger, Kurt Sontheimer or Maurice Duverger, Finer was critical of the new movement, yet to quote his words: 'some of it was enormously appealing to me, particularly its demand for a "systematic politics" that should include non-Western as well as Western systems and its call to search for "patterns of uniformity and difference."' 'This implied', to follow Finer's quotation from the paper he himself submitted to the Florence Round Table, that

> in maintaining that [...] governmental data are susceptible of classification, analysis and comparison, and that they can be shown to exhibit causal inter-relationships, the vital claim is being made, albeit implicitly, that governmental phenomena are not unique to time and place and circumstance; and thereby they are differentiated sharply from the category of *historical* data. This claim was to sever Political Science from History.

He then formulated the considerable change which took place in his mind in the 1950s in the following paragraph:

> With hindsight, I can now see how these three components – my own new-minted notion of what 'politics' is, the pluralist group approach and the desire to fit non-Western forms into my frame of comparison, blended together and generated in me a new outlook on political study. I brought non-Western societies into my core course, and began to perceive states as falling into great families. More: once I transferred my attention from the institutionalised polities of the Western and the Communist worlds to the highly fluid political forms in the Third World, politics (a form of social behaviour) visibly dissociated itself from government, i.e., from the nexus of structures that purport to channel it. My new outlook took me beyond a mere taxonomy of regimes: it made possible a deeper understanding of the nature of political behaviour as such. It was from this standpoint that the course of lectures emerged which, much later, were to become the basis for *Comparative Government* (1970). (Finer 1980b: 353–354)

Enough, so far, on what one might term Finer's period of formation and reorientation which was to make him the special political scientist he was to be.

FINER'S PROFESSIONAL CAREER

Taking a leaf from Finer's working methods, one could say that after demobilisation in 1946, his professional life can be divided into four appointments, and five stages. First, he spent four years as a lecturer and junior fellow at Balliol College in Oxford (1946–1950). He then moved, secondly, to 'a handful of army huts on a bleak and sodden hillside in the Midlands in order to found, from scratch, an entire department of Political Institutions' (Finer 1980b: 352) in the new University College of North Staffordshire, soon to be Keele University, ending up as deputy vice-chancellor in 1962–1964. From there, in 1966, he went on, thirdly, to chair the Department of Government of the University of Manchester. As one of his junior colleagues of the time was to remark, this department had just been depleted by the departure for Edinburgh of its prominent Head of Department, W. J. M. Mackenzie, and of a large number of staff Mackenzie had trained who went to fill the rapidly growing number of chairs in the blossoming provincial universities. Hence, Finer had to build for the second time a department with new staff, aided this time, however, by a number of more senior colleagues such as Ghita Ionescu, the founder and editor of the highly readable journal of comparative politics, *Government and Oppostion.* Having successfully done so, he moved over in 1974 to the Gladstone Professorship in Government and Public Administration at the University of Oxford which had been vacated by that prominent scholar on constitutionalism, federalism, and legislatures, [Sir] Kenneth Wheare. The Gladstone Chair (which went with a fellowship at All Souls) had considerable prestige, but carried little power or patronage. If Finer was able to put a special stamp on the two Departments he directed previously, there was little chance of his doing so for the political science curriculum at Oxford, that 'democratic' university, where real power rests with the colleges and their tutors. Incidentally, he also failed in his ardent desire to see Giovanni Sartori appointed to the Oxford Chichele Chair of Political Philosophy. The attempt apparently fell one vote short in the nomination committee (Sartori 1997: 97). Finer retired from the Gladstone Chair in 1982. If this meant leaving his fourth appointment, it brings us to the fifth stage of his professional life: his retirement project of writing *The History of Government from the Earliest Time*s, which, notwithstanding failing health, he had nearly finished before his death in 1993.

THE TEACHER

Finer was an exceptionally gifted teacher. I first saw him closely in action in 1958–1959, when he came over regularly from the English Midlands to the Institute of Social Studies in The Hague. This Institute, established by the joint Dutch Universities as an international graduate school on development studies, attracted students (many, in fact, mid-career civil servants) mainly from Third World Countries. The major subjects in a deliberately interdisciplinary programme were economics, sociology and public administration (widening over time towards political science). Sammy would arrive by night-boat and would face an audience barely awake. He sat himself cross-legged on a table, often wearing a particularly colourful waist-coat, staring the group down. And then he pronounced: 'You are the stupidest, sleepiest audience I have seen for a long time'. 'If you want attention from the public,' he remarked gleefully afterwards, 'you must insult them'. I was a young assistant at the time, and was charged with instructing course participants in other fields of learning in elementary political science and administration. It made me aware of the considerable challenge and difficulties which a general introductory course represents.

Finer made things easier for me by lending me his own extensive lecture notes. 'You see,' he said, 'when I had to teach for the first time, I worked and I worked day and night. And this preparation has served me ever since.' His notes were both comprehensive and detailed, divided systematically by points and sub-points. Although it was often said that Sammy Finer taught when he talked – and talking he did incessantly – he would never enter a class-room unprepared. He was also very much aware of the different types of audiences he would face, adjusting his presentation accordingly. He loved the rhetorical challenge of the large introductory classes attended by hundreds of students at Manchester, but was also particularly successful in smaller seminars. I attended the latter frequently, when he taught pre-doctoral students at the just-opened European University Institute (EUI) in Florence in 1977. I asked him later to participate in a new venture, a Summer School on Comparative European Politics for university lecturers from all over Europe, organised at the EUI in the hot summer of 1979. The programme deliberately centred on country studies as well as comparative themes. Finer's taking apart of British politics in a week-long seminar for gifted young academics from other lands, combining the elementary with the most advanced information and approaches, was a model of what trenchant teaching should be.

If one seeks to account for his gift as a lecturer, there was of course the gift of speech, the command of language (at time using words lovingly which others had to look up in dictionaries), the erudition, the wit, the delight of performing. But there was always also the thorough preparation, the systematic order of presentation, the ever-fresh *engagement* with genuine political phenomena. Finer was often critical of other lecturers, famous scholars or not. 'There's no such thing as a boring subject, only too many boring lecturers', he said. Or to quote his wife: 'taking an interest, and, especially *being interesting*, called in his view for a solid base of meticulous hard work to be fashioned into appropriate lectures via a lively dose of imagination.' And as she noted later: 'I can affirm that there was little accidental about Sam's so-called "natural flair" for lecturing to large lay audiences. He deserved to be good at it because he took the task seriously, loved it and really worked at it' (Jones Finer 1994: 578–9).

THE TRUE SCHOLAR

In sketching Finer's development as a scholar, we noted that until middle age his published work was mainly concerned with British politics. This remained true even when he was inspired by American authors like David Truman to engage in the study of pressure groups. In this he did not immediately follow his brother Herman, who had turned towards comparative analyses much earlier in life, and had made his greatest mark accordingly. But then came the change, under the twin factors of the need to set up the Keele department, and his direct contact in the early 1950s with the call for a new comparative politics coming from the Evanston Seminar. In describing this change, Finer said with so many words that this made him develop 'a comparative government course which demoted "British Constitution" from its paradigmatic status to a subordinate role as merely one among a cluster of similar or, alternatively, contrasting regimes' (Finer 1980b: 353). This was indeed a drastic change. It did not prevent him from taking sides in political controversies (such as the British debate on the Suez intervention of 1956 which made him break with Labour). Nor did it hold him back him from reacting strongly to the stop-and-go politics from alternating single-party governments, which made him give up the 'intellectual convictions of a life-time'[5], rejecting what he was to term, 'Adversary Politics' and embracing the case for proportional representation. Yet, although moved by his domestic concern about what he felt to be the degeneration of the two-party system, he did so by drawing in a number of European scholars who were asked to analyse their experience with different electoral systems. Both in the resulting book *Adversary Politics and Electoral Reform* (1975), and in his later highly critical *The Changing British Party System 1945–1979* (1980), which originated as part of an international project on *Recent Changes in European Party Systems*, there was a clear element of comparative appreciation.

One volume planned within the latter project was Paolo Farneti's *The Italian Party System* (1985). Farneti was to have come to All Souls College in 1980, where he was to work on an early, still rough manuscript in Finer's stimulating company. When he was killed in a car accident, Finer set out to edit the manuscript into a publishable book, an act of rare collegiality.[6]

Although the turn towards the much wider canvass of contemporary states first, the history of governments later, was to be the hall-mark of Finer's academic work and greatness, student needs and the pull of the academic market were such that British politics remained at least one major subject in the actual publication of Finer's work. One finds special sections on Britain, the US, France and the USSR in Finer's *Comparative Government* (1970), and a very interesting chapter on the Constitution of Britain (which does not have a written constitution) in his book *Five Constitutions* (1979) which contains the written constitutions of the USA, France, Germany and the 1936 and 1977 constitutions of the USSR.

Yet, the shift towards comparative study which began in Finer's case in the 1950s was lasting and profound. It is possible to see his earliest comparative volume *The Man on Horseback* as a particular *Exkurs*, combining an intriguing question with Finer's World War II experience in the military. However, already in this book the range and learning is astounding, showing the twin qualities of scholarship and hard work which were to characterise his later books. From then on to the publication of *Comparative Government* (1970) the enduring shift occurred in Finer's working methods. He deliberately moved away from an exclusive concentration on the larger liberal democracies to a systematic inventorising of the various political systems of his day. His method was mainly one of classification, relying on his general learning, concentrated reading of secondary literature, and the constant checking and re-checking of reference works. His wife Catherine Jones Finer was to remark:

> [F]or Sam, the devising of frameworks, tables, charts, matrices etc. was of the essence (not to say the entertainment) of being a comparativist per se, as against (for example) an area specialist. The skill and value of the comparativist lay in the quality of the comparison he/she had the insight and imagination to think of, check out, properly construct and thence strive to account for; never 'just' to observe. Creative, in the sense of constructive, thought-provoking concepts, definitions and distinctions to be drawn. It was also, by definition, an activity which called for wide-ranging experience – and/or a capacity to acquire wide-ranging familiarity with *other's* experience right across a discipline or subject; coupled finally with an ability to draw on and draw together such experience in an integrative fashion. (Jones Finer 1994: 578–9)

In developing his comparative work, Finer was to take strong issue with the prevailing structural-functionalism and systems theory which dominated the approach towards comparative politics at the time. He wrote a strong attack against the great master of such an approach in what was for him a somewhat unusual methodological critical essay 'Almond's Concept of the "Political System": a textual critique' (Finer 1969). The major thrust of the argument was twofold: the element of sociological reductionism he saw in the dominant development theories, and the tendency to dissolve government into a black box. To quote from his own summary, comparing the effects of Marxism and systems theory:

> Neither 'school' allows any autonomy for politics or political behaviour. Both, in very different ways, see it as some sort of epiphenomenon. It is quite idle to say how this is reflected in Marxism, so universally is it known. But the shape it took in American mainstream political science does provoke me to comment. It is best illustrated by that well known 'model' of the political process which shows a circle consisting of Inputs – Black Box – Outputs – feedback – inputs *und so weiter.* Wittingly or unwittingly, the use, or rather abuse, of this model resulted in a crass sociological reductionism. The institutions of government, the framework of constitutions, the territorial

distribution of authority, the machinery for executing it and the like were all relegated to the status of the 'black box' *(videlicet* the so-called 'conversion mechanism') and attention was instead concentrated on the inputs. [...] Politics was reduced, á la Parsons, to the steering of impulses which came from the outside, or from what was called the 'environment' – from the religious or the cultural or the economic sectors of a society. The state, one species of the genus 'political system', was retranslated as the political system, Law became translated as 'rule'. The will of a Stalin became a withinput. The consequence was work which was ostensibly about political behaviour and political institutions but in practice was a mini-sociology; or, even worse, a set of generalisations across societies so diverse, as the Nuer or Esquimaux are compared with the USA, that they became wholly banal (Finer 1980b: 358).

Although he distinguished 'government' and 'politics', his main concern remained with the former throughout his life.[7] He retained the term 'government' in the title of his two major works, published respectively in 1970 and posthumously in 1997. His shorthand definition of government was 'institutionalised politics'. Spending time on bringing out *Five Constitutions* with its elaborate indices needed no apology. He was caustic about 'continental jurists [describing] themselves as "political scientists"'. They continue their barren recitals, make a desert and call it 'politology,' he once wrote. But in the same breath he maintained that 'out of this public law tradition came great names like Carré de Malberg, Hauriou, Esmein, Duguit and Barthélemy whose luminous minds far transcended mechanical legalism' (Finer 1980b: 351).

For a time his *Comparative Government,* the product of his years of teaching at Manchester, seemed to satisfy him. But as political developments made some of his schemata and classifications questionable, he started in his late sixties, with a heart attack already behind him, on the most ambitious project of his life: *The History of Government from the Earliest Times.* The idea came to him in a flash, he has testified, and the fact that nobody in his view had ever attempted such a thing, was all the more challenging. At the outset he shared some of the problems of this venture in a brilliant address (Finer 1983) and he left additional notes for the future editor of his work, whether himself or others (Finer 1997, vol. 1: 1–94). He developed new criteria and ways of analysing different systems, and worked tirelessly on both the specifics of the governments included in 5000 years of history, and such understanding as could be drawn from them. In the process he devoured books and other sources, consulting experts in Oxford and elsewhere both on suggested reading and their understanding of the working of regimes with which they were familiar. He studied his many polities with his characteristic combination of hard work and perception. During one visit to him I remember him saying: 'I am working on Rome now. I have consulted those who should know. The fact is they don't, because they do not understand government. It took me three-and- a-half weeks to find out!'

Finer once exclaimed 'This [*The History*] is the most exciting venture of my life' (Jones Finer 1994: 585). He did not aim at 'encyclopaedic perfection', stating 'this is going to be my interpretation, not a compilation' (Jones Finer 1994: 586). His comparative work was intended to harvest insight in generalities, not particularities (1994: 582). Yet one cannot help feeling that the Odyssey which brought him to many a strange land was if not motivated, at least made more satisfying because he had that insatiable curiosity about all forms of government. The common element in all of Finer's work was his genuine fascination with governmental and political phenomena, rather than the specific (and often restrictive) theories or methodologies of political science. Just as he had a remarkable gift to develop definitions or classifications, he was also ever ready to jettison or replace them for the sake of a better fit. For all his knowledge of the work of others, political scientists, historians, sociologists, economists or what not, he remained the quintessential individualist. Certainly his earlier work testified to ad hoc interests rather than a desire to arrive at overall generalities. In 1974 he remarked to an interviewer that 'he had no great prospective design for any future books. I believe in the knock-on principle in life' (Kavanagh 1984: 17). As this was between the publication of *Comparative Government* (1970) and *The History of Government* which he began in the early 1980s, this is, in hindsight, a somewhat ironical statement. Yet, there is also the constant exhilaration with work at hand, whatever the subject. This was true for the earlier years. Whether writing *Chadwick*, or debunking the doctrine of individual ministerial responsibility, being immersed in the role of the police or of pressure groups, studying backbench opinion in the House of Commons or military take-overs in Third World countries, bringing out the writings of Pareto (1966) or publishing and indexing *Five Constitutions* (1979), there is always the same enthusiasm, the tireless energy, the strong imagination, the never-ending wish to probe and understand. And the same characteristics carried him along later in his ever-widening study of the varieties of governments, in time and in space.

In this respect it is interesting to note his criteria for singling out the governments he sought to treat in *The History of Government*. He distinguished four categories:

1. those 'so outstanding by their sheer durability, or by the number of people they governed, or by their contemporary power and repute, that no serious history could omit them';
2. 'polities that should be studied precisely because they *are* archetypes';
3. 'some polities [which] obey neither of the two criteria, but nevertheless have a claim to be recognised because they invented a form, or technique, or a process which was adopted, either at the time or subsequently, by other polities'; and
4. any polity 'that is already a variant on others already dealt with, but of so vivid or of so strange a shape that to dwell on it illuminates in a wondrous way the general type'.

In short: the historically great and mighty polities, the archetypical polities, the innovators great or small, and finally, 'the vivid variant' (Finer 1983). Notably the third and fourth categories speak clearly for Finer's fascination not only with the generalities, but also with particular cases.

As a trained historian, Finer had, of course, an excellent eye for 'particularities'. Yet, his real drive remained to be on the look-out for *regularities* across the range of reported experience. This demanded comparative analysis. Classification was his main analytical instrument, and he laid great stress on the need for clear concepts. But given his wide knowledge of contemporary affairs and deliberate turn towards historical diversities, this meant that he found it necessary to revise his own schemata again and again. Most other scholars would tend to foreclose their findings. Not so Sammy Finer, who ploughed ever new terrain, helped by his immense erudition, his never flagging curiosity, his constant willingness to learn, re-think and reformulate. Few people could hope to follow him on that path. To quote Kavanagh and through him the man himself, Finer had 'a particular talent [...] to perceive emerging patterns in his data quickly. He once referred to this as the ability to make "an intuitive leap" from data to analysis, interpretation and explanation' (Finer 1983: 10). He did not see it as the goal of political science to become a science like the natural sciences. Earlier he had remarked that fields like biology or meteorology were not sciences in that sense. Later he rejected even that comparison as irrelevant. He has summed up his achievements in the following terms: 'When I reflect on what I have been doing in my work, it seems, at the end of the day, something that I can express variously as: *interpreting*, a body of factual knowledge; or, if you will, making a *pattern* out of it; or, most simply and probably, most comprehensively, making *sense* out of it' (Finer 1980b: 363).

Finer in fact remained an individualist *pur sang*. He never belonged to a particular school, nor did he form or leave one. Although his great gifts of exposition ensured that his writings were always revealing and significant, its lasting effect was less in his models, typologies or classifications than in one's increased awareness of the importance and subtleties of political relationships.

Early in my life Jan Barents, whose assistant I was in the University of Amsterdam in the early 1950s, suggested that the most agreeable way to study the realities of government and politics was to read the memoirs and biographies of British politicians. Clearly, this counsel was not so much intended as a means to arrive at generalities, but to sensitise one to the world of government. Reading the life-time's work of Finer does the same, but does so in a manner of incomparable richness and wonder.

Notes

1 (Finer 1962: 5) Ibidem, p. 6: 'The wonder, therefore, is not why [the military] rebels against its civilian master, but why it ever obeys them.'
2 See Finer, 1997, vol. 1, 59–72. Finer returned to the role of the military in Third World Countries also in his 'Militari e politica nel terzo mondo' (1980c).
3 With essays by Isabel de Madariaga, Catherine Jones Finer, Julius Gould, Ghita Ionescu, Arend Lijphart, Roger Williams, Geraint Parry and Vernon Bogdanor (de Madariaga et al. 1994).

4   For a summary volume on this Round Table, see Heckscher 1957. Finer has referred to his own contribution to the Florence Round Table several times, notably in his essay in 'A Generation of Political Thought'. It was never published in its original English version, but see the Italian translation (Finer 1954).
5   This remark is taken from the jacket of *Adversary Politics and Electoral Reform* (Finer 1975b).
6   For details of the way in which the English and Italian editions of this volume came about through the successive efforts of Finer and Alfio Mastropaolo, necessitating translation and retranslation, see Foreword to Farneti 1985.
7   For a sensitive analysis see Ionescu 1994.

REFERENCES

Farneti, P. (1985) *The Italian Party System (1945–1980)*, eds. S. E. Finer and A. Mastropaolo; with foreword by Hans Daalder, London: F. Pinter.

Finer, H. (1923) *Representative Government and a Parliament of Industry; A Study of the German Federal Economic Council*, London: Allen and Unwin.

(1932) *The Theory and Practice of Modern Government*, 2 vols., London: Methuen.

(1949; first edition 1934) *The Theory and Practice of Modern Government*, second abridged edition, New York: Holt.

(1956) *Governments of Greater European Powers*, New York: Holt.

Finer, S. E. (1950) *A Primer of Public Administration,* London: Frederick Muller.

(1952) *The Life and Times of Sir Edwin Chadwick*, London: Methuen.

(1954) 'Metodo, Ambito e Fini dello Studio Comparato dei Sistemi Politici', in *Studi Politici,* 3 (1): 26–43.

(1956) 'The Individual Responsibility of Ministers', *Public Administration,* 34: 377–96.

(1958) *Anonymous Empire; A Study of the Lobby in Great Britain*, London: Pall Mall.

(1962) *The Man on Horseback; The Role of the Military in Politics*, London: Pall Mall.

(1966) (ed.) *Vilfredo Pareto; Sociological Writings*, London: Pall Mall.

(1969) 'Almond's Concept of the Political System; A Textual Critique', *Government and Opposition,* 5: 3–21.

(1970) *Comparative Government*, London: Allen Lane/Penguin Press.

(1975a) 'State- and Nation-Building in Europe; The Role of the Military', in C. Tilly (ed.), *The Formation of National States in Western Europe*, Princeton: Princeton University Press.

(1975b) (ed.) *Adversary Politics and Electoral Reform*, London: Anthony Wigram.

(1979) (ed.) *Five Constitutions; Contrast and Comparisons*, Harmondsworth: Penguin.

(1980a) *The Changing British Party System (1945–79)*, Washington

D.C.: American Enterprise Institute.

(1980b) 'Political Science; An Idiosyncratic Retrospect of a Putative Discipline', *Government and Opposition,* 15: 346–63.

(1980c) 'Militari e politica nel terzo mondo', *Rivista Italiana di Scienza Politica,* 10 (1): 5-50.

(1983) 'Perspectives in the World History of Government – A Prolegomenon', *Government and Opposition,* 18: 3–22.

(1997) *The History of Government from the Earliest Times,* 3 vols., Oxford: Oxford University Press.

Finer, S. E., Bartholomew, D. and Berrington, H. (1961) *Backbench Opinion in the House of Commons,* Oxford: Pergamon.

Finer S. E. and Maud, J. M. R. (1953) *Local Government in England and Wales,* Oxford: Oxford University Press.

Gould, J. (1994) 'Sammy Finer- Scholar and Human Being: A Pupil Remembers', *Government and Opposition,* 29: 587–600.

Heckscher, G. (1957) *The Study of Comparative Government and Politics,* London: Allen and Unwin.

Ionescu, G. (1994) 'New and Old Perspectives on Government', *Government and Opposition,* 29: 601–620.

Jones Finer, C. (1994) 'S. E. Finer: A Memoir', *Government and Opposition,* 29: 574–586.

Kavanagh, D. (1984) 'Personality, Politics and Government; S. E. Finer', in D. Kavanagh and G. Peele (eds.), *Comparative Government and Politics; Essays in Honour of S. E. Finer,* London: Heinemann.

Kavanagh, D. (1997) 'The Fusion of History and Politics: The Case of S. E. Finer', in H. Daalder (ed.), *Comparative European Politics; The Story of a Profession,* London: Pinter.

Kavanagh, D. and Peele, G. (eds.) (1984) *Comparative Government and Politics; Essays in Honor of S. E. Finer,* London: Heinemann.

Macridis, R. C. and Cox, R. (1953) 'Research in Comparative Politics', *The American Political Science Review,* 47: 641–675.

Madariaga, I. de et al. (1994) *S. E. Finer.* Special issue of *Government and Opposition,* 29: 564–695.

Sartori, G. (1997) 'Chance, Luck and Stubbornness', in H. Daalder (ed.), *Comparative European Politics; The Story of a Profession,* London, Pinter.

chapter five | Samuel P. Huntington: Political Order and the Clash of Civilizations
Gianfranco Pasquino

INTRODUCTION

The greatness of a scholar in political science, as in the other social sciences, may be measured not only by the originality and the systematic approach of his contributions, but also by his ability to put forward new themes that structure and re-structure the agenda for political research, thus obliging others to discuss his ideas and findings and to debate his interpretations and the practical proposals he makes. By satisfying these criteria Samuel P. Huntington (New York, 1927) gained and retained a central role for himself right from the start of his scientific production, and not in American Political Science alone. In the best tradition of Harvard, the University where he obtained his PhD in 1951 and where he returned to settle in 1962, following three years at Columbia University, he dealt with both wide-reaching themes and issues that were of more immediate and controversial concern. The in-depth analysis characteristic of his work led to his ability to come up with specific solutions.

Robert Putnam at the end of a brief but focused outline of Samuel P. Huntington's career, written to celebrate the latter's nomination as President of the American Political Science Association in 1986, discussed the scholar's work and scientific production with reference to three 'tensions' common to American political science (and not so commonly found in other traditions of political science). The first is a tension that Putnam describes as a 'productive tension', that between the American origins of political science and a broader, comparative perspective. The second is a 'painful tension' between liberal values and conservative instincts or leanings. The third is a 'creative tension' between the appeals of social theory and those of applied policy-making. Putnam concluded that these three tensions have contributed to Huntington's scholarship being of 'exceptional quality' (Putnam 1986: 845).

In this chapter I argue, through reference to both his books and most important articles, that Huntington has often dealt with subjects that have already been explored by other authors, some of whom have produced in-depth and varied studies, such as on political development and democratisation. Notwithstanding this, the specific, and therefore original, contribution of Huntington lies in the fact that he was able to give new direction to preceding reflections and research, often turning dominant ideas upside down and thus indicating new ways of thinking. Lastly, while I in no way believe that Huntington went looking for notoriety for his scientific production, especially in the short term, he was nonetheless fully aware of this possibility (Huntington 1988), and nearly all his books, with the exception of works concerned with certain themes of foreign policy and national security, have had a significant impact on aspects of policy-making that were anything but secondary.

Huntington has had five principal areas of interest over his roughly 50-year career as a political scientist. These are, in the order in which he dealt with them and which produced his most important works:

a) the political role of the military;
b) United States' policy;
c) political development;
d) democratisation;
e) civilisations and international political order.

Naturally these themes overlap and sometimes are interwoven and re-emerge as each has triggered in the author new interpretations or led him to re-elaborate or redefine previous thoughts. I would, for example, give singular importance to the 'clash of civilisations' (Huntington 1996) as I believe that the combination of phenomena relevant to modernisation and democratisation with those concerning the dynamics of coalitions between states and cultures and their impact on the international political order, offers an analytical perspective of policy-making that is both original and of great importance, as well as being highly controversial, as are so many of Huntington's works.

Lastly, I wish to stress that the themes the author chose to tackle were closely linked to the most important political issues of that specific moment in time. Huntington's research has never been isolated or unrelated to the period in which he was producing and publishing it. Rather, it is a product of the period and inspired by contemporary issues without being influenced by them. I would also re-emphasise that his work redefined the problems as they were seen at the time and frequently offered practical solutions.

I will deal with the five themes in the chronological order indicated above, mirroring the sequence of the works published by Huntington and thus following the development of his research interests, even though the cumulative effect of knowledge means that in each successive publication the author uses the insights acquired in previous studies.

THE SOLDIER AND THE STATE

The central theme of the book, *The Soldier and the State* (Huntington 1957) is made clear by Huntington himself both in the choice of sub-title *The Theory and Politics of Civil-Military Relations* and in his introduction: the analysis of a significant change in perspective with regard to the role of the military. The central thesis of the volume is that in the United States of the mid-1950s, in the middle of the Cold War, it was no longer necessary to define the problem by referring to the question of whether the model of civil-military relations was compatible or not with the liberal-democratic values of the American tradition. Rather, it needed to be readdressed with reference to the security needs of the United States, and therefore directed towards the identification of an improved model of civil-military relations in order to ensure those needs. To perform this task, Huntington applied a procedure to which he would remain faithful in all his subsequent production, and with excellent results. First, he seeks the necessary historical background for his analysis and his interpretations; second, he makes ample use of comparisons both to gain a stronger foundation for his generalisations and to assess their validity; third, he formulates generalisations that are able to 'travel' far beyond the specific cases analysed. A closer look at the contents of the book shows how the central problem is to understand and explain how political power can manage to obtain the subordination of the military to choices the political authorities must make and ensure that the military organisation puts these choices into practice.

When Huntington wrote the book, two other famous scholars had already tackled the problem of the political role of the military more or less directly. The contrast with the first, the eminent political scientist Harold D. Lasswell, was inevitable. In fact, Huntington faced it head on. On the other hand, a clash with the second author, the then equally eminent sociologist C. Wright Mills, was avoided, though I could not say whether this was deliberate or not. However, it is a pity that no comparison is made with Mill's thesis that claimed that the higher echelons of the military belong to the United States power elite, a hypothesis that was not at all unlikely, formulated as it was right in the middle of the Cold War and with a General, Dwight D Eisenhower, in the White House. President Eisenhower himself was critical of the 'military-industrial complex'. In fact Mill's thesis gave rise to an important sociological and political debate between elitists and pluralists. The explanation for this lack of comparison can probably be found in the different perspectives adopted by Huntington and Mills. Mills is concerned with limited democracy in a system that is dominated by a power elite that includes the military at its core, and thus his perspective is concerned with the effects on domestic politics. Huntington, on the other hand, is interested in evaluating how the military can contribute to national security and how, despite the importance of the task entrusted to it, the military accepts being subordinated to civil, political power. The military becomes neither part of the power elite, nor does it have power in its own right. It contributes, through a particular relationship with civilians, to the construction of a balanced and satisfactory social order. In this light, perhaps with an excessive faith in military qualities, the comparison between West Point and the nearby village of Highland Falls, two ideals almost of American values, is extremely suggestive (Huntington 1957: 464–6).

Undoubtedly, Lasswell (1941, 1951) would in no way have agreed with the idealisation of West Point. In fact, in that prestigious military academy he could have found a number of elements to support his thesis of a 'garrison state'. It is therefore perhaps not surprising that at the end of the book, in a post-script added specifically for this reason but maybe rather limited in scope for an issue of such importance, Huntington clearly rejects the hypothesis of a garrison state (1941: 346). Nonetheless, he did consider the thesis sufficiently interesting and meaningful to update and re-edit his original essay and add a version of it to a collection which he edited himself some years later (Lasswell 1962). His criticisms of Lasswells's essay, which are rather harsh, focus on two elements: first, the lack of rigour in defining the conditions that lead to the garrison state; second, the inadequate assessment of the content of military values, the unconvincing elaboration of the (im)possibility of militarisation in a liberal society and an insufficient understanding of civil-military relations. The last element is the one on which Huntington's analysis is based and which shows most originality. Huntington distinguishes between two types of civil control: subjective and objective. The *subjective* control subordinates the military to an institution: the Crown, the Presidency, the Parliament or to a social class, for example, the aristocracy or, at least in theory, the proletariat. The subjective civil control permits, or rather is based on, the maximisation of the power of a group of civilians over the military, especially when the military are not yet professionalised. In a statement destined to arouse much controversy Huntington claims that even in a democracy

> the military may undermine civilian control and acquire great political power through the legitimate processes and institutions of democratic government and politics (1957: 83).

This argument is quite similar to that put forward by C. Wright Mills who in the mid-1950s, famously and controversially, claimed that the warlords were still in a strong position to influence US politicians. In any case, the military were part of the 'ruling elite'. In a situation of subjective civilian control the military has the possibility of deciding if it wishes to support a group of civilians, and if so, which group. Thus the military has a political role that goes/would go beyond its military role.

The second type of control, which is the type Huntington would wish for, is defined as *objective*.

> Subjective civilian control achieves its end by civilianising the military, making them the mirror of the state. Objective civilian control achieves its end by militarising the military, making them the tool of the state (1957: 83).

These theses have been criticised in different ways at different times and strongly by Samuel Finer (1976: 20–4) and Alfred Stepan (2001). Both note, though in different ways, that an increased professionalism of the military in no way decreases or hinders military intervention in political life, but rather that an increase in specialist knowledge not only in war but also in geo-politics may be an element that could encourage the military to free itself from the control of civilian politicians, who are often considered less 'professional' than the military. Finer develops his interpretation by making reference to levels of political culture and government legitimacy which open up to or preclude military intervention in the political sphere, explicitly claiming, however, that the military's professionalism is in no way a deterrent to intervention. Rather, as Stepan argues, in Latin America in the early 1960s, it was indeed the new professionalism of the military that not only pushed it into intervening in politics but also led it to stay in government. The military was convinced that it not only possessed specific military capabilities as a manager of violence but also a more generalised ability to lead the country or at least to lead it better (less conflict, less corruption, less division) than the civilian politicians. Although some of the criticisms are undoubtedly on the mark, Huntington's book did have the decided merit of presenting the problem of the ways in which civilians manage to control the military in a manner that was concrete, effective and lasting, on the one hand, by recognising the professionalism of the military, and on the other by maintaining the legitimacy of the government. It is a problem that does not appear to have found a definitive solution either as regards the professionalism of the military, or the legitimacy of governments, for most of the time since the publication of Huntington's book. Certainly no solution was apparent up to ten years ago in Latin America and even nowadays in Africa, or even less so in the Middle East. In fact, in both Africa and the Middle East many regimes are necessarily defined either as civil-military or military-civilian, depending on which part dominates the other, and the balance is always temporary and marked by conflict.

SOCIAL MODERNISATION AND POLITICAL ORDER

The Soldier and the State opened up an area of debate that has rightly seen much development and to which Huntington himself returned, enlarging it further with reference not only to the political role of the military but to its experience in government throughout the period of social modernisation and, perhaps, of political development of the systems in Latin America, Asia and Africa. *Political Order in Changing Societies* (Huntington 1968, reprinted 1996 without variations) is certainly for many aspects Huntington's best book and at the same time can be considered one of the most intelligent, provocative and important texts of political science in the post-war period. Huntington's analysis emerges from a fundamental dissatisfaction with the plethora of optimistic studies on the perspectives for change in the many political systems that had gained independence after differing periods of colonisation and which were starting out on a process of modernisation and, again perhaps, political development, as though these two elements were not only inevitable but were destined to continue.

Huntington, by contrast, notes that the possible link between socio-economic modernisation and political development is not necessarily positive. Modernisation does not independently, automatically and inevitably produce political development. Rather, if the institutionalised organisations and procedures do not manage to produce a sufficient degree of *institutionalisation*, the consequences of an accelerated process of socio-economic modernisation will certainly produce political decadence. Only institutionalised organisations and procedures can accept, accommodate and channel socio-economic modernisation, and even promote it, by permitting growth of political participation and the strengthening of the political order.[2] If this does not occur socio-economic modernisation produces tensions and conflicts that can lead not to development but to the decay of political institutions.

This introduction to the analysis of modernisation and development is an extraordinarily important contribution. In fact, Huntington manages to perform two tasks: on the one hand, he contrasts a sort of socio-economic determinism that was very widespread in the decade in which he was writing, and on the other he refocuses the issue on political variables, procedures and institutions, thus

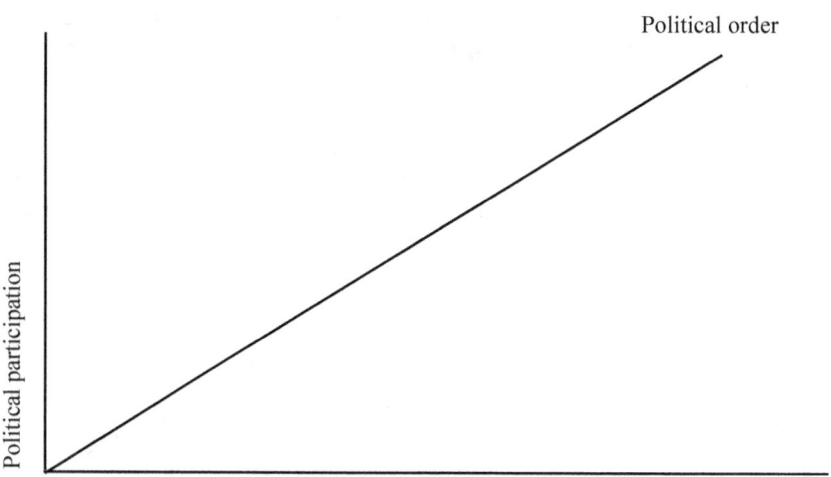

Legend: Each point on the diagonal marks the fulfilment of political order at different levels of political participation. All the points above the diagonal indicate the existence of a praetorian society in which the degree of political participation is above the ability of the institutions to meet its demands. All the points below the diagonal indicate the existence of authoritarian regimes in which the institutions limit or suppress political participation.

Figure 1: Participation, institutionalisation and political order

highlighting the difficulty of the task of building a political order at various levels of political participation. Political decadence is the inevitable consequence of the absence of political order, that is to say of a balanced relationship between the degree of political participation on the one hand and the level of political institutionalisation on the other. In Figure 1 I propose a way of visualising and interpreting this complex relationship.

The concern over the political order, which was already present in *The Soldier and the State*, and the attention devoted to political participation become thereon central to Huntington's analyses, even when they are extended to societies that are already modernised and that, for various reasons, may be considered politically developed. As far as the political systems where socio-economic and political transformation is underway, in a phrase that has remained rightly famous both for its precision and simplicity, Huntington provides a snapshot of the societies in which political order is completely lacking and in which, given the ratio of forces, military intervention in politics is more likely, in fact almost certain: 'The wealthy bribe; students riot; workers strike; mobs demonstrate; and the military coup' (1957: 196). Moreover, he distinguishes clearly between the types of military control – 'oligarchic', 'radical' or 'mass' – which will come about on the basis of the different levels of political participation in each society, as well as their consequences for the different military governments as regards their duration, their efficiency, the need to resort to violence and repression, and the times and ways in which power will be returned to civilians. The decisive importance of military organisations in developing countries does not depend on their specific and absolute power. In the wake of the thinking developed in *The Soldier and the State*, Huntington emphasises that the potential and real power of military organisations is, in fact, linked to the degree of development of the political and social system. Even a military organisation that is not particularly broad, strong or competent, in other words not very professional by its own definition, may be able to intervene in the political sphere when the level of political participation is low and society is lacking in organisation. In fact, in this case social and civil resistance will be limited and ineffective. Furthermore, the military intervenes with a clear objective which is only in a small way linked to the real or perceived needs of its organisation but which, on the other hand, concerns society and the political system. As Huntington writes (1957: 194), perhaps rather too succinctly: 'military explanations do not explain military interventions'. Explanations of military interventions in politics are not part of the military language, i.e., they are essentially or exclusively organisational/corporative issues. To argue this, Huntington claims that the aim of the military, which may also obtain personal and organisational advantages from its incursion into the political sphere, is the creation of political order in a system that would otherwise be exposed to disruption from the rich, students, workers and the masses, and which would have a negative effect on the stability and workings of the political system.

Should it be necessary to set out a strategy of alliances that would permit the military to restore order, Huntington suggests that the most useful allies who wish to be characterised as modernisers are the peasants. Through an effective agrarian reform, carried out by the military, the political, social and economic system would be stabilised and could be further modernised. *Numbers* (peasants) plus *Guns* (military) equals political order: this is the recipe prepared by Huntington, who considers the potential alliance of *Numbers* and *Brains* (intellectuals), as revolutionary as well as relatively infrequent. Highly unlikely, or almost impossible, is an alliance between intellectuals and the military who are generally rival protagonists for obtaining a decisive and influential political role. Since the publication of *Political Order in Changing Societies*, no scholar has been able to avoid reference and comparison to the role of the military in politics as presented by Huntington.[3] Even today, after a quarter of a century, the generalisations Huntington set out continue to permit an understanding of the military interventions in the political sphere and an awareness of the military's behaviour in government and its attempts to return to the barracks.

The lasting concern for political order, which is so important that it appears in the title of the book both here, and in later analyses, will lay Huntington open to criticism from progressive scholars, which is, however, seldom completely convincing and never formulated in an equally systematic way. I mean by this that among the studies on modernisation and political development no 'progressive Huntington' exists. Rather, Huntington could quite reasonably claim the honour of having indicated the only way in which change could become positive, i.e., 'progress', by building political order through an intelligent regulation of political participation. In fact, the political order that Huntington thinks should be sought after is, in other contexts, an essential precondition for the construction and maintenance of a situation which makes it possible to pursue other individual and collective goals, starting from freedom which can only be guaranteed by order and in an order.

Of its numerous merits, *Political Order in Changing Societies* has one that is fundamental and which has had an enormous impact, even though this has not always produced the indispensable reorientation of research and theorising throughout the sector of modernisation and political development, which at that time was in full and turbulent growth.[4] In an earlier and very influential article Huntington (1965) had struck at the heart of one, almost certainly the greatest, flaw, in the literature on political development: that of considering that once any process of socio-economic modernisation is underway, it will continue, even through periods of difficulty and perhaps over a long time, until it is completed, i.e., until such time as a sufficiently politically stable and economically vital system has been built. By demonstrating with a richness of data and examples that there was a flaw in this reasoning, that is to say that far from ensuring development, many countries that had entered the sphere of socio-economic modernisation could, on the other hand, as previously demonstrated, be destroyed by the decadence of their inadequate institutions, Huntington swept away entire book shelves of optimistic and self-satisfied analyses. The two key variables which he used and which were to reappear in the study of 'developed' political systems, are political participation and political institutionalisation (the result, as anticipated above, is the bringing about/bringing back of political order). The equation is, in a certain sense, very simple. If the degree of social mobilisation and political participation exceeds the degree of institutionalisation and organisation of political procedures then tensions will arise which will, if they are not controlled and reduced, end up producing political decadence. In the case of political systems that have begun the change, this decadence manifests itself as chronic instability and leads to an inability to produce any type of lasting modernisation. In the case of democracies, this decadence can be seen as a real crisis of governability. Huntington's conclusion, which had to some degree been explicit in *Political Order* and was further evident in the advice given in his role as political advisor during the Vietnam War, (and was later openly proclaimed in the essay written for the *Trilateral),* was provocative and undoubtedly controversial: to limit, control, discourage and reduce political participation.

In the face of conspicuous social mobilisation and given that it is difficult rapidly and significantly to increase the level of institutionalisation of the organisations and political procedures in a democratic regime, in order to achieve a satisfactory equilibrium it would appear indispensable to find a means of controlling, discouraging and even reducing any excessive political participation. Naturally, behind this proposal – that was absolutely unthinkable for progressives and probably judged to be unworkable both from a technical and political point of view even by the majority of conservatives – there lies a precise political vision: 'Men can have, certainly, order without freedom, but they cannot have freedom without order. Authority must exist before it can be limited' (Huntington 1968: 7–8, cited by Putnam 1986). The creation of political order can, in certain circumstances and situations, require the limitation of freedom, for example, regarding political participation. If disorder reaches the stage of the destruction of authority there can be no meaningful political participation. Instead, there will be a praetorian society in which the intervention of the military becomes more than just a practical possibility. The incredibly intense political debate aroused by the way in which Huntington posed this problem overshadowed his important attempt to define and give a precise connotation to the concept of 'institutionalisation'. Huntington defines it as the process by which organisations and procedures acquire worth and stability (1968: 12) and proposes to measure its level with reference to four indicators: adaptability, complexity, autonomy and coherence.

A number of different criticisms have been made both of Huntington's definition and operationalisation of the concept of institutionalisation; in particular, that the indicators overlap considerably and that there is incongruence and even contradictions. This is not the right place to go into the criticisms and evaluate how justified they were. What matters is, on the one hand, the attempt Huntington made to achieve greater analytical precision and to give predictive power to his hypotheses, and on the other, to draw attention to the fact that only institutionalised organisations and procedures are able to 'accommodate' growing levels of political participation and translate its pressure and demands into processes of political development. In addition to military organisations, Huntington argues (once again in an anti-conformist and provocative way and going against the dominant consensus of opinion on the possibility of building democratic and competitive situations), that political order can also be produced by a single party, and more than this, that the single-party system offers a satisfactory solution both with regard to the stabilisation of the political order and as an answer to the problems of social mobilisation. In certain conditions the single party reduces complexity and governs it. Obviously, the political order produced by a single party is not a democratic political order. However, as Huntington (1970) argued in his lengthy introduction to an important collection of original essays on variations of single-party systems, these party systems have, at least for a certain period, played a part in the structuring or restructuring of their respective societies. The different ways in which they carried out this restructuring – with the 'exclusive' single parties quashing participation and excluding opponents, while the 'revolutionary' single parties increased participation and then absorbed it by taking control of it – strongly conditioned their dynamics and the fulfilment or otherwise of their pledges. Thus, the exclusive parties failed when they were seen to be unable to control socio-economic modernisation, while the failure of the revolutionary single parties became evident when the promised modernisation was seen to be completely lacking in substance. In both cases, though for opposite reasons, Huntington's prophetic conclusions, based on a solid generalisation of cause and effect, were proved to be valid when systems collapsed in the face of change. This is what happened from Franco's Spain to Brezhnev's Soviet Union.

DEMOCRACY IN AMERICA

Partly in order to answer a number of questions regarding military security and defence strategy in the United States, but especially because he was interested in the dynamics of change in political systems, Huntington chose to work with Zbigniew Brzezinski on a comparative analysis of the American and Soviet political systems (Brzezinski and Huntington 1964). Huntington and Brzezinski had been colleagues from the former's early days as a student at Harvard, then later as a researcher and lecturer at Columbia University before Huntington's definitive return to Harvard. The study was carried out within the context of the dominant thesis of the time which tended to look for certain convergences between industrialised political systems, but the analysis of these two political scientists rejected the possibility of any convergence, by putting forward the opposing argument of a much more probable evolution of the two political systems that was in keeping with their political history and which took into account the different weight of political and socio-economic factors. On the basis of the knowledge of that time, a period in which U.S. and Soviet relations were improving, Brzezinski and Huntington predicted gradual adjustments and slow change, with no dramatic events likely to occur. However, at least in the United States, more than one dramatic event was about to be witnessed, with the others following on the first in rapid succession: the assassination of President John F. Kennedy; the war in Vietnam; the assassinations of the leader of the Black Movement, Martin Luther King, and then of the Democratic candidate to the Presidency, Robert F. Kennedy; the forced resignation of the Republican President, Richard M. Nixon, to avoid impeachment; and throughout all this the wide-spread, prolonged and turbulent student movement which mobilised many other sectors of society and which, together with other phenomena, cast doubts on the very workings of American democracy.

Having already focused his attention on some general trends (Huntington 1971) his observations were further triggered by a debate which started with the publication of two important volumes written respectively by Brzezinski (1970) and by a Harvard colleague, Daniel Bell (1973). Following these, Huntington (1974a) reflected both on the ways in which it is possible to predict the development of a society and especially, on what the role of politics should be in a post-industrial society. Huntington's prediction, partly influenced by the events of the time, and partly because he had always tended to emphasise the need to restore political order, was that post-industrial society would require a political order with greater authority and greater deference, with a clear hierarchy, and politics which we would today define as less timid (if politics can ever be described as timid, or permit itself to be so) and tougher. The most explicit, precise and articulated description of the challenges facing democratic politics and of the solutions that would be both desirable and possible, is to be found in the chapter on the United States in the 'Report on the Governability of Democracies', prepared for the Trilateral Commission and published as a volume in 1975 (and in a slightly abridged version in Huntington (1975b) and in a short essay (1975a)). Once again, the thesis is simple but powerful, logically argued and, I would suggest, deliberately provocative and non-conformist. And, once again, the structure of the explanation is as linear as it is efficient, based on the central core of the relationship between the various levels of participation and the ability of the governmental structures to provide a fruitful response to the socio-political demands while maintaining political order. More precisely, Huntington believed that the problems facing democracy in the United States were the result of a sudden and exaggerated increase in political participation that had led to a polarisation of political opinions and a lack of faith in authority. As the authorities had been unable to cope adequately with the demands deriving from this political participation the effect had been, in addition to a growing distrust of authority, a decrease in the citizens' sense of efficiency, and a sort of reaction to this. On this same subject Hirschman (1982) offered an alternative progressive interpretation of the cycles of involvement that is both refreshing and stimulating.

In fact, when twenty-five years later Huntington (2000: *xxiv*) looked back at this essay, he could not help noting with a certain self-satisfaction that the deregulation and self-limitation of governments, as well as certain social and economic policies enacted by Margaret Thatcher (1979–1990) and Ronald Reagan (1980–1988), were perfectly in line with both his prognosis and diagnosis. Moreover, although his conclusions were generalised they were a good deal more pessimistic: 1) democracy is not merely one way in which an authority can govern and it cannot necessarily be applied universally; 2) the efficient working of a democratic political system requires a certain lack of activity or interest of a number of individuals or groups; 3) just as there are desirable limits to economic growth so there are potentially desirable limits to the indefinite expansion of political democracy (Huntington 1977: 109–10), and this led to the prediction that democracy would suffer a crisis were no countermeasures taken. These conclusions were widely criticised above all by those who hold that democracy should be a universal value to be extended to all, but also by those convinced that democracy works better if all groups can vigorously express their preferences and ensure their interests are taken into account. For these academics and politicians alike, the solution to the 'overloading' of democracy cannot be the demobilisation of the electorate and discouraging it from participation in the political process. Rather, they would suggest, the solution would be in the setting up of improved political and institutional structures to accommodate the expression of preferences and interests and to filter and channel them into the decision-making processes, in other words, the institutionalisation of organisations and political procedures, as indeed Huntington himself suggested in *Political Order*. Herein lies the real point which should be debated, though unfortunately many of Huntington's critics, some of whom have preferred to write on the crisis of capitalism, did not take it up or discuss it further.

Huntington returns to the analysis of political development many times, retracing certain themes, reviewing later research and new knowledge (Huntington and Dominguez 1975) and suggesting new paths for comparison (Huntington 1987; for a later overall review see Hagopian 2000). In the meantime, however, his interest had shifted to other themes on which he would expand, equipped with the knowledge and insights gained through his study and writings on participation and order, development and decadence. No American political scientist can allow himself to ignore completely his own political system. American political science is often accused of provincialism (sometimes rightly so, especially in regard to the perspectives used); however, it has continued to produce scholars able to address wider issues within which the domestic and foreign policy of the United States is considered, with notable analytical advantages. Huntington, who is not an empirical political scientist interested only in elections, parties, the Congress and the U.S. Presidency, acquired widespread and enduring fame thanks, as we have seen, to his brilliant essay on political order in changing societies. Even when studying the military Huntington showed himself to be above all interested in the building and working of institutions and their relationship with ideas. Thus, when he decided to deal specifically with the United States his approach combined the analysis of institutions with that of ideas, that is to say the relation that runs between institutions and ideals. This approach had already been hinted at in *Political Order* when he performed an interesting comparison between the United States and Europe, and in particular the Great Britain of the Tudors.

Huntington's fruitful and well-tried procedure is to write an article (Huntington

1974b) that contains in a nutshell a wider theme which is explored and which prepares the soil from which a book will eventually develop (Huntington, 1981). The thesis is simple, according to some critics, too simple even. In American politics there is an irreparable and fundamental gulf between ideals and institutions. It is a gulf that is destined to last as the ideals of freedom, equality and democracy can never be completely achieved with the institutions that exist, even though they may be reformed from time to time. American politics are not principally conditioned by socio-economic factors nor reflected in them. American politics are, however, marked by clashes of values, by moral passions and conflicts between groups that promote their own interests while attempting to fulfil the American ideals (1981: 11–12). The gap between the promises of the American ideal and the performance of the institutions may be large and provoke disappointment. This disappointment inevitably manifests itself, not because there is a betrayal, but only because there is hope (1981: 262). Compared to the darker vision of politics in post-industrial society and in a much more critical way than the essay prepared for the *Trilateral*, 'The Promise of Disharmony' has a characteristic that can only be called justificationist. In short, the American political system is all right as it is because the promise, however unobtainable it may be, has maintained all its charge, it propulsive impulse. The American political system does, nevertheless, offer protection to citizens' rights and a level of democracy that is clearly greater than that of any other political system. Once the student revolts of 1968 (which the book recognises as having been inspired by an ideal passion), the war in Vietnam, the crisis of governability (provoked by the behaviour and resulting resignation of Nixon) have all been consigned to history, this Harvard scholar, on the one hand, almost rejoices in the possibility of a new political phase, that of Reaganism, and on the other hand, appears to bide his time. The American ideals will always be out of reach for American institutions, but there may be moments in which this gulf between ideals and institutions seems much smaller.

THE WAVES OF DEMOCRATISATION

Huntington's greatest concern when dealing with the analysis of the processes of political development, more than with political democracy itself, was, as we have seen, the building of political order which he considers as an indispensable premise for the establishment of democracy. The first important studies on the transition from authoritarianism began to appear in the early 1980s (especially O'Donnell *et al.* 1986), but the problem of 'democratisation' was posed, amongst tensions and expectations, concerns and hopes. Huntington's first exploration of the issue (1984) surveyed the general beliefs and theories that existed, at the same time as warning against over optimistic expectations. The conclusion, however, which was coherent with his traditional analytical pessimism ('it could be that the limits of democratic development have already been reached' (1984: 218)), was to be revealed as fallacious in the years immediately following. Despite this, the article he wrote in 1984 was not a casual piece of writing, but the mark of an early interest in the theme that was to become all-absorbing and practically dominant from the end of the 1980s (for an overview see Bunce 2000). In any case, the questions raised in the article regarding the economic, social and cultural prerequisites and concerning the international context, were the right ones and Huntington was to return to them in a much broader research project, *The Third Wave* (1991). The reference to the role of the *élites* was equally important: 'the ability of the *élites* to reach compromises makes democracy possible; the tendency of *élites* to take revenge makes democracy desirable – for the *élites*.' (Huntington 1984: 212)

Huntington brings at least two original perspectives to the study of the processes, that is to say of the waves, of democracy. The first perspective, which has always been congenial to him and which distinguishes him from the other political scientists of his generation, can be seen from his choice of considering a problem within a greater historical context, or of exploiting to the full his historical knowledge. This is why Huntington's analysis of the waves of democracy begins from the earliest processes of democracy. He is convinced that there is much they can teach us as, apart from anything else, they provide us with more cases to study and provide us with a comparative vision over a longer period of time. The second perspective is again typical of Huntington as a scholar, but perhaps also of Huntington as a man. Whether you choose to call it realism or pessimism, Huntington is faithful to, and expresses, a vision which not only refuses to accept *tout court* the existence of 'magnificent and progressive destinies' developing positively and without interruption, but also attempts to identify and emphasise the difficulties, the problems, the crises, the actual breakdowns in the process towards democracy, the upsets, the backlashes and, to stick with his metaphor, the turnings of the tide. In this case, too, the aim is to reach a greater and better understanding. Is it more likely that political systems that have experienced democracy, even a complicated democracy that ultimately failed, will return to democracy and be consolidated, or can democracy be learned from scratch, and if so, how? Is it possible that this factor of 'habituation', despite the important indications Rustow (1970) gave, counts for little or nothing in the building of democracies? Do only the builders of democracy learn, or do their opponents, the destroyers of democracy, learn also, so that eventually the habituations will cancel each other out?

Of the most widespread generalisations on both the appearance and length of democracies, there is one that links the level of socio-economic development positively to the creation and the maintenance of democratic regimes. Recently, however, certain scholars (in particular, Przeworski *et al.* 2000) have criticised the importance of this link and even whether it exists, notably by claiming that democracies may appear at *any* level of socio-economic development, the problem rather being whether 'poor' democracies would be likely to survive. The relatively underdeveloped democratic regimes tend to succumb more easily to economic crises compared to consolidated regimes. Huntington's arguments are particularly effective because they manage, on the one hand, to avoid any type of socio-economic determinism, and on the other, underline the real importance of political factors. Once again, he does this with concise conclusions which manage to sum up complicated and detailed analyses that are rich in data and problems: 'economic development makes democracy possible; political leadership makes it real' (Huntington 1993: 316). In this way, all analyses of democratic processes are encouraged to give a sufficient consideration to each of the social and economic factors, as well as to the quality of political leadership. From the careful and fertile combination of the two elements are derived forecasts, that are not only more reliable than previous studies as regards the potential for democracy, but also possible strategies which Huntington, in fact, sets out in chapter after chapter in his book, like a 'democratic Machiavelli', as he himself puts it. The outcome is a complex explanation which takes account of many factors and which is, surprisingly, more optimistic regarding the future of democracy and of the democratic process that might be expected on the basis of Huntington's usual attitude. However, the basic difficulties remain in large areas of the world which the author sums up as follows: 'In China the obstacles to democratisation in 1990 were political, economic and cultural; in Africa they were overwhelmingly economic; in the rapidly developing countries of East Asia and in many Islamic countries they were primarily cultural' (1993: 315).

When Huntington formulated his conclusions on the waves of democracy and on the conditions facilitating them (Rustow 1970) he hinted at a problem that had already been on his mind for some time: the relationship between religion and politics in building of old and new democracies. Religion merits much attention in the analysis of political systems and their dynamics, whether as facilitating factors, such as in the case of the Protestant religion and later, at the end of the twentieth century after the Second Vatican Council, the Catholic religion, or as powerful brakes to democracy, such as in the cases of Islamism and Confucianism. The key question was therefore posed, and the answer began to emerge through Huntington's classic approach to research, first sowing the seeds in an article.

THE CLASH OF CIVILISATIONS

It was indeed, once again, an article that proved to be provocative and controversial as it was influential, sparking off a debate and on a possible, and more or less imminent, 'clash of civilisations' (Huntington 1993). It is not just the meaning, but the aims and even the overall approach of Huntington's book (1996) which have been widely misinterpreted, either deliberately or through ignorance. The title, designed to capture the imagination, received more attention than the content which is, in fact, indicated in the subtitle. As we noted earlier, the issues of national security, military defence and strategies had always been one of Huntington's concerns (Huntington was part of the Harvard Nuclear Study Group which had produced an important essay during the second wave of the Cold War between the United States and the Soviet Union in the early 1980s: Carnesale *et al.* (1983)). Incidentally, as well as having actively taken part in the publication of the journal

The Public Interest, Huntington had also founded another journal, *Foreign Policy*, about 15 years earlier. In the 'clash of civilisations' the geo-strategic concerns become the central issue and the framework used produces an analysis of the solitude of the American superpower (Huntington, 1999). The book aims to explain what type of 'new world order' is being created and why, as well as its possible consequences. It is an ambitious attempt at interpreting the profound dynamics that followed the disappearance of the Soviet Union in the form of an end of the ideological conflict between the East and West (and not, as quietly debated with Francis Fukuyama, the end of 'history': 'societies that assume that their history has ended [...] are usually societies whose history is about to decline' (Huntington 1996: 449)), and which, despite the fact that a real North-South conflict never materialised, continue to produce conflict, and not only at a local level. These dynamics, furthermore, noticeably condition the nature of alliances. If the political and military alliances of the single states are no longer forced to rotate around the dominant East-West axis, but each one is free within limits to choose its own allies, what choices are both practical and lasting? Huntington's answer is that the world is realigning around civilisations that have the initial advantage of having basic elements in common.

The definition of the term 'civilisation' leads to the first difficulty in the analysis. Huntington claims that 'a civilisation is the broadest cultural entity' (1996: 43) and that 'culture is the common theme in virtually every definition of civilisation' (1996: 42). If 'blood, language, religion and way of life' (1996: 42) are elements that distinguish a civilisation, from that of the classical Greek civilisation onwards, 'of all the objective elements which define civilisations, however, the most important usually is religion' (1996: 42). Yet when the author characterises civilisation more precisely there are two elements that distinguish western civilisation from others. The first element is individualism; the second is the separation between spiritual and temporal powers. With one of the typically incisive phrases that Huntington uses to conjure up an idea, he emphasises that,

> In Islam God is Caesar; in China and Japan Caesar is God; in the Orthodox world, God is Caesar's junior partner. The separation and recurring clashes between Church and State that typify Western civilisation have existed in no other civilisation. (1996: 70)

In the conflicts in which culture, inspired above all by religion, is the driving force, clashes become inevitable. In contrast to the conflicts based on the distribution of resources, it is not possible to negotiate on matters of identity, culture or civilisation. The leading states of each civilisation will be forced to confront each other in terms of identity and culture. What to Huntington seems certain is that the American identity possesses clear components: 'liberty, democracy, individualism, equality before the law, constitutionalism, private property' (1996: 305); or, as he wrote elsewhere, 'the essence of Western civilisation is the Magna Carta, not the Magna Mac'. Yet, at another point he says this identity is threatened by 'groups within Western societies' (1996: 304). Some of these groups, 'wish to create a country of many civilisations, which is to say a country not belonging to any civilisation and lacking a cultural core. History shows that no country so constituted can long endure as a coherent society' (1996: 306). However, a 'multicultural America is impossible because a non-Western America is not American' (1996: 318).

For many reasons the clash of civilisations has become a reality. It is self-delusional to think that modernisation on the one hand, and the spread of democracy on the other, will influence the Islamic and Confucian civilisations that Huntington sees as being those most likely to represent a danger through aggressive expansionism. In fact, in both the Islamic and Chinese worlds, modernisation develops without, or in reaction to, westernisation. Moreover, the spread of democracy, which has not even started in the Arab and Islamic civilisations, is a process that is counterproductive in its concrete effects. Thus,

> as Western leaders realise that democratic processes in non-Western societies often produce governments unfriendly to the West, they both attempt to influence those elections and to lose their enthusiasm for promoting democracy in those societies. (1996: 198)

The attempt to spread Western values, believing that they are universal values, indicates a willingness to re-launch colonialism, which intended more or less knowingly to impose Western values as universal values. Specifically, 'imperialism is the necessary, logical consequence of universalism' (1996: 310). Any temptation that is 'imperialist/universalist' must be abandoned: in 'a multi-civilisational world the constructive course is to renounce universalism, accept diversity and seek commonalities' (1996: 318). It is thus clear that Huntington can in no way be considered a promoter of a clash of civilisations (rather, he could be considered a Cassandra that is ignored, in the noble tradition of Western civilisation). I see overall four possible positions that can be discerned regarding the desirability and probability of such a clash, which are summarised in Table 1.

	Probable	Improbable
Desirable	Osama bin Laden	fundamentalists
Undesirable	Huntington	multiculturalists

Table 1: Clash of civilisations

It should be emphasised that, despite the views expressed by many people who have not even read the book, Huntington never suggests that a clash of civilisations is desirable, even though he fears this clash may come about, as he clearly states in many parts of the book. Despite the radical differences between the civilisations, however, a clash may still be avoided if two conditions are met: first, an 'understanding and cooperation between the political, spiritual and intellectual leaders' of the major civilisations; and second, the building of an 'international order based on civilisations' (1996: 321). Leaving aside the recent unilateral politics of the United States (as well as European anti-Americanism), Huntington warns quite clearly that 'in the clash of civilisations, Europe and America will hang together or hang separately' (1996: 321). Nor does he ignore the risks: 'the dangerous clashes of the future are likely to arise from the interaction of Western arrogance, Islamic intolerance and Sinic assertiveness' (1996: 183). However, Huntington has no doubts as to which civilisations run the greater risk. When rewriting a passage from the article which gave the title to the book and which most annoyed his critics, who were however unable to refuse it, he states: 'Islam's borders are bloody, and so are its innards. The Muslim propensity towards violent conflict is also suggested by the degree to which Muslim societies are militarised' (1996: 258).

The Clash of Civilisations is a profound, complex and challenging book, which has all too often been analysed superficially, and even more frequently, been misunderstood. This is why I judged it necessary to quote widely from the original text. The profoundness and complexity of the book is the result of an analysis that builds on many of the themes that Huntington had previously discussed at length on different occasions, such as modernisation, political order, the spread of democracy, the link between values and institutions. When these issues are placed in the context of world politics at the beginning of the third millennium, they become interesting and controversial, stimulating and prickly. This does not make them any less important or meaningful. Huntington has set out an agenda for debate that cannot be ignored either at a scientific, or (even less so) a political level.

CONCLUSION

I have already emphasised that no American political scientist can neglect analysis of his or her own political system, even if it is not the central subject of his research. Nonetheless, too many American political scientists tend to limit their research only to their own political system and, in a certain sense, however well equipped they are as regards methodology, they impoverish that research. By contrast, Huntington has, from the beginning of his career, managed to combine a detailed analysis of the American political system, or specific parts of it such as the military and the Congress, with a comparison of other systems. Moreover, he has succeeded in enriching this comparative analysis by exploiting his knowledge of the American situation and switching between the two to refine further his concepts. I believe that in this regard the use of the relationship between participation and political institutionalisation was particularly important and revealing. First, this relationship was used by Huntington as a central concept in his analysis of political development in situations in which the excess of expectations produced by uncontrolled political participation, which cannot be channelled into adaptable independent and coherent institutions, leads to political decadence. Next, he identified two possible vicious circles – too much mobilisation and too little institutionalisation; too little political order and too little socio-economic modernisation – in developing countries, and he then went on to tackle the problem of the crisis of American democracy when faced with a sudden increase in political participation. In the developing countries, instead, the mixture between socio-economic modernisation, political participation and demands for equality can lead to, on the one hand, a technocratic model (more development and less socio-economic equality), and on the other, a populist model (greater socio-economic equality and less development) (Huntington and Nelson 1976: 24–5). In the United States, where the conflict between development and equality is endemic in a certain sense, the problem lies in adapting the institutions to probable and repeated waves of political participation, or as would seem to have happened in a homeopathic way, in using the institutions to limit and possibly discourage the excess (but by how much and concerning which participation?). Inevitably, the study of political development has led Huntington to an analysis of democracy itself. In particular, Huntington was drawn this way from many points, one of which was his important observations on the gulf existing between the promises of the American ideals and the performance of the institutions of the American political system. When his attention is directed to the processes of democratisation Huntington goes beyond a narrow perspective and looks for an explanation within an historical perspective that includes and takes account of many processes of democratisation and the outcome of each, however fragile and unconsolidated.

Huntington's specific contribution is two-fold and as clear as it is important. On the one hand, it consists of an argued and documented refusal to take for granted that democracy, once achieved, is destined to last, or that any political system that becomes democratic will never be subject to processes of crisis or collapse. If the terms were not so unattractive one could describe such a reversion as a form of 'de-democratisation', or in any case as an involution of democracy when there is no actual collapse. It is indeed the same, powerful notion that led to the warning not to consider all processes of modernisation as irreversible preliminary steps towards development. As in the sphere of political development, where there is always a danger of potential political decadence, so with democratisation the danger is a backlash, or a return to a non-democratic system. At the height of the third wave of democracy a phenomenon appeared that attracted Huntington's interest both from an analytical and political point of view: the existence of a hard (and broad) core of countries that not only resisted democratisation, but had in fact not even begun on the path of democratisation. In a world which Huntington sees as being caught up in the processes of globalisation, and which cannot be limited purely to the commercial and financial spheres, the presence of this hard core of Arab and Muslim states that resist democratisation is a danger and a challenge for the democracies. It implies a potential clash of culture and civilisations, one that may come about, is not unavoidable, and would certainly be very dangerous.

The book, *The Clash of Civilisations* is the mature outcome of a path followed by Huntington through the identification of the most important political phenomena involving all the countries of the world. Through his constant use of comparison, by considering historical phenomena and weighing up their importance at different times, Huntington has managed not only to give new direction to an analytical perspective but has formulated generalisations and interpretations of both heuristic and predictive value. Probably his greatest contribution consists in his extraordinary ability to come up with simple explanations to highly complex problems: political decadence depends on the imbalance between participation and order; American political disharmony is the consequence of unavoidable tensions between ideals and institutions; democratisation is the result of the happy combination of socio-economic development and a capacity for political leadership; and lastly, the international disorder of recent years can be explained by the strengthening of identities that has led to a potential clash of civilisations. Thanks to the clear explicative structure of his books and the importance of their themes, the works of Samuel P. Huntington continue rightly to be an important, and often essential, source of learning.

Notes

1 I am grateful to Robert Putnam for commenting on an earlier draft of this chapter and suggesting some important improvements.
2 I have discussed this specific point at length in Pasquino (1970: 146–183).
3 See, for example, two of the most interesting studies on the subject, Perlmutter (1977) and Nordlinger (1977), who in one way or another, when criticising or appreciating, are much in his debt.
4 For an analysis of the theories and books produced in that period, I would be so bold as to suggest Pasquino (1970).

REFERENCES

Bell, D. (1973) *The Coming of Post-Industrial Society*, New York: Basic Books.

Brzezinski, Z. (1970) *Between Two Ages; America's Role in the Technotronic Era*, New York: Viking Press.

Brzezinski, Z. and Huntington, S. P. (1964) *Political Power: USA/USSR*, New York: Viking Press.

Bunce, V. (2000) 'Comparative Democratisation; Big and Bounded Generalisations', *Comparative Political Studies,* 33 (6–7): 703–34.

Carnesale, A., Doty, P., Hoffmann, S., Huntington, S. P., Nye, S. S. Jr. and Sagan, S. D. (1983) *Living with Nuclear Weapons*, Cambridge, Mass: Harvard University Press.

Finer, S. E. (1976 [1962]) *The Man on Horseback; The Role of the Military in Politics*, Harmondsworth: Penguin Books.
Hagopian, F. (2000) 'Political Development, Revisited', in *Comparative Political Studies,* 33 (6–7): 880–911.
Hirschman, A. O. (1982) *Shifting Involvements; Private Interests and Public Action*, Princeton: Princeton University Press.
Huntington, S. P. (1957) *The Soldier and the State; The Theory and Politics of Civil-Military Relations*, Cambridge, Mass: Harvard University Press.
— (1965) 'Political Development and Political Decay', in *World Politics,* 17 (3): 386–430.
— (1968) *Political Order in Changing Societies*, New Haven/London: Yale University Press.
— (1970) 'Social and Institutional Dynamics of One-Party Systems', in S. P. Huntington and C. H. Moore (eds.), *Authoritarian Politics in Modern Society; The Dynamics of One-Party Systems*, New York, Basic Books.
— (1971) 'The Change to Change; Modernisation, Development, and Politics', *Comparative Politics,* 3: 283–332.
— (1974a) 'Post-Industrial Politics; How Benign Will It Be', *Comparative Politics,* 6: 163–91.
— (1974b) 'Paradigms of American Politics: Beyond the One, the Two, and the Many', *Political Science Quarterly,* 89 (1): 1–26.
— (1975a) 'The Democratic Distemper', *The Public Interest,* 41: 9–38.
— (1975b) 'United States of America', in M. Crozier, S. P. Huntington and J. Watanuki, *The Crisis of Democracy; Report on the Governability of Democracies to the Trilateral Commission*, New York: New York University Press.
— (1977) 'The Soldier and the State in the 1970s', in A. J. Goodpaster and S. P. Huntington, *Civil-Military Relations*, Washington, D.C.: American Enterprise Institute.
— (1981) *American Politics; The Promise of Disharmony*, Cambridge, Mass./London: The Belknap Press of Harvard University Press.
— (1984) 'Will More Countries Become Democratic?', *Political Science Quarterly,* 99 (2): 193–218.
— (1987) 'The Goals of Development', in M. Weiner and S. P. Huntington (eds.), *Understanding Political Development*, Boston: Little Brown.
— (1988) 'One Soul at a Time: Political Science and Political Reform', *American Political Science Review,* 82 (1): 3–10.
— (1991) *The Third Wave; Democratisation in the Late Twentieth Century*, Norman/London: University of Oklahoma Press.
— (1993) 'The Clash of Civilisations?', *Foreign Affairs,* 72 (3): 22–49.
— (1996) *The Clash of Civilisations and the Remaking of World Order*, New York: Simon and Schuster.
— (1999) 'The Lonely Superpower', *Foreign Affairs,* 78 (2): 35–49.
— (2000) 'Foreword', in S. J. Pharr and R. D. Putnam (eds.), *Disaffected*

Democracies; What's Troubling the Trilateral Countries?, Princeton: Princeton University Press.

Huntington, S. P. and Dominguez, J. I. (1975) 'Political Development', in F. I. Greenstein and N. W. Polsby (eds.), *Handbook of Political Science*, Reading, Mass: Addison Wesley, vol. III.

Huntington, S. P. and Nelson, J. M. (1976) *No Easy Choice; Political Participation in Developing Countries*, Cambridge, Mass: Harvard University Press.

Lasswell, H. D. (1941) 'The Garrison State', *American Journal of Sociology*, 46: 455–68 (reprinted in *The Analysis of Political Behaviour; An Empirical Approach*, London: Routledge and Kegan Paul, 1947).

— (1951) 'Does the Garrison State Threaten Civil Rights?', *Annals of the American Academy of Political and Social Science* 275: 111–116.

— (1962) 'The Garrison State Hypothesis', in S. P. Huntington (ed.), *Changing Patterns of Military Politics*, New York: Free Press.

Mills, C. W. (1956) *The Power Elite*, New York: Oxford University Press; Italian translation: *L'élite del potere*, Milano: Feltrinelli, 1959.

Nordlinger, E. A. (1977) *Soldiers in Politics; Military Coup and Governments*, Englewood Cliffs, NJ: Prentice-Hall.

O'Donnell, G., Schmitter, P. and Whitehead, L. (eds.) (1986) *Transitions from Authoritarian Rule; Prospects for Democracy*, Baltimore: Johns Hopkins University Press, 4 vols.

Pasquino, G. (1970) *Modernizzazione e sviluppo politico*, Bologna: il Mulino.

Perlmutter, A. (1977) *The Military and Politics in Modern Times*, New Haven/London: Yale University Press.

Przeworski, A., Alvarez, M. E., Cheibub, J. A. and Limongi, F. (2000) *Democracy and Development; Political Institutions and Well-Being in the World, 1950–1990*, Cambridge: Cambridge University Press.

Putnam, R. D. (1986) 'Samuel P. Huntington: An Appreciation', *PS*, 19 (4) 837–845.

Rustow, D. A. (1970) 'Transitions to Democracy; Toward a Dynamic Model', *Comparative Politics*, 2 (3): 337–363.

Stepan, A. (2001) 'The New Professionalism of Internal Warfare and Military Role Expansion', in *Arguing Comparative Politics*, Oxford/New York: Oxford University Press.

chapter six | Juan J. Linz: An Intellectual and Personal Biography of the 'Maestro-Compositore'

Philippe C. Schmitter

If by *'maestro'* one means someone who assembles a large group of sub-ordinates and then conducts them to play the music of someone else, Juan José Linz is not and has never been a *'maestro.'* He is and has always been a *'compositore'* – someone who writes and plays his own music. However, since he has frequently assembled a few associates and both written and conducted music with them, let us call him a *'maestro-compositore'* of political sociology/science.

Let me first display some basic facts about our 'maestro-compositore'. Juan José Linz Storch de Gracia was born on 24 December 1926 in Bonn, Germany. He holds the following advanced degrees: Licenciado en Ciencias Políticas y Económicas, Universidad de Madrid, 1947; Licenciado en Derecho, Universidad de Madrid, 1948; and PhD in Sociology, Columbia University, 1959, as well as: 'doctor honoris causa,' of Universidad del País Basco, 2002; University of Oslo, 2000; Philipps-Universität zu Marburg, 1992; Universidad Autónoma de Madrid, 1992; Georgetown University, 1992; Universidad de Granada, 1976; the Johan Skytte Prize in Political Science from Uppsala University, 1996, and the Premio Principe de Austurias de Ciencias Sociales, 1987; and other honours and awards too numerous to list. He started his professional career as an Assistant Professor of Sociology at Columbia University, 1960–66, before being promoted to Associate Professor of Sociology, Columbia University, 1966–68. He then moved to become Professor of Sociology and Political Science at Yale University, 1968–1977, then Pelatiah Perit Professor of Political and Social Science at Yale University, 1977–89, and finally Sterling Professor of Political and Social Science at Yale University, 1989 – present. He has also held innumerable visiting professorships in Europe and the United States of America.

In addition to over 200 book chapters and articles, his major publications include: *Roberto Michels, Political Sociology, and the Future of Democracy* (with H. Chehabi), 2006; *Fascismo, autoritarismo, totalitarismo: Connessioni e differenze*, 2003; *Totalitarian and Authoritarian Regimes*, 2000; (with H. Chehabi, eds.), *Sultanistic Regimes*, 1998; (with A. Stepan), *Problems of Democratic Transition and Consolidation*, 1996; (with Y. Shain, eds.), *Between States: Interim Governments and Democratic Transitions*, 1995; (with A. Valenzuela, eds.), *The*

Failure of Presidential Democracy, 2 vols., 1994; (with L. Diamond and S. M. Lipset, eds.), *Democracy in Developing Areas: Latin America*, 1989; (with L. Diamond and S. M. Lipset, eds.), *Democracy in Developing Areas: Asia*, 1989; (with L. Diamond and S. M. Lipset, eds.), *Democracy in Developing Areas: Africa*, 1988; (with J. R. Montero, eds.) *Crisis y cambio: Electores y partido en la España de los años ochenta*, 1986; (with M. Gomez-Reino, D. Vila and F. A. Orizo, eds.), *Informe Sociológico sobre cambio político en España*, 1976–81; (with A. Stepan, eds.), *The Breakdown of Democratic Regimes*, 1978; and (with A. de Miguel), *Los Empresarios ante el poder Público*, 1966.

This abbreviated *Curriculum Vitae* illustrates something that Juan Linz has in common with many of the best 'comparativists' of his generation, i.e. training and professional activity in both Europe and the United States. He has a more unusual family background, i.e. the German and Spanish nationalities of his parents and his early education exclusively in (Franquista) Spain. In his generation of internationally renowned sociologists and political scientists, Juan Linz is the lone Spaniard. His subsequent academic trajectory has also been rather unusual (for the USA), i.e. regular professorial positions in only two American universities (Columbia and Yale) – with almost 35 consecutive years of service at the latter! This is a trait that he shares with his colleague, Robert Dahl, and with Samuel Huntington at Harvard. Most American 'maestri' have moved much more frequently in their quest for fame (and higher salaries).

Second, the CV demonstrates Linz's enormous productivity and his obvious preference for writing articles rather than books.[1] If I am not mistaken, he received tenure from Columbia University and the full professorship at Yale before having published a 'real' book. And when they did begin to flow, more or less after his having edited the landmark *The Breakdown of Democratic Regimes* in 1978,[2] the books typically took the form of a volume with chapters by various authors, edited jointly with one of his students or younger colleagues and built around an article previously written by Linz himself. Every time the theme was first set by him – the role of interim governments, the peculiarities of sultanistic regimes, the relation between transition and consolidation of democracy, the weakness of presidentialism, and of course, the machinations behind the breakdown of democracy – and then explicated, elaborated and extended by his collaborators. At the present moment, Linz is again working with Alfred Stepan, this time on a joint project that may accomplish something that I have always thought impossible, namely, to make the topic of 'comparative federalism' interesting, innovative and relevant.

Third, and what the CV can show only less clearly, is Linz's extraordinary capacity to exploit conceptualization and empirical research about a single country to build a very loyal following among comparativists in several world regions – Western (and, more recently, Eastern) Europe and Latin America in particular, but also Asia and Africa. Considering that his point of departure was a country, Spain, that no one was interested in or could even classify until the mid-1970s, the achievement is all the more remarkable. Most comparativist '*maestri*' have rooted their scholarship in some polity or polities that really mattered and for which there were both a significant secondary literature and a thriving social science community – not in a polity that was long considered a pariah and that had limited academic production and freedom.[3]

A DIFFERENT BEGINNING

I remember Seymour Martin Lipset introducing me to the work of Juan Linz in a seminar at Berkeley by telling me that he had 'the most cited doctoral dissertation never published.' Naturally, as a budding political sociologist, I was curious and managed to get hold of a copy of this hidden masterpiece, 'The Social Bases of Political Parties in West Germany.' I must admit that I was under-whelmed – if only because, as a very junior graduate student coming from study in Switzerland, I was rebelling against what was the rising orthodoxy of the time, namely, something called 'behavioralism' and Linz's analysis of secondary data was a flagrant (if excellent) example of that orthodoxy.[4] In other of his early (this time, published) articles, Juan Linz explored a subtle (at the time, I considered it 'too eclectic') mixture of individualistic-social psychological-survey based data and collective-social structural-aggregate based data in an effort to explain 'the social bases of politics' – very much in line with the seminal analysis, *Political Man*, written by his (and my) mentor, Seymour Martin Lipset. From this first encounter with Linz, I picked up two eccentric themes (neither of which convinced me at the time): (1) the persistent importance of religion for explaining political behaviour; and (2) the need to pay attention to regional breakdowns when analyzing survey or aggregate data. If I am not mistaken, Linz was the first political sociologist to emphasize the sub-national level of social structure, religious practice and political behaviour in his 'Within Nation Differences and Comparisons: the Eight Spains.'[5] Americanists had already discovered the potential payoff in comparing the 50 US states, but their message had not penetrated to those of us interested in more exotic settings and, in any case, none of us believed that the range of variance within America was that significant.

One major shift in intellectual trajectory for Linz (and the reason for my first face-to-face encounter with him) had come a bit earlier, when he published the first of several seminal essays in which he exploited the Spanish case to reach out to the broader audience of comparativists. For those of us working on Latin America, his 'An Authoritarian Regime: The Case of Spain' came as a revelation (Allardt and Littunen 1964).

> Political systems with limited, not responsible, political pluralism, without elaborate and guiding ideology, but with distinctive mentalities, without extensive or intensive political mobilisation, except at some moments in their development, and in which a leader or occasionally a small group exercises

power within formally ill-defined limits but actually quite predictable ones. (Linz 1964: 255)

That is the definition that caught my attention – and that of so many other Latin Americanists. In retrospect, I find it difficult to explain why this characterization of the Franquista regime in Spain became so influential. For one thing, it was completely unsystematic and out of tune with the theoretical orthodoxy of the times. According to the 'structural-functionalism' pioneered by Gabriel Almond and the Social Science Research Council's (SSRC) Committee on Comparative Politics, all regimes had to perform a fixed number of specified 'functions' if they were to persist. Any 'valid' definition of regime types, therefore, should have been based on institutional variation in the performance of those – usually four – functions.[6] Linz's was purely inductive and devoid of any pre-established link to prevailing theory. Its multiple characteristics came unaccompanied by any explicit conceptual justification – just a concise description of what Linz considered the most salient traits of a polity that he knew well. In other words, it was not an 'ideal type,' but a 'constructive type' and, therefore, of strictly limited applicability.

For another thing, the multiple items composing the definition were virtually impossible to measure quantitatively and, worse, came with a confusing set of caveats. So, its pluralism was 'limited, not responsible.' Its 'elaborate and guiding ideology' was non-existent, but replaced by something called 'distinctive mentalities.' Political mobilisation was 'neither extensive nor intensive,' but it nevertheless did occur 'at some points.' Finally, and most confusingly, the limits of rule by a leader (or by a small group) were 'formally ill-defined,' but 'actually quite predictable.'

My hunch is that, if this definition were inserted into an examination in methodology, any reasonably well-trained doctoral candidate would be able to demolish it in very short order. Key terms were left either under-specified (e.g. did 'political pluralism' refer only to parties or to interest associations or both?) or over-rated (e.g. were the ideologies of other regime-types really so 'elaborate and guiding' and how did they differ from mere 'mentalities' in Spain?). How could one possibly identify a distinctive regime-type – even a 'constructive' and not an 'ideal' one – without specifying who the rulers were, how they acquired their status as rulers or how they managed to handle the problem of succession in power? All we were told was that there was a leader or a small group exercising power, but that is something one should expect of all regimes according to Mosca, Pareto *et seq*. Placed in its (1960s) context, it is obvious that Linz was more concerned with drawing a distinction between 'authoritarian' and 'totalitarian' regimes than with distinguishing either from 'democratic' ones. Indeed, many polities that described themselves as 'liberal & democratic' could just as well have been classified as 'liberal & authoritarian' according to an unbiased assessment of the multiple variables contained in Linz's definition. It should, therefore, come as no surprise that once scholars got around to measuring some of these traits, there turned out to be many more 'authoritarian' than either 'totalitarian' or 'democratic' regimes.[7]

A WIDER OPENING

E pur si muove! Despite all these manifest imperfections and the blatant 'Hispano-centricity' of his definition, Linz opened up a Pandora's Box of thinking about regime-level analysis and, eventually, about regime change. By leaving aside (at least, temporarily) his exclusively behaviouralist concentration on individual values and social structures, and by focusing in a historical manner on the very notion of 'political regime' as a determinant of party systems and other collective outcomes and by simultaneously breaking with the prevailing classification system, he effectively re-designed the way that many of us saw Latin America. The situation that obsessed us, namely, military and civilian dictatorships, was not something produced 'behaviourally' by a supposedly 'Iberian' political culture or by an allegedly 'Hispano-colonial' or 'dependent' social structure, but an outcome of a particular configuration of power with its own rules, forms of repression, degrees of (sporadic) mobilisation, and ways of justifying itself ideologically. Along with Spain, Portugal and many Third World countries, Latin American polities were neither incompletely totalitarian nor embryonically democratic, but persistently authoritarian, and that had implications for how their respective political cultures were manipulated, and for how their respective status and class systems were formed and deformed. We may have struggled with the way in which Linz initially specified its generic properties, but we quickly realized that he was offering us a very important conceptual innovation.

By co-incidence, Juan Linz was invited to Brazil in 1967 when I was doing my field research there and I was 'assigned' by Candido Mendes to squire him about Rio de Janeiro. Instead of showing him the usual sociological sights, I literally kidnapped him and sat him down for a three hour conversation just off the beach in Copacabana (fortunately, Linz showed no apparent interest in the beach itself). We went over every detail of his 'An Authoritarian Regime: Spain' article and to my relief he even accepted some of the modifications that I had proposed to make it fit not just the current military dictatorship in Brazil, but several previous manifestations of authoritarian rule in that country and elsewhere in Latin America. I remember how relieved I was when he acknowledged that what I was calling 'corporatism' might be an appropriate synonym for what he had labelled as 'limited pluralism'.[8]

We met a second time on Brazilian 'turf' – at a conference organized by Alfred Stepan at Yale. I had written a paper on 'The Portugalization of Brazil?' intended in part (correctly, as it turned out) to provoke the ire of the ruling military dictators. My contention was that a series of 'Additional Acts,' substantive policies and informal practices beginning in 1968 were laying the basis for the perpetuation of authoritarian rule into the indefinite future – thereby, reducing giant Brazil to the status of little Portugal. Linz's paper argued that the Brazilian military dictatorship was only in an 'authoritarian situation' and that it was unlikely to be able to institutionalize itself in power as Franco and Salazaar had done some thirty to twenty-five years earlier. In retrospect, his assessment was closer to the mark than mine. The generals did remain in power for almost another 20 years and they proved capable of imposing a very gradual and selective change of regime upon their country, but Linz was right that they never were capable of putting together that self-reinforcing set of traits that he had observed in Spain and Portugal.[9]

When it began in 1975, Juan Linz was particularly well prepared to cope personally and intellectually with Spain's transition to democracy. His early work had relied heavily on mass public attitudes and 'developmental' structural constraints, but the book he had edited with Alfred Stepan on *The Breakdown of Democratic Regimes* brought out a more 'political' mode of analysis with a strong emphasis on 'agency,' i.e., on the role of actor choices in the 'undermining' and, subsequently, 'crafting' of new institutions. A strict application of the orthodox attitudinal/structural approach would quickly have led him to question the very probability of democratising Spain in the mid-1970s. That country, while more developed than neighbouring Portugal and perhaps more attitudinally pluralist given its tumultuous past and regional diversity, nevertheless, had none of the so-called 'pre-requisites' for liberal democracy emphasized by the then prevailing literature – to which Linz, *via* his association with Lipset, had made an important contribution. The less deterministic and more voluntaristic 'political' approach embedded in the *Breakdown* book represented something of an epistemic shift in his thinking and opened up the possibility that the Spaniards just might be able to pull off such a successful regime change. I can remember a period of 18 months from mid-1974 to end-1975 when Linz and I met each other at least half dozen times on panels at conferences and colloquia trying to explain to each other and various audiences why Spain and Portugal – two countries allegedly with so many cultural, historical and developmental traits in common – were in the midst of such different transitions. The obvious explanation concerned the modes of transition. Portugal has been 'liberated by golpe,' i.e. by a very small and audacious group of junior Army officers who were facing the imminent prospect of defeat in one of the country's several colonial wars – ironically, the one in Guinée-Bissau that was by far the least important (Schmitter, 1975). Following that unexpected event, came a massive popular mobilisation that drove regime change far beyond its political realm into those of economic ownership, social status and cultural hegemony. Spain, having been deprived of its colonies and its imperial illusions at the end of the 19th Century, had no such prospect of being liberated by its military. Indeed, the potential difficulty there was the inverse: how to prevent an 'inactive' military from reacting negatively to the prospect of 'liberation by stealth,' i.e. through pacting among civilian politicians, now that Franco had died. Not only had popular mobilisation been successfully contained by elites, but also the very tumult and radicalism of what was happening in Portugal made Spanish elites act even more cautiously. In short, we had a fascinating case for 'perverse diffusion' in which the late-comer was trying to avoid what had just happened to the front-runner.

But Linz emphasized a second factor that had not initially occurred to me, namely, a 'dog that had failed to bark' at the regime level in Portugal. When Salazaar had fallen off his chair and been replaced by Caetano in 1969, the latter's efforts at liberalizing the prevailing autocratic system were weak and unsuccessful – unlike the case in Spain, where a similar attempt had occurred much earlier (1958) and gone much further so that by the time Franco died in 1975 the country was already firmly anchored economically and socially in Europe. The Portuguese (at least, its aging political elite) still harboured illusions of imperial grandeur and riches, and had not yet unequivocally committed themselves to being 'just' Europeans. What made the *Revolução* such a radical break was not only the widespread and protracted popular mobilisation it triggered, but also the dramatic withdrawal from Angola, Mozambique and Guinée-Bissau and the huge influx of refugees back to the *métropole* that this occasioned. Portugal became equivocally democratic and unequivocally European at the very same time. Spain had already undergone a prior (and gradual) transition.[10] Regardless of whether we were successful in capturing the reasons for their momentary difference, Linz and I were in complete agreement on one thing: both countries would eventually become consolidated, western, representative, liberal democracies – but they would get there by taking different paths! From this rather fortuitous collaboration came a hypothesis that guided much of my subsequent research on democratisation, namely, that there were many ways in which a polity could 'transit' from autocracy and there was no guarantee that any of them would lead to democracy, but there was a distinct possibility of 'equifinality' – i.e., of ending up with the roughly same generic type of regime. What Terry Karl and I later called 'the modes of transition' were more likely to influence the type of democracy that managed to consolidate itself than whether the outcome would be democratic (Karl and Schmitter 1991).

A MASSIVE EXTENSION

The massive comparative study on *Problems of Democratic Transition and Consolidation* that Linz and Alfred Stepan published in 1996 has become **the** point of reference for scholars working on the outcome of recent regime changes. Based on cases ranging from Southern Europe to the Southern Cone of Latin America to Central and Eastern Europe and the Republics of the former Soviet Union, the empirical coverage is prodigious and the theoretical approach is prolix. Alone, the 'analytical narratives' of 15 countries attempting democratisation represent a major contribution. Instead of the 'stylized facts' selectively strung together by rational-choicers to make the best possible case for their deductive presuppositions or the 'quantitative compilations' comprehensively gathered by number-crunchers to provide the largest possible database for their probabilistic inferences, Linz and Stepan digest an immense amount of raw and processed material (in several languages), order it loosely according to a broad set of interpretive categories, compile a rich narrative full of complex linkages and sequences, and then proceed to draw insightful conclusions from each case. And then they do something that has been much advocated by generalists and excoriated by area specialists. They draw further comparisons across world regions – Southern Europe, South America, and Post-Communist Europe. Linz has always been a peculiar combination of a dyed-in-the-wool country specialist who also dares to make cross-regional comparisons. No one that I know in the discipline has done more to insist that political sociologists need to know the language, history and culture of the units that they are analyzing while, at the same time, insisting that they contrast and test their findings against a wide range of cases with quite different languages, histories and cultures – and not just their 'regional' neighbours. Perhaps because this 'method-*cum*-design' is so demanding, Juan Linz has had so few imitators, even if so many of us admire him for both his erudition and his audacity.

In terms of substance, Linz and Stepan introduce several independent variables in their national and cross-regional analyses that were overlooked or discounted in earlier versions of 'transitology', e.g. degree of stateness, distribution of ethno-linguistic/national identities and variation in the international context. And they make a compelling case for their relevance, especially in post-communist settings. Strictly speaking, however, they do not pretend to offer 'a theory of democratisation.' Linz can only rarely be associated with something as bounded and tightly structured as a theory.[11] Rather, his approach (very similar to that adopted in the *Breakdown of Democracy* essay) is to lay out (in an 83 page introduction!) an extensive set of rather capacious categories with which to order the voluminous information generated by the process of regime change and with which it should be possible to evaluate whether the outcome of regime change will be a consolidated democracy.

Linz and Stepan are (characteristically) profligate in their definition of the dependent variable. According to them, the consolidation of democracy is composed of three layers:

1) behavioural;
2) attitudinal; and
3) constitutional.

No explicit hypotheses about the temporal or causal relationship among these three components are made, but what presumably produces this outcome is the capacity of all of them collectively to generate an enduring political situation in which 'democracy has become the only game in town.' Needless to say, this is not equivalent to 'the end of history.' Even the most consolidated of democracies can subsequently become deconsolidated. Nor do Linz and Stepan imply that only one type of democracy is being consolidated (although there is no explicit treatment of what different types of democracy might be currently 'on offer'). From the case-studies, it becomes apparent that the 'quality' of the democracies that have emerged does vary considerably, even if they do not explicitly address this controversial issue.

Linz's definition of democratic consolidation shares many of the characteristics we observed above with the definition he earlier developed of an authoritarian regime. It is not just cumbersome and difficult to operationalise, but its 'layered' components may not be equally significant in any particular case and they are almost certainly not co-variant in any necessary fashion. What are we to make of the frequency distribution of attitudinal responses to such vague questions as 'Is democracy preferable to any other regime?' And, why should we rely so much on the behavioural fact that there are 'no significant groups seriously attempt[ing] to overthrow the democratic regime or secede from the state?' Ironically, it was Juan Linz, in his introductory contribution to *The Breakdown of Democratic Regimes* who argued that, not infrequently, the most dangerous opponents of democracies have been precisely those actors who think of themselves as democrats and who are convinced that they are just struggling to save or to improve democracy. If so, just because virtually no contemporary neo-democracies have sizeable and explicitly anti-democratic parties (not even ex-communists qualify any longer), one should not draw the inference that, therefore, they are all securely consolidated. And what about the many countries where attitudes are very sceptical about democracy as it is experienced by mass publics and, yet, no overtly anti-democratic parties attract a significant following and most citizens and politicians behave according to constitutional norms?

In my own work on consolidation, I have focused exclusively on the third dimension (although I would hesitate to call it 'constitutional' since so many of the most important and regularly followed core procedures of any democracy are not included in such a formal and unique document). My strategy has been to concentrate on the process whereby politicians do or do not reach agreement on mutually acceptable rules of the game regulating their competition and cooperation in a select number of what I call 'partial regimes' (Schmitter 1998). Only subsequently, once these rules have been consolidated, would I advocate taking into account the 'behavioural and attitudinal' implications they may have. Obviously, this implies the hypothesis that the process of consolidation first requires that rulers be ensnared (*piégés* is the better French expression) into playing politics according to certain generically democratic rules and, only then, is there any reason to expect that citizens will follow up by picking the 'proper' parties and conforming to the 'proper' values. How reliable can attitudes in favour of democracy and behaviours with regard to parties be when held by persons who do not yet know what the rules are going to be and, therefore, cannot have experienced their effects? There can, of course, be exceptions – for example, when the period of autocratic rule has been short and the memories of previous democratic practices still quite salient in the minds of the public – but these should be recognized as such and not allowed to obfuscate the more generic process.

A second problem emerges in the way Linz and Stepan have defined and measured the dependent variable in each of the case studies. Laudably, they have tried to specify the exact moments at which regime transition ends and at which consolidation occurs. For example, in the admittedly peculiar case of Portugal, both are alleged to have happened on a single day: August 12, 1982! Elsewhere, transition ends and only later does consolidation begin, according to them. But what if these two processes normally tend to be both more separate and more overlapping – and to stretch out over a longer period? Merely ratifying a constitution (or eliminating certain autocratic reserve powers in a previous constitution, as Portugal did on that momentous day in 1982) might not ensure that core procedures have been agreed upon and implemented effectively. They do not mention it, but Portugal had to go through a second, even more substantial, revision of its constitutional provisions on property ownership and economic management in 1989. Linz and Stepan are certainly correct in arguing that, contrary to scholars from Samuel Huntington to Adam Przeworski, it is not enough just that elections be regularly held and 'freely and fairly' conducted, but they seem to be agnostic on what these other arrangements are. For example, does the consolidation of modern democracy require 'crafting' mutually acceptable rules concerning such things as bargaining between capital and labour and guarantees for different forms of property and assurances about minimal social protection – or is it sufficient that actors choose between presidential or parliamentary executives and federal or unitary territorial formats, as their subsequent research suggests?

If all this were not already complicated enough, Linz and Stepan, then, argue that in order for the three layers to combine and guarantee democracy's status as 'the only game in town' for the indefinite future, no less than five different arenas have to reinforce each other and bring about such an outcome:

1) civil society;
2) political society;
3) rule of law;
4) state apparatus; and
5) economic society.

Some of these causal factors are not exclusive to democracy (e.g. state apparatus and economic society); some are more specifically democratic (e.g. civil society and, perhaps political society); others refer more to the unit in which the regime exists (e.g. state apparatus and rule of law); and, finally, some refer to (presumably) pre-political prerequisites (e.g. economic society and, perhaps, the rule of law). As is so often the case with Linz's (and Stepan's) work, the discussion substantiating the relevance of each of these arenas is full of insightful historical observations drawn from a wealth of cases. What is not so usual is their utilization of a 'functional' language of necessity, implying that one arena is somehow needed in order for another to operate effectively – without, however, their specifying how much of each is required or when one must precede the other. I am convinced that a quick glance at most 'real-existing' liberal democracies would reveal not only considerable variance in the form and content of all five arenas, but also that not all of them necessarily function to reinforce each other.

In the final segment of their theoretical introduction on 'Actors and Contexts,' Linz and Stepan come closest to producing an orthodox, i.e. probabilistic and falsifiable, theory about regime consolidation. They link specific, empirically observable, conditions such as:

1) the institutional composition and leadership type of the *ancien régime*;
2) the identity and degree of control of those who initiate the transition;

3) the foreign policies of neighbouring polities (especially, those of regional hegemons);
4) the *Zeitgeist* of plausible political ideologies at a particular moment in time;
5) the probability of political learning *via* diffusion from one democratising experience to another;
6) the impact of economic performance on regime legitimacy (where they offer a much more subtle argument than the usual linear one); and
7) the type of constitution-making environment to the differential likelihood of success in consolidating democracy. In the subsequent case studies, the complex (and often unique) interactions between these actors and their contexts are narrated in greater detail and exploited to produce more discrete estimates of whether a particular country is on the way to consolidating 'its' appropriate form of democracy.

In this, his latest major *opus*, Linz (along with his co-author) has done nothing less than to lay the foundation for a new sub-discipline of political science, which I have labelled (much to the distaste of many): 'consolidology.' The stones are certainly numerous and large enough, but only use (and misuse) by subsequent scholars will determine whether they are sufficient to bear all of the weight and chiselling that they will subject it to. As has been his distinctive style in the past, Linz has constructed his foundation by respecting the complexities and contingencies involved in such a difficult and contentious process. He has not resorted to stylizing actor preferences and trivializing their choices. He has not just coded a mass of data, estimated their associations and drawn probabilistic inferences. And, a bit more surprisingly, he has not even succumbed to the temptation to suggest 'quick fixes' on the route to consolidating democracy.

I say this because in his more recent work, Linz has become very institutionalist – in the best sense of the word, that is to say, 'historical institutionalist.' He is much too knowledgeable about and sensitive to the importance of embedding actors in their past sequences of interaction (and not just in a time series or an iteration of the same game) to attribute much importance to the 'stylised facts', 'Pareto-Optimal Outcomes' and 'Nash Equilibria' of so-called 'neo-institutionalists'. He has been following up (with Stepan and other collaborators) a series of hunches about how specific institutions – interim governments, presidential/parliamentary executive formats, sultanistic regimes and, most recently, federalist arrangements – have an (allegedly) similar relation to the positive or negative outcome of democratisation. Although he has never presented them as 'silver bullets' or 'quick fixes,' Linz has claimed that parliamentarism (Linz 1990b) and federalism (Linz 1999) lead to good outcomes, while interim governments (Linz and Shain 1995) and presidentialism do not (Linz 1990a; Linz and Valenzuela 1994). And 'sultanism' is definitely, according to him, a bad place to start from (Linz and Chehabi 1998).

Frankly, I find this quest a bit puzzling for someone trained as a political sociologist. I had always presumed that one of the first credos of this breed of social scientist was that no rule, law, formal institution or informal arrangement would have the same effect regardless of the social/historical context into which it was inserted. My initial assumption has been – and I thought that I had learned it from Linz et al. – that 'it [i.e. the impact] depends' and that one of our goals was to find out why polities with the same generic institutional configuration tended to vary so much in their stability, effectiveness, durability, legitimacy, and so forth.

And my second assumption was that the explanation for such diversity usually resided in the differences in how, when and in what sequence these configurations had come about historically.

FIVE PRINCIPLES OF INTERPRETATION

Therefore, I conclude this brief intellectual biography by specifying what are the lessons that I have personally learned from reading the works, listening to the presentations, participating in the panels and just plain conversing with Juan Linz over the years. Alas, I have never formally been his student or co-author, but I do consider him as one of my most significant mentors.

By my calculation, I owe him for five major principles of macro-historical interpretation. I have tried (no doubt, not always successfully) to use them consistently in my own work. To the best of my knowledge, he has never written any of them down explicitly. I am not even sure that he would recognize his authorship of them or subscribe to all of them. Rather, these principles are the sort of 'jewels' that Linz so generously (if not always consciously) distributes between the lines of his written work and during his oral interventions at conferences and in seminars. They are often hard for his listeners to pick out since they are frequently buried under an avalanche of factual material and excursions into tangential issues that make up his inimitable style of lecturing. They are also the product of long experience with and an encyclopaedic knowledge of politics and society. Juan Linz has had many collaborators and students, but he has had few imitators, and unfortunately I am not one of them.

> *'Things are not now what they once were.'* This is a particularly odd maxim for someone who is so deeply 'historical' in his knowledge and approach. Most card-carrying historians spend a lot of effort trying to convince people that nothing has changed and, therefore, only by knowing what has gone on 'way back when' can anyone possibly understand what is happening in the present. Ironically, I learned this from Linz with regard to political parties – a preoccupation of his since his very earliest writings. At some point in a discussion, he let drop the observation that 'parties are not what they used to be and do not expect them to accomplish what they did in earlier instances of democratisation.' I took this to heart and even built it into the title of an essay of mine dissenting from the usual orthodoxy among political scientists studying democratisation that 'once you get the parties right, the rest will fall into place' (Schmitter 2001).

'Things that bring about the demise of something are not what bring about its successor.' I suppose that this principle should be attributed to Fritz Stern, Linz's colleague in history at Columbia, but I learned it from Linz himself. Its *locus classicus* was the Weimar Republic. While it is plausible to argue that by 1931 the democratic republic was doomed and its demise was 'over-determined' by a rather obvious set of convergent factors, this does not explain why its demise was followed by National Socialism. Some of the same factors may have entered into the complex chain of causality, but so did lots of novel ones. Hence, when Linz analysed the breakdown of democracy, he did not also claim that this explained the nature or type of the autocracy that followed. Nor was the subsequent demise of authoritarian regimes in Southern Europe and Latin America to be understood simply as an inversion of the causal factors behind the previous regime change. Guillermo O'Donnell and I explicitly made this point in our *Transitions from Authoritarian Rule: Tentative Conclusions about Uncertain Democracies* and carried it further when we hypothesized that the actors responsible for bringing about the demise of autocracy were not usually those who played a leading role in the consolidation of democracy (O'Donnell and Schmitter 1986).

'Things can only be analyzed after they have first been classified.' Juan Linz has always been a vigorous (if not always systematic) classifier. He is responsible not only for 'discovering' the distinctive characteristics of authoritarian (as opposed to democratic and totalitarian) regimes, but he has devoted a great deal of attention to the identification of sub-types within this initial breakdown. He is even the inventor of the first (and perhaps only) three-dimensional typology in political science.[12] There is virtually not a recent book or article of Linz's that does not begin with either a full classification system or a major conceptual distinction (say, between parliamentary and presidential executives). The implication is that it is only by first discerning the generic category to which the case or cases belong at that particular time that it is possible to set up a comparison and draw valid inferences about causality. Moreover, if one combines this maxim with the first one, the task is also to place cases not only in their apposite category but also in their relevant time period. Linz, as I interpret him, has rarely wasted his time in the search for 'the universal laws of political motion.' Implicitly, he tells us to be content as scientists with partial subsets of cases in which it is possible to control (approximately) for specified structural, cultural, temporal and ideational aspects of context and only then plunge inductively into the data in the search for empirically grounded patterns and associations.

'Things cause another thing (especially, regime change) by narrowing or widening the range of possible variation that the other thing can take on.' I may be exaggerating this principle. In his work, Linz certainly recognizes a plurality of causal mechanisms including the good old fashioned one of direct, necessary and sufficient effect, but one of most original arguments in his essay in the *Breakdown* book concerns the way in which the worst enemies of democracy were often its self-proclaimed defenders and their noxious effect was to reduce the range of responses in the future by engaging in policies that narrowed the range of possible defences in the present. Admittedly, this is not an easy inference to prove in positivistic terms. One has to engage in very problematic counter-factual assertions just to make the point and there will always be other actions of individuals or collectivities that can be claimed to have had a narrowing or widening impact. I, however, found this maxim important for explaining why autocratic rulers so frequently mis-calculated the effects of their actions. They took decisions based on incomplete information or wrong assumptions and then found themselves less capable of using repressive measures in response. Inversely, it could be argued that actors in the democratic opposition occasionally took decisions during the highly uncertain moments of the transition that inadvertently opened up spaces and opportunities for their opponents in the future. Of course, all such phenomena can be described under the capacious rubrique of 'unintended consequences,' but viewed through this specific focus of causal narrowing and widening the distinctively political nature of choice becomes more apparent – and illustrates quite well why orthodox notions of rational (economic) choice are so inappropriate.

'Things rarely end up for the best; therefore, it is better to accept the second best outcome.' This is a normative principle, not one of conceptualisation, case selection or empirical inference. Linz has the natural instincts of an anti-revolutionary conservative, but not of a reactionary. He knows that things have to change and even welcomes change – but always within measure and never dramatically or irreversibly. Most of all, he is instinctively suspicious of actors who claim that their enlightened intention (or superior grasp of history) will bring about such a remarkable improvement in society or polity that this justifies the application of coercion or violent repression. Needless to say, this instinctual cautiousness must stem from his experiences during and after the Spanish Civil War (and, for a brief period, in Nazi Germany), although he does not dwell at any length on the subject in his intellectual autobiography (Linz, 1997). Linz is a scholar who is unusually erudite, but also aware of the limitations of scholarly (and his own) knowledge. On those (not frequent) occasions when he has publicly proffered advice to politicians, as when he argued for a '*ruptura pactada*' during the Spanish transition or, subsequently, when he favoured an '*estado de las autonomias*' rather than either a unitary state or full-fledged federalism, Linz has been a 'satisficer' not an optimiser. It would not be an exaggeration (I believe) to call him 'a

normative theorist (but never an apologist) for the second best.' I personally admire the extraordinary consistency of his values over a long and eventful career, not to mention his remarkable tolerance for others (such as myself) who have not always agreed with his opinions and interpretations.

So, I recommend the *persona et opere* of Juan J. Linz to all students of political science and not just to those who are members of the small club of comparative political sociologists. He is a *maestro-compositore* who has taken an original Spanish melody (admittedly a complicated *zarzuela*) and used it as the source of inspiration for employing virtually the full range of available instruments and for exploring a wide range of substantive themes. Baroque at heart, never a romantic or a modernist, he has managed to produce a unique set of classic works that will be capable of enlightening us into the foreseeable future.

Notes

1 I should, however, point out that some of Juan Linz's articles are as long as many scholars' books, especially when one includes the footnotes. Linz is famous among comparativists for his voluminous and encyclopaedic footnotes. I cannot also resist pointing out that, in this era when young scholars are obsessively concerned with placing as many articles as possible in 'major, peer-refereed journals,' very few of Linz's articles fit into that category. He has never (to my knowledge) published an article in the American Political Science Review and, even more insulting to the American hegemony of the discipline, very many of his articles have been written or only appear in a language other than English! Insomma, Linz has followed a career trajectory that no one would dare recommend to someone entering the profession today – and yet, he is one of the most cited and influential figures in contemporary political science.

2 The timing of this book (1978) is an other perfect illustration of the Hegelian principle that 'owls only fly after dusk,' i.e. that social scientists only understand and write about phenomena when they are in decline. Just as Linz and Stepan collaborated on transitions from democracy to autocracy, the political world was headed in the opposite direction – a shift in fortuna that Linz himself picked up very quickly and, so to speak, intimately as Spain began to move toward democracy after the death of Francisco Franco in 1975.

3 Here is something else that the CV cannot say. Juan Linz is living proof that incessant smoking of some of the most noxious and foul-smelling cigarettes in the world may not be so hazardous to your (mental) health. For all I know, he may even give those thousands of Ducados some credit for his remarkable acuity and capacity to concentrate on difficult and weighty 'matters of state.'

4 One of my main complaints about 'behavioralism' was its dependence not only upon individual attitudes (sometimes, presumptuously called 'values'), but also upon a limited range of historical data and assumptions. What mattered were the attitudes captured in a mass sample survey at a particular moment, not why these respondents came to acquire these attitudes and what previous forces affected their choices. Linz may have started out in this vein, but he very quickly recognized the significance of time-series attitudinal data. In Spain, due to his long association with the Centro de Investigaciones Sociologicas and his role as the founder of a private survey research firm, DATA S.A., he played a crucial and pioneering role in the development of this technique of data-gathering and ensured its historical continuity, starting during the regime of Francisco Franco. Of all of the more than fifty countries that have transited from autocracy towards democracy since 1974, we know far more about the long-term evolution of mass and elite attitudes in Spain than in any of the others.

5 In Merritt and Rokkan, 1966. His friend and colleague, Stein Rokkan, had earlier emphasized the distinction between 'center and periphery' as a persistent source of cleavage in the emergence of European states, but Linz took that insight further by specifying the multiplicity of 'peripheries' and the ways in which they could generate quite different problems for state-builders or regime-consolidators.

6 Presumably, they were derived directly or indirectly from the GAIL functions proposed by Talcott Parsons (1951).

7 Although it does not explicitly measure the traits mentioned by Linz, the annual scores produced by Freedom House do bear some generic similarity to them. In its early versions, the number of 'partially free' countries widely outnumbered the 'not free' and 'free' ones. (Gastill 1990).

8 I was completely unaware at the time that Linz (in collaboration with Amando de Miguel) had just finished a small book (virtually introuvable then and now) on *Los Empresarios ante el Poder Publico* (1966). My dissertation dealt (in part) with the same issue in Brazil – although I approached it through the study of business interest associations, while Linz focused mainly on opinions of individual businessmen in an innovative elite survey. At the time, this was a very unexploited topic, whatever the approach taken, and thus Linz deserves recognition as a pioneer in the field of the empirical study of 'business and politics' – even if virtually no one has read or utilized the little book that he and Amando de Miguel wrote.

9 These essays can be found in Stepan 1973.

10 For Linz's thoughts on this comparison, see Linz 1981 and 1977. For my comparative thoughts on Portugal, see Schmitter 1999.

11 This may explain something that has puzzled me when I began thinking about writing this chapter. I consulted what is considered by some to be the most definitive statement of the current status of the discipline of political science, Goodin and Klingemann, 1996. The name of Juan Linz does not appear in the list of 'luminaries' (Appendix A1.C) who are most frequently cited by its various authors, implying that he has made little or no contribution to the discipline as a whole. Even more bizarre, he is barely mentioned in any of the four chapters on comparative politics, not even in the one devoted specifically to studies of democratisation! Since I find this manifestly absurd, my first reaction was to blame it on the rather skewed composition of those who were chosen to write the chapters. But this may not be sufficient. Several of those with whom he has had close working relations do get cited: e.g. S. M. Lipset, S. Rokkan, R. Dahl, A. Lijphart, G. Sartori. My assumption is that scholars who can be associated with a particular 'causal theory' or 'novel method,' tend to get greater recognition. Someone like Linz who offers an 'approach' (and one that is very difficult to imitate) and who breaks more new ground by innovating conceptually than by offering a comprehensive explanation of some particular topic are less likely to make the list of 'notables,' even if on the basis of citations or influence on doctoral research, his or her impact has been much greater.

12 Linz 1975. NB the page count of the chapter – 236 – more than many books! I suspect that it may be the longest article ever published in political science or sociology.

REFERENCES

Allardt, E. and Littunen, Y. (eds.) (1964) *Cleavages, Ideologies and Party Systems: Contributions to Comparative Political Sociology*, Helsinki: The Academic Bookstore.

Gastill, R. (ed.), *Freedom in the World: Political Rights and Civil Liberties, 1987–8*, New York: Freedom House.

Goodin, R. E and Klingemann, H. D. (eds.) (1996) *A New Handbook of Political Science*, Oxford: Oxford University Press.

Karl, T. L. and Schmitter, P. C. (1991) 'Modes of Transition in Latin America, Southern and Eastern Europe', *International Social Science Journal*, 128: 269–84.

Linz, J. (1964) 'An Authoritarian Regime: The Case of Spain', in E. Allardt and Y. Littunen (eds.) *Cleavages, Ideologies, and Party Systems: Contributions to Comparative Political Sociology*, Helsinki: Transactions of the Westermarck Society.

(1966) *Los empresarios ante el poder público: el liderazgo y los grupos de intereses en el empresariado español*, (edited by A. de Miguel), Madrid: Instituto de Estudios Políticos.

(1975) 'Totalitarian and Authoritarian Regimes,' in F. Greenstein and N. Polsby (eds.), *Handbook of Political Science*, Reading, MA: Addison-Wesley.

(1977) 'Spain and Portugal: Critical Choices,' in D. S. Landes (ed.), *Western Europe: The Trails of Partnership*, Lexington, MA: D. C. Heath.

(1981) 'Some Comparative Thoughts on the Transition to Democracy in Portugal and Spain', in J. B. de Macedo and S. Serfaty (eds.), *Portugal since the Revolution*, Boulder, Col.: Westview Press.

(1990a) 'Perils of Presidentialism,' *Journal of Democracy*, 1 (1): 51–69.

(1990b) 'The Virtues of Parliamentarism,' *Journal of Democracy*, 1 (4): 84–92.

(1997) 'Between Nations and Disciplines: personal experience and intellectual understanding of societies and political regimes,' in H. Daalder (ed.), *Comparative European Politics: The Story of a Profession*, London: Pinter.

(1999) 'Democracia, multinacionalismo y federalismo', *Revista Española de Ciencia Política*, Vol. 1 (1): 7–49.

(2000) *Totalitarian and Authoritarian Regimes*, Boulder, Col.: Lynne Rienner.

(2003) *Fascismo, autoritarismo, totalitarismo: connessioni e differenze*, Rome: Ideazione Editrice.

(2006) *Roberto Michels, Political Sociology, and the Future of Democracy* (edited by H. Chehabi), New Brunswick, NJ: Transaction Publishers.

Linz, J. and Chehabi, H. (eds.) (1998) *Sultanistic Regimes*, Baltimore: The Johns

Hopkins University Press.
Linz, J. and de Miguel, A. (1966) *Los Empresarios ante el poder Público. El Liderazgo y los Grupos de Intereses en el Empresariado Español*, Madrid: Instituto de Estudios Políticos.
Linz, J., Diamond, L. and Lipset, S. L. (eds.) (1988) *Democracy in Developing Areas: Africa*, Boulder, Col.: Lynne Rienner; London: Adamantine Press.
(1989) *Democracy in Developing Areas: Latin America*, Boulder, Col.: Lynne Rienner; London: Adamantine Press.
(1989) *Democracy in Developing Areas: Asia*, Boulder, Col.: Lynne Rienner; London: Adamantine Press.
Linz, J., Gomez-Reino, M., Vila, D. and Orizo, F. A. (1981) *Informe Sociológico sobre el cambio político en España 1975–1981: IV Informe FOESSA, Vol. I.*, Madrid: Euroamérica.
Linz, J. and Montero, J. R. (eds.) (1986) *Crisis y cambio: Electores y partido en la España de los años ochenta*, Madrid: Centro de Estudios Constitucionales.
Linz, J. and Shain, Y. (eds.) (1995) *Between States: Interim Governments and Democratic Transitions*, Cambridge: Cambridge University Press.
Linz, J. and Stepan, A. (eds.) (1978) *The Breakdown of Democratic Regimes*, 4 Vol., Baltimore: The Johns Hopkins University Press.
(1996) *Problems of Democratic Transition and Consolidation: Southern Europe, South America and Post-Communist Europe*, Baltimore: The Johns Hopkins University Press.
Linz, J. and Valenzuela, A. (eds.) (1994) *The Failure of Presidential Democracy*, 2 Vol., Baltimore: The Johns Hopkins University Press.
Merritt, R. and Rokkan, S. (eds.) (1966) *Comparing Nations*, New Haven: Yale University Press.
O'Donnell, G. and Schmitter, P. C. (1986) *Transitions from Authoritarian Rule: Tentative Conclusions about Uncertain Democracies*, Baltimore, MD: Johns Hopkins University Press.
Parsons, T. (1951) *The Social System,* London: Routledge and Kegan Paul.
Schmitter, P. C. (1975) 'Liberation by Golpe: Retrospective Thoughts on the Demise of Authoritarian Rule in Portugal', *Armed Forces and Society* 2 (1): 5–33. Reprinted in: H. Bienen and D. Morrell (eds.) *Political Participation Under Military Regimes*, Beverly Hills: Sage Publications, 1976.
(1998) 'Some Basic Assumptions about the Consolidation of Democracy', in T. Inoguchi *et al.* (eds.), *The Changing Nature of Democracy*, Tokyo: United Nations University Press.
(1999) 'The democratization of Portugal in its comparative perspective', in F. Rosas (ed.), *Portugal e a Transição para a Democracia (1974–1976)*, Lisboa: Edições Colibri/Fundação Mário Soares e Instituto de História Contemporânea da Univ. Nova de Lisboa.

—— (2001) 'Parties Are Not What They Once Were,' in L. Diamond and R. Gunther (eds.), *Political Parties and Democracy*, Baltimore, MD: Johns Hopkins University Press.

Stepan, A. (ed.) (1973) *Authoritarian Brazil: Origins, Policies and Future,* New Haven: Yale University Press.

chapter seven | Seymour Martin Lipset: Modernisation, Social Structure and Political Culture as Factors in Democratic Thought

Ursula Hoffmann-Lange

INTRODUCTION

Seymour Martin Lipset was doubtlessly one of the foremost social scientists of the 20th Century, 'who has shaped, arguably more than any other contemporary social scientist, the study of the conditions, values, and institutions of democracy in the United States and throughout the world' (Marks 1995: 765). His contributions to political science and sociology are outstanding. He is the only person to have served as both president of the American Sociological Association (1992–93) and the American Political Science Association (1979–80). He was also president or vice president of numerous other American and international professional associations, e.g. the International Society of Political Psychology, the World Association for Public Opinion Research, and the Society for Comparative Research. His professional activities attest to the broad spectrum of Lipset's academic interest, spanning areas from comparative politics to social stratification. Lipset received numerous honours, e.g. fellowships at prestigious academic institutions such as the Center for Advanced Study at Stanford, prizes from professional associations, and no less than seven honorary PhDs.

Lipset was born in New York City on 18 March 1922. He studied at the City College of New York where he completed his BA in 1943. He received a Ph.D. from Columbia University in 1949. He held chairs and other academic appointments at several prestigious universities and research schools: at the University of California at Berkeley (1948–50 and 1956-66), Columbia University (1950–56), Harvard University (1965–75), Stanford University (1975–90) and finally George Mason University (1990–2004). He remained active both as a Senior Fellow at the Hoover Institution at Stanford and as Professor at George Mason University until 2001 when he suffered a stroke. He died on 31 December 2006. Upon his death, his eminence as a social scientist was acknowledged in countless obituaries published by newspapers (e.g. *New York Times, Washington Post, Guardian*), academic journals (e.g. *the Journal of Democracy,* 2007) and the institutions at which he had worked and taught (e.g. *Hoover Digest*), praising his contribution to the social sciences and his exceptional personality as an academic mentor for generations of graduate students, many of whom themselves later became noted scholars.

His dissertation on 'Agrarian Socialism' (1950) won Lipset early and wide acclaim in the profession, and some of his subsequent publications became classic texts that are still in print. *Political Man* (1960) is probably Lipset's most widely known political science text. It has been translated into 20 other languages and has sold more than 400,000 copies (Diamond 2007). Among the 24 books that he authored or co-authored are seminal works such as *Union Democracy* (1953, with Martin Trow and James S. Coleman), *Social Mobility in Industrial Society* (1959, with Reinhard Bendix), *The First New Nation* (1963, 1979), *The Politics of Unreason* (1970, with Earl Raab), *Continental Divide* (1990), and *American Exceptionalism* (1996a). His last book, *It Didn't Happen Here; Why Socialism Failed in the United States* (with Gary Marks), was published in 2000.

Two of the 28 books he edited or co-edited have become classics too: *Class, Status and Power* (1953, with Reinhard Bendix), *Party Systems and Voter Alignments* (1967, with Stein Rokkan), as have the four volumes of the *Encyclopedia of Democracy* (1995). In addition to his books, more than 500 articles attest to his enormous productivity.

During his years at Columbia and Berkeley, Lipset became acquainted with other young scholars who themselves later became noted social scientists, among them two with whom he continued a life-long collaboration: Juan Linz and Reinhard Bendix. With Reinhard Bendix, his colleague at Berkeley, he co-authored important contributions to the theory of social stratification and mobility, and with Juan Linz he co-edited several volumes on politics and democracy in developing countries. He also worked with other preeminent scholars such as James Coleman, Larry Diamond, David Riesman, Stein Rokkan, Neil Smelser and Martin Trow. All of these scholars defy a simple classification as either sociologists or political scientists. Instead, they have emphasised the interrelations between social structure, political institutions and culture. It is therefore not surprising that Lipset played an important role in two organisations that have been instrumental to the development of political sociology. The first is the Bureau of Applied Social Research at Columbia University (now the Institute for Social and Economic Research and Policy, ISERP), founded by Paul Lazarsfeld in 1941[1]. The other is the joint Research Committee on Political Sociology of IPSA and ISA, co-founded and chaired by Lipset from 1960 to 1970.

Lipset's academic merits have been widely acknowledged (e.g. Marks 1995). On the occasion of Lipset's 70th birthday, Gary Marks and Larry Diamond edited a *Festschrift* honouring Lipset's work, which appeared as a special issue of the *American Behavioral Scientist* in 1992.

Not all of Lipset's work has been purely academic, though. In fact, as a young man he joined the Trotskyist movement and, even after leaving the radical left, he continued to support liberal causes. He was an active member of the Anti-Defamation League, chaired the National Commission of B'nai B'rith Hillel Foundation (1980–83), was Vice Chair of the Center for Peace in the Middle East (1981–1991) and Chair of The United Jewish Appeal (1985–1987). In fact, in his autobiographical sketch (Lipset 1996b) he notes that it was his political activism that made him give up his original intention to become a dentist and to begin studying sociology instead.

Lipset made important contributions to many fields of social science, yet at the same time his work has one single focus: the preconditions, stability and performance of democracy (cf. Marks and Diamond 1992). His preoccupation with the factors that contribute to democratisation and democratic stability began when Lipset was a student and continued to dominate his work for the rest of his life. He realised early on that studying democracy requires a broad comparative perspective. Therefore, he used relevant materials on most world regions, i.e., North America, Latin America, Europe, East Asia, as well as developing countries. However, he not only studied many countries, but also took into account a broad variety of social and political factors that affect the working of democracy:
- socio-economic development
- social stratification and social mobility
- political culture
- intermediary organisations
- social movements
- intellectuals and academics
- political parties
- electoral competition and voting
- political leadership

Lipset's thinking about democracy was deeply influenced by European social scientists. Paul Lazarsfeld was his teacher and doctoral mentor at Columbia University, and much of Lipset's work is grounded in ideas developed by Max Weber, Alexis de Tocqueville, Robert Michels, Joseph Schumpeter, Karl Marx and Aristotle. As a committed young socialist, he started out investigating factors that were conducive to the success of the socialist movement. However, since he was equally committed to democratic principles, he soon realised the fundamental conflict between these two ideals. While working on his dissertation on the Cooperative Commonwealth Federation (CCF), a Marxist socialist movement that came to power in the Canadian province of Saskatchewan in the 1930s, he concluded that the discrepancy between the socialist programme and the pragmatic policies pursued by the CCF was the inevitable result of democratic politics, which require political parties to appeal to a broad constituency and to work out compromises with economically powerful groups (Schwartz 1998).

Lipset's methodological approach may be characterised as empirically informed social theory. Throughout his long career, he made ample use of empirical data. However, he was never an empirical researcher in the sense of devoting most of his time to data collection and data analysis, at least not after leaving Columbia University in 1956. His empirical books were all written with co-authors who, it seems, took responsibility for the data part of these projects. Lipset himself used empirical data primarily as supporting evidence for his theoretical arguments.

Since it is virtually impossible to provide a comprehensive overview of the broad range of topics covered by Lipset's work, the following account is necessarily selective and subjective. Nevertheless, it illustrates the broad scope of his scholarly interests and highlights some of the important theoretical insights he contributed to the advancement of the social sciences in the second half of the 20th century.

REQUISITES OF DEMOCRACY: SOCIO-ECONOMIC DEVELOPMENT, EFFECTIVENESS, AND LEGITIMACY

Socio-Economic Development and Democracy
In his seminal article on 'Some Social Requisites of Democracy: Economic Development and Political Legitimacy' which was first published in the *American Science Review* in 1959 and reprinted in *Political Man*, Lipset put forward the idea of a direct relationship between socio-economic development and democracy. To demonstrate the validity of his assumption, he studied the effects of several indicators:
– standard of living: per capita income, access to medical care, motorisation
– access to communication media: telephones, radios, newspaper circulation
– industrialisation: workforce in agriculture, energy consumption
– education: literacy and level of formal education
– urbanisation

Lipset compared stable democracies to unstable democracies and dictatorships in two groups of countries, the first group being Europe and the English-speaking world, the second Latin America. He demonstrated substantial differences between democratic and non-democratic countries in both regions with respect to the above indicators. In trying to account for the statistical relationship he had found, Lipset argued that it was not wealth as such, but rather two factors that are closely associated with economic development, i.e. the more equitable distribution of the national income in developed societies and the higher level of formal education. Both of them foster values of political moderation and tolerance.

The expectation that socio-economic modernisation would more or less automatically lead to democratisation was later thrown into doubt by other authors who pointed out that the relationship between economic development and democracy is not as close as Lipset had assumed. Japan and Germany before

1945 were powerful counter-examples, as well as the communist countries of central eastern Europe which enjoyed fairly high levels of socio-economic development and yet remained firmly under the grip of a totalitarian regime (e.g. Lepsius 1969). In *The Third Wave*, summarising the empirical findings of the last decades, Samuel Huntington stated that many different variables had been shown to influence democratisation (1991: 37). He therefore concluded that no single factor is sufficient to explain the development of democracy and that the 'causes of democratisation differ substantially from one place to another and from one time to another' (1991: 38). According to Huntington, socio-economic development was a decisive factor only in the first wave of democratisation. For the second wave, political and military factors (occupation by the Western Allies and decolonisation) were more important, while for the third wave, starting in 1975, 'declining legitimacy and the performance dilemma' were decisive (1991: 46ff.). Huntington concludes: 'Economic factors have significant impact on democratisation but they are not determinative. An overall correlation exists between the level of economic development and democracy yet no level or pattern of economic development is in itself either necessary or sufficient to bring about democratisation' (1991: 59).

The views of Huntington and Lipset are not incompatible, though. It is obvious that statistical explanations are probabilistic rather than deterministic, and Huntington's analysis of the relationship between economic development and democratisation confirms rather than disclaims Lipset because Huntington's data show that the bulk of the democratisations of the third wave occurred at an intermediate level of socio-economic development. However, Lipset's assumption of a simple relationship between the two factors requires some qualification. Huntington's detailed analysis suggests that socio-economic development should primarily be considered as a facilitating factor while other factors play a role as well (1991: 62).

In his 1992 article for Lipset's *Festschrift*, Larry Diamond states that Lipset's assertion of a direct relationship between economic development and democracy has been subjected to extensive empirical examination, both quantitative and qualitative, and that these studies have generally supported the existence of a strong causal relationship, even though that relationship is not as linear as Lipset implied and has also varied across periods. Moreover, although the evidence confirms that GNP remains the single most important predictor of democracy, Diamond argues that the Human Development Index (HDI), which primarily relies on educational level and life expectancy, has higher explanatory power. Diamond therefore recommends a modest reformulation of Lipset's thesis in the following way: 'The more well-to-do the people of a country, on average, the more likely they will favor, achieve, and maintain a democratic system for their country' (1992: 468). Lipset would probably not mind this reformulation because it is perfectly compatible with his way of reasoning. In fact, he himself emphasised the existence of a close link between education and democratic political culture.

The evolutionary theory of democracy developed by Tatu Vanhanen (1997 and 2003) has likewise built on Lipset's prior work. He assumed that it is the decentralisation of power resources rather than economic development that is the main causal factor facilitating the development of democracy. While the two are empirically closely associated, Vanhanen argues that the decentralisation of power resources is the more fundamental factor:

> When the level of economic development rises, various economic resources usually become more widely distributed and the number of economic interest groups increases. Thus the underlying factor behind the positive correlation between the level of economic development and democracy is in the distribution of power resources. Economic development is only a special case of the underlying causal factor (resource distribution). (1997: 25)

It is worth noting that Vanhanen's *Index of Power Resources* includes many variables Lipset had already included in his 1959 essay, i.e., urbanisation, industrialisation, literacy, and the percentage of citizens with university education. Empirically, Vanhanen goes further than Lipset, though, by measuring the distribution of power resources directly with three indices: occupational diversification, knowledge distribution and the distribution of economic power resources. Thus, Vanhanen has actually used most of Lipset's requisites of democracy in his study. His index can therefore be considered as a straightforward operationalisation of what Lipset had in mind.[2]

MARKET ECONOMY

Lipset always argued that a market economy is an important precondition of democracy. 'The fewer economic resources the state can directly control, the greater the possibilities for a free polity' (1994: 3). If the economy is controlled by political elites, political power becomes the only source of status and wealth which in turn will foster political corruption. Moreover, Lipset also emphasised that the existence of a free market economy was a relevant factor for the early institutionalisation of democracy in the United States:

> In the late eighteenth and early nineteenth century world, democratisation had its best chance for success in the United States. There the links between the polity and the economy were much more limited and truncated than anywhere else, thus satisfying another major condition for democracy. The elites did not get their economic advantages from a powerful controlling state, but rather from the land and other possessions. (Lipset 1998: 2)

This quotation also demonstrates that Lipset later abandoned the socialist ideals of his youth.

EFFECTIVENESS AND LEGITIMACY

Lipset's analysis of effectiveness and legitimacy as preconditions of democratic stability, analysed in another chapter of *Political Man*, is probably as well-known as his chapter on the social requisites of democracy. At the beginning of this chapter, Lipset defines effectiveness as the ability of the political system to 'satisfy the basic functions of government as most of the population and such powerful groups within it as big business or the armed forces see them' (1960: 77), i.e., the ability of governments to accommodate the demands of different subgroups and strata within the citizenry. Later on in the book, however, Lipset uses a much narrower concept of effectiveness, as the following quotation shows:

> In the modern world, such effectiveness means primarily constant economic development. Those nations which have adapted most successfully to the requirements of an industrial system have the fewest internal political strains, and have either preserved their traditional legitimacy or developed strong new symbols. (1960: 82)

Thus, he redefines effectiveness as primarily involving successful economic policy, and this is also how the concept of effectiveness has been understood ever since.[3]

Lipset's analysis of the relationship between effectiveness and legitimacy has become conventional wisdom in the social sciences. His famous fourfold table identifies four different types of polities (1960: 81):

	Effectiveness +	Effectiveness −
Legitimacy +	A	B
Legitimacy −	C	D

Consolidated democracies (A) (United States, Sweden, and Britain) are high on both effectiveness and legitimacy. Polities lacking in both (D) are inherently unstable und prone to breaking down unless upheld by force, such as Communist Hungary or the German Democratic Republic. Austria and Germany during the 1920s are mentioned as examples of relatively effective democracies which lacked legitimacy (C) because their systems of government were not held to be 'legitimate by large and powerful segments of its [their] population' (1960: 81). Societies of type C, however, may eventually develop into consolidated democracies, since 'prolonged effectiveness over a number of generations may give legitimacy to a political system' (1960: 82). Lipset thus assumed that effectiveness may engender legitimacy in the long run, and he hoped that this would be the path followed by new democracies: 'In large measure, the survival of the new political democracies of Asia and Africa will depend on their ability to meet the needs of their populations over a prolonged period, which will probably mean their ability to cope with industrialisation' (1960: 82ff.).

Type B is particularly interesting because high legitimacy is presumed to function as a safety valve, stabilising democracies even in times of poor economic performance or other crises: 'When the effectiveness of various governments broke down in the 1930s, those societies which were high on the scale of legitimacy remained democratic, while such countries as Germany, Austria, and Spain lost their freedom, and France narrowly escaped a similar fate' (1960: 82). Even though Lipset did not provide any examples of this type, it can be assumed that he had the country examples of type A in mind which had also been deeply affected by the Great Depression without suffering from severe political crises.

SOCIAL STRUCTURE

Being a social scientist and not an economist, Lipset did not believe that economic factors had a direct effect on the political order. Instead, he emphasised their indirect effects. He considered industrialisation and economic success as only two among several factors to be taken into account in analyses of democratic development and emphasised that the social concomitants of industrialisation are more immediately related to democracy, among them urbanisation, rising levels of education, the rise of a large middle class and a decrease in economic inequality.

SOCIO-ECONOMIC DEVELOPMENT AND SOCIAL STRATIFICATION

In his writings on social stratification, Lipset argued that the existence of a large middle class, educational opportunities and a high level of social mobility are important preconditions for a democratic polity, an idea he traced back to Aristotle, Montesquieu, Locke, and Hobbes. These attributes of modernisation first materialised in the United States and have contributed to America's role as a leader in modernity until today. At the same time, the development of the United States has also disproved the expectation of Marxist theorists that the United States as the economically most advanced country would lead the rest of the world on its road to socialism. In his 2001 article, 'The Decline of Class Ideologies. The End of Political Exceptionalism?', Lipset claims that,

> the continued inability of socialists to create a viable movement in the United States was a major embarrassment to Marxist theorists, who assumed that the superstructure of a society, which encompasses political behavior, is a function of the underlying economic and technological systems. (2001: 251).

Lipset concluded that only the first part of this prediction turned out to be correct. While social and political developments in the United States have indeed always preceded those in other countries, the assumption that industrialisation would inevitably lead to socialism was far from the mark.

Lipset went on to state that the second part of the Marxist assumption was not only erroneous, but predicted the opposite of what had actually happened. Instead of a continued growth of the working class and a deepening of economic inequalities, the distribution of income and occupational skills has changed from a pyramidal shape (▲) to one that resembles a diamond (♦). This, in turn, has forced the political parties of the left to appeal to the growing middle strata rather than limiting their efforts to the declining numbers of industrial workers (2001: 253). Lipset also linked the decreasing membership figures of labour unions and the declining class consciousness in the socio-economically most advanced societies to these changes in social stratification.

The changing class structure is closely associated with rising levels of social mobility. As traditional class barriers break down, opportunities for social mobility increase. Even the members of the less privileged strata become less class conscious than before and believe in individual rather than collective social advancement. Therefore, leftist parties are increasingly forced to emphasise equal opportunities rather than redistribution:

> In the past, Socialist parties created extensive welfare states that required a steadily increasing proportion of the gross domestic product to go to the government, in some cases reaching over one-half. Today, however, the same parties recognise that they simply cannot compete on the world market unless they reduce government expenditures. Their electoral situation forces them to press for the voter support of the middle-class and affluent skilled workers and high tech employees. (2001: 260)

Thus, the 'Old World Left' is no longer serving as a model for the American Left, but instead 'is now becoming more like the American' (2001: 262).

Lipset further assumed that social mobility is at least indirectly related to democracy, because it implies that meritocratic rather than ascriptive factors become the main determinants of social status. At the same time, equality of opportunity is a central tenet of a democratic political order. Moreover, Lipset argued that the belief in the meritocratic character of society increases the probability that individuals will accept even a high degree of economic inequality. In his introduction to the paperback edition of *The First New Nation* (1979), Lipset cited a study by Robert Hauser which showed that the rates of social mobility have always been much higher in the United States than in other countries, thus confirming the meritocratic character of the United States.

However, Lipset was never an uncritical observer of his own country. Until the 1970s, he repeatedly criticised the fact that certain segments of the American population were deprived of equal life chances and that 'the promise of equality remains a mockery for many mature blacks and women, as well as for members of some ethnic minorities, particularly American Indians and persons of Spanish origin' (1979: *xxix*). In later publications, however, he acknowledged considerable improvements in the situation of African Americans since the 1960s. At the same time, he also argued against the introduction of quotas for hiring minorities as a means of achieving equality of opportunity because he thought that quotas were not only incompatible with the emphasis on individual responsibility, which is deeply engrained in American culture, but were in fact counter-productive:

> Yet, the repeated emphasis on how little progress has been made serves to sustain the argument that purposeful social action designed to benefit blacks simply does not work, that there are factors inherent in the black situation which prevent them from getting ahead. Not only most whites, but many blacks have absorbed such negative self-images. Americans believe that what determines success or failure is hard work, regardless of whether a person is black or white. Hence if blacks fail, it follows that it is largely their own fault. (1996a: 132)

Instead, Lipset recommended measures which he considered to be more in line with American political culture than affirmative action programmes:

> To rebuild the national consensus on civil rights and racial justice, affirmative action should be refocused, not discarded. It is clear, for example, that quotas of special preferences will not help the poorly educated and unskilled to secure good jobs. [...] To succeed in postindustrial society requires good education. Extending and vastly improving education in the ghettos, from very early Head Start Programs, to financial incentives for students, teachers, and successful schools, to expanding apprentice programs that combine classroom instruction and on-the-job training, are the directions to be followed for children and school-age youth. (1996a: 149)

These quotes also confirm that Lipset had two different reasons for analysing the situation of African Americans in the United States, a practical and a scholarly one. It was already mentioned that as a young man he was a committed human rights activist. Even later, he continued publicly to denounce perceived violations of civil liberties. As a scholar, he was interested in studying the effects of policies designed to improve the living conditions of underprivileged groups. He compared, for instance, the different conceptual approaches to removing social barriers for underprivileged segments of the population in the United States and continental Europe. While the American culture emphasises equal rights and educational opportunities, the European culture has for long been preoccupied with relieving poverty. Lipset claimed that this cultural difference explains the fundamentally different approaches to welfare policies in the United States and Europe and is also the reason why American welfare expenditures are much lower and poverty levels much higher than in other highly industrialised countries (1996a: 72ff.).

Lipset explicitly distinguished three aspects of economic inequality: access to education and consumer goods, distribution of wealth and distribution of income. He acknowledged that access to education and to consumer goods has improved in the United States, thus providing more opportunities for the social and political participation of the lower classes. At the same time, 'the variations in *income* in the United States are among the highest in the world' (1979: 326). Lipset considered large inequalities in income as justifiable on meritocratic grounds, while he believed that gross inequality in access to educational opportunities inhibits democratic development. With respect to the distribution of wealth, he stated that democratic societies are characterised by a more equitable distribution than non-democratic societies. However, he did not attempt to specify just how much economic inequality a democracy can sustain.

EDUCATION

For Lipset, the education system was important for two reasons: because of its contribution to economic success, and because it provides the most important basis for the application of meritocratic criteria for the attainment of social status in society. He emphasised that the United States has always spent a higher percentage of its GDP on education than other developed nations, 'while Europe has devoted more resources to welfare' (1996a: 117). Moreover, Lipset argued that the United States has always been far ahead of other nations in terms of literacy and in the percentage of young people attending institutions of higher education. He considered such higher investments in the education system as a means to make up for lower welfare expenditures, and claimed, at least implicitly, that the former will eventually contribute more to the general welfare of the country than the latter. Moreover, access to educational opportunities was for him a major precondition for high levels of social mobility since education is closely associated with social status.

CROSS-CUTTING CLEAVAGES

In their introduction to the *Festschrift* for Lipset, Gary Marks and Larry Diamond emphasise that the notion of cross-cutting cleavages, reducing the intensity of political conflict is one of Lipset's 'enduring contributions to our understanding of democratic stability' (1992: 355). In *Political Man*, Lipset developed this argument in the context of a broader theory of political development, stating that the differences in the political development of Western nations depended, to a significant degree, on the historical sequence in which these nations had to cope with three fundamental issues:
- the place of religion within the nation

- the admission of the lower strata to full political and economic citizenship and the right of collective bargaining
- the continued struggle over the distribution of wealth.

Were these issues dealt with one by one, with each more or less solved before the next arose, or did the problems accumulate, so that traditional sources of cleavage mixed with newer ones? Resolving tensions one at a time contributes to a stable political system; carrying over issues from one historical period to another makes for a political atmosphere characterised by bitterness and frustration rather than tolerance and compromise. (1960: 83)

Lipset argued that the moderating effect of cross-cutting cleavages is also confirmed by behavioral studies showing that individuals or groups who are isolated from people with other points of view are more prone to back extremist movements, e.g. workers in isolated industries and farmers. He specifically referred to electoral studies that had provided evidence that individuals under cross-pressure are less likely to vote and to develop political commitments. Lipset acknowledged that the assumption of a moderating effect of cross-pressure had been developed by others, giving credit to Georg Simmel's analysis of intersecting social circles, to the electoral studies of Paul Lazarsfeld (cf. Lazarsfeld *et al.* 1944; Berelson *et al.* 1954) and to pluralist theoreticians such as David Truman and Robert Dahl. Nevertheless, given the enormous impact of *Political Man* as a political science text, it is fair to say that Lipset popularised the idea that cross-cutting cleavages contribute to promoting democratic stability:

> Multiple and politically inconsistent affiliations, loyalties, and stimuli reduce the emotion and aggressiveness involved in political choice [...]. The available evidence suggests that the chances for stable democracy are enhanced to the extent that groups and individuals have a number of cross-cutting, politically relevant affiliations. To the degree that a significant proportion of the population is pulled among conflicting forces, its members have an interest in reducing the intensity of political conflict (1960: 88ff.).

THE ROLE OF VOLUNTARY ASSOCIATIONS

Lipset was not the first scholar to emphasise the relevance of intermediary organisations to democracy. Nevertheless, *Union Democracy* (1956) was certainly the first detailed study of the internal structure of a labour union. This seminal study was carried out at the Bureau of Applied Social Research in collaboration with Martin Trow and James Coleman. Lipset's decision to study the International Typographical Union (ITU) was because of its peculiar structure. The ITU differed from other labour unions by its fairly high level of rank-and-file involvement in union affairs that was in turn facilitated by a wealth of opportunities for informal communication among its members. It maintained social clubs, sport clubs, veterans' groups etc. Last, but not least, the ITU was set apart by the existence of an internal two-party system, i.e., two well-established, though not formally recognised factions competing regularly in intra-organisational elections. The decision to study the ITU also had an autobiographical reason, as Lipset explained in his memoirs, since his father was a member of the ITU. So Lipset had learned about this peculiar labour union already as a child (cf. Lipset 1996b).

Union Democracy is at once a case study and much more than just that. It can be considered as a major contribution to democratic theory with respect to two fundamental aspects, the role of voluntary associations and the question of intra-organisational democracy.

VOLUNTARY ASSOCIATIONS AND DEMOCRACY

With regard to the first aspect, *Union Democracy* explicitly builds on the theory of pluralist democracy and its complement, the theory of mass society. Later studies of voluntary associations focussed on other aspects instead, e.g. corporatism or the integration of associations into networks of political power. It was only in the 1990s that academic interest in the role of voluntary associations, as an essential element for democratic polities, was revived, mainly as a consequence of two independent political developments: the breakdown of state socialism in Eastern Europe, and the dwindling membership figures of traditional voluntary associations in post-industrial democracies. Since the 1990s, numerous publications on the relevance of civil society have appeared. While not explicitly referring to *Union Democracy*, two of Robert Putnam's recent books have emphasised the importance of voluntary associations, i.e., *social capital*, for the viability of democracy (1993 and 2000).

Given the renewed interest in the role of voluntary associations, it is worthwhile re-reading *Union Democracy*, as one will be surprised how many of the arguments regarding the beneficial effects of a functioning civil society can already be found there. *Union Democracy* emphasises that voluntary associations serve two important functions:
- 'external power functions': they foster the development of political opposition within the larger community by serving as arenas for generating new ideas, as communication networks, as a basis for the training of future leaders, and as a basis of opposition to the central authority;
- 'internal functions': they generate political involvement among their members. (1956: 89ff.)

Voluntary associations therefore contribute to the integration of their members into the wider community. The authors of *Union Democracy* distinguished three different types of societies with respect to political mobilisation:

A. *Nonexistence of secondary organizations*, or a *mass society*, helps maintain a *conservative oligarchy*, such as is found in South American dictatorships, in Europe before the nineteenth century, or in the average stable trade union

B. *Existence of secondary organisations*
  1. *controlled* by the government helps maintain *revolutionary totalitarianism*, intent on making changes within the society which it governs, as in Nazi Germany or Soviet Russia
  2. *independent* of the government helps maintain *democracy*, such as is found within the ITU or in the United States or most European democracies. (1956: 89)

The second type of society was characteristic of central-eastern European countries before 1990. The existing *mass organisations* with more or less compulsory membership primarily served the purpose of mass mobilisation under tight control of the state. Since they did not enjoy much autonomy, they were unable to serve as a basis for independent citizen activity and for the political mobilisation of opposition. The United States, on the other hand, has always belonged to the third type of country. Already in the first half of the 19th century, Tocqueville emphasised the role of the rich associational life in the United States as a distinguishing characteristic of American Society. This is also the reason why Robert Putnam, in *Bowling Alone* (2000), has expressed concern about the potentially devastating effects of the decline in *social capital* for the future of American democracy.

INTRA-ORGANISATIONAL DEMOCRACY

Union Democracy also analysed the causes of the formation and continued stability of intra-organisational democracy in the ITU. The authors explicitly referred to Michels' *iron law of oligarchy* and tried to identify the reasons why the ITU was not dominated by an oligarchic leadership that was so characteristic of most other mass organisations. They identified a number of causes, some of them due to the peculiar working conditions of printers at the time, some of a more general nature. In particular, the following specific conditions of the occupational community of printers were discussed in the book:

- printers enjoyed a high prestige among blue-collar workers, and high prestige in turn provides a motivation to socialise with colleagues;
- the printing industry's system of hiring additional workers on an ad hoc basis among those who were present at the beginning of shifts, forced printers who were looking for a job to show up and spend time at the local union premises;
- the frequency of night work fostered the development of informal social relations among the workers. (1956: 158)

Moreover, the ITU had also developed a democratic organisational culture. The existence of a two-party system was widely accepted within the ITU, even though it was not officially acknowledged in the union statutes. At the same time, there was agreement among the members that the two-party system did not weaken the effective representation of the printers' interests vis-à-vis employers.

Another important factor was the creation of the ITU from below, i.e., the central organisation was only founded after strong local and regional branches had already been in existence. At the same time, however, the authors emphasised that the development of democracy in the ITU was by no means an inevitable result of structural factors:

> Democracy in the ITU was thus no necessary consequence of a particular set of static factors, but rather was favoured from the beginning by numerous factors and even more strongly favoured as time went on and numerous events added to the systems's stability. (1956: 441)

The authors therefore concluded that structural factors only determine, the probabilities that given historical events can result in an enduring institutional pattern such as a two-party system. Social structure thus constitutes a *potential* for democracy, a potential which, however, may be realised only under certain historical circumstances. (1956: 447ff.)

Ultimately, *Union Democracy* confirmed three basic tenets of democratic theory. First, that the development of democracy is always the result of a combination of favourable structural conditions and facilitating situational factors. Second, that once established, democracy is likely to become self-perpetuating. Last, but not least, that the institutionalisation of party competition is a decisive factor in the continued functioning of (intra-organisational) democracy.

More than fifty years after it was first published, *Union Democracy* remains a classic text worth reading.[4] It is at the same time a detailed case study based on empirical data, and a theoretical study. Even following decades of empirical social research, the availability today of more refined research instruments and much more convenient techniques for data analysis, the book can be considered as an exemplary academic study, combining a historical analysis of the ITU, a structural analysis of the working conditions of the printing craft, and an analysis of two surveys of printers and local union officials. The book abounds with tables and graphs documenting the empirical evidence, and includes a detailed methodological appendix, describing sampling procedures and index construction. Even though the ITU has long ceased to exist, the insights gained by the study are of lasting theoretical importance.

POLITICAL PARTIES

Since Lipset considered electoral competition as a central characteristic of democracy, he also wrote extensively on political parties. In *The First New Nation*, he analysed how the fundamental precondition for a competitive party system, the acceptance of organised opposition, developed in the United States. As in other new democracies that came into existence through a revolutionary process, the American founding fathers were united by their desire for independence from (British) colonial rule. Soon after achieving independence, however, unity gave way to the development of conflicts over how the country should be governed. Such a development is not uncommon, as Joseph Ellis notes in his book, *Founding Brothers*:

> With the American Revolution, as with all revolutions, different factions came together in common cause to overthrow the reigning regime, then discovered in the aftermath of their triumph that they had fundamentally different and politically incompatible notions of what they intended. (Ellis 2002: 15)

Lipset analysed the early appearance of organised political parties in the United States and identified the unwillingness of the Federalists to accept their role as opposition party in the emerging two-party system as the main reason for their demise.

Besides emphasising the fundamental importance of party competition, Lipset also studied the relevance of political cleavages. In collaboration with Stein Rokkan he analysed the cleavage structures that became decisive for the formation of western European party systems. They co-edited the volume *Party Systems and Voter Alignments* (1967), and their comprehensive co-authored introductory chapter to that volume has become a classic text on European party systems. Even today, political scientists working on political parties continue to refer to that chapter. However, while it can be assumed that Lipset was genuinely interested in the questions analysed in that volume, he was not a Europeanist, and it is probably fair to conclude that the basic ideas developed in the introductory chapter were those of Rokkan rather than Lipset. Yet, Lipset's academic reputation probably contributed a great deal to its success in the United States.

POLITICAL CULTURE

Political culture features prominently in Lipset's work. In *Political Man*, Lipset devoted several chapters to questions of democratic legitimacy, working-class authoritarianism, support for fascist movements, and voting behaviour. Moreover, Lipset's books on the United States and American Exceptionalism were primarily devoted to analysing the peculiarities of American political culture, i.e. religious traditions, individualism, and support for equality of opportunity. It seems remarkable, therefore, that although *Political Man* was published three years before *The Civic Culture* (Almond and Verba 1963), Almond and Verba developed their ideas without reference to Lipset's work. In the index of *The Civic Culture*, Lipset is only mentioned twice. Thus, despite the fact that these authors studied similar research questions, they largely ignored each other's work.

THE ROLE OF SECULAR RELIGION IN THE UNITED STATES

In his writings on *American Exceptionalism*, Lipset repeatedly emphasised the peculiarities of American religiosity. First and foremost he mentioned the contrast between the enormous importance Americans have always attributed to religion and the religious pluralism of American society. He argued that it was precisely the co-existence of numerous religious communities which led to the decision to include the principle of a strict separation of state and church in the American constitution. Religion was thereby explicitly defined as a private matter, thus precluding any interference of the government in religious activities. At the same time, it also required tolerance vis-à-vis other religions (1979: 155).[5]

Lipset claimed that the separation of church and state reinforces democratic practices in three ways. First, American churches have always been purely voluntary organisations which in turn requires churches to cater to the demands of their local supporters:

> The withdrawal of government support from religion made American Protestantism unique in the Christian world. The United States became the first nation in which religious groups were viewed as purely voluntary associations. To exist, American churches had to compete in the marketplace for support. (1979: 160)

Secondly, the Protestant sects prevalent in the United States were mostly congregationalist and practiced self-government: 'Congregationalism, with its stress on self-government within the church, contributed to secular self-government in the form of the New England town meeting' (1979: 160). Congregationalist ministers were therefore more supportive of the American revolution than the established churches (Episcopalian and Catholic) which tended to side with the Tories.

A third characteristic of American religiosity is the emphasis on individual morality:

> American Protestantism, with its emphasis on the personal achievement of grace, reinforced the stress on personal achievement which was dominant in the secular value system. Both sets of values stressed individual responsibility, both rejected hereditary status. (1979: 162)

Religious doctrines therefore reinforced the *anti-aristocratic tendencies* in American society, and the emphasis on the personal attainment of grace has been 'the religious parallel to the secular emphasis on equality of opportunity' (1979: 163).

However, Lipset also argued that American religion has problematic implications for American foreign policy. It implies something Lipset called *utopian moralism*, which stands in stark contrast to the tolerance that is otherwise characteristic of the American political culture (1990: 76ff.):

> The need to assuage the sense of personal responsibility has meant that Americans have been particularly wont to support movements for the elimination of evil by violent means if necessary. (1979: 163)

Lipset argued that it fosters a propensity for moralistic crusades and an inclination to denounce the other side as being an agent of Satan:

> Americans have been unique in their emphasis on non-recognition of 'evil' foreign regimes. The principle is related to the insistence that wars must end with the unconditional surrender of the Satanic enemy. The United States rarely sees itself merely defending national interests. Foreign conflicts invariably involve a battle of good versus evil. (1990: 78ff.)

Lipset thought that this millennialism inherent in the American *civic religion* helps explain a pervasive feature of American foreign policy that has always been difficult to understand for Europeans who tend to view foreign policy as something to be handled pragmatically.

INDIVIDUALISM, EGALITARIANISM, ACHIEVEMENT, AND MERITOCRATIC VALUES

Throughout his writings on American political culture, Lipset emphasised that individualism is the most distinctive value of American political culture. Lipset devoted most of his book, *Continental Divide,* to analysing the differences between a revolutionary nation based on individualistic values (USA) and a counter-revolutionary nation that has never overcome a preoccupation with deference towards traditional authorities and collectivism (Canada). The book analyses the implications of this basic difference for a broad variety of social and political phenomena, e.g. constitutional provisions, the judicial system, the economy, the treatment of minorities, social policies, welfare policies, etc.

In his analysis of American exceptionalism, Lipset repeatedly stated that the 'emphasis on competitive individualism' has been responsible for the enormous economic success of the United States (1996a: 58):

> The United States, almost from its start, has had an expanding economic system. The nineteenth-century American economy, as compared to the European ones, was characterised by more market freedom, more individual landownership, and a higher wage income structure – all sustained by the national classical liberal ideology. From the Revolution on, it was the laissez-faire country par excellence. Unlike the situation in many European

countries, in which economic materialism was viewed by the traditional aristocracy and the church as conducive to vulgar behavior and immorality, in the United States hard work and economic ambition were perceived as the proper activity of a moral person. (1996a: 54)

Egalitarianism and achievement are two other American values responsible for the uniqueness of the United States. Egalitarianism is mainly understood as equality before the law, egalitarian social relations and equality of opportunity. Lipset concurred with Tocqueville's observation that 'regardless of steep inequalities, Americans did not require the lower strata to acknowledge their inferiority' (1990: 24). This implies that status differences do not play much of a role in social interactions. Moreover, the emphasis on egalitarian social relations also explains the lack of deference towards persons of high status or public authorities (1979: 211). Lipset claimed that it is the combination of individualism, egalitarianism and emphasis on achievement that has contributed to the acceptance of a free market economy and considerable inequality of income in the United States.

Lipset saw the contradictory nature of these two values as constituting the basis of the political conflict between liberals and conservatives who attribute different priorities to them. While liberals stress egalitarianism and the 'social injustice that flows from unfettered individualism', conservatives tend to 'enshrine individual freedom and the social need for mobility and achievement as values "endangered" by the collectivism inherent in liberal nostrums' (1979: *xxxiii*).

In his book on *American Exceptionalism*, Lipset also analysed the downside of the American emphasis on achievement, i.e., higher crime rates and lower government support for the underprivileged. He explained the high crime rate in the United States by referring to Robert Merton, his teacher at Columbia University, who had developed the idea that a discrepancy between valued ends and a lack of legal means to achieve those ends, may result in anomie and deviant behaviour: 'The greater lawlessness and corruption in the United States can also be attributed in part to a stronger emphasis on achievement' (1990: 94).[6]

POLITICAL MODERATION AND POLITICAL EXTREMISM

Lipset considered political moderation to be a result of the modernisation process and an important factor of democratic stability. He claimed that political moderation and tolerance are fostered by two concomitants of the modernisation process, education and cross-cutting cleavages. In *Political Man,* he provided empirical evidence for the positive effect of education on social and political tolerance (1960: 56 and 109ff.). The close association between education and tolerance has since been confirmed in so many other studies that it can be considered as a kind of social law (e.g. Almond and Verba 1963; Barnes and Kaase 1979; Inglehart 1997).

Another influential chapter of *Political Man* discussed extremist movements.

In '"Fascism" – Left, Right, and Centre' (1960), Lipset advanced a general theory of political extremism, even though the article primarily focused on fascist movements. He began with the assumption that rapid social change contributes to the development of political dissatisfaction and therefore fosters the formation of extremist political movements, which can be seen as 'a response of different strata of the population to the social effects of industrialisation at different stages of its development' (1960 137ff.). 'They appeal to the disgruntled and the psychologically homeless, to the personal failures, the socially isolated, the economically insecure, the uneducated, unsophisticated, and authoritarian persons at every level of society' (1960: 175).

Lipset also argued that members of the old middle class are particularly susceptible to the appeals of right-wing extremist movements because their relative status had declined in the wake of industrialisation and this had fostered feelings of resentment against the modern way of life (1960: 136). Members of the traditional middle class felt threatened by both leftist demands for economic redistribution and their own diminished economic prospects. While Lipset was not the first author to put forward this idea, his essay certainly contributed to its popularisation:

> It is not surprising, therefore, that under certain conditions small businessmen turn to extremist political movements, either fascism or anti-parliamentary populism, which in one way or another express contempt for parliamentary democracy. These movements answer some of the same needs as the more conventional liberal parties; they are an outlet for the stratification strains of the middle class in a mature industrial order. But while liberalism attempts to cope with the problems by legitimate social changes and 'reforms' ('reforms' which would, to be sure, reverse the modernisation process), fascism and populism propose to solve the problems by taking over the state and running it in a way which will restore the old middle classes' economic security and high standing in society, and at the same time reduce the power and status of big capital and big labour. (1960: 137)

POLITICAL LEADERSHIP

Lipset is much less known for his contribution to the theory of political leadership. However, in his book, *The First New Nation* he skillfully analysed George Washington's role as a charismatic leader who was instrumental and probably indispensable in establishing a national authority in the United States. Starting out from Max Weber's distinction between traditional, rational-legal and charismatic authority, Lipset argued that the political institutions of new nations do not normally enjoy a great deal of legitimacy and that they therefore have to rely on charismatic authority as a source of legitimacy. Charismatic authority has several features that make it well suited to the needs of new nations: 'It requires neither time nor a rational set of rules, and is highly flexible' (1979: 18). However, charismatic authority is also inherently unstable and has to give way to rational-legal authority if a young nation is to survive.

Lipset argued that George Washington contributed to engendering faith in the viability of the American constitution. He specifically mentioned four aspects of Washington's leadership that were particularly important in this respect:

1. His prestige was so great that he commanded the loyalty of the leaders of the different factions as well as the general populace. Thus, in a political entity marked by much cleavage he, in his own person, provided a basis for unity.
2. He was strongly committed to the principles of constitutional government and exercised a paternal guidance upon those involved in developing the machinery of government.
3. He stayed in power long enough to permit the crystallisation of factions into embryonic parties.
4. He set a precedent as to how the problem of succession should be managed, by voluntarily retiring from office. (1979: 22ff.)

In this analysis of Washington's role in the consolidation of American democracy, Lipset applied Max Weber's rather abstract theory of charismatic leadership to a concrete example and explained why many new nations fail, even if they have a charismatic leader. This is because most of these leaders fulfill only the first of these four functions.

Modern historiography has confirmed Lipset's evaluation of Washington's role and supports his conclusion that the political institutions of the new American nation were initially so feeble that only a charismatic leader could ensure their survival: 'Without a republican king at the start, [...] the new quasi nation called the United States would never have enjoyed the opportunity to achieve its long-run destiny' (Ellis 2002: 155). Moreover, Ellis has also emphasised that Washington's voluntary retirement was 'crucial in establishing the republican principle of rotation in office' (Ellis 2002: 122).

Lipset's analysis of political leadership underscores once more the importance he attributed to historical contingency. He acknowledged that structural and cultural variables are insufficient for explaining political developments, and that the survival of the United States, as the first new nation, was primarily due to a coincidence of favourable structural conditions and the good fortune to have had a group of political leaders who were capable of creating a workable set of republican institutions that were without precedent at the time.[7]

CONCLUSION

Seymour Martin Lipset was certainly one of the most productive and innovative social scientists of the 20th century. It is hardly possible to overrate his contribution to democratic theory. An analysis of his work shows that Lipset considered democracy as the result of a complex constellation of interrelated factors. He emphasised that socio-economic modernisation fosters the development of a broad middle class and cultural diversity which in turn provide the basis for the development of a democratic political culture. Lipset also studied the sociological and cultural developments associated with modernisation in great depth.

Democratisation and the conditions for stable democracy preoccupied Lipset's thinking for many decades. He developed his basic ideas when he was fairly young and continued to refine them over the years, making them ever more succinct. Most of his basic assumptions have been confirmed by later research and with more elaborate data than was available at the time Lipset developed them. Moreover, the assumptions were also supported by political developments he could not have foreseen. The breakdown of communism in central and eastern Europe is a telling example of the inherent instability of regimes that are low in terms of both political legitimacy and effectiveness.

The reason why Lipset did not have to revise his basic assumptions has to do with the fact that most of his work was devoted to advancing an interrelated set of theoretical ideas and illustrating them with a wealth of empirical data. His ingenuity in collecting supporting evidence from many different countries and sources is awesome. As mentioned at the beginning of this chapter, many of his ideas have become so commonplace that we are hardly aware that Lipset was the first scholar to present them, or at least to phrase them as theoretical propositions in the way that they are still known today.

Notes
1   In his commemoration of Lazarsfeld's 100th birthday, Devitt (2001) hails the ground-breaking studies that came out of the Bureau, which blended several fields of scholarship, such as economics, mathematics, sociology, social psychology, and political science. He specifically mentions *Union Democracy* by Lipset, Trow and Coleman.
2   This is confirmed by Lipset's more recent article 'The Social Requisites of Democracy Revisited', in which he states 'that the more the sources of power, status and wealth are concentrated in the state, the harder it is to institutionalise democracy', because a centralisation of resources implies that 'the political struggle tends to approach a zero-sum game' (1993: 4).
3   However, Lipset himself mentions the case of a well-governed colony as an example of high effectiveness, yet low legitimacy. Thus, the original concept was obviously meant to imply a well-functioning public administration as well.
4   Michael Goldfield (1998) also lauds the book's combination of 'meticulous empirical examination of history and data, with an interest in the broadest of social and political questions.'
5   Lipset argued that this even results in greater tolerance toward irreligion, i.e., agnosticism and atheism (1979: 153ff.).
6   Lipset assumed that egalitarianism also contributes to higher crime rates in the United States: 'Generalised deference is not accorded to the state or those at the top in the United States;

therefore, there is a greater propensity to redefine or ignore the rules' (1990: 94).
7   This is again supported by Ellis who emphasises that the historical actors themselves felt uncertain as regards their ability to establish a new system of government (2002: 9). He explicitly mentions a number of liabilities that made the success of the new nation doubtful. The most important of these was certainly that no one had ever established a republican government on the scale of the United States. Moreover, the country had no common history as a nation. At the same time, the intellectual legacy of the revolution stigmatised a concentration of political power, making it difficult to establish a central authority (Ellis 2002: 11).

REFERENCES

Almond, G. A. and Verba, S. (1963) *The Civic Culture*, Boston: Little, Brown.
Barnes, S. H., Kaase, M. *et al.* (1979) *Political Action; Mass Participation in Five Western Democracies*, Beverly Hills: Sage Publications.
Bendix, R. and Lipset, S. M. (1959) *Social Mobility in Industrial Society*, Berkeley: University of California Press.
Berelson, B., Lazarsfeld P. F., McPhee, W. N. (1954) *Voting*, Chicago: The University of Chicago Press.
Devitt, J. (2001) 'ISERP to Celebrate the Work of Columbia Sociologist Paul F. Lazarsfeld', *Columbia News*.
    www.columbia.edu/cu/news/01/09/lazarsfeld.html
Diamond, L. (1992) 'Economic Development and Democracy Revisited', *American Behavioral Scientist,* 35: 450–99.
    (2007) 'A Giant among Teachers', *Hoover Digest*, No. 1.
Ellis, J. J. (2002) *Founding Brothers; The Revolutionary Generation*, New York: Vintage Books.
Goldfield, M. (1998) 'Lipset's Union Democracy After 40 Years', *Extensions*, Special Orders 98, www.ou.edu/special/albertctr/extensions/sp98/contents.html.
Huntington, S. P. (1991) *The Third Wave; Democratisation in the Late Twentieth Century*, Norman: University of Oklahoma Press.
Inglehart, R. (1997) *Modernisation and Post-Modernisation*, Princeton: Princeton University Press.
Journal of Democracy (2007) 'Seymour Martin Lipset (1922–2006)', *Journal of Democracy,* 18: 185–8.
Lazarsfeld, P. F., Berelson, B. and Gaudet, H. (1944) *The People's Choice*, New York: Duell, Sloan & Pearce.
Lepsius, M. R. (1969) 'Demokratie in Deutschland als Historisch-Soziologisches Problem', in T. W. Adorno (ed.), *Spätkapitalismus oder Industriegesellschaft*, Stuttgart: Enke.
Lipset, S. M. (1950) *Agrarian Socialism*, Berkeley: University of California Press.
    (1960) *Political Man*, London: Heinemann.
    (1979) [1963] *The First New Nation; The United States in Historical*

and Comparative Perspective. Expanded Paperback edition. New York: Norton.

(1990) *Continental Divide; The Values and Institutions of the United States and Canada*, New York: Routledge.

(1993) 'The Social Requisites of Democracy Revisited', *American Sociological Review*, 59: 1–22.

(1996a) *American Exceptionalism; A Double-Edged Sword*, New York: Norton.

(1996b) 'Steady Work; An Academic Memoir', *Annual Review of Sociology*, 22: 1–27 (also available on www.seymourmartinlipset.org).

(1998) 'Excerpts from Three Lectures on Democracy'. (The 1997 Julian J. Rothbaum Distinguished Lecture in Representative Government). *Extensions*, Special Orders 98.www.ou.edu/special/albertctr/extensions/sp98/contents.html

(2001) 'The Decline of Class Ideologies; The End of Political Exceptionalism?', in T. N. Clark and S. M. Lipset (eds.), *The Breakdown of Class Politics; A Debate on Post-Industrial Stratification*, Baltimore: Johns Hopkins Press.

Lipset, S. M. and Bendix, R. (eds.) (1953) *Class, Status and Power; Social Stratification in Comparative Perspective*, Glencoe: The Free Press.

(1966) 'The Field of Political Sociology', in L. A. Coser (ed.), *Political Sociology*, New York: Harper & Row.

Lipset, S. M., Diamond, L. and Linz, J. (eds.) (1995) *Encyclopedia of Democracy*, 4 vols., Boulder: Lynn Rienner.

Lipset, S. M. and Marks, G. (2000) *It Didn't Happen Here; Why Socialism Failed in the United States*, New York: W.W. Norton.

Lipset, S. M. and Raab, E. (1970) *The Politics of Unreason; Extremism in America 1790–1970*, New York: Harper & Row.

Lipset, S. M. and Rokkan, S. (1967) 'Cleavage Structures, Party Systems, and Voter Alignments: An Introduction', in S. M. Lipset and S. Rokkan (eds.), *Party Systems and Voter Alignments; Cross-National Perspectives*, New York: The Free Press.

Lipset, S. M., Trow, M. and Coleman, J. (1956) *Union Democracy*, Garden City: Doubleday (Anchor Books).

Marks, G. (1995) 'Lipset, Seymour Martin', in S. M. Lipset (ed.), *The Encyclopedia of Democracy*, Vol. III., London: Routledge.

Marks, G. and Diamond, L. (1992) 'Seymour Martin Lipset and the Study of Democracy', *American Behavioural Scientist*, 35 (4/5): 352–62.

Putnam, R. D. (1993) *Making Democracy Work*, Princeton: Princeton University Press.

(2000) *Bowling Alone; The Collapse and Revival of American Community*, New York: Simon & Schuster.

Schwartz, M. A. (1998) 'Democracy and Agrarian Socialism', *Extensions*, Special Orders 98. www.ou.edu/special/albertctr/extensions/sp98/contents.html.

Vanhanen, T. (1997) *Prospects of Democracy*, London: Routledge.
    (2003) *Democratisation; A Comparative Analysis of 170 Countries*, London: Routledge.

chapter eight | Giovanni Sartori: Democracy, Parties, Institutions[1]

Gianfranco Pasquino

(RE-)FOUNDING POLITICAL SCIENCE

There was no political science in Italy before Giovanni Sartori. Often identified with three major scholars, the founders of the so-called 'school' of the ruling class – that is, Gaetano Mosca, Vilfredo Pareto, and Roberto Michels – the significance of Italian political science had rapidly disappeared in their passing away, without taking roots in Italian academia.[2] There had been no need for Fascism to get rid of scholars engaged in political analysis of any kind. The Italian situation was not at all comparable with that of Germany where a thriving political science could survive abroad. While Mosca, Pareto, and Michels had had different scholarly affiliations (constitutional law, economics, political thought), they shared one important negative aspect. They left no disciples. Quietly, what had existed of political science in Italy simply withered away without a trace. As a consequence, from the 1930s until the end of the 1950s, the study of political elites and the ruling class school was appropriated fundamentally by historians of political thought and, later on, by a handful of political sociologists. No surprise, then, that Sartori was instrumental in organising an important IPSA colloquium on elites 'I significati del termine "elite"' (Sartori 1961). He also wrote on Michels, 'Democrazia, burocrazia e oligarchia nei partiti' (Sartori 1960). Sartori's degree came from the Facoltà di Scienze Politiche 'Cesare Alfieri' of Florence where he was trained in political philosophy and the theory of the State. He went on to teach courses in Political Science, but no chair was available in that field. Hence, in 1963 he was obliged to win first a chair in Sociology, quickly renamed, so that in 1996 he could become full professor of Political Science at the University of Florence.[3] By that time he had already engaged in a difficult, time-consuming, uphill battle to give Political Science academic recognition and an appropriate place in the Italian university system. He had published several scholarly articles arguing in favour of the specific identity of Political Science and its original contributions to the scientific study of politics, quite different from the knowledge to be acquired through constitutional law, political philosophy (there was not much political theory in Italy at that time), political history, and the sociology of politics. Most of his essays were later reprinted in book form (Sartori 1979) and provide the foundation for his methodological guidelines.

By the end of the 1960s, thanks to the support and prestige of two other important scholars, Norberto Bobbio and Gianfranco Miglio, though themselves not strictly political scientists, the battle for the establishment of autonomous Departments (Facoltà) of Political Sciences was finally won. In the meantime, Sartori had received funding for training young graduate students and had founded the Centro Studi di Politica Comparata where most of the first generation of Italian political scientists were recruited. The first published product of the group was a quite successful collection of important articles: *Antologia di scienza politica* edited by Sartori (1971a) himself who wrote a very provocative introductory essay. A competing centre was established in Turin under the academic supervision of Norberto Bobbio.[4] In 1971 the Centro Studi di Politica Comparata launched the journal *Rivista Italiana di Scienza Politica*. Sartori served as editor for 33 years until the end of 2003 when he donated the journal to the Società Italiana di Scienza Politica (SISP, Italian Political Science Association) whose founding he had strongly encouraged in the late 1960s. Finally, his scholarly organisational commitment culminated in the establishment of the Department of Political and Social Science at the European University Institute (EUI) in Florence (1974–1976). Tired of fighting against the Italian university bureaucracy and disgusted with the way the Italian university system was run, in 1976 Sartori decided to accept the chair in Political Science at Stanford University left vacant by the retirement of Gabriel Almond. After three years, he moved to Columbia to become the Albert Schweitzer Professor in the Humanities, since 1994, Emeritus.

THE AUTHOR OF PATH BREAKING BOOKS

Sartori's strenuous devotion to the inauguration and development of political science was constantly accompanied by a steady flow of conspicuous and important publications. It is often said that even excellent scholars write just one important book in their lifetime and that all subsequent publications constitute fundamentally an elaboration of its dominant theme. This is certainly not so in the case of Sartori's overall intellectual trajectory and his many publications (a distinction he shares with a handful of contemporary political scientists). Moreover, one can easily detect in Sartori's sequence of publications a theoretically consistent and methodologically aware research design. Finally, much before the comparative method became fashionable in political science, though still today rarely convincingly applied and utilised, Sartori formulated the conditions to be respected for meaningful and fertile comparative studies. His very frequently quoted article 'Concept Misformation in Comparative Politics' (Sartori 1970)[5], remains one of the most important readings for all those who engage in comparative analysis and whose aim is the production of significant, competent, and replicable studies. That, indeed, political science could find in the comparative method its own preferable tool for research and theoretical purposes, was also argued by Sartori, in the long and thorough opening article of the *Rivista Italiana di Scienza Politica*: 'La politica comparata: premesse e problemi' (Sartori 1971b), which can be fruitfully complemented by 'Comparing and Miscomparing' (Sartori 1991). Unfortunately, in too many instances, so-called comparative studies are little more than juxtapositions of phenomena, processes, regimes, and political systems that do not contribute much of value to our knowledge of the complexity of politics or help us to make theoretical advances.

Sartori would also remark that the limits of contemporary comparative studies derive to a large extent from two major drawbacks. The first is a poor and inadequate conceptualisation that translates itself into the misleading, when not simply wrong, use of (what is inadequate) political terminology. The most important example is the confusion between 'mobilisation' and 'participation'. The first term indicates a situation in which individuals are, more or less forcefully, constrained, from above or by exogenous phenomena, to act in a less than spontaneous manner. Hence, in a variety of forms, mobilisation characterises non-democratic regimes and refers to what the 'subjects' are allowed, encouraged or obliged to do by the rulers. The second term, participation, belongs to and is practised exclusively in democratic regimes. It is spontaneous and depends on the free will and autonomous decisions of interested citizens. Largely constitutive of democratic situations, participation is the lymph of all democratic regimes, and its quality and quantity determine the excellence of those democracies. Obviously, participation has little affinity with mobilisation. Indeed, in several cases, the two types of activities should be located almost as opposites. A similar attempt at clarifying another important concept whose usefulness was being prematurely denied can be found in the article on 'Totalitarianism' (Sartori 1993).

As this example clearly indicates (and there are others too), the terminology of politics and political science runs the inevitable risk of being/becoming value-laden. For this reason, Sartori launched a complex enterprise to restore the precise meanings of the most important of the political terms: COCTA (Committee on Conceptual and Terminological Analysis). This is one endeavour in which Sartori has most certainly not had the kind of success for which he was hoping. Even the book he edited (Sartori 1984), though containing some remarkable reconstructions of several important political concepts, is very rarely quoted.[6] His own sustained effort in 'cleaning' and defining the most important concepts can be found in a rich and several times enlarged and reprinted book (Sartori 1995).

The second drawback, not just of comparative politics, but of contemporary political science in general, against which Sartori has been fighting, is the premature quantification of political science. Once the terminology and the concepts have been accurately defined, Sartori is not at all opposed to quantification, even though he does not believe that all political phenomena could systematically be better analysed, interpreted, and explained by using mathematical tools and formulae. His overall attitude towards quantification has been precisely stated in a couple of very important sentences: 'Measures are all the more useful and necessary the more we have first identified the problems, mapped the cases, and suggested causal explanations, that is, the more they are entered under well-circumscribed sets of nominal qualifications and assumptions. Words *alone* beat numbers alone. Words *with* numbers beat words alone. And numbers make sense, much greater sense, *within* verbal theory' (1976: 319, original emphasis).

At the time, the 'quantomaniacs' were a visible, though not particularly powerful, group. Subsequently, the supporters of so-called positive political theory emerged, as well as the practitioners of different varieties of rational choice theory who have challenged what they would call traditional political science. Here is not the appropriate occasion for an exhaustive comparison between Sartori's not so traditional contributions and those of the rational choice scholars.

ON DEMOCRACY

For the moment, I will confine myself to a few remarks deriving from those of Sartori's books devoted to the extremely important topic of democracy, which have been surprisingly neglected by rational choice scholars. In fact, Sartori has written four quite different books on democracy: *Democrazia e definizioni* (1957, reprinted several times); *Democratic Theory* (1962, 1965), his own translation and thorough revision of the previous Italian book, *The Theory of Democracy Revisited* (2 volumes 1987); and *Democrazia; Cosa è* (1993, 2007). All these books contain a combination of historical and conceptual, empirical and theoretical material appropriately highlighted and revised for the different audiences, times and problems to be analysed. Just one consideration will suffice.

It is quite a different task to reflect on democracy before and after the collapse of international communism. However, the fundamental problem of the definition of what democracy has been, is, and will be, is of the utmost importance. Here, it is appropriate to illuminate Sartori's position toward Communism and Marxism. His conception of democracy is shaped by an in-depth analysis of the conditions that allow, create, promote, and protect liberty. Hence, Communism must be rejected as a political phenomenon that has curtailed and destroyed liberty. As to Marxism, Sartori rejects it because, on the one hand, it does not constitute a falsifiable theory, according to the criteria suggested by Popper, and, on the other, it fails to give any appreciable space to political factors; worse, it does not recognise the autonomy of politics.

It is difficult to underestimate the amount of historical knowledge, conceptual clarity, innovative theorising that scholars and students can find in Sartori's books on democracy. The success of his 1957 book in Italy (and of the 1962 American translation) can be explained with reference to the fact that Sartori challenged all received wisdom and all manipulative definitions of democracy, especially those that were, in fact, subverting the true meaning of the concept and of reality, such as 'popular democracy', 'guided democracy', and so on. Two elements of his analysis of democracy stand out. The first is that Sartori does not simply offer his interpretation of what democracy is, should be, promises to be, succeeds in being. At all points, he compares his interpretation with those formulated by all the other important scholars in the field, especially the elitists and the 'participationists', highlighting their respective strengths and weaknesses. In addition, building on Schumpeter's 'competitive theory of democracy' and Carl J. Friedrich's 'anticipated reactions', Sartori comes to the formulation of his own theory based on competition and accountability. More precisely, he indicates and shows that the teams of leaders who have entered into an electoral competition with the goal of winning political power will have a vital interest in attempting to remain, both in government and in opposition, accountable to all citizens because they will run again and will want to win office again. In addition, it will be as much in their interest to encourage participation as it will be in the interest of the citizens to decide when, where and how much to participate in order to support one team and to defeat the other team(s) and to communicate their preferences. Therefore, far from being 'elitist', Schumpeter's theory can easily accommodate whatever amount of participation to which the citizens may want to commit themselves and, far from being insulated against citizens' pressures, the winning team and the opposition will keep their eyes and their ears open to the demands coming from the voters because their responsiveness most certainly affects their re-election chances.

The second outstanding element of Sartori's analysis of democracy is grounded in an extremely important dynamic distinction between *real* and *ideal* democracies. There is always a tension between what existing, that is, 'real' democratic regimes can offer and provide to their citizens and what citizens and scholars alike believe that democracy ought to achieve. Aware of this constitutive tension, all scholars are encouraged to analyse democracy both descriptively and prescriptively, utilising clear concepts and precise empirical indicators. Fully recognising the importance of information and of the role of public opinion in the working of contemporary democracies, Sartori has critically examined the role of television in manipulating and debasing political issues and processes, first in a short, poignant article (1989), then in a booklet *Homo Videns* (1997b), translated into several languages. The existence of a wide, well-informed, autonomous public opinion is a hallmark of viable democratic regimes that significantly improves the quality of democratic performance.

ON PARTIES

In modern/contemporary democracies, political competition takes place, as Schumpeter wrote, among teams of elites. Today, those teams have generally all transformed themselves into more or less cohesively organised parties. As a matter of fact, parties remain the dominant component of contemporary democracies. As Elmer E. Schattschneider (1942; 1960) put it several decades ago, all democracies must be, and in practice are, 'party democracies'. Moreover, he would certainly add that party democracies are of superior quality to democracies where parties are weak and not in a position to play a significant, paramount role. It is likely that, for his part, Sartori would agree. Indeed, I am in no doubt that his *Parties and Party Systems* (1976) derived initially and fundamentally from his concern with the working of democracy. He was also motivated by his dissatisfaction – bordering, as he wrote, on unhappiness – with the content of the dominant book in the field: Maurice Duverger's *Political Parties* (1951). In addition, although Italy does not figure prominently in his prize-winning book (Sartori 2004: reprinted in the Classics Series of the European Consortium for Political Research), the lively debate on the nature of the Italian party system and the type of competition between the governing Christian Democrats and the opposition Communist Party certainly stimulated his theoretical imagination.

Here, a digression is in order because Sartori was quite critical of Giorgio Galli's definition of the Italian party system as an 'imperfect two-party system' (Galli, 1966)[7] and above all of its concrete, and very different, implications for the dynamics of Italian politics. Relentlessly, he argued that the Italian party system was a case of polarised pluralism whose 'mechanics' were negatively affecting the entire political system and that could be improved only once the Italian Communist Party (PCI) had ceased being 'anti-system' (his many articles and essays on the subject, only some of which have been published in English, can be found in Sartori 1982). While Italy has not yet achieved a situation resembling that of a two-party system, and may never do so, the events of the 1990s, that is, above all, the profound political and programmatic transformation (almost disappearance) of the PCI, have proved Sartori right and by now the Italian party system is, at least from the perspective of its 'mechanics', sufficiently 'depolarised', but also somewhat 'destructured', while, from the perspective of format, it has become a case of a limited multiparty system.

Sartori's most important and probably enduring contributions in his extraordinary book on parties and party systems range from the analysis of party competition (including a chapter critical of Downs, *An Economic Theory of Democracy*) to party classification; from the criteria for counting political parties and for defining the nature of their competition to a clarification of the format and the dynamics (or mechanics, as he defines it) of all types of party systems. Even today there does not seem to exist a similarly ambitious and successful enterprise. *Parties and Party Systems* is not merely an exercise in classification, but also an excellent example of how to construct a typology. It contains a theory of party competition and the transformation of the party system that is clearly, imaginatively, and convincingly formulated in Chapter 9. Here, I will simply deal with the essence of Sartori's contributions and show why they all retain paramount importance more than 30 years after publication (for a more extended treatment see Pasquino 2005a).

First, with party competition, Sartori argues that it is simply not true that there is a natural tendency towards 'bipolarism' (*dualisme*, in Duverger's definition). Indeed, there are several instances of party systems in which the existence of a strong political party located at the centre of the political alignment prevents the emergence of bipolar competition. It is also not true that all parties will converge toward the centre, as Anthony Downs famously claimed, because extreme parties may retain a strong interest in attracting centrist voters away from the centre, but may also have an even stronger interest in not taking the risk of losing their own 'extremist' supporters, possibly to abstention, if not to a splinter party originated by their own very convergence towards the centre/central party. As a consequence, Sartori suggests that in extreme multiparty systems, neither bipolar competition nor a convergence towards the centre are likely to characterise the dynamics of the party system and the behaviour of voters. Hence, polarised multiparty systems will experience neither bipolar competition nor alternation in office. If they survive the joint challenge coming both from the extreme left and the extreme right, they will still find themselves functioning at very low performance levels.

Until Sartori, the traditional, most often used and quasi unique criterion for the classification of party systems had simply been the number of parties: one, two, many. Sartori drastically redefined all classifications by adding a new, qualitative criterion. Scholars ought to count those parties that *do* count, that is, that are in a position to exercise some influence on the functioning of the party system. Parties are (or become) *relevant* under two conditions: either, if and when they participate in governmental coalitions, or, if and when their influence is felt on the formation, the working, and the dissolution of those coalitions, even if they do not take part in them. It is my belief that this qualitative criterion, though difficult to manage because it requires a considerable amount of knowledge of the political and party systems of the various countries, remains by far superior to all the few alternatives devised afterwards. I will limit myself to only one example.

Several scholars writing in the 1970s and early 1980s have often referred to the German party system (Christian Democrats, CDU; Social-Democrats, SPD; and Liberals, FDP), by obviously looking only at the percentage of votes, as a two and a half party system. Scholars utilising the Laakso and Taagepera (1979) effective number of parties index would find little difference between the party system of the United Kingdom (Conservatives, Labour, Liberals) and that of Germany. Indeed, superficially applying a simple numerical criterion both party systems appeared characterised by the existence of about three effective parties in the 1949–1987 period. By confining themselves to counting the number of parties in those two political systems (and several other examples could be added), too many scholars were simply missing the crucial difference concerning the concrete and practical dynamics of those two party systems. In the United Kingdom, only two parties, the Labour and the Conservative, could win governmental power while the Liberal Party was in no position to influence either the formation of any government or the formulation of governmental policy. It was not, as Sartori would put it, 'relevant'. In Germany, by contrast, the relatively small Liberal Party was, from the beginning of the Bundesrepublik, not just relevant, but even decisive in the formation of all governments, with the exception of the 1966–1969 Grand Coalition. The German Liberals were so significant that they played a decisive role initially, in producing the first alternation in government by giving their support to the Social-Democrats in 1969 and, then, by re-instating a coalition with the Christian Democrats in 1982 (remember that Sartori's book was published in 1976).

The difference in the mechanics of the two-party systems could not be less important. The British party system was and has remained a two-party system, while the German party system must be classified as an important case of a limited and moderate multiparty system. The subsequent evolution of both party systems is also revealing. In 2008 there are five relevant parties in the German party system, whose dynamics continue, therefore, to be quite different from the British two-party system where the political relevance of the Liberals can essentially be discounted (from a systemic point of view). There is no doubt that Sartori has been proved unequivocally right in distinguishing the dynamics of the British party system from its German counterpart as qualitatively different, and that his theory contains enough predictive power regarding the transformation of different types of party systems.

Predictive theories, of the kind advocated by Sartori, serve the purpose of predicting consequences from the existence of a clearly defined set of conditions. The validity of Sartori's classification of party systems can also be tested with reference to his analysis of the characteristics of the pragmatic-hegemonic party system of Mexico. Limiting oneself to counting the number of existing (whether 'effective' or not) parties, the Mexican party system might be defined (much to the surprise of all Mexicans) as a moderate multiparty system. Obviously, this was never Sartori's view and interpretation. Even in those situations in which one party succeeds in governing alone for a rather long period of time, scholars need to apply precise criteria to define which type of party system actually exists. First, however, one must draw a clear line between competitive and non-competitive party systems. Among non-competitive party systems, one finds single-party systems where there is exclusively one party, that is powerful enough to prevent the appearance of any other party, and hegemonic party systems where more than one party is allowed to exist, but only one party controls political power in less than competitive elections. Poland and Mexico represent two different examples of non-competitive hegemonic party systems: the first is a case of an *ideological hegemonic* party system; the second is *pragmatic hegemonic*.

Single-party systems are generally unable to accommodate political change. They are bound to collapse, as in the fate suffered by the Communist Party of the Soviet Union. Hegemonic party systems may encounter a more favourable future. Indeed, in both Poland and Mexico there has been a difficult but real evolution towards a competitive party system. Sartori's theory (or 'framework' as he modestly put it) has successfully confronted the most important test, that is, it has convincingly proved to be endowed with predictive power. Once more, the combination of the two criteria for counting existing political parties, that is, their number and their relevance, has served the purpose of better identifying the party systems, correctly analysing their dynamics and thus predicting their likely transformation.

Unfortunately, Sartori lost the manuscript containing his analysis of party organisations. One chapter was much later retrieved and published (Sartori, 2005) thanks to Peter Mair who has also provided an incisive presentation. What I believe is of paramount importance and lasting significance in Sartori's analysis of party types, is the emphasis on the variety of organisational models and their relationship to the performance of political functions. No discussion of Sartori's theory of parties can be considered satisfactory that does not give some space to his rejection of all sociological explanations of the birth and nature of political parties. More precisely, Sartori (1969: 84) has openly challenged all interpretations constructed on a social class basis: 'class behaviour presupposes a party that not only feeds, incessantly, the "class image", but also a party that provides the structural cement of "class reality"'. This extremely important statement opens the way to many possible avenues of research on the appearance of political parties (on this point, see especially Boix 2007).

ON CONSTITUTIONAL ENGINEERING

The last major scholarly book by Sartori is *Comparative Constitutional Engineering*. Published in 1994, it has been translated into many languages and has been reprinted several times (the Italian edition has gone through five different versions with several additions). It is a concise, timely, extremely perceptive and profound analysis of the most important mechanisms and institutions of contemporary political systems, especially of the electoral formulae and their consequences and of the nature and working of presidential, parliamentary, and semi-presidential governments. I would like to highlight three special merits of Sartori's book. The first is that Sartori, who had already written in the past a very illuminating article on the relationship between electoral systems and party systems (Sartori 1968), produces a set of advice useful for all countries that are attempting to construct viable democratic institutions (as was the case in that period). By so doing (and this is the second merit), he also contributes to so-called neo-institutionalism, that is to the (re)discovery by US scholars of the role played by institutions, rules, and procedures. This rediscovery, preceded ten years before by the school that can be defined by the title of a somewhat naïve book, *Bringing the State Back in* (Evans et al. 1985), appears to be, from the perspective of French, German, Italian, and Spanish scholars (and, no doubt, of all Latin American scholars as well), a rather curious phenomenon.

Neither the State nor governmental, representative, bureaucratic institutions had ever disappeared from the analyses of politics on the European (and Latin American) continents. And, defining and differentiating presidentialism, parliamentarism, and semi-presidentialism, Sartori has participated influentially in the debate on the quality and consequences of the various types of governing and representative institutions, pointing to their advantages and disadvantages. Finally, in *Comparative Constitutional Engineering* (1994) more than in his many other books, Sartori formulates and elucidates his position on the paramount intellectual task of political science. To the extent that political scientists are capable of constructing generalisations, providing explanations, and formulating probabilistic theories, they ought to engage in the debate concerning the improvement of political systems. The knowledge acquired by political scientists can not only be put to good use, it should be put to the test of empirical reality. Indeed, from Aristotle to Machiavelli, political scientists have felt that it is their intellectual task to apply their knowledge and have not refrained from offering advice. The best of contemporary political science possesses enough comparative knowledge that can be, under certain conditions, applied with success. All this said, Sartori has always and deliberately kept himself clear of any specific political or partisan commitment. His books and articles speak out as to his favourite type of political system. His intellectual independence stands above and beyond any doubt and has allowed him to gain the credibility that derives from his knowledge.

Nevertheless, having returned to Italy from the USA, where he held for almost 20 years the Albert Schweitzer Chair in the Humanities at Columbia University, Sartori has turned into a passionate commentator on Italian political events and a relentless critic of the Italian political class. His columns in one of Italy's most important dailies *Il Corriere della Sera* have been collected, together with similar pieces published elsewhere, in a splendid, rich and provocative volume, *Mala Tempora* (2004) followed by *Mala Costituzione e Altri Malanni* (2006) and, most recently, by *Il Sultanato* (2009). To no avail. There is no improvement in sight for the Italian political system, but Sartori's teachings and writings make for extremely rewarding reading and constitute a precious and powerful testimony of what great political scientists can contribute both to the understanding of a difficult and troubled political situation and, perhaps, even to some possible solutions.

Notes
1 An earlier version of this chapter was published with the title 'The Political Science of Giovanni Sartori' (Pasquino, 2005c).
2 On their contributions see the book by another 'maestro' of Italian political science, Norberto Bobbio (1996), that constitutes a 'must read'.
3 He himself has reported on his difficult times in Sartori, 1997a.
4 For additional details see G. Sola, 2005: 23–69.
5 Together with several important methodological and substantive pieces, it has just been reprinted in Collier and Gerring, 2008.
6 'Consensus' by George S. Graham, 'Development' by Fred W. Riggs, 'Ethnicity' by Robert H. Jackson, 'Integration' by Henry Teune, 'Political Culture' by Glenda M. Patrick, 'Power' by Jan Erik Lane and Hans Stenlund, and 'Revolution' by Christoph M. Katowski.
7 Much of the material on which Galli relied can be found in Galli and Prandi, 1970.

REFERENCES

Bobbio, N. (1996) *Saggi sulla scienza politica in Italia*, Roma-Bari: Laterza.
Boix, C. (2007) 'The Emergence of Parties and Party Systems', in C. Boix and S. Stokes (eds.), *The Oxford Handbook of Comparative Politics*, Oxford: Oxford University Press.
Collier, D. and Gerring, J. (eds.) (2008) *Concepts & Methods in Social Science; Giovanni Sartori & His Legacy*, London/New York: Routledge.
Evans, P. B., Rueschemeyer, D. and Skocpol, T. (eds.) (1985) *Bringing the State Back in*, Cambridge: Cambridge University Press.
Galli, G. (1966) *Il Bipartitismo Imperfetto*, Bologna: il Mulino.
Galli, G. and Prandi, A. (1970) *Patterns of Political Participation in Italy*, New Haven and London: Yale University Press.
Laakso, M. and Taagepera, R. (1979) '"Effective" Number of Parties; A Measure with Application to West Europe', *Comparative Political Studies,* 12 (April): 3–27.
Pasquino, G. (2005a) 'La teoria dei sistemi di partito', in G. Pasquino, *La Scienza Politica di Giovanni Sartori*, Bologna: il Mulino.
(2005b) *La Scienza Politica di Giovanni Sartori*, Bologna: il Mulino.
(2005c) 'The Political Science of Giovanni Sartori', *European Political Science,* 4 (1): 33–41.
Sartori, G. (1957) *Democrazia e Definizioni*, Bologna: il Mulino.
(1960) 'Democrazia, burocrazia e oligarchia nei partiti', *Rassegna Italiana di Sociologia,* 3: 119–136.
(1961) 'I significati del termine "elite"', in AA.VV., *Le Elite Politiche*, Bari: Laterza, pp. 94–99.
(1962) *Democratic Theory*, Detroit: Wayne University Press.
(1968) 'Political Development and Political Engineering', in J. D. Montgomery and A. O. Hirschman (eds.), *Public Policy*, Cambridge, Mass: Harvard University Press, vol. XVII.
(1969) 'From the sociology of politics to political sociology', in S. M. Lipset (ed.), *Politics and the Social Sciences*, New York/London/Toronto: Oxford University Press.
(1970) 'Concept Misformation in Comparative Politics', in *American Political Science Review,* 64 (4): 1033–53.
(1971a) *Antologia di Scienza Politica*, Bologna: il Mulino.
(1971b) 'La politica comparata; premesse e problemi', *Rivista Italiana di Scienza Politica,* 1 (1): 7–66.
(1976) *Parties and Party Systems; A Framework for Analysis*, Cambridge: Cambridge University Press.
(2005) *Parties and Party Systems; A Framework for Analysis*, Essex: ECPR Press.
(1979) *La politica; Logica e Metodo in Scienze Sociali*, Milan: SugarCo.

(1982) *Teoria dei Partiti e Caso Italiano*, Milan: SugarCo.

(1984) (ed.) *Social Science Concepts; A Systematic Analysis*, London: Sage.

(1987) *The Theory of Democracy Revisited*, Chatham, N.J: Chatham House Publishers, 2 vols.

(1989) 'Video Power', *Government and Opposition,* 24 (1): 39–53.

(1991) 'Comparing and Miscomparing', *Journal of Theoretical Politics,* 3 (3): 243–57.

(1993) 'Totalitarianism, Model Mania, and Learning from Error', *Journal of Theoretical Politics,* 5 (1): 5–22.

(1993 [2007]) *Democrazia; Cosa è*, Milan: Rizzoli.

(1994) *Comparative Constitutional Engineering; An Inquiry into Structures, Incentives and Outcomes*, London: Macmillan.

(1995) *Elementi di Teoria Politica*, Bologna: il Mulino.

(1997a) 'Chance, luck, and stubbornness', in H. Daalder (ed.), Comparative European Politics; The Story of a Profession, London and New York: Pinter.

(1997b) *Homo Videns; Televisione e post-pensiero*, Roma-Bari: Laterza.

(2004) *Mala Tempora*, Roma-Bari: Laterza.

(2005) 'Party Types, Organisations and Functions', *West European Politics,* 28 (1): 5–32.

(2006) *Mala Costituzione e Altri Malanni*, Roma-Bari: Laterza.

(2009) *Il Sultanato*, Roma-Bari: Laterza.

Schattschneider, E. E. (1942) *Party Government*, New York: Farrar and Rinehart.

(1960) *The Semi-Sovereign People: A Realist's View of Democracy in America*, New York: Holt, Rinehart, and Winston.

Sola, G. (2005) 'La rinascita della scienza politica' in G. Pasquino (ed.), *La Scienza Politica di Giovanni Sartori*, Bologna: il Mulino.

chapter nine | Sidney Verba: His Voice[1]
Keiko Ono and Clyde Wilcox

INTRODUCTION

Sidney Verba is working on a new book, in collaboration with Henry Brady and Kay Schlozman. Verba is 76, and many would expect him to step back from original research and to write synthetic essays about the history of the discipline. After all, he was present at the start of the behavioural movement in comparative government – a co-author of *The Civic Culture*. Moreover, during the last decade he published two major books on civic voluntarism and political participation that totalled nearly 1100 pages (Verba, Schlozman and Brady 1995; Burns, Schlozman and Verba 2001). He also managed to publish four articles in the *American Political Science Review*, three in *Journal of Politics*, two in *American Journal of Political Science*, and one each in the *British Journal of Political Science* and the *Journal of Theoretical Politics*. This level of productivity is remarkable for scholars of any age. Surely no one would object if he took a break.

Verba's contributions to the discipline have been widely recognised. In the past decade he has been awarded the James Madison Award by the American Political Science Association (APSA) – given every three years for a career contribution to political science. He won two separate awards named after his late contemporary Warren Miller – one given by the APSA Organised Section on Voting and Public Opinion, for a Career contribution to the study of public opinion and elections, and the other given by the Inter-University Consortium for Political and Social Research (ICPSR) for distinguished contribution to the social sciences. He was more recently awarded the Johann Skytte Prize by the University of Uppsala for a distinguished contribution to political science. All of these retrospective prizes would seem to imply that it is time to take stock of Verba's career, and to look backward not forward.[2]

Yet Verba is not ready to step back from original research. Indeed, he told an interviewer for the *Harvard Crimson* that his only hobby is doing statistical analysis of social science data (Marks 2003). His next project, again co-authored with Kay Schlozman and Henry Brady, has all of the making of a career capstone. The volume will focus on equality – the theme that has tied together so many of his projects over the years. Verba says that this book will be more broadly theoretical – 'without mind-numbing statistics' – and that the book will 'not be grounded in a particular dataset'. But he is also building another remarkable dataset, of 22,000 interest groups, including their lobbying activity, their campaign contributions, their issue agenda, and other characteristics.

CAREER PATHS AND CHAOS

It is easy to create a narrative of Verba's career that would stress the continuity of his projects, and how each seems to build from earlier research. Seen from the outside, his career appears to have been carefully planned. Indeed, Verba seems to have been tatting together the various threads of his career to create a lace web of research on participation and equality. All roads appear to lead to his new project, but Verba tells the story a bit differently. In fact, chaos theory seems an appropriate lens through which to look at the early stages of his career.

Chaos theory suggests that small variations in initial conditions result in huge, dynamic transformations in concluding events. The most memorable formulation of chaos theory is the dictum that if a butterfly beats its wings in China, it rains in Central Park.[3] Applied to academic careers, chaos theory might suggest that there are many potential career paths that might result for any individual if the initial conditions for that career were varied.

For Sidney Verba, the 'butterfly beating its wings' is a too-pastoral metaphor for the anti-communist crusade of Senator Joe McCarthy. After receiving a BA degree in history and literature, Verba wanted to enter the Foreign Service. He entered the Woodrow Wilson School to study international relations, but McCarthy's Red Scare made the Foreign Service seem much less attractive. He gradually drifted to the political science department, where he took a course with Gabriel Almond, and became interested in Almond's efforts to study comparative politics as a truly comparative enterprise. When Almond offered him a research assistantship, Verba accepted, in part because his wife was pregnant and could no longer be counted on to support the family through her teaching job. At the time, he viewed the assistantship as a job, and did not perceive the importance of the project.

His assignment was to work on an ambitious cross-national survey project that eventually resulted in the publication of the *The Civic Culture*. Verba had to learn survey research and statistical analysis. His interest in the project grew quickly, and he soon became entranced by the theory and methods of the project. He says that he became co-author of the book without fully understanding the importance of the project, nor the role it would have in launching his career. Almond was an important mentor to Verba. At Almond's funeral, Verba summed up Almond's influence on his career:

> Gabriel was my teacher, my mentor, then my collaborator at Princeton, then my colleague here at Stanford, and for most of my adult life my friend, and

my role model. As a teacher he taught me about political science; as a mentor, he taught me how to do political science; as a collaborator, he taught me how to work intensely with others, how exhilarating that can be, how to disagree and how to it stick out and overcome disagreements; as a colleague he taught me how to build and maintain institutions as he built the political science department at Stanford, as a friend, he taught me the value of friendship and how to maintain it, how to be concerned about others, and as a role model he taught me how to be a serious scholar; but much more important how to be a serious human being. Surely Gabriel was a serious scholar during an active academic life and an equally active retirement – a role model one only hopes one can emulate. But he was always much more. He knew that life was much more than learning and books. Gabriel was a role model for scholarship, but more important he was a role model for *enschlichkeit*.

From Verba's collaboration with Almond in *The Civic Culture*, he says that one project tended to follow another, and that he was not following any well laid-out career strategy. Yet his career can also be seen as a web of connected important projects on related themes. In the U.S., universities consider teaching, collegiality and service, and most importantly research, in evaluating colleagues for tenure and promotion. It is often claimed that these three factors are of equal weight, though in reality research is the most important. Before discussing Verba's research, then, it is useful to briefly consider his teaching and service.

TEACHING: VERBA AS MENTOR

If one measure of a scholar is the quality of students he or she trains, then Verba ranks as one of the most influential mentors in the field.[4] Indeed, in his letter nominating Verba to be president of APSA, Bingham Powell singles out not only his scholarship, but also his teaching, noting that 'If possible, Verba is even more influential as teacher and critic than as a published scholar.' Among the list of Verba's students are names such as Norman Nie, Kay Schlozman, Kristi Andersen, John Petrocik, Carole Uhlaner, Goldie Shabad, Michael Dawson, Gerald Gamm, and Nancy Burns – all influential scholars at top universities. His advocacy on behalf of his students is legendary – he calls or e-mails on behalf of even those students for whom he is but a dissertation reader, not mentor.

Verba has co-authored with his students and offered them opportunities to author chapters in his books. Indeed, his students are co-authors on some of the most important books in the discipline over the past 20 years. Verba is modest about this arrangement, noting only that,

> I have been very lucky in having found some really bright people to work with. It has always been a valuable and rewarding experience, and the results have been better than we could have done alone.

But Verba's former students are full of praise for him as a mentor, and as a collaborator. Goldie Shabad of the Ohio State University noted that Verba's mentorship extended not only when she was a student, but throughout her career. Indeed, we contacted more than half a dozen of his former students, and each of them referred to him as a continuing personal friend. Many said that they tried to do the same things as mentor that they learned from Verba. Kristi Andersen of the University of Syracuse (whose dissertation won the APSA award as best in American politics), echoed themes that emerged in the comments of several of his former students when she noted that,

> Sidney did what I try to do – provide whatever support is needed but essentially let people make their own mistakes and enjoy their own intellectual discoveries. No micromanaging. And he has always given me the sense that I'm making the right choices.

COLLEGIALITY: VERBA AS COLLABORATOR, COLLEAGUE, AND INSTITUTION BUILDER

Verba has written with many scholars over the years, and they universally praise him as a collaborator. Kay Schlozman, J. Joseph Moakley Professor and Chair of Political Science at Boston College and one of Verba's former students and frequent collaborators, writes of her collaboration with her former mentor and contemporary collaborator:

> Over the years Sidney has had many research collaborators. I am sure that all of us would tell similar stories about why it is such a privilege to work with him. Sidney's brains are legendary. Nobody knows better how to coax an interesting political story out of survey data. But anyone who has ever written with him also knows that Sidney's appetite for work is limitless. Not only is he willing to log long hours, he does not cherry pick the interesting tasks and leave for the rest of us all the nitty-gritty, hands-on, detail work on which good scholarship – regardless of field – must rest. Sidney runs data, meets with research assistants, reads journal articles, and checks page proof.

> Not only does Sidney know how to work, he knows when to stop. One of the most important lessons I learned during our first joint project more years ago than I care to acknowledge is to recognise the point of diminishing returns. Many an academic has foundered because of an ability to let go of an imperfect dissertation or book manuscript. Sidney has the wisdom to discern when the improvement in quality is not sufficient to justify continued effort.

Sidney always touts the virtues of working together by saying that 'Collaboration allows you to do a fraction of the work, claim all the credit, and get none of the blame.' Sidney Verba's co-authors know that he does more than his fraction of the work, claims less than his share of the credit, and nobody ever has to take any blame.

Bingham Powell of the University of Rochester praised Verba as collegial critic in his nomination of him to be president of the American Political Science Association.

In my personal experience he is the best and most helpful scholarly critic that I know. There is simply no one who is better able to take a rough piece of work, see immediately the heart of its argument, and suggest how it might be improved.

The major figures in academic fields not only leave behind influential scholarship and train good students, they also contribute to the discipline in service and by helping to build institutions. Verba has served as president of the American Political Science Association, and served on many disciplinary committees. Verba has organised numerous national and international conferences, and served as one of the few political scientists on the National Academy of Sciences.

He served as chair of his department at Harvard, which he helped to rebuild. He also served for a time as dean, and on many University-wide committees. Kenneth Shepsle notes that 'Whenever there is a hot potato, an administrator somewhere in Harvard looks for Sid.' Gary King notes that 'Sid [...] can get together warring factions with a few disarming comments, and settle disputes before anyone realises that they are over.' Verba brings formidable skills to this task, including a legendary sense of humour that is always positive. Several of his colleagues merely note that he is a 'mensch'.

Perhaps his most important service role at Harvard was as head of the Library, a position he held for more than 20 years. He helped integrate Harvard's many libraries to allow easier access by the University community, and also to make the Harvard collections available to a global community through the Library Digital Initiative. Because of Verba's work, projects like the Open Collections Program make key documents available through the Internet.

Verba has contributed to the discipline in another way. He has collected many important datasets in the U.S. and in other countries. In many countries, he helped to build research teams that became prominent in establishing contemporary political science there. Always his data are archived for use by the scholarly community in a prompt manner – indeed the data from the massive study of activists in the 1990s was available while his first book from the project was still cooling from the presses.

SCHOLARSHIP

Taking stock of Verba's scholarship is a daunting task. He is one of the most frequently cited scholars of his or any generation, in both American politics and comparative areas (Masuoka *et al.* 2007). He has produced an extensive volume of exemplary work that makes important theoretical arguments, and that tests hypotheses with creative methods and complex new datasets.

The range of his projects is remarkable. In his own words, Verba has always been interested in 'individual behavior, elite behavior in context, and individual behavior not for its own sake, but individual behavior in terms of the functioning of democracy,' and his scholarly contributions reflect that. Paul Sniderman began his intellectual biography of Verba in 1994 by noting:

> It is common practice to divide the study of politics into two – normative and empirical; then into three – American, comparative, and international; then into two again – substantive and methodological; then into two yet again – micro vs. macro, and having defined this 2 x 3 x 2 x 2 disciplinary matrix, we then tell graduate students to specialise. It is, most obviously, the rare distinction of Sidney Verba to have made fundamental contributions to very nearly every location in this 24-cell matrix. (Sniderman 1994: 574)

Sniderman goes on to list and categorise the various publications by Verba through 1994, before the bulk of publications from his most recent project. Verba's breadth is remarkable. In his early opus is a collection of theoretical essays on the international political system, to which Verba contributed a chapter on the rationality assumption in international relations theory (Verba 1961b). He co-edited books with Lucian Pye and others on political development. He has published a methodological treatise on qualitative research, and a theoretical piece in the *Journal of Theoretical Politics*.

But most of Verba's scholarship, and his most important contributions, are in the fields of American and comparative politics. Verba is one of the rare political scientists who is able to integrate American politics with comparative politics. Most comparative work ignores the US case, labeling it as exceptional, or an outlier. Yet the US is not just any outlier, and some of the trends that once seemed exceptional in American politics (conscience votes in legislatures, declining voter turnout, weakening partisan ties) have become evident in Europe and elsewhere. Verba has been involved in three large cross-national projects, in each of which the US is a key case. Indeed, he has twice first published a book on a topic in the U.S., and then a couple of years later written a broader comparative study on the same topic. He is a leading figure in both American and comparative politics, and even when his research is focused exclusively on the American case, its theory and data are of interest to students of comparative politics.

It is perhaps most useful to explore Verba's intellectual career chronologically, and then to conclude with thoughts on the broader themes in his work. Verba has produced seminal scholarly research in every decade from the 1960s through the 1990s. We will of course focus on the major works, but also point to lesser known but important scholarship. Sniderman notes in his history of Verba's work that:

> With his first wave of work, Sidney had distinguished himself in his generation. Yet what was truly to set him apart was that, having won the principal honors of his profession [...] he then embarked on a second wave of work, more deeply considered, further reaching, and more imaginative than the first. (1994: 577)

Sniderman published his biography in 1994, just as Verba began publishing from his third wave of scholarship, which is even *more* deeply considered and imaginative than that of the 1980s. And Verba clearly has plans to publish important work in the new millennium as well.

EARLY WORKS

Verba's first book, *Small Groups and Political Behavior; A Study of Leadership* (Verba 1961a) is quite different from most of his other work. Drawing on experimental studies, Verba explores leadership in a variety of face-to-face groups, including families. Although much of his later work examines the role of social and political groups on political participation, this relationship is explored in large random-sample surveys.

Sniderman calls attention to Verba's discussion of the dilemma that leaders face in dealing with small group norms – they must conform enough to maintain their leadership role, but be able to deviate enough to provide innovative leadership. He notes that the book reflects 'the crucial themes of the role of citizens, the responsibility of leadership, and the dilemmas of political representation.' (Sniderman 1994: 575).

There are other themes in this early work that persist across Verba's career. The role of families is explored at some length, a theme that would return in his most recent book on gender roles. More importantly, Verba spends considerable time talking about participation in small groups – how individuals are socialised to participate, and how that participation leads group members to give more support to the group's leaders. Membership in voluntary associations is a principal theme of Verba's work in the 1990s, and the notion that participation leads to support for leaders is one that is suggestive of the broader exploration of system support in *The Civic Culture*.

Small Groups and Political Behavior is out of print, and it is rooted in the social science of its day (e.g. the book discusses authoritarianism at some length). But it remains an insightful set of essays, valuable more for its theorising than its evidence. Despite its age this remains an influential book: it shows up in the *Social Science Citation Index* with fully 51 citations since 1981 – that is, beginning some 20 years after publication and counting forward.

'THE CIVIC CULTURE', AND RELATED PROJECTS

The book that launched Verba's career was *The Civic Culture* (Almond and Verba 1963). The volume is clearly a foundational one in comparative politics, and it was immediately controversial for its theory, its methods, and perhaps most of all for its ambitions. At the time most comparative politics scholars focused on developing a deep understanding of a single country or perhaps region – learning the language, the culture, the history, and the players. *The Civic Culture* compared five countries using a single survey instrument – one that did not focus on the issues most salient to each country, but instead sought to measure similar concepts using identically worded survey instruments translated literally into the language of five separate countries. To those who insist that a scholar live in a country and study it for years before writing about it, Verba has reportedly quipped that he believes that political scientists should never write about a country that they had not at least flown over. Almond and Verba consulted closely with country specialists, but their broadly comparative approach was nonetheless controversial.

Almond and Verba had large theoretical ambitions. The book began with the claim that 'This is a study of the political culture of democracy and the social structures and processes that sustain it.' Rooted in the concerns for stability that came from the rise of Nazism, Fascism, and Communism, the study seeks to explain democratic stability, using political cultural variables, and social structures and processes. For a time in the 1970s and 1980s, *The Civic Culture* seemed less relevant to a generation of graduate students who found its theoretical roots in Parsons and other European sociologists dated, and its concern for democratic stability an artefact of the anxieties of the age. Yet today, as new democracies teeter in Latin America, Asia, Eastern Europe, Africa, and elsewhere, the question of what sustains democracy, takes on a new importance. Recent studies have looked toward many of the attitudes and orientations discussed in *The Civic Culture* as important determinants of the stability of new democracies, although they have couched this analysis in the language of civil society (e.g. Howard 2003). Indeed, Verba received queries from social scientists in the new democracies of Eastern Europe in 1989 about a replication of the *The Civic Culture*, but he advised against it (Verba 1997).

Almond and Verba argued that a civic culture was central to democratic stability, and that this culture was characterised by a constellation of citizen attitudes. The 'allegiant participant culture' is the product of socialisation, but unlike other works of the era, Almond and Verba included not only childhood socialisation but also early adult learning.

Echoing themes that would preoccupy Verba all of his career, the authors predict a coming 'participation explosion' but note that 'what mode of participation will be uncertain.' (1963: 4). But a participation explosion is not necessarily to be desired, for excessive participation can signal an unstable system. Instead, it is critically important for citizens to provide regime support (see Pateman 1980 for a critique). Indeed, Almond and Verba note that in Britain (one of the two successful, stable democracies), the citizens take a subject, deferential role, and although this is not optimal, the authors imply that the active participatory role of the US citizen may not be ideal either. Yet both were seen as superior to the civic cultures in Germany, Italy, and Mexico, where there were much lower levels of social and interpersonal trust, and of regime support. Ideally, the civic culture needed the values of passivity, trust, and deference to authority. This need not mean that citizens blindly accept government edicts, but rather that they provide the regime with sufficient support for it to govern.

The surveys sought to measure support for democratic procedures and norms, efficacy (sense of civic competence), the perceived obligation to participate, participation in groups and politics, and also civic virtues such as generosity. These attitudes were explored not only across nations, but across classes, genders, and parties within and across nations. Almond and Verba sought to 'spell out methodically the mixture of attitudes that support a democratic system.' (1963: 505). The authors anticipated that time and increased education would increase the levels of civic culture in Germany, Italy, and Mexico, but instead history has shown that the levels of political trust in the U.S. and Britain have declined (Verba 1980). Moreover, Italian and German democracy have survived for the 40 years since the publication of the book, and Mexican democracy is healthier today than then, suggesting that the attitudes that Almond and Verba studied might not be essential to democratic stability.

Some 40 years after publication, *The Civic Culture* seems 'outsized in its theoretical ambition' (Sniderman 1994). Verba himself refers to the study as 'bold,' 'incautious' and even 'foolhardy' (Verba 1980: 394–5). Yet it was precisely this boldness, indeed the incaution that allowed *The Civic Culture* to become so influential. It invited rebuttal, and provoked democratic theorists, but that stimulated many ongoing conversations. Verba quotes Pareto as saying 'Give me fruitful error, bursting with the seeds of its own correction' (Verba 1997: 283). *The Civic Culture* certainly inspired those who sought to uncover its error, but also those who were excited by the possibilities that it revealed. The book inspired many later studies of cross-national political attitudes and behaviour, for it suggested that rigorous comparative work could be done in the behavioural tradition.

Sniderman also notes that the book was 'outsized in its empirical reach'. The magnitude of the project is worth conveying to graduate students, who often complain if a dataset cannot be downloaded in SPSS format immediately. In a time when survey research firms were not common in other countries, Almond and Verba hired their own survey teams, whose work was a bit uneven. With no established research protocols to guide them, they designed and had translated the survey instruments, in consultation with country specialists. And like other quantitative work at the time, they performed their analysis on punch cards that were sorted by an IBM 101 counter-sorter. Verba notes that they were 'making it up as they went along'.

The *Civic Culture* was a very influential exemplar. It demonstrated that cross-national studies of individual citizens could be done and done rigorously. The data from the volume were pored over by scholars and students of the day, and generated many publications by those who re-analysed the data (e.g. Nie *et al.* 1969a, 1969b). Indeed, Giuseppe Di Palma (1970) published a re-analysis of the data in book form, embedded in more historical analysis. These were the primary data on comparative mass politics until the release of Verba's cross-national participation study in the 1970s. In a time when vast quantities of data languish largely unexplored, it is difficult to explain to students the importance of this initial dataset.

Several themes in *The Civic Culture* would emerge later as central to Verba's work. The book explored the relationship between education and various civic attitudes, and between education and participation. It was in *The Civic Culture* data that Verba first noted the heavy socio-economic bias associated with political participation, a theme that was to become central to his later work. *The Civic Culture* also explored gender differences – an innovative topic at a time when the discipline was dominated by men, and a topic that would become the focus of his most recent book.

Verba followed up *The Civic Culture* with an edited book on civic culture and development (Pye and Verba 1965), and with a book on comparative survey analysis (Rokkan, Verba, Viet, and Almassy 1969). In 1980, Almond and Verba published an edited volume that included important critiques of the book, and country specific discussions (see Sani 1980 for a discussion of Italy).

Late in the 1960s, Verba did an unrelated study of public attitudes toward Vietnam, writing an article and later a book (Rosenberg *et al.* 1970). It was his only foray into political advocacy, and the initial press release led to an angry response by conservative columnists Rowland Evans and Robert Novak, who called the work dishonest and incompetent. The survey is one of the best on public attitudes toward the war, however, and the data are archived at the ICPSR.

THE PARTICIPATION PROJECT OF THE 1970S

In the 1970s, Verba began a second major project that eventually led to four books, this time focusing squarely on political participation. Although the most famous publication from the project focused on the U.S. case, the project involved the collection of data in seven countries. Unlike *The Civic Culture*, the participation project involved similar but not identical surveys in each country – allowing for questions that were relevant to the specific country context.

In 1971, Verba published two books from this project. *The Modes of Democratic Participation* developed in some detail the principal modes of participation identified by factor analysis from the survey data (Verba, Nie, and Kim 1971). After wondering in *The Civic Culture* what mode of participation would come to dominate, Verba and his colleagues showed empirically that there were multiple modes (discussed below).

Verba also co-authored a volume that focused on a two nation comparison between India and the US (Verba, Ahmed and Bhatt 1971). After the broad comparison in *The Civic Culture*, this volume adopted a much more focused comparison, taking advantage of the interesting contrast between race and caste in the two societies. Although African Americans and Dalits both occupied similar location in status hierarchies, their absolute positions were different and so were the ideologies that supported this stratification. By limiting the focus of the study, and narrowing the comparison to two countries, Verba and his colleagues were able to develop a much richer description of the racial/caste politics in each society without sacrificing the methodological rigour of his other comparative work.

The authors discuss the social movements that have mobilised these disadvantaged groups, and the nature of group consciousness that helps to motivate participation in each country. They report that group consciousness was far more developed among blacks in the US, while the Dalits were fragmented by geography, language, and subgroup identification, and lacked the resources to form a leadership cadre. In hindsight, the book makes a major mistake in ignoring the contrasting role of religion in the two cases. In the U.S., African Americans transformed a Christian faith that whites had used to justify their enslavement into a resource for resistance and liberation – and a source of institutions that both provided leadership and also infrastructure. The Harijans were unable to effect a similar transformation of Hinduism, since they are defined out of the religion and denied access to Hindu temples. Instead, they would have had to have converted to some other religion – Islam, Buddhism, etc. to build religious resources. By ignoring the role of religion in this comparison, Verba and colleagues were squarely in the mainstream of the discipline at the time. In his later works, however, Verba has explored the role of churches in building participatory resources.

Participation in America (Verba and Nie 1972) won the Gladys Kammerer Award from the American Political Science Association for the best book in American politics. In this, and an earlier volume, Verba and Nie develop and test a typology of types of political participation. Whereas many studies before and after focused primarily on voting, these studies distinguished between a range of participatory acts based on the amount of pressure and information required, the scope of the outcome, the amount of conflict involved, and the difficulty of the act. These dimensions resulted in a typology of participatory acts that included voting, campaign activity, co-operative activity and social contacting, and particularised contacting.

The factor analysis of survey data confirms these modes of participation, and analysis of the factor scores revealed that campaign activity and co-operative activity are very different modes of political engagement. From this analysis, the authors developed a typology of participants – one far more nuanced than previous works that had assumed that all participation was additive. The most intriguing result was that 'Communalists' and 'Campaigners' were distinctive groups that were almost mirror images of one another. Communalists were active in local affairs, building social capital and working co-operatively with others for a common good. Campaigners in contrast enjoyed the conflict of elections, and presumably prefer to solve community problems by electing those who will pursue their favoured policies. Yet community building and campaigning need not be exclusive activities, for slightly more than one in ten were 'complete activists,' engaging in all kinds of participatory acts.

Participation in America started with the fundamental assumption that those with the most resources – especially education, income, and occupational prestige – were more likely to participate in politics. The 'socio-economic model' was not terribly surprising – *The Civic Culture* had stressed the role of education in moulding attitudes that can lead to participation, and *The American Voter* had shown that education was a strong predictor of voting. What *was* novel was the way that Nie and Verba used the socio-economic model as a baseline, against which the impact of other factors could be assessed. Although socio-economic status directly explained only around 4% of the variance in overall participation, when combined with the civic orientations that socio-economic status (and especially education) produces, the baseline model explained roughly a quarter of the variance.

From this baseline, Verba and Nie were able to create 'corrected' participation scores for various subgroups – that is, an estimate of the level of participation that might incur if members of a particular group had the same levels of education, income, and occupational prestige as others. They showed, for example, that the decrease in participation among the elderly is somewhat exaggerated in the bivariate data, because the oldest Americans were much less well-educated than their younger counterparts.

The most interesting of these adjustments was on race. The book was written after the civil rights movement had sought to build black identity and consciousness in the 1960s, and Verba and Nie found that once the socio-economic disadvantage of African Americans was controlled, blacks participated at a higher rate than whites. Moreover, it was only among those African Americans who mentioned race as a source of conflict in their community (a component of group consciousness) that participation was elevated.

The increased level of participation among blacks was concentrated among campaign activities and communal activities, not voting. Yet even after controls for socio-economic status (SES), blacks were less likely to engage in particularised contacting. The authors showed that African Americans were less likely to engage in particularised contacting because they were more pessimistic about whether they would be listened to by government should they try to request aid.

In the final section, Verba and Nie explore issues that would prove central to Verba's later scholarship – the connections between citizens and elites, and the role of participatory inequality in producing other forms of inequality. The authors conclude that increased participation by the advantaged elements in American society leads to increased attentiveness by government officials. This distortion of the democratic process would become a major theme in Verba's work in the 1990s.

Participation in America continues to be widely cited, averaging 25–30 citations per year during the 1990s, and appears on most graduate syllabi for courses in mass politics, although it is now more than 30 years old. It remains a seminal work, and it is an especially useful pedagogical tool. The detailed analysis in Chapter 4 remains one of the best exemplars of factor analysis for graduate instruction, for it is thorough and painstaking in detail. Although confirmatory factor analysis has replaced exploratory analysis as the tool of choice for determining the dimensionality of variables, the underlying logic of the entire process is laid out clearly here. Moreover, the second half of the book provides a useful way to teach the importance of systematic controls to graduate students just beginning their studies.

The comparative element of the participation study was expressed most centrally in *Participation and Political Equality* (Verba, Nie, and Kim 1987). This seven nation study – of the U.S., Austria, the Netherlands, Japan, India, Yugoslavia, and Nigeria, broke new ground by including one country with a communist government and another in which a democratically elected government had been overthrown by a military coup. Verba *et al.* confirm the basic structure of participatory acts described in *Participation in America*, and apply the same general socio-economic model. But the countries in the study had quite different political institutions, and these institutions could facilitate or hinder various types of participation. The authors were able to explore deviations from the basic model (e.g. in the Netherlands religious parties had the ability to mobilise their members beyond what the SES model would suggest), and to examine partisan and left-right differences in mobilisation. They find that in countries where parties and other institutions play an important role in mobilising campaigners, there is less of a class bias in voting. The book included a clever analysis of both individual and institutional paths to participation, and managed to explore the interaction between these paths and the various modes of participation in each country. Once again the data from this project became an important source of articles by others.

Several themes from this set of studies would become the focus of Verba's work in the 1990s. Taken together, these works showed that differences in rates of participation had consequences, and that advantaged groups were more likely to vote and participate than others. Verba addressed gender and racial differences in participation, and the role of group consciousness in mobilisation.

THE CHANGING AMERICAN VOTER

In the same decade that he published four books and several articles from the comparative participation project, Verba also co-authored *The Changing American Voter* with two of his former graduate students. Published in 1976, the book won the Woodrow Wilson Prize for the best book in Political Science (all fields). The Michigan model of voting developed by Campbell, Converse, Miller and Stokes (1960) in *The American Voter* had dominated the study of electoral behaviour, and continues to exert a strong influence today. Nie, Verba, and Petrocik sought to develop a more political explanation of electoral behaviour, rooted in the issues and controversies of the 1960s and early 1970s.

The American Voter was based on elections in the 1950s. This was a stolid era in American politics, where partisan loyalties were passed from parent to child, and where most political issues lacked emotional punch. In the list of issues that Campbell *et al.* considered in their analysis of potential issue voting, were such things as rural electrification – clearly a powerful issue to those in rural areas who lacked electricity, but hardly an issue likely to shock the majority of citizens into political action.

After the publication of *The American Voter*, the civil rights movement marched against angry mobs, fire hoses and attack dogs, demanding equal rights and integration. The Vietnam War escalated, and students who faced the possibility of being drafted occupied buildings and came to Washington to protest against the war, including one attempt to levitate the Pentagon. Young women began to demand equal access to education and jobs, and more equal treatment in general from society. Some marched with banners stating that 'A Woman Needs a Man the Way a Fish Needs a Bicycle.' The widespread proliferation of marijuana and other drugs, a sexual revolution powered by the pill, and new styles of clothing and hair led to a backlash by cultural conservatives, and angry confrontations between hardhats and hippies. As the baby boom worked its way through adolescence, the large number of teenaged males meant higher rates of violent crime, and calls for greater efforts at social control. Clearly, the 1960s and early 1970s were a more politically charged era than the 1950s, and it seemed reasonable that the new issues would lead to a new engagement by the public.

Moreover, the period between 1960 and 1972 had two ideologically extreme candidates (Goldwater and McGovern) – one on the right, one on the left. Goldwater embraced the label conservative (and even extremist), and McGovern did not run from the liberal label. The 1968 election had a strong third party bid by George Wallace, whose economic populism was combined with militant nationalism and support for racial segregation. These elections invited citizens to think in ideological terms, and to consider politics more systematically than in the 1950s, when Eisenhower ran as a war hero and grandfather.

The Changing American Voter sought to explore the impact of new issues, and new people (that is, generational replacement) on the relatively static world described by Campbell *et al.* Nie, Verba and Petrocik traced declines in partisanship, and increases in ideological thinking, issue constraint, and issue voting. They argued that as party loyalties eroded and elections became more centred on candidates, the new generation of voters was free to respond to the new issues of the day. This would be reflected in voting behaviour when candidates offered clear choices (and not echoes) to the public.

The claim that issue constraint had increased in the 1960s prompted two methodological critiques, centred on the change in National Election Studies (NES) question wording in 1964 – precisely the year that Nie *et al.* had reported the most rapid increase. In two experiments published in the same issue of *The American Journal of Political Science*, Sullivan *et al.* (1978) and Bishop *et al.* (1978) demonstrated beyond doubt that the increases in consistency were due to the changes in question wording, and not to changing political debates. The implication of Sullivan, Piereson and Marcus in particular is that constraint was always higher than Converse (1964) had reported, because the poor design of previous questions induced errors that the anchored seven-point scales avoided.

These methodological critiques are clever and convincing, and appear often in graduate syllabi. Yet they should not obscure the larger truth of the claims of *The Changing American Voter*. Partisan ties did weaken in the 1960s and 1970s, and a new cohort of voters with different priorities and issue concerns did emerge. New issues (especially abortion) have transformed partisan loyalties, and mobilised previously apolitical citizens (Adams 1997; Maxwell 2002). And the trend for party activists to be more extreme than inactive partisans has greatly increased, leading to a polarisation that has clearly resonated with voters (Jacobson 2000).

RESEARCH ON ATTITUDES TOWARD EQUALITY

In the late 1970s and throughout the 1980s, Verba and his colleagues explored public attitudes toward inequality. He began with a study of attitudes toward unemployment (Schlozman and Verba 1979). The failure of the economically disadvantaged in the US to press for redistributive policies has been called the 'dog that didn't bark' in American politics (Hochschild 1981), and the group that might seem most likely to actually bark would be those who once had jobs (and therefore have at least some skills and resources) but lost them during a recession. In the late 1970s, the US experienced 'stagflation' – stagnant growth and high levels of inflation that led to an unemployment rate of greater than 8% in the middle of the decade.[5] US rates of unemployment in this period were higher than those in Canada, Italy, Britain, the Netherlands, France, West Germany, Japan and Sweden.

Yet in 1975, with unemployment at 8.5%, only three demonstrations of the unemployed were reported. Schlozman and Verba surveyed 1370 randomly selected urban labour force participants, and 571 of the urban unemployed. Their ultimate explanation involved a realistically complex combination of free rider constraints (it is more rational to invest your time in a job search than in building a movement of the unemployed), a general acceptance of the individualistic American ethos, and the lack of resources among the unemployed. Perhaps more importantly, they found that those who are affected by unemployment and those who make unemployment policy, often take positions that deviate from self interest because of their more general beliefs about social justice and equality. Schlozman and Verba trace the patterns of these attitudes across class and racial lines, with fascinating results.

The importance of beliefs about fairness and equality in explaining the seeming acquiescence of the unemployed led directly to two books about attitudes toward inequality – one centered on the US (Verba and Orren 1985) and the other comparative (Verba *et al.* 1987). These books come from a large multinational survey of elites, drawn from business, labour, agriculture, intellectuals, the media, political parties, college youth, and special issue groups (blacks and feminists in the US). These books uncovered many nuanced patterns of attitudes towards political equality. The comparative book was a fascinating study of three very different countries – the US, Sweden, and Japan – with very different conceptions of equality.

PARTICIPATION AND EQUALITY STUDIES OF THE 1990S

By the end of the 1980s Verba had completed three remarkable sets of American and comparative studies. Over the previous two decades, he had explored the attitudes and orientations that sustain democracy in *The Civic Culture*, had examined the modes of participation of citizens in the US and elsewhere, and had considered in a preliminary way the implication of the socio-economic skew in participation. In the 1980s, Verba had explored ideas of equality, and how various groups (the unemployed, average citizens and elites) think about these issues. In the 1990s he was to combine these three concerns – democratic sustainability, participation and equality – into a remarkable set of papers and books that have had a major impact on the field and are considered mandatory reading in most courses on participation. The work had such a widespread impact on public debate that the American Public Broadcasting Service (PBS) aired a special on the topic.

Like many of Verba's projects, this involved a remarkable dataset. The investigators began by surveying some 15,000 individuals with a questionnaire that helped them to identify those who are active in some way in civic or political life, and to ask those activists special sets of questions. This resulted in more than 2,500 long, personal interviews. The dataset is complex and not simple to use, but like most of Verba's other projects, the data are rich and still very valuable to social scientists even after Verba and his colleagues have published two large books and many articles from the data.

In these projects Verba and his colleagues investigate the sources of civic and political activism, and the impact of that activism on equality in the US. By focusing not only on political participation but also on civic voluntarism, the work connected to some of the concerns about democratic stability in *The Civic Culture*. By the early 1990s, democratic theorists were reminding scholars of the importance of a voluntary sector in sustaining democracies. The publication of Robert Putnam's *Making Democracy Work* (Putnam 1994) brought the discussion of the importance of civil society to the fore. Putnam argued that civil society was an essential ingredient to effective regional government in Italy.

Although *Voice and Equality* does not focus on the importance of civic voluntarism, its publication caught almost precisely the wave of interest in civil society that was cresting in the mid 1990s. Instead of the classic rational choice view of participation as an irrational act, Verba and his colleagues argue that voluntary participation in America is common, and thus the question to be explained is not 'why would anyone participate' but rather 'why do some not participate?' Here Verba *et al.* offer three basic explanations:

Because they can't – they lack the resources necessary for participation
They don't want to – they have little interest in politics or civic life
Nobody asked – because they are not part of networks of solicitation

Of the three, Verba and his colleagues focus the greatest part of their attention on the first explanation. Here Verba revisits the SES model from his earlier 1970s studies, and argues that although SES provides a useful baseline from which to measure deviations in rates of participation, it is an inadequate explanation of participation. In its place, Verba focuses on the resources that are required for participation – civic skills, time, and money among others, and how those resources are acquired.

The book makes a convincing argument that better educated Americans are likely to have better social skills that enable effective participation. This includes the ability to make coherent and effective arguments, the ability to participate effectively in a group discussion, to organise your time effectively to take on additional tasks and responsibilities, etc. Although education, workplace learning and socialisation are the principal ways that these skills are acquired, involvement in some types of civic groups can also help citizens develop these skills (for an elaboration of the causal model, see Brady *et al.* 1995). In the US, churches are the most important source of these skills for lower SES citizens. This is especially true for African Americans, who have higher rates of church attendance and are more likely to be involved in evangelical Protestant churches that have many roles for the laity. Churches are not singled out by theory, but instead by empirical results. In other societies unions might well provide these critical skills to working class families, but in the US unions are quite weak and only a small portion of the working class belong to a union.

Verba and his colleagues also focus on the recruitment of activists – and the role of solicitation in increasing participation rates. Recruitment networks are understudied in American politics, and quite important in political contributing (Brown *et al.* 1995). Verba's data show that half of those asked to become involved in community activities agree to do so. This does not mean that half of all citizens are willing to do this kind of work, of course, because solicitors are skilled in identifying likely volunteers and do not bother to ask those who are unlikely to participate. Yet it does suggest that there may be many citizens who would be willing to be active if they were asked (only 19% had been asked to be involved in community activity). Moreover, it adds an additional element to the explanation of the upper SES bias to participation – for citizens ask their neighbours and friends to participate, thereby recreating the social contours of the activist elite in exaggerated form (Brady *et al.* 1999).

Verba and his colleagues also explore the consequences of the unequal rates of participation in the US. In an extended discussion of the concept of representation, they introduce the concept of 'participatory distortion' to describe the misrepresentation of public views that comes from the amplified voice given to those who participate regularly. When policymakers mingle regularly with participatory elites, they hear a very different set of policy preferences and positions than they would hear if they mingled regularly with average citizens. Here Verba gives a much more elegant theoretical treatment to themes that had begun to crop up in his work as early as *The Civic Culture* and especially in *Participation in America.*

Participatory distortion is significant in all kinds of political participation, but it is especially important in the case of campaign contributions (see also Francia *et al.* 2003). Although time volunteered to a campaign or interest group is both limited (all citizens have only 24 hours in their day) and the basic resource is distributed equally, campaign contributions in the US have until very recently been unlimited in size, and in the US income and wealth are very unevenly distributed. And although campaign contributors have diverse policy views that are polarised along party lines, the priorities of liberal elites are more likely to be post-material issues such as abortion rights and the environment rather than programmes that help poor and working families (Verba *et al.* 1993).

Voice and Equality inspired a rare review symposium in the *American Political Science Review.* The introduction to the three reviews declared the book 'a modern masterpiece,' but each reviewer had a slightly different perspective on the book. John Aldrich (1997) argues for a different conceptualisation of various acts of participation – that only by constructing 'domain specific' models of understanding can a positive theory of participation be forged. Jane Mansbridge (1997) stresses the positive benefits of participation – the way that participating enhances citizen capacity (see also Warren 2000). Jennifer Hochschild (1997) highlights results that imply that even among African Americans and Latinos, activists have different policy preference and priorities to non-activists, and puzzles over the lack of a connection between participation and racial and ethnic consciousness in these communities. The book was awarded the Philip Converse Prize from the APSA Section on Elections, Public Opinion, and Political Behaviour in 2007.

Several of the articles from the Voice and Equality project focused on gender differences in participation, a topic to which Verba turned in his most recent book. In this book, Burns, Schlozman and Verba (2001) begin with the dataset from *Voice and Equality,* but they re-interviewed 609 activists, and for the 382 respondents who were married, they conducted separate interviews with their spouse. Their book, *The Private Roots of Public Action* won the Victoria Schuck Award from the APSA for the best book on women and politics.

Their work addresses the puzzle of the continuing gender gap in political participation in the US, three decades after the feminist movement and at a time when young women and men take equality more or less for granted. Women's participation rates are only slightly lower than men in most areas (and higher in church-related voluntarism), but women are much less likely than men to give money to campaigns, a participatory act that Verba and colleagues had shown was a special source of participatory distortion in *Voice and Equality*. Although women vote slightly more often than men in most elections, they are less likely to be volunteers for political parties, or to be active in groups that seek to improve communities – areas where the literature has long assumed that women were more active.

The authors perform 'outcomes analysis' which enables them to investigate the influence of different levels of a particular explanatory variable (e.g. education) as well as the differential impact that this variable may have on men and women (that is, education may matter more to women than to men, or vice versa). They find little support for some traditional explanations of the gender gap in participation – that the double burden of labour force participation and homemaking gives women little time to be involved in politics, that childrearing leaves little psychological energy to devote to politics, and that patriarchal families raise their daughters to be more politically passive.

Instead, the authors conclude that women's lower rate of participation comes from a combination of small effects – deficits in education and other resources, for example, and lower levels of interest in politics. They also uncover some subtle gender differences – for example, churches primarily help women gain civic skills, because men are more likely to acquire them at work. They also note that women in elected office tend to increase women's interest in politics, and their participation rate increases with their interest. This implies that women's participation rates may increase over the next few decades, as women become increasingly well represented in state legislatures and Congress (Thomas and Wilcox 1998).

A DIVERSION INTO METHODS

Verba collaborated on one other book in the 1990s, quite outside the regular path of his scholarship. Together with Gary King and Robert Keohane, Verba wrote a useful volume on qualitative methodology (King *et al.* 1994). Although Verba's career has been marked by rigorous statistical analysis of large and complex datasets, some of the most interesting theoretical questions in political science cannot be explored with large surveys. In this useful text, King *et al.* explore the logic of social science and descriptive inference, of various models of causality, or what to observe and errors to avoid, and how to increase the number of observations. The book is very useful for scholars, and is an invaluable teaching tool as well.

VERBA'S VOICE

Verba's productivity establishes him as first among equals in the profession, but what is his unique voice? Several threads connect Verba's work across the decades, some methodological, and some substantive. Many of Verba's most important projects involve the collection of large, complex datasets that are uniquely formulated to answer the questions that he poses, but that ultimately prove useful for many other purposes to scores of other scholars. The five-nation survey of *The Civic Culture*, the seven-nation survey of political participation, the oversample of attitudes of the unemployed, the cross-national survey of elite attitudes toward equality, and the more recent massive survey of activists – all are important contributions for the data alone. Few scholars have ever attempted to build a single dataset of the complexity of these, much less this many diverse projects.

Verba's work is also characterised by methodological rigour, methodological inventiveness, but not by a methodological straitjacket. Verba carefully explores the data in these studies, finding the underlying structure of attitudes and tracing differences across many overlapping groups. The books and articles are packed with analysis of data that is subtle, insightful, and often quite clever. In *Participation in America*, for example, with simple tables Verba shows that after controlling for socio-economic status, blacks in the South were significantly less likely to vote than whites, and blacks in the North were significantly more likely to vote.

Verba asks questions that are not merely of theoretical interest to the study of political science, but of fundamental relevance to society as well. The twin themes of equality and participation, and the important intersection between these two concepts, remain critically important to both theories of democracy and also to the conduct of American politics. In the 2000s, the US slashed its income taxes on the wealthy, and at the same time imposed limits on health care for the poor. There is no political scientist in the US or elsewhere who is better able to explain tragic policy combination than Verba. His research tells us much not only about why the US has adopted these policies, but why the working class and the poor are not in the streets objecting to these policies. At a time when empirical political science is routinely condemned for asking only unimportant questions that can be easily answered with data, Verba stands out as a rebuttal to the charge – as someone who asks a hard question, then does the hard work to find the data that can help to answer the question.

The normative beliefs underlying his work are evident and deeply felt. Verba has been concerned with inequality all of his life, and his research has led him to focus on the role of differential rates of political participation on equality. He says that inequality is 'one of the biggest real political issues in the USA today.' He traces his interest in the topic to his Depression era childhood, growing up in a working class immigrant neighbourhood, a child of shopkeepers who worshiped FDR (President Franklin Roosevelt). Verba's unique voice is in part an exploration of the lack of voice accorded to some social groups. Instead of exploring the upper class accent of the choir (Schattschneider 1960), he focuses on the voices missing from the choir.

Verba explicitly acknowledges the normative underpinnings of his work (Verba 2003, 2006). He explores the positive and negative aspects of equal participation, and the reasons for inequality (Verba 2006). His conclusion makes clear his commitment to equality:

This paper has focused on the equality of citizen participation, and the reasons why we want it. It also makes clear that we will not get it soon. This is no reason not to continue trying. (Verba 2003)

> [...] achieving fully equal voice as input – the criterion chosen for this analysis – is difficult, unlikely, and may have negative consequences associated with it. Nevertheless, I argue that it is a goal worth striving for if one wants a polity that will be considered fair by those living in it (2006: 517).

Verba's former student Goldie Shabad says that this was the most important lesson that she learned from Verba as a student – of combining 'important normative concerns with rigorous empirical analysis of substantive issues.' Shabad says that this is the element of Verba's mentorship that she most copies with her own students.

Verba's answers are not simple ones. The explanation for the continuing gender gap in political participation is not one that can be easily summarised in a slogan, or a blurb on the back of a book. Instead, the authors carefully dissect the participation gap, showing how its sources differ for different participatory acts, and how a number of factors combine to create the gap. Verba's work is always careful, and methodical. The argument is laid out, alternative explanations proposed and assessed, evidence sifted, and an answer proposed.

This does not make for brief volumes. The two volumes that Verba produced in the 1990s combine to total more than 1000 pages. Luckily, Verba writes with an elegance that keeps readers turning those pages. Last year one of my students remarked that *Voice and Equality* was the most readable 600 page book that she had ever read – and in fact the most readable book in the entire term among a set of far slimmer volumes. Sniderman elegantly captures the strength of Verba's prose:

> Most obviously, Sidney has a gift for analytic narrative. The metaphor implicit here – between survey researcher and novelist – may strike some readers as inapt. If so, they would have missed a vital part of what makes Sidney's books singular: they are narratives of ideas. [...] The result is the capacity to develop an argument of uncommon complexity, step by step and in as much empirical detail as necessary, without sacrificing or obscuring the larger causal – and political themes. I am not aware of a contemporary social scientist, writing at full length, with a capacity to organise and convey complex quantitative results with comparable expository flair and analytical force [...] (1994: 578).

In 2004, Verba joined with the American Political Science Association Task Force on Inequality and American Democracy, and was co-author on 'Inequalities of Political Voice,' one of the Task Force's important position papers (Schlozman *et al.* 2004). Yet he has stated that his next book will be the culmination of his work on equality. It is tempting to declare that this will be the capstone of his career, but Verba likes to keep gathering and analysing data. In an interview in 2003 he said that 'I've always thought of political science as a craft. I like sort of creating arguments, putting pieces together, think of it much more as kind of craftsmanship, rather than, high level fancy thing.' He is likely to continue to practice the craft and turn out important scholarship for years to come.

Notes
1. We would like to thank Sidney Verba for a personal interview and an extended e-mail exchange, and Kristi Andersen, John Bailey, Bing Powell, Kay Schlozman, Goldie Shabad, and Robert Keohane for their insight.
2. Verba was also recognised as one of the 'Tweediest' professors by M Magazine, which he reports is the only award that got him respect from his children (Marks 2003).
3. The more formal formulation comes from a lecture by Edward Lorentz in 1972 at the meeting of the American Association for the Advancement of Science in Washington, D.C. The lecture was entitled 'Predictability: Does the Flap of a Butterfly's Wings in Brazil set off a Tornado in Texas?'
4. But Verba's first class had precisely no students (Marks 2003).
5. In the US, unemployment rates include only those in the labour force. In the case of those who are unemployed, only those who have actively sought work in the past two weeks are considered. Thus the unemployment rate understates the real level of unemployment, for 'discouraged workers' may want jobs but have lost their will to apply for them.

REFERENCES

Adams, G. (1997) 'Abortion; Evidence of an Issue Evolution', *American Journal of Political Science,* 41: 718–37.

Aldrich, J. H. (1997) 'Positive Theory and Voice and Equality', *American Political Science Review,* 91: 421–3.

Almond, G. and Verba. S. (1963) *The Civic Culture; Political Attitudes and Democracy in Five Nations*, Princeton: Princeton University Press.

(1980) *The Civic Culture Revisited*, Newbury Park: Sage.

Bishop, G. F., Tuchfarber, A. J. and Oldendick, R. W. (1978) 'Change in the Structure of American Political Attitudes; The Nagging Question about Question Wording', *American Journal of Political Science,* 22: 250–69.

Brady, H. E., Verba, S. and Schlozman, K. L. (1995) 'Beyond SES: A Resource Model of Political Participation', *American Political Science Review,* 89: 271–94.

Brady, H. E., Schlozman, K. L. and Verba, S. (1999) 'Prospecting for Participants: Rational Expectations and the Recruitment for Activists', *American Political Science Review,* 93: 153–68.

Brown, C. Jr., Powell, L. and Wilcox, C. (1995) *Serious Money; Contributing and Fundraising in Presidential Elections*, New York: Cambridge University Press.

Burns, N., Verba, S. and Schlozman, K. L. (2001) *The Private Roots of Public Action; Gender, Equality, and Political Participation,* Cambridge: Harvard University Press.

Campbell, A., Converse, P., Miller, W. and Stokes, D. (1960) *The American Voter*, New York: Wiley.

Converse, P. E. (1964) 'The Nature of Mass Beliefs Systems', in D. Apter (eds.) *Ideology and Discontent*, New York: Wiley.

Di Palma, G. (1970) *Apathy and Participation; Mass Politics in Western Societies*, New York: Free Press.

Francia, P., Green, J. C., Herrnson, P. S., Powell, L. and Wilcox, C. (2003) *The Financiers of Congressional Elections; Investors, Ideologues, and Intimates.* New York: Columbia University Press.

Hochschild, J. (1997) 'Practical Politics and Voice and Equality', *American Political Science Review*, 91: 425–427.

(1981) *What's Fair? American Beliefs about Distributive Justice*, Cambridge: Harvard University Press.

Howard, M. M. (2003) *The Weakness of Civil Society in Post-Communist Europe*, New York: Cambridge University Press.

Jacobson, G. (2000) 'Party Polarisation in National Politics; The Electoral Connection', in J. R. Bond and R. Fleisher (eds.) *Polarised Politics; Congress and the President in a Partisan Era*, Washington, DC: CQ Press.

King, G., Keohane, R. O. and Verba, S. (1994) *Designing Social Inquiry*, Princeton: Princeton University Press.

Mansbridge, J. (1997) 'Normative Theory and Voice and Equality', *American Political Science Review*, 91: 423–425.

Marks, S. M. (2003) 'Professor Juggles, Mediates', *The Harvard Crimson Online*, www.thecrimson.com/article.aspx?ref=348200 accessed 6/12/03.

Masuoka, N., Grofman, B. and Feld, S. L. (2007) 'The Political Science 400: A 20 Year Update', *PS*, January, pp. 133–45.

Maxwell, C. J. (2002) *Pro-Life Activists in America; Meaning, Motivation, and Direct Action*, New York: Cambridge University Press.

Nie, N. H., Bingham Powell, G. Jr. and Prewitt, K. (1969a) 'Social Structure and Political Participation; Developmental Relationships, Part I', *American Political Science Review*, 63: 361–78.

(1969b) 'Social Structure and Political Participation; Developmental Relationships, Part 2', *American Political Science Review*, 63: 808–32.

Pateman, C. (1980) 'The Civic Culture; A Philosophical Critique', in G. Almond and S. Verba (eds.) *The Civic Culture Revisited*, Newbury Park: Sage.

Putnam, R. (1993) *Making Democracy Work; Civic Traditions in Modern Italy*, Princeton, New Jersey: Princeton University Press.

Pye, L. and Verba, S. (1965) *Political Culture and Political Development*, Princeton, New Jersey: Princeton University Press.

Rokkan, S., Verba, S., Viet, J. and Almassy, E. (1969) *Comparative Survey Analysis*, The Hague: Mouton.

Rosenberg, M. J, Verba, S. and Converse, P. E. (1970) *Vietnam and the Silent Majority*, New York: Harper & Row.

Sani, G. (1980) 'The Political Culture of Italy: Continuity and Change', in *The Civic Culture Revisited*, Newbury Park: Sage.
Schattschneider, E. E. (1960) *The Semi-Sovereign People; a Realist's View of Democracy in America,* New York: Holt, Rinehart and Winston.
Sullivan, J. L. Piereson, J. E. and Marcus, G. E. (1978) 'Ideological Constraint in the Mass Public; A Methodological Critique and Some New Findings', *American Journal of Political Science,* 22: 233–49.
Schlozman, K. L., Page, B. I., Verba, S. and Fiorina, M. P. (2004) 'Inequalities of Political Voice', *American Political Science Association,*www.apsanet.org/imgtest/voicememo.pdf
Schlozman, K. L. and Verba, S. (1979) *Injury to Insult; Unemployment, Class, and Political Response,* Cambridge: Harvard University Press.
Sniderman, P. M. (1994) 'Sidney Verba; An Intellectual Biography', *PS: Political Science & Politics*, September: 574–579.
Thomas, S. and Wilcox, C. (1998) *Women and Elective Office; Past, Present, and Future,* New York: Oxford University Press.
Verba, S. (1961a) *Small Groups and Political Behavior: A Study of Leadership*, Princeton: Princeton University Press.
—— (1961b) 'Assumptions of Rationality and Non-Rationality in Models of the International System', in K. Knorr and S. Verba (eds.) *The International System; Theoretical Essays*, Princeton: Princeton University Press.
—— (1980) 'On Revisiting the Civic Culture; A Personal Postscript', in G. Almond and S. Verba (eds.) *The Civic Culture Revisited,* Newbury Park: Sage.
—— (1997) 'The Civic Culture and Beyond; Citizens, Subjects, and Survey Research in Comparative Politics', in H. Daalder (ed.) *Comparative European Politics; A History of the Profession,* London: Pinter.
—— (2003) 'Would the Dream of Political Equality Turn into a Nightmare? Why Might We Not', *Perspectives on Political Science,* 1 (4): 663–79.
—— (2006) 'Fairness, Equality, and Democracy; Three Big Words', *Social Research,* 73: 499–540.
Verba, S., Ahmed, B., Bhatt, A. (1971) *Caste, Race, and Politics; a Comparative Study of India and the United States,* Beverly Hills: Sage.
Verba, S., Kelman, S., Orren, G. R., Miyake, I., Watanuki, J., Kabashima, I. and Donald Feree, G. Jr. (1987) *Elites and the Idea of Equality; A Comparison of Japan, Sweden, and the United States*, Cambridge: Harvard University Press.
Verba, S. and Nie, N. (1972) *Participation in America*, New York: Harper & Row.
Verba, S., Nie, N. and Kim, J. (1971) *The Modes of Democratic Participation; a Cross-National Comparison,* Beverly Hills: Sage.
—— (1987) *Participation and Political Equality; a Seven-Nation Comparison,* Chicago: University of Chicago Press.
Verba, S., and Orren, G. R. (1985) *Equality in America; The View from the Top,*

Cambridge: Harvard University Press.
Verba, S., Schlozman, K. L. and Brady, H. (1995) *Voice and Equality; Civic Voluntarism in American Politics,* Cambridge: Harvard University Press.
Verba, S., Schlozman, K. L. Brady, H. and Nie, N. (1993) 'Citizen Activity; Who Participates? What do they Say?' *American Political Science Review,* 87: 303–18.
Warren, M. (2000) *Democracy and Association*, Princeton, New Jersey: Princeton University Press.

chapter ten | Aaron Wildavsky: Civic Passion and Scientific Commitment
Giorgio Freddi

THE FIELD OF PUBLIC ADMINISTRATION

Aaron Wildavsky's scholarly output is veritably prodigious and astoundingly multifaceted: his bibliography includes 45 books (of which seven are posthumous) and more than two hundred essays, articles, and chapters in collective works. The task I aim to fulfill here is twofold: first, to outline and characterize Wildavsky's scientific profile and, second, to underline the specificity of his contribution to, and impact on, political science. Thus, in the context of his exceedingly large and diversified production, I focus on Wildavsky's contribution to the field of Public Administration and related areas. This means overlooking his brilliant excursions in such disciplinary fields and research areas such as: international relations (Wildavsky 1965b; 1983a; 1983b; Seabury and Wildavsky 1969; Friedland *et al.* 1975a; 1975b); regime transitions in post-Communist political systems (Clark and Wildavsky 1990); general political theory (Wildavsky 1967; 1971; 1991b); historical reconstructions of political and administrative institutions (Webber and Wildavsky 1986); political parties (Wildavsky 1959; 1962a); federalism (Wildavsky 1962b; 1967); the American presidency (Wildavsky 1959–60; 1965a; 1969; 1982; 1991a; Wildavsky and Ellis 1989), not to mention biblical analysis and interpretation (Wildavsky 1984; 1993a).

If we review the development and the sequence of the theoretical and empirical positions taken by Wildavsky chronologically, we are led to conclude that his original matrix is represented by the old field of Public Administration, mistakenly perceived and hastily described, in many an academic quarter, as obsolete and marginal against the background of contemporary political science. It has been a premature indictment: in the creative path reopened by Wildavsky, some of the original approaches of Public Administration play a central role in the discipline of political science. However, if we were to depict Wildavsky as the world leader in Public Administration, we would end up portraying him as a sedate and traditional scholar, entirely misrepresenting the dynamic thrust and innovative direction of his *curriculum studiorum*. I am now going to show how Wildavsky, born to academic life as a student of Public Administration, managed to revolutionise the ways to approach that venerable field of research.

A few words about the working style and the profound motivations of our author are in order here. We know that in all fields of scientific investigation, even the most theoretically and technically sophisticated, the personality of the individual scientist, and the values with which he identifies, play a dominant role both in choosing the empirical referents to be investigated and in shaping the approaches to be adopted in the research process.

Wildavsky was passionately interested in politics, in the different ways in which power is deployed, and in their effects. More specifically, he was particularly interested in problems of collective relevance, in their impacts on individual freedom, and in how political action formulates and implements solutions to those problems. He was not, then, a laid-back and systematic thinker absorbed in building theoretical paradigms and methodological strategies. By this I do not, in any way, mean that Wildavsky was disinterested in theory building and methodological design. The opposite is true (as can be gathered especially by the discussion set forth in the fourth and fifth sections of this chapter), but when he approached methodological and theoretical themes, he saw them as elegant and parsimonious instruments in problem solving processes.

As noted above, the first – in chronological order – thematic influence on Wildavsky's scientific evolution is represented by the field of Public Administration. The late 1950s and early 1960s, when Wildavsky was first a graduate student at Yale, and then a young teacher at Oberlin University, were centrally important years in the renewal of the old and tired Public Administration, where one could distinguish two very different and distinct gradients. The older one, a product of the beginnings of American political science, had been authoritatively pioneered by Woodrow Wilson, first a professor of Public Administration in the Department of Politics at Princeton, then president of that university, later Governor of New Jersey, and finally President of the United States (1913–21). Wilson was a moderniser of the discipline of political science and, at the same time, a great reformer of public institutions. In the 1880s, when his academic career began, the Jacksonian spoils system had reached its highest point of inefficiency, ineffectiveness, and corruption, so much as to constitute a serious threat for democratic legitimacy. As an academic moderniser as well as an administrative reformer, Wilson had a very specific model in mind: the Prussian bureaucracy and its supporting theoretical framework, labeled in Germany as 'general theory of public law'. This theory hinges on the assumption that in constitutional and representative political systems there is total separation between, on the one hand, elected and politically appointed organs which, as the sole repositories of sovereignty, enjoy an integral decisional monopoly and, on the other hand, a permanent professional bureaucracy, operationally defined as merely charged with the technical execution of the law from an impartial and politically neutral posture or *überparteilich*.

In Continental Europe, the theory of separation between politics and administration has served the indispensable function of justifying the coexistence of representative assemblies – that, by their very nature, involve the possibility of alternating political majorities – with the stable professional bureaucracies 'inherited', so to speak, from the old regime (Freddi 1986: 158–62). In Wilsonian America, on the contrary, the theory of separation came to perform a very different function. Not the justification of the administrative *status quo*, but the formulation of a radical programme meant to extirpate the spoils system and to replace it with the harmonious collaboration, in the words of Wilson, between the art of politics and the science of administration.

The theoretical framework shaped by Wilson to set forth his definition of the separation between politics and administration does, to quite an extent, anticipate the functionalist theory of political action some sixty years before it became an integral part of the conceptual arsenal of political science. In fact Wilson argued that the theory of the tripartite separation of powers no longer succeeded, a century after the enactment of the constitution, in describing and explaining the workings of government and the political system, as witnessed by the daily spectacle of each of the three branches impinging on the prerogatives of the others. One could no longer realistically speak of three branches but, rather, of two *functions*: on the one hand, the political function of authoritative decision-making and, on the other, the administrative function of executing decisions according to criteria of efficiency and economy.

The second, relatively more recent, gradient of the old Public Administration is represented by the study of the organisational dimension of public bureaucracies, developed in accord with the guidelines provided by the school of scientific management, strictly modeled after Taylorism. This approach to the study of governmental administration was very productive and fecund until the 1940s and, true to its tayloristic posture, was oriented to produce operational prescriptions, rather than empirically verify hypotheses about behavioural regularities.

In the late 1940s the discipline of Public Administration had become more and more sterile: the Wilsonian legacy had become stifling, deteriorating into a formalistic and acritically axiological position, removed from the empiricist ferments that, in those days, were renewing political science. It was a discipline in disarray which rapidly gained a new profile, thanks to the creative labours of such authors as Appleby (1949), Lipset (1950), Selznick (1949) and Waldo (1948), who guided larger and larger numbers of scholars to the redefinition of administration as an extension of politics, as another political actor in governmental decision-making. A crisis of equal gravity and irreversible direction had also struck the scientific management movement, reduced to uttering dogmatic and untested propositions and operational principles, devastatingly ridiculed as 'proverbs' by Herbert Simon (1947). This crisis, however, caused, in a relatively short time, many an innovator to open a new path leading to an empirically-oriented non-normative theory of organisation.

So far I have summarily outlined the scientific circumstances in which the young Wildavsky was beginning his career. A context with a very high potential for innovation with which he fully identified and which he immediately undertook to enrich and expand, as shown by the inclusion in his research work of a profound understanding of electoral processes, leadership, social stratification, as well as the complex interactions between formal and informal roles taking place in policy-making. As examples of these properties of Wildavsky's research output, one should mention his continued collaboration, every fourth year, to *Presidential Elections* [1], the book *Leadership in a Small Town* [2] (Wildavsky 1964a), and his investigation, with Heclo as a co-author (Heclo and Wildavsky 1981), of the ways in which the Permanent Secretaries of White Hall decide how to spend billions of pounds, paying little attention to the economic, financial, and operational dimensions of their decisions, while being almost exclusively interested in keeping the political consensus among the 'Mandarins' heading government departments.

The incredibly vast repertoire of methods, theoretical paradigms, and empirical referents one detects in Wildavsky's research activity can be concisely illustrated by listing and reviewing the numerous acknowledgments that he received from various institutions and associations. Thus, in 1975, he was the first scholar to receive the Charles M. Merriam Award in recognition of his ability in applying the theories developed by political science to the practice of politics and government. In 1982 the American Society for Public Administration bestowed on him the Dwight Waldo Award for his contributions to the literature of Public Administration. In 1984 the Policy Studies Association conferred on him the Harold Lasswell Award. He has been a member of the National Academy for Public Policy Analysis and Management, Fellow of the American Academy of Arts and Sciences, and President of the American Political Science Association.

INCREMENTALISM

If we wish to give a conceptually rigorous order to the numerous themes, referents and insights woven into the multicoloured tapestry metaphorically represented by Wildavsky's life work, some terms are critically important in characterising the fundamental thrusts of his research. 'Incrementalism' is the first such term that needs to be discussed here. A scholar so greatly interested in problem solving, so bent on pursuing the dynamics of the political system's outputs, and one who totally identified with the notion that administration is the continuation of politics with other means, was likely to adopt – following the basic assumptions of Harold Lasswell's view of the political process – the structure and functions of budgeting as the greatest link between politics and administration. The major output of this line of research was the publication of *The Politics of the Budgetary Process* (1964b) (now in its seventh edition). The scientific impact of this slim volume on the theory and practice of public budgeting was so revolutionary and path-breaking that it led to the disavowal of the then dominant and unchallenged synoptic approach to budget analysis (Smithies 1955) and to its replacement by the perspective of incrementalism.

Breakthroughs and insights that had recently enriched the theoretical repertoire of political science had created a situation ripe for Wildavsky's treatment of budgeting, and two such insights and breakthroughs are particularly meaningful for an understanding of the impact of his innovative work. The first such intellectual source was very close to Wildavsky's experience as a graduate student at Yale. Those were the years when Charles Lindblom was looking forward to moving from the department of economics to that of political science. Central to Lindblom's decision was his lucid and stimulating analysis of a comprehensive and, at the same time, incremental decisional system which, in the case of public bureaucracies, he famously rendered as 'muddling through' (Lindblom 1959; 1965; 1979). The second intellectual source, a permanent inspirational influence, is represented by the revolutionary approach to the interpretation of decisional processes generated by Herbert Simon. Wildavsky was one among the first political scientists – as a young scholar and throughout his scientific maturity – to absorb the shock of the new theory of decision-making, and utilise it systematically in his work.

To summarise, *The Politics of the Budgetary Process* is a most coherent demonstration of the assumption whereby administration is linked to politics *via* a continuous and combinative nexus. The several editions of the book, each one of them amply reviewed and partially revised, have multiplied its explanatory power. The process of formulation and implementation of the budget has been employed to tackle a number of problematic issues such as how to control the government, how to reorganise public administration, as well as the models and practices of governmental planning. By successive extensions of his budgetary theory and by further increasing its explanatory potential, Wildavsky and his many co-authors have produced an impressive sequence of books, articles, and essays. Hence, we have several technically sophisticated contributions dealing with budgeting and public finance which have led to both macro- and micro-analyses of the American and English cases, and of some developing nations (Wildavsky 1966; 1975; 1980b; 1988b; Davis *et al.* 1966; Caiden and Wildavsky 1974).

We also have the works that have opened and illustrated the great season of Wildavsky as a policy-analyst, concerned with a myriad of empirical referents and intellectual issues. Here I merely give a list of examples in an attempt to offer an idea of the breadth and depth of his investigations: what happens to federal programmes once they have fulfilled their goals? (Wildavsky 1976); the peculiarities of public works practices in the area of recreational projects (Nienaber and Wildavsky 1973); the policies for the development of reliable estimates of the quantity of oil and natural gas in the United States (Wildavsky and Tennenbaum 1981); the policies of international trade during the oil shock of the 1970s (Friedland *et al.* 1975b); the public vs. private dilemma in energy policies (Levy *et al.* 1974); how you do policy research (Wildavsky 1980a) and how you teach it (Wildavsky 1993b).

IMPLEMENTATION

The discussion developed so far, quite logically calls attention to the second term which is of central importance in characterising the Wildavskian contribution to political science: implementation. This term is also the title of one of his most important and cited works (Jeffrey Pressman being the co-author): *Implementation* (Pressman and Wildavsky 1973).

The importance and relevance of this book go far beyond its substantive research subject (the plan implemented by a federal agency, the Economic Development Administration, in order to promote the creation of jobs in a high unemployment area in Northern California). There are two dimensions that have deservedly given this book the reputation of a classic. In the first place, *Implementation* is the very fertile spearhead of a large literature which enjoys the authoritative status of a semi-autonomous sub discipline – implementation research – in the field of public policy. Research carried out in this subfield has elaborated concepts and approaches of great empirical and analytical saliency such as (to give just an impressionistic illustration) implementation deficit, top-down, bottom-up, policy community, policy network, policy legacy, iron triangle, policy evaluation (Bardach 1977; Barrett and Fudge 1981; Berman 1978; Elmore 1979–80; Hargrove 1975; Majone and Wildavsky 1978; Mazmanian and Sabatier 1983; Ripley and Franklin 1986; Sabatier 1986; Van Meter and Van Horn 1975).

Secondly, one must underline how the conceptual framework of *Implementation* fulfilled, and continues to fulfill, the function of a paradigmatic model in public policy research. Let us see why. The first studies of public policy analysis, which appeared in the mid-1960s, were received with some perplexity and moderate enthusiasm by both political scientists at large and by 'public administrationists'. The field of public policy analysis, objectively innovative and revolutionary in uncovering and investigating informal architectures of decisional power, invisible (or at least not seen) until then, began to invalidate the existing assumption that the study of public decision-making ceased with the investigation of the inner workings of public bureaucracies (which, as everybody knew, were supposed to be in charge of the output functions of the political system). This position had become deeply rooted in a scholarly context that had fully accepted the view that public administration is little more than a phase of the political process. In other words, it seemed that no conceptual room was left for a more pinpointed dissection of the workings of power.

This explains why, at the inception of public policy analysis in the academic arena, confronted with the new perspectives advanced by the policy analysts – not infrequently perceived as being arrogantly petulant – the academic establishment reacted with censorious disdain. It is true that since then, the relationship between tradition and innovation has somewhat improved, but it is equally true that we observe now an excessive autonomy and premature separation of policy studies vis-à-vis the main body of political science, with negative consequences for both.

Implementation is, among many things, an excellent and prescriptive example of how to avoid premature clashes which end up throwing out the baby with the bathwater. In fact, the research model utilised by Pressman and Wildavsky, while giving full value to the most recent and up-to-date developments in the field of Public Administration, at the same time succeeded in merging and combining them with the intuitions and concepts born out of the disciplinary propensities of public policy analysis: in short, a very insightful model of continuity, for theoretically ambitious research ventures in public policy.

POLITICAL CULTURE

'Political culture' is the third term denoting Wildavsky's intellectual and scientific voyage. It is the theme central to the last ten years of his life and signals his passage, as a political scientist, from a position close to the input and suggestions of economics, to an interest in those offered by anthropology – as shown by his long scholarly relationship with Mary Douglas.

We must clarify at the outset that the theoretical definition and the operational utilisation of culture as developed in the research carried out by Wildavsky, his associates and collaborators, differed markedly from those of the structural-functional approach which emerged and was prominent in the late 1950s and 1960s, and greatly influenced the work of scholars such as Almond (1952; 1955; 1960), Almond and Powell (1966), and Eckstein and Apter (1963).

On the one hand, the functionalists employ the concept of 'political culture' and its empirical operationalisation at a macroscopic level in order to throw light on the deep-seated and comprehensive dimensions of political action. They seek answers to questions such as: what makes a political system stable or unstable? and what conditions explain radical differences in political performance? Wildavsky, on the other hand, applies his theory of political culture to describe and interpret political and social action at a level of utmost specificity, with an emphasis on individual decisions and policies. He seeks answers to this question: why is it that various political systems, confronted with the same problem, adopt different approaches and end up adopting considerably diverging solutions? (Wildavsky 1988a; Douglas and Wildavsky 1982; Thompson *et al.* 1990). If we wish to receive appropriate answers to this kind of question – so runs Wildavsky's argument – we must utilise the tool represented by cultural analysis. In fact, the analytical tools provided by economics are not up to the job because they neglect the values and preferences of the actors. Preferences and values are deemed to be exogenous vis-à-vis the system being investigated. From the vantage point of cultural analysis, on the contrary, values and preferences are endogenous, and are disclosed by the ways in which collective actors build, modify, and destroy their institutions. In other words, when we observe different patterns of action employed to solve a given problem, the explanation is embedded in social life. The starting point, therefore, is a conceptualisation of the notion of culture as the collection of shared values legitimating social practice.

In Wildavsky's theory there are two basic dimensions of culture that can be summarily described as follows:

a) *The type of groups articulating culture.* A group is *strong* when it is coherent and inflexibly separated from other groups and, at the same time, decisions are rigidly binding on all members of the group. A group is *weak*, conversely, when its boundaries are permeable and its members can make individual decisions;

b) *The rules and prescriptions directing* group activities can be *many* (in which case individual members tend to be strictly guided by a large number of rules), or *few* (in which case, individual members make decisions at their own discretion).

If we use these two variables to construct a double-entry table we obtain a quadripartite typology, from which four ideal types emerge. They can be succinctly presented as follows:

a) *Competitive Individualism.* Competitive individualism is characterised by few prescriptions and weak boundaries. Its only fundamental rule is that coercion – defined as limits on transactions – is confined to the protection of people and their property. In other words, individuals are free to pursue their own interest, which means that competitive individualism is a risk-oriented market culture. From the political and institutional points of view, the definition of equality emerging from this model is that of equality of opportunities, which is tantamount to saying that individuals have the right to be different in status, income, prestige and so forth.

b) *Hierarchical Collectivism.* Hierarchical collectivism is the opposite end of individualism: here we have strongly bounded groups with many roles and rules. Against a background of status stratification, hierarchies assign and divide tasks painstakingly, so that each status lives by the rules imposed on it. Power distribution is obviously asymmetrical but not necessarily authoritarian, and risk is accepted, but only in terms of collective participation and responsibility. The notion of equality is emblematic of the general set-up seen so far: indeed, legal equality – operationally definable as the right shared by all members of this culture to be treated equally by the judge and by the tax collector – is tantamount to saying that socio-economic differences among individuals are immutable through time.

c) *Sectarian Egalitarianism.* While the two ideal models just discussed can easily be linked to historically tangible referents (capitalism in a constitutional polity and Weberian bureaucracy in a corporatist society), in the case of this model, not so easily recognisable at first sight, let us identify some historical referents which are not immediately necessarily recognisable: the Puritans; the anarchist movement; the *kibbutz*. Here the groups are very cohesive but have the fewest possible rules and prescriptions. Social organisation is in every respect voluntary, so that no one has the right to give orders to others. Equality of conditions or results is emphasised for, without authority, this is the only way in which individuals belonging to the same community can relate to one another. Not only must material gains be redistributed among group members, but social differences among them must be diminished.

d) *Impotent Fatalism*. This last ideal model is characterised by weak and easily penetrable groups and by an exceedingly high quantity of personal rules over which people have no control whatsoever. For the members of this culture there is no reciprocity, no mutuality, no sharing. Indeed, having no access to power, people believe either in luck or in submission and, consequently, do not take risks for themselves or for others because this is their fate. The model of fatalism, highly relevant to the anthropological contributions of Mary Douglas – who, as noted, has been Wildavsky's major co-author in cultural research – has rarely been put to use by Wildavsky, who has been mostly interested in investigating highly modernised contexts.

It is close to impossible, in the space of this chapter, to render complete justice to the explanatory complexity of Wildavsky's approach to the study of culture. The gist of his applied theory is represented by the analytical attention deployed to identify the means adopted and the results obtained by a culture in achieving the indispensable level of coherence between social structure on one side, and prescriptions and rules on the other. A satisfactory level of coherence in a culture allows its adherents to figure out principles for mitigating envy, placing blame, securing accountability, taking or avoiding risks and, last but not least, achieving the right kind of equality: equality of opportunities for the individualists (i.e., the right to be different on the basis of merit); legal equality, or certainty of the law, for the collectivists (which ends up perpetuating socio-economic differences); and equality of conditions and in results for the sectarians. At this point, we can ask a critically important question: how will different cultural models react to situations with a high level of ambiguity? Collectivists will resort to hyper-regulation, even at the cost of inefficiency. Individualists will go for criteria of competitive selection and redundant experimentation, with a strong preference for self-regulation. Egalitarians, who loathe competition as the very root of individual differences, will favour non-authoritative and non-discriminative criteria of distribution and, like the collectivists, be ready to absorb the high costs of inefficiency.

Obviously, for Wildavsky, as was learned from Max Weber, ideal-typical models are conceptual tools and not empirical propositions. When doing empirical research guided by ideal models, one runs into the so called hybrid types, that is, concrete situations where the elegantly geometric traits of ideal-typical models are combined according to different ratios, emphasising some and playing down others. Wildavsky, working at several comparative projects, has elaborated two main hybrid types, the former aimed at capturing European conditions and situations, the latter focused on explaining so called American exceptionalism.

Thus, in Europe one observes a strong collectivist tradition, a moderate extent of individualism and, altogether, more or less incisive propensities to sectarian egalitarianism. Nearly all European political systems have undergone historical development marked by a strong sense of sovereignty and an institutional tradition where hierarchy and bureaucracy play a major role. However, two partially different cultural configurations can be distinguished, depending on whether the preferred value is legal equality (usually where the political arena is controlled by moderate parties), or a more sectarian equality of conditions and results (which tends to take place in stable social democracies). In any case, the prevailing regime is (neo)-corporatism.

An entirely different picture can be seen on the other side of the Atlantic Ocean: American political culture flows from a combination where collectivism is practically non-existent (historically the United States has no tradition of institutionalised hierarchy), individualism is very strong, and sectarian egalitarianism unmistakably active. The peculiar quality of American historical development explains why sectarianism is so powerful. As is well known, Protestant sects contributed valiantly to the construction of the polity and, in so doing, injected into it an intense distrust vis-à-vis governmental power. Since then, a government which was weak, but nevertheless coherently regarded with suspicion as the very cause of inequality became a hallmark of the American Republic, as was exemplified in democratic populism. Throughout most of the 19th century there were no instances of conflict between the sectarian ideology and competitive individualism. As long as governments continued to be weak, the market place seemed to be capable of guaranteeing the conditions, for both equality of opportunities and equality of conditions and results. Toward the end of the 19th century, the establishment and consolidation of the giant stock corporation caused the happy coincidence between the two cultures to disintegrate.

End of the century monopolies were perceived as impenetrable hierarchies generating higher and higher measures of inequality to such an extent that the sectarian component of political culture, while remaining wary of all and any form of authority, came to terms with political power advocating governmental intervention in the economy and society as a countermeasure. Many historical instances of this trend could be mentioned; for example, antitrust legislation, draconian legal controls of industrial products and a very active and pragmatic environmental movement.

In concluding this section, we might ask a very pertinent question: what is the relevance of the Wildavskian approach to culture for the study of public policy? There is no doubt that the comparative cultural approach discussed here had, and continues to have, a major impact on a branch of the discipline – the largest in terms of his contributions to the literature – that can be concisely denoted as empirical-inductive with a strong theoretical and explanatory emphasis. Even a cursory review of policy studies shows that academics who practice in this field tend to favour empirical and comparative analyses, very often with explicit references to Wildavsky's works.

THE CULTURAL MODEL IN ACTION

It is well known that the proof of the pudding is in the eating and so I will give an illustration of the capacity of the Wildavskian model to tackle the complexity of empirical data, and to reveal continuities and consistencies. Wildavsky, either alone or with collaborators, has published some 50 works (books, articles, essays, and chapters in collections) where the theoretical model discussed thus far has been tested empirically on numerous referents.

The publication I have chosen to illustrate this model is a good representative example of Wildavsky's working style. While this is the main reason for my choice, I must add that there is another subjective factor at work here: I too have done research on the same empirical referent. The publication in question is *Doing More and Using Less; Utilisation of Research as a Result of a Regime* (Wildavsky 1986). The subject of this work, comparatively analysed in the most important democratic and postindustrial political systems, is constituted by the policies formulated and implemented in order to protect human health from the effects of chemical products and chemical production processes. The central question our author wants to answer is as follows:

> Why does the United States produce so much more research into chemical contamination and use so little, whereas European nations and the Japanese produce much less, but make much greater use of their knowledge? Why, to add an element of complexity, do the others rely more on politics and less on research – though when they rely on research it does matter – while the United States relies both on research and on politics, but neither reaches agreement nor uses the bulk of research results? (Wildavsky 1986: 5)

We may begin to answer these questions by taking into consideration a series of factors which are of help in drawing a first distinction between trends prevailing in the major European political systems on the one hand, and in the United States, on the other. In Europe, even though there are structural and regulatory differences in France, Germany and the United Kingdom, a common trend can be discerned that we call 'remedial' and, at the same time, 'collaborative'. Legislatures and *ad hoc* executive agencies, when confronted with episodes of chemical contamination, react with remedial intentions only after disastrous events have occurred. Scientific research, generally of quite modest calibre, is carried out by a very limited number of (repeatedly used) experts, who act as permanent fiduciaries of the government. Customarily, research operations take a long time to be completed and once a scientific verdict has been made available, the decision process goes into motion according to criteria – as we have seen – marked by collaboration involving not only *ad hoc* governmental agencies but also representatives of those charged with contamination, as well as representatives of the trade unions. The significance of this neo-corporatist arrangement is quite clear. The goal of pursuing adequate protection from chemical contamination must be compatible with another objective: the government's need to ensure that both employment and the national economy's ability to compete internationally will not be negatively affected. In other words, the agencies which have been assigned the task of environmental protection must do their duty without endangering interests that would normally be regarded as incompatible with their institutional goal.

Implementation is assigned to administrative agencies, with little or no room left for judicial intervention, in a process that varies between nations. Thus in Germany very detailed rules are negotiated and bargained at length between governmental agencies and the potential polluters, with the intent of producing norms and prescriptions capable of automatic application. In the United Kingdom solutions are reached through a very informal style of negotiation among the relevant actors, leading to what are referred to as 'gentlemen's agreements'. In France, in view of the very authoritative stance of public administration, and of the historical and legislated tradition of strict and watchful governmental control over organised interests, one could very well describe the relationship reached between *ad hoc* agencies and the business concerns involved in environmental action as a quasi-protectorate.

The American picture, on the contrary, is characterised by a consolidated trend that can be denoted as *proactive* and, simultaneously, *adversarial*. The term 'proactive' clearly signifies that public intervention to control potential contaminative chemical production and the building of chemical plants takes place at the planning stage and not after the occurrence of calamitous events – it is not by chance that the United States is the home of environmental impact evaluation.

Interventions are carried out by technical agencies of great scientific and technological quality – such as the Environmental Protection Agency (EPA). Actions are put forward with extraordinary swiftness, in an aggressive and 'adversarial' manner. However, the swiftness of the decision process contrasts strongly with the slow and time-consuming implementation stage. Judicial and quasi-judicial procedures protract the conflict between regulators and those regulated inordinately. This is why judges play a central role and thus, in spite of the great amounts of high quality scientific and technological research displayed in these proceedings, conflict resolution tends to be politically rather than scientifically articulated.

The antithesis vis-à-vis the European style is quite evident. The structure expected to protect the public from the risk of chemical contamination, the EPA, pursues single-mindedly the goal of protection, while the safeguarding of the ability of national industrial concerns to compete in the international economy, and the goal of full employment, are not part of its mission.

Though the description given above is admittedly compact and tight to the extreme, we have nevertheless reached an interesting conclusion about the ways in which governments intervene to counteract chemical contamination. We are dealing here with democratic post-industrial systems, which share a common constitutional and institutional set-up, are faced with the same environmental problems produced by the same causes, and have access to the same scientific and technological know-how. And yet, contrary to our expectations, they end up opting for remarkably different solutions. The interpretation of these surprising differences can be given – following Wildavsky – in prevailingly cultural terms.

The four political systems we have been using as representative examples in our previous analysis – France, Germany, the United Kingdom, and the United States – have succeeded, admittedly by applying different criteria, in institutionalising innovative capacities in problem-solving. In other words, other things being equal, the *ad hoc* agencies that have been framed to provide environmental protection, do manage correctly to identify pollution sources and to initiate appropriate action. So, we can take for granted that our four political systems can avail themselves of an environmental police with adequate technological and scientific knowledge and personnel.

Now let us try to explain why, even in the presence of these critically important and shared properties, there are, from one to the other of our political systems, operational differences of such magnitude. In the United States pollution is perceived as a by-product of industrial capitalism – a cultural model strenuously rejected by the sectarian and egalitarian components – while in Europe pollution is regarded as a collective problem, a solution to which must be found *via* the coordinated participation of all social forces, all of them more or less partaking of a hierarchical tradition.

In the United States, when a very threatening and comprehensive emergency occurs, the reaction takes the form of a pluralistic and, at the same time, antagonistic problem-solving posture, activated by that web of voluntary associations so famously evidenced by Alexis de Tocqueville. In Europe, granted that there is a degree of variety from one political system to the next, voluntary associations are fragile almost everywhere and not deeply embedded in the culture. In their place we see those thriving patterns of discreet and velvety consultations by means of which top industrial groups, very large trade unions and governmental agencies, protected by well-tested bureaucratic procedures, slowly move towards the solution to a problem. In other words, we have here that particular form of interest articulation known as neo-corporatism. This mode of problem-solving would be absolutely unthinkable in the United States where the strong sectarian component of political culture would consider it as evidence of corruption and of elitist conspiracy.

What has been argued so far leads to a plausible explanation of the different modes exhibited by our political systems so far as the utilisation of science and technology is concerned. Political cultures with a major sectarian component painstakingly look for the very first symptoms of incipient danger, long before they emerge with undoubted evidence. Precisely because the sectarian components maintain, quite frequently with ample margins of justification, that both the government and the industrial complex show a propensity to minimise situations of potential danger, they favour proactive policies, utilising science and technology as anticipatory strategies. If, as a consequence of this approach, industrial capitalism experiences delays and losses in production and profits, this is the right price to pay. After all, whoever is guilty of causing situations of risk and danger for the public, deserves to be punished.

An entirely different picture is uncovered when we focus our attention on regimes with prevailingly hierarchic and collectivist cultures. There is no doubt about the concern of these regimes with environmental damage, but they put equal, simultaneous, and contextual emphasis on other problems as well, such as economic development, unemployment, inflation and ability to compete in the international market place. All this induces them to proceed slowly, to request lengthy studies and (often duplicated) research, and even to ignore evident symptoms of danger, delaying action until the evidence is overwhelming.

CUMULATIVENESS

It was no simple task, and yet I hope that I have managed to capture the quintessential elements, dimensions, and interests of Aaron Wildavsky. In so doing I have been forced to make difficult choices that have caused me to neglect many alluring pages on federalism, the American presidency, post-Communism and, why not, Moses and Joseph.

In concluding, I wish to call attention to a very important attitude exhibited by Wildavsky in assessing what he considered to be the central objective, both theoretical and practical, of our discipline: how to recognise and make advances in problem-solving with regard to the major collective issues of our time, and the impact of those issues on individual liberties. Wildavsky has applied himself to this impervious task by rigorously pursuing a research style likely to augment the probability that knowledge produced by political science is cumulative. By cumulative, I do not mean here a technical and epistemological definition of the term but, rather, an approach that is likely to strengthen mutually, and exploit to the full, most of the complementarities between paradigms and methods elaborated by political scientists. In other words, he advocated creating the conditions for intellectual collaboration where, very frequently and unfortunately, we encounter situations of hostile incommunicability.

To summarise, Wildavsky – who liked to say ' our discipline may not be so great, but it looks to me that we know much more than we did thirty years ago' – has consistently cultivated an intellectual style that guided him, by juxtapositions, adjustments, and corrections, to seek the gradual growth of the explanatory power of this or that model. Nelson Polsby (1994: 37) has admirably captured this trait of Wildavsky's scholarship in these words:

> Aaron's approach to truth was incremental, a distillation of the method of successive approximations. One of the secrets of his productivity was that he tended to publish each approximation. Scholarship for Aaron was a public process, a social process, fit for many hands. It's a powerful idea, and a very sensible solution to the classic problem of the blind men and the elephant:

If you get enough blind men working on the same problem, and coordinate them properly, the elephant actually emerges. And so in Aaron's style of work we see not only multiple approximations but also many collaborators, disciples, and correspondents drawn in scholarly enterprise.

NOTES

1 *Presidential Elections,* first published in 1964 and, since then, every fourth year (Polsby and Wildavsky 1964).
2 *Leadership in a Small Town* is the first example of Wildavsky's propensity and ability to involve his students in research projects. When he began his academic career at Oberlin University, he was mindful of the large research project that Robert Dahl was conducting in New Haven, investigating the power structure of that town. Wildavsky led his students in intensive research to reproduce, in parallel, in the town of Oberlin, what Dahl was doing in New Haven.

REFERENCES

Almond, G. A. (1952) 'A Comparative Study of Interest Groups and the Political Process', *American Political Science Review,* 52: 275–89.
— (1955) 'Comparative Political System', *Journal of Politics,* 40: 1042–9.
— (1960) 'A Functional Approach to Comparative Politics', in G. A. Almond and S. G. Coleman, *The Politics of Developing Areas,* Princeton, Princeton University Press.
Almond, G. A. and Powell, G. B. (1966) *Comparative Politics,* Boston: Little Brown; trad. it. *Politica Comparata,* Bologna, il Mulino, 1970.
Appleby, P. H. (1949) *Policy and Administration,* Tuscaloosa, Ala: University of Alabama Press.
Bardach, E. (1977) *The Implementation Game; What Happens after a Bill Becomes a Law,* Cambridge, Mass: MIT Press.
Barrett, S. and Fudge, C. (eds.) (1981) *Policy and Action; Essays on Implementation of Public Policy,* London: Methuen.
Berman, P. (1978) 'The Study of Macro and Micro-Implementation', *Public Policy,* 2 (2): 157–84.
Caiden, N. and Wildavsky, A. (1974) *Planning and Budgeting in Poor Countries,* New York: John Wiley & Sons.
Clark, J. and Wildavsky, A. (1990) *The Moral Collapse of Communism; Poland as a Cautionary Tale,* San Francisco: ICS Press.
Davis, O., Dempster, M. A. H. and Wildavsky, A. (1966) 'A Theory of the Budgetary Process', *American Political Science Review,* 60 (3): 529–47.
Douglas, M. and Wildavsky, A. (1982) *Risk and Culture; An Essay on the Selection of Technological and Environmental Dangers,* Berkeley/Los Angeles: University of California Press.

Eckstein, H. and Apter, D. E. (1963) *Comparative Politics*, New York: Free Press.
Elmore, R. (1979–80) 'Backward Mapping, Implementation Research and Policy Dimensions', *Political Science Quarterly,* 94 (4): 601–16.
Freddi, G. (1986) 'Bureaucratic Rationalities and the Prospect for Party Government, in F. Castles and R. Widenmann, *Visions and Realities of Party Government*, Berlin and New York: Walter de Gruyter.
Friedland, E., Seabury, P. and Wildavsky, A. (1975a) 'Oil and the Decline of Western Power', *Political Science Quarterly,* 90 (3): 437–50.
—— (1975b) *The Great Detente Disaster; Oil and the Decline of American Foreign Policy*, New York: Basic Books.
Hargrove, E. (1975) *The Missing Link; The Study of the Implementation of Social Policy*, Washington, DC: Urban Institute.
Heclo, H. and Wildavsky, A. (1981) *The Private Government of Public Money*, Berkeley, Los Angeles: University of California Press.
Levy, F., Meltsner, A. and Wildavsky, A. (1974) *Urban Outcomes*, Berkeley/Los Angeles: University of California Press.
Lindblom, C. E. (1959) 'The Science of Muddling Through', *Public Administration Review,* 19: 78–88.
—— 1965) *The Intelligence of Democracy; Decision Making Through Mutual Adjustment*, New York: Free Press.
—— (1979) 'Still Muddling Not Yet Through', *Public Administration Review,* 39: 517–26.
Lipset, S. M. (1950) *Agrarian Socialism*, Berkeley: University of California Press.
Majone, G. and Wildavsky, A. (1978) 'Implementation as Evolution', *Policy Studies Review Annual,* 2: 103–117.
Mazmanian, D. and Sabatier, P. (1983) *Implementation and Public Policy*, Glenview: Scott, Foresman & C.
Nienaber, J. and Wildavsky, A. (1973) *The Budgeting and Evaluation of Federal Recreation Programs; Or, Money Doesn't Grow on Trees*, New York: Basic Books.
Pressman, J. and Wildavsky, A. (1973) *Implementation*, Berkeley/Los Angeles: University of California Press (3rd ed. 1994).
Polsby N. (1994) 'Remarks by Nelson Polsby', in *Aaron Wildavsky 1930–1993*, Berkeley, University of California: Institute of Governmental Studies.
Polsby, N. and Wildavsky, A. (1964) *Presidential Elections; The Strategies of American Electoral Politics*, New York: Scribner's Sons.
Ripley, R. and Franklin, G. (1986) *Policy Implementation and Bureaucracy*, Chicago: Dorsey Press.
Sabatier, P. (1986) 'Top-Down and Bottom-Up Approaches to Implementation Research; A Critical Analysis and Suggested Synthesis', *Journal of Public Policy,* 6 (1): 21–48.
Seabury, P. and Wildavsky, A. (eds.) (1969) *US Foreign Policy Perspectives and*

Proposals for the 1970s, New York: McGraw-Hill.
Selznick, P.A. (1949), *TVA and the Grass Roots*, New York: Harper & Row.
(1957) *Leadership in Administration*, New York: Harper & Row.
Simon, H. (1947) *Administrative Behavior*, New York: Macmillan; trad. it. *Il Comportamento Amministrativo*, Bologna: il Mulino, 1958.
Smithies, A. (1955) *The Budgeting Process in the United States*, New York: McGraw-Hill.
Thompson, M., Ellis, R. and Wildavsky, A. (1990) *Cultural Theory*, Boulder, Col: Westview Press.
Van Meter, D. and Van Horn, C. (1975) 'The Policy Implementation Process; A Conceptual Framework', *Administration and Society*, 6 (4): 445–88.
Waldo, D. (1948) *The Administrative State*, New York: Ronald Press.
Webber, C. and Wildavsky, A. (1986) *A History of Taxation and Expenditure in the Western World*, New York: Simon and Schuster.
Wildavsky, A. (1959) 'A Methodological Critique of Duverger's Political Parties', *Journal of Politics*, 21 (2): 303–318.
1959–60) 'Choosing the Lesser Evil; The Policy-Maker and the Problem of Presidential Disability', *Parliamentary Affairs*, 13 (1): 25–37.
(1962a) 'On the Superiority of National Conventions', *Review of Politics*, 24 (3): 307–19.
(1962b) *Dixon-Yates; A Study in Power Politics*, New Haven: Yale University Press.
(1964a) *Leadership in a Small Town*, Totowa, NJ: Bedminster Press.
(1964b) *The Politics of the Budgetary Process*, Boston: Little, Brown.
(1965a) 'The Goldwater Phenomenon; Purists, Politicians and the Two-Party System', *Review of Politics*, 27 (3): 386–413.
(1965b) 'Practical Consequences of the Theoretical Study of Defence Policy', *Public Administration Review*, 25 (1): 90–103.
(1966) 'The Political Economy of Efficiency; Cost-Benefit Analysis, Systems Analysis, and Program Budgeting', *Public Administration Review*, 6 (4): 292–310.
(1967) 'Aesthetic Power or the Triumph of the Sensitive Minority Over the Vulgar Mass; A Political Analysis of the New Economics', *Daedalus*, 96: 1115–28.
(1969) (ed.) *The Presidency*, Boston: Little, Brown.
(1971) *The Revolt Against the Masses and Other Essays on Politics and Public Policy*, New York: Basic Books.
(1975) *Budgeting; A Comparative Theory of Budgetary Processes*, Boston: Little, Brown.
(1976) 'Doing Better and Feeling Worse; The Political Pathology of Health Policy', *Daedalus*, 96: 105–23.
(1980a) *Speaking Truth to Power; The Art and Craft of Policy Analysis*, Boston: Little, Brown.
(1980b) *How to Limit Government Spending*, Berkeley/Los Angeles:

University of California Press.

(1982) 'Putting the Presidency on Automatic Pilot', in K. W. Thompson (ed.), *The American Presidency; Principles and Problems*, Washington, DC: University Press of America, Vol. 1.

(1983a) 'Dilemmas of American Foreign Policy', in A. Wildavsky (ed.) *Beyond Containment*, San Francisco: ICS Press.

(1983b) (ed.) *Beyond Containment; Alternative American Policies Toward the Soviet Union*, San Francisco: ICS Press.

(1984) *The Nursing Father; Moses as a Political Leader*, Tuscaloosa, Ala: University of Alabama Press.

(1986) 'Doing More and Using Less; Utilisation of Research as a Result of a Regime', *Rivista Trimestrale di Scienza dell'Amministrazione*, 4: 3–48.

(1988a) *Searching for Safety*, New Brunswick, NJ: Transaction Publishers.

(1988b), *The New Politics of the Budgetary Process*, New Brunswick, NJ, Transaction Publishers.

(1991a) *The Beleaguered Presidency*, New Brunswick, NJ: Transaction Publishers.

(1991b) *The Rise of Radical Egalitarianism*, Washington, DC: American University Press.

(1993a) *Assimilation versus Separation; Joseph the Administrator and the Politics of Religion in Biblical Israel*, New Brunswick, NJ: Transaction Publishers.

(1993b) *Craftways; On the Organisation of Scholarly Work*, New Brunswick, NJ: Transaction Publishers.

Wildavsky, A. and Ellis, R. (1989) *Dilemmas of Presidential Leadership From Washington Through Lincoln*, New Brunswick, NJ: Transaction Publishers.

Wildavsky, A. and Tennenbaum, E. (1981) *The Politics of Mistrust; Estimating American Oil and Gas Resources*, Beverly Hills, Calif: Sage.

chapter eleven | Morgenthau: Political Theory and Practical Philosophy
Angelo Panebianco

INTRODUCTION

Undoubtedly Hans Morgenthau was the most widely read and most influential theorist of international relations in the second half of the 20th century.[1] Even now, no political scientist could neglect the study of his writings and no lecturer in international relations could pass over an explanation of Morgenthau's theories. This is still true even if his work, alongside its undeniable merits, has numerous flaws that have been stressed by his critics over time. There are many reasons why Morgenthau's thinking was so influential both inside and beyond the American universities (and hence in European ones as well) for at least three decades after the Second World War. I will refer to two of them here.

The first reason is that Morgenthau, a German Jew who arrived in the United States in 1937, was, as stressed by Stanley Hoffmann (1977), one of the main scholars responsible for the renewed interest in internationalist studies between the end of the Second World War and the beginning of the Cold War, thanks to the success of his early publications in America. This achievement was due to the fact that, as we shall see, Morgenthau was able to adapt a long line of prestigious European thinking on political realism, of which he was both the heir and the representative, to the sensibilities of the American academic public. This interpretation suggests that Morgenthau, seen in this light, demonstrated how political realism and the doctrine of state power could be reconciled with the American democratic creed.

The second reason is that the American administration or political establishment (or at least part of it, especially that part which is normally identified as the foreign policy community), was, at the end of the Second World War, looking for a general vision of international politics that would make it in some way possible to justify the new role that America was taking on in the world. Morgenthau, with his ferocious criticism of the liberal conceptions of foreign policy that dominated America in the pre-war period, and his emphasis on the impossibility for any great power to step outside the game of power politics, offered precisely the interpretation of international politics that America needed at that time.

Obviously, he was not the only one to do so. For example, there was George Kennan (1954) and Walter Lippmann (1943).[2] However, Morgenthau had a decided advantage over men such as Kennan or Lippmann: he was able to exploit a knowledge of European political thinking that had no rivals in the American world at that time and thus to win the title of the best theoretician of international relations (especially after the publication in 1948 of *Politics Among Nations*, his most important book). He was also a theoretician who was readable for non-academics.

The influence of Morgenthau's ideas, which according to contemporaries was widespread even among those working in the area of foreign policy (and not only in America, as the former British diplomat and exponent of the English school of international relations, Adam Watson, made clear)[3], was a result of the fact that he aimed to build a theory that would be useful in practical foreign policy, capable of guiding and inspiring it; at least, this was the author's intention. This point is linked to the limits, real or presumed, of Morgenthau's theory that have triggered the reactions of generations of critics. Morgenthau is no Kenneth Waltz (to cite the most famous realist theoretician of international politics of the generation following Morgenthau). Nor can he be considered an 'internationalist' counterpart of David Easton. Morgenthau, on the other hand, is the builder of a theory which we could initially, roughly describe as policy-oriented (actually, as we shall see later, it is more correctly described as a practical philosophy of policy and of international relations in particular). This theory was designed to influence the perceptions, evaluations and choices of heads of state. One of the most common criticisms made against Morgenthau is that this ambition caused him to mix both factual judgements with value judgements, and explanations with obligations.

A further point that should be emphasised is that Morgenthau's ideas certainly influenced many a young American diplomat's vision of international politics during the post-war period (if only because those diplomats had inevitably come across Morgenthau's books either as university students or later when preparing for a career in the diplomatic service). Nevertheless, relations between Morgenthau and the American administration were, throughout his long career, almost always bad, and characterized more by conflict that co-operation (especially following his brief experience as advisor to the Department of State between the late 1940s and the early 1950s). Even leaving aside the issue of the Vietnam War (Morgenthau was strongly against American intervention in Indochina, for reasons that were later shown to be well-founded) his evaluations of the foreign policy of successive American presidents, from Truman onwards, were always highly critical.

Morgenthau was always torn between the desire to advise the Prince, and the decidedly incompatible wish to retain his own intellectual independence and autonomy as a scientific researcher. He was, throughout his academic career, an unheeded advisor: the American foreign policy community bowed to his intellectual stature and his standing, but for the most part, ignored his advice. Thus it was to be his general theory that was influential (if indeed it was), and not his interpretations, judgements and advice on specific issues facing the American administration.

This chapter focuses on Morgenthau as a classical scholar of political science. The argument that I will uphold and attempt to defend is that Morgenthau's ideas underwent a paradoxical fate. In fact, Morgenthau's scientific reputation rests on theses (those on power, national interest, power politics, power balances, etc.) that are *not* particularly original, whereas other theses of his which are, if not original, are certainly much more interesting and in certain aspects, are ahead of their time, and are rarely discussed or cited by political scientists.

POWER POLITICS

The internationalist theory of Morgenthau as illustrated in his most famous work, and the one to which he owes his fame, *Politics Among Nations*, is not an original theory. The main virtue of *Politics Among Nations* is that it created a European doctrine on state power (as well as its corollary of the balance of power) that, dating back to the eighteenth and nineteenth centuries, was made accessible to the American public through updating and adaptation to the new historical context. In particular, Morgenthau adapted a line of thinking that can be traced back to Leopold von Ranke and his pupils in Germany in the nineteenth century, and made it palatable to the American public. It could be said that *Politics Among Nations*, together with *Gleigewicht oder Hegemonie*, by the German historian Ludwig Dehio (1948), was one of the last successful fruits of this early doctrine.

Certainly, in no way do I wish to diminish the value of Morgenthau's work. *Politics Among Nations* (in its first edition published in 1948, and even more so in the later editions) is a precious work, which should still be read by anyone studying international politics. It is rich in analyses of the history of international politics and contains many convincing observations on the 'regularity' of the behaviour of states.[4] Nonetheless, the fact remains that the framework is not new.[5]

What is, however, original is Morgenthau's ability to draw from a wide range of intellectual sources, taking what he needs each time by exploiting his knowledge of both the history of political thinking and international politics, to 'prove' the theory. Indeed, it is this feature that to an extent explains the continuing interest in this work. Morgenthau's political realism, which is illustrated as a set of 'principles' (presented in the book's opening pages), is essentially based on the thinking of Thucydides and Machiavelli. Above all it is from Thucydides and Machiavelli that he picks up the idea that the observation of history may permit a scholar to identify the laws of politics, laws that in turn, owe their continuing validity to the fact that human nature does not change over time or space. 'Political realism', writes Morgenthau, 'believes that politics, like society in general, is governed by objective laws that have their roots in human nature.' He then continues: 'Realism, believing as it does in the objectivity of the laws of politics, must also believe in the possibility of developing a rational theory, however imperfectly and one-sidedly, of these objective laws' (1985: 4).[6] Power politics has its basis in an aspect of human nature ('thirst for power'), that is common to all men.

From Machiavelli too, and from the seventeenth century doctrine on the reasons of state and that of the eighteenth century on state power, Morgenthau takes another of the principles of political realism, i.e. what makes it possible to identify politics as a distinct sphere of action from that of economics, culture, ethics, etc. is that the category of interest is defined in terms of power. Morgenthau follows in the steps of those dealing with the reason of state, in distinguishing between interests and passions (see Hirschman 1977; Ornaghi and Cotellessa 2000) and in recognising the particular interest pursued by political actors as being power. Without this concept, Morgenthau claims, we would have no way of creating a theory of international or indeed domestic politics, as there would be no criteria for distinguishing between political and non-political facts.

The concept of interest defined as power is, in fact, for Morgenthau (as indeed for the authors that inspired him) not only an instrument of analysis, but also a guiding compass. Politics inspired by interest is a politics that attempts to minimize the role of and impact of the many irrational factors (the 'passions' of eighteenth century language) that have so much importance in politics. Politics moved by interest, defined in terms of power, is therefore for Morgenthau, a synonym of *rational* politics. And in Morgenthau's opinion, rational politics is always good politics because it minimises risks and is inspired by the rules of political caution. As is clear from this passage, in Morgenthau's theory the interpretative-descriptive and normative components are inextricably linked.

On these foundations Morgenthau constructs what he defines as a 'theory' of international relations with a function similar to that of a map, i.e. it may be used to guide us through political facts and make them comprehensible. Without going into the details of a theory which, at least in general terms, is well-known I intend to recall its principal points. The key concepts are those of power politics and national interest. Power politics for Morgenthau is not only the means and end of political action, but also a psychological relationship between those that exercise it and those that submit to it. In foreign policy, moreover, power is defined in terms of national interest. National interest consists of stable elements which are constant over time (linked for example to the opportunities and risks deriving from the geographical position of a state, or to its cultural traditions) and transient elements linked to historical circumstances. It should be noted here that the majority of Morgenthau's critics comment negatively on the use he makes of the concepts of political power and national interest (see Claude 1962; Aron 1962). Politics (which in Morgenthau's view is always a synonym for the battle for power) both within a state and at an international level, can be traced back to three fundamental types: politics can be aimed at the retaining of power, or at increasing it or at showing it off. Hence the well-known distinction between *status quo* politics, imperialist politics and prestige politics.

The power of a state is made up of many elements, some of which are material such as wealth and military force, while others are not material, such as cultural traditions and the degree of moral cohesion of the different states. The battle for power has as its necessary corollary the balance of power (both within states and in the international system), a principle that is always active when in a society (either national or international) there are a certain number of independent units present.

Despite the highly articulate expression of the theory of power politics (which takes up the first half of *Politics Among Nations*) given by Morgenthau, and despite his undeniable ability to adapt it to the needs of a twentieth century public, there is nothing really original in the theses set out above. They are all already present in the seventeenth, eighteenth and nineteenth century authors from whom Morgenthau draws his inspiration. On the other hand, the second half of the book is more original, where Morgenthau deals with the so-called limits on national power: morals, rights, public opinion and international organisations. If, on the one hand, Morgenthau shows, in keeping with the principles of political realism, how wrong the traditional liberal vision is (he refers above all to Wilsonism), insofar as it expects to exploit morals, rights and international organisations to neutralise power politics, on the other hand he also wishes to demonstrate that within certain limits these same factors may to an extent moderate power politics, making it more 'civilised' so to speak. This is where Morgenthau makes the strongest attempt to adapt the doctrine of power politics to the American political mind. If it is not possible to neutralise power politics as liberals like Wilson would have, it is at least possible to control it, to stop it releasing energies that are too destructive. Morals, rights and international organisations can, in the twentieth century, moderate power politics just as solidarity between the dynasties of sovereigns and homogeneity between the cultures and lifestyles of the aristocracies did in the eighteenth century. Moreover, this concession of Morgenthau's to American liberal sensibility is balanced in the closing chapters of the book with a very old-fashioned apology of diplomacy, considered as the main instrument of a rational foreign policy, which in Morgenthau's case always means that its aim is to defend national interest while respecting the precepts of political caution.

The debate on the merits and flaws of *Politics Among Nations* has never ceased. The book brought Morgenthau many supporters but also a large number of ferocious critics. The book also influenced his output over the following thirty years in two ways. Firstly, Morgenthau went on to use the theory set out in *Politics Among Nations* over the years to examine and assess American foreign policy and the main international issues of his times. Secondly, he was to devote many pages of his work to replying to the critics of *Politics Among Nations*, in an attempt to clear up misunderstandings about his position. It is, for example, noteworthy that Morgenthau was often labelled by superficial readers as a more or less cynical supporter of *Realpolitik* and political amorality. In fact, as we shall see, he dedicated much effort throughout his life to analysing the theme that interested him most, if not obsessed him: the complex and difficult relationship between ethics and politics.

THE RELUCTANT SUPERPOWER AND THE DOCTRINE OF NATIONAL INTEREST

The theory set out in *Politics Among Nations* was used by Morgenthau to criticise the intellectual premises on which American foreign policy was based. Morgenthau believed his first task was to show to the intellectuals and politicians of his adopted country the mistakes in the liberal conception of international politics, which at the time was dominant in the United States, and the disastrous results such a conception could produce. From 1950, when his book *In Defense of the National Interest* was published (his most far-reaching book on American foreign policy) and for the rest of his life, Morgenthau dedicated a very large part of his work to this theme. According to Morgenthau, America at the beginning of the 1950s was completely unprepared to take on with realism, caution and efficiency the tasks which its new role as superpower thrust upon it. The reason for this was the political culture of the country as it had been forged by the circumstances of history.

The fundamental problem is that America, like any other state, 'possesses' a national interest which is (relatively) permanent and which can be objectively identified, but because of its political culture the state fails to recognise this. The outcome is mistaken choices in foreign policy which do not respect the requirement to defend the American national interest. In order to guarantee survival in a world characterised by the anarchy of states and to defend its own institutions and lifestyle, America should accept the idea that these objectives can be achieved only when there is a clear understanding of what is the American national interest in various parts of the world. It should, for example, recognise sincerely and without false moralism that America's national interest requires that it retain its position as the dominant, unrivalled power of the American continent. It should also recognise that on the two main stages of Europe and Asia its national interest lies above all in maintaining the balance of power. However, an inadequate understanding of the nature of international politics and of America's duties in the world means it does not make the right choices.

The paradox, in Morgenthau's view, is that America's inability to recognise its own interest, and to act on it, is not a genetic disease. The Founding Fathers, in contrast to the American politicians of the late nineteenth and through the twentieth centuries, had clearly identified American national interests. Above all Alexander Hamilton and George Washington (in his 'Farewell Address') had based American foreign policy on realistic foundations and this permitted America to look after its own interests in the international arena with relative efficiency in the early nineteenth century.

Morgenthau distinguishes three phases in the history of American foreign policy. A realistic phase started with the Founding Fathers, in which America carefully and wisely defended those advantages bestowed on it by its geography and history: the possibility to prosper and defend its independence without being dragged into the disastrous power struggles that bloodied the European continent.

The Monroe doctrine was also an outcrop of the realism inspired by the founding fathers. The following phase is described by Morgenthau as the ideological phase, whose champions were Thomas Jefferson and Quincy Adams. Jefferson and Adams, and especially the latter, were political moralists who associated the call of the great liberal principles with ruthless policies. Morgenthau talks of ideology because the liberal principles were used in this phase in an ideological way to rationalize and justify policies that aimed to satisfy national interests.

The third, utopian, phase had a number of faces e.g. that of President McKinley who declared war on Spain for the Philippines while being totally ignorant of national interests and moved only by abstract moral principles. The utopian phase reached its peak with Wilsonism. The failure of Wilson's foreign policy was the result of a vision of foreign policy that flew in the face of the hard laws of international politics. The failures of this period were to lead, as a reaction, to the isolationism of the period between the two world wars, which was as unrealistic as Wilson's earlier policy. America's isolationist policy, which left a political vacuum in the international system, was partly to contribute to the catastrophe of the Second World War.

Moralism (which presumes to judge policies on the basis of abstract moral criteria), legalism (which presumes to boil international politics down to a group of questions of law) and internationalism (which presumes to deny the reality of division in the world and the power struggles between nations in the name of liberal cosmopolitanism) are the legacies of Wilsonism and are responsible for many catastrophic errors in American foreign policy. The first of these mistakes was to consider the conflict of the Second World War as a battle between good and evil. Thus Roosevelt insisted on the unconditional surrender of Germany which led to the disastrous outcome for American national interests of the division of Germany and the occupation of Eastern Europe by the Soviet Union.

According to Morgenthau the Americans repeated a similar mistake in 1950 in the middle of the Cold War: incapable of seeing international politics in its true light, they confused a struggle for power with a battle between good (American liberal democracy) and evil (Soviet Communism). The inability to think of politics in terms of power politics and the refusal to recognise the inherent 'morality' of any action taken in the national interest, led the United States to commit errors when dealing with complex problems. If the struggle for power is not recognised for what it is, the inevitable mistake when you come up against it is to consider it as an exclusively military matter: evil exists and must therefore be fought and destroyed. However, the military solution is not always the right answer. For example, Morgenthau says, while it was right to tackle the European problem in terms of a military solution (in Europe the real problem was to 'limit' Soviet imperialism), the same was not true in Asia. There was a real political and social revolution underway there and Soviet imperialism was not the problem on that continent. Both in its relations with China and the fighting of the war in Korea the United States committed serious mistakes. A political and social revolution cannot be handled by military means; other means are necessary. What was needed above all was an open-minded political response to the demands for social rights and a careful and continued fight, using both cultural weapons and propaganda, to win over minds. The real political realist does not, in Morgenthau's opinion, always resort to the use of military force whatever the circumstances. Rather, he is aware of the nature of politics and its laws, and analyses the varying circumstances in order to identify the best means of resolving them.

While the mistakes of American foreign policy may be above all the result of the dominance of the liberal conception, the workings of the democratic institutions also bear no small part of the responsibility for these mistakes. In *The Purpose of American Politics* (1960)[7] Morgenthau reminds us that a government that is in the hands of public opinion and that is incapable of taking decisions that are considered 'unpopular' is a non-existent government that abdicates its duties. As public opinion does not exist except as an effect of the choices of government, it is the duty of democratic leadership to form and guide it by making responsible choices whose value may be publicly argued as being in line with the national interest.[8]

POLITICAL SCIENCE AS A PRACTICAL PHILOSOPHY

Apart from the two Morgenthaus we have seen so far, that of the theoretician of power politics and the critic of American foreign policy, there is another Morgenthau who, in my opinion, is the most interesting of the three. This is the Morgenthau who is much less well-known and debated, the one who reflects on the nature of social sciences, on the relationships between science and philosophy, on the duties of political science, on the relation between social science and the practice of politics, as well as the moral conditions that exist in relation to political actions. This is the author of *Scientific Man vs. Power Politics* (published in 1946), who resurfaces in essays devoted to this theme over a period of thirty years. This is the Morgenthau who attempts to draw up a general theory of politics, by reinterpreting in a creative way his much loved classics of political thinking, which would help to understand the politics of his day and to provide an intelligent and cautious guide to action. Naturally, there is a close link between the theoretician of power politics, the scholar of American foreign policy and the political theoretician, as it is through his political theorising that Morgenthau hopes to position his analyses and conceptions of international politics within a strong philosophical-political framework

Scientific Man vs. Power Politics is a book that is deliberately non-conformist. His aim is to be provocative and argumentative. Morgenthau wants to destroy two myths. First of all he wants to show that the liberal vision of foreign policy that dominated pre-war politics and which even in 1946 continued to influence scholars and practitioners of American foreign policy, was inherently wrong. As one of the veterans of the Weimar Republic who had managed to flee from Nazism he wants to explain why the liberal vision of international politics, with its horror of power politics and its belief in the possibility of a harmony of interests between nations, and its unchallenging faith in the pacifying virtues of international law and trade, failed dramatically when faced with the harsh reality of international politics, and to demonstrate that this could lead Western democracies towards new disasters if not definitively and quickly abandoned.

The second myth which Morgenthau wants to destroy in the book, and which is of greater interest, is what he regards as a mistaken view – and which he believes to be a view commonly held among social scientists – of the nature of social science and its relationship to policy practice. Morgenthau gives the name of rationalism to the ideology dating back to the seventeenth and eighteenth centuries which he wants to refute, and the name of scientism to the variation on rationalism which he sees as being so widespread in the twentieth century.

This book, whose general principles have been often misunderstood, won Morgenthau fame (justly so) as an enemy of Wilsonism, and more generally of the liberal conception of international politics. However, he was also unjustly labelled as an opponent of social science and an exponent of the 'traditionalist' family of enemies of science. Actually, Morgenthau limits himself to the criticism of scientism, an ideology which on the one hand compares the social and the natural sciences, and on the other, sees the history of mankind as a type of scientific laboratory and considers political problems as scientific problems which can therefore be resolved scientifically. What Morgenthau is criticizing here, (just as Friedrich von Hayek does a few years later in 1952 in *The Counter-Revolution of Science*) is the idea, which comes from positivism (going back therefore to Saint-Simon and Comte, and even further back than that), that all political problems can be resolved using the solutions offered by applied social science. This belief was widely held in America at the time. Many of the theses presented by Morgenthau in his book of 1946 are nowadays considered common sense, but it was not so at the time. That is why when the book came out the criticisms against it outnumbered the praise.

Morgenthau's attack on scientism, however, advances on two fronts. Firstly, he protests against the idea that explanations in social sciences can be based on the physical-determinist model of causality. He notes:

> The difference between social sciences in this respect is obvious. The natural sciences are in doubt as to whether or not certain causes will occur, but they foretell with a high degree of certainty that upon a certain typical cause a certain typical effect will follow. The social sciences, on the contrary, are in doubt as to the occurrence not only of the causes but also of the effects, once a cause has taken place. (Morgenthau 1974: 131)

This occurs, Morgenthau argues, because while experimental natural sciences can work on isolated causes which operate on motionless objects, the social sciences 'deal with interminable chains of causes and effects, each of which, by being a reacting effect is the cause of another reacting effect, and so forth ad infinitum' (1974: 129).

From a synchronic point of view every social phenomenon is the result of multiple causes (hence all the single-cause theories of the social sciences are fallacious in Morgenthau's opinion). From a diachronic viewpoint every social phenomenon is the product of a potentially infinite chain of cause and effect which social sciences, unlike the natural sciences, can never isolate or separate from each other. One of the consequences of the impossibility of applying the physical-determinist model of cause and effect is that predictions are hardly ever possible in the social sciences. Morgenthau believes this makes applied social science less credible.

Morgenthau continues by underlining the fact that scientism is mistaken in imagining it possible for men to be guided in their reactions by reason alone (so that it would suffice that science indicated the right path for men then to take). Morgenthau quotes Hume to remind his readers that men are guided by passions and interests and that reason often plays a minor role when decisions are taken. Morgenthau further argues that even the social scientist himself is influenced by passions and interests, and his research can never be wholly protected against the conditioning influence of historical circumstances. Lastly, he reminds us that the social sciences are part of the social world they study and so are influenced by it and influence it in turn, in unpredictable ways, due to the effects of the knowledge generated by the social sciences themselves on human behaviour (a thesis, I would note, that is very close to the so-called Thomas theorem whereby prophecies are self-fulfilling or self-defeating).

I have so far dealt with Morgenthau's *pars destruens*; however, there is also a *pars construens*. Morgenthau wants to criticize scientism but *not* science. It is only his conception of social science that is different from that of most of his contemporaries. The researcher must always bear in mind the strong limits that weigh on the social sciences, for the reasons already stated, and from which they can never escape. The study of science, according to Morgenthau, means the search for 'laws' (that is to say constants) that guide human behaviour. Some of these laws, though few of them, are universal (the laws of power politics are one example) and depend on certain invariable characteristics of human nature, as we have seen. However, nearly all of the laws, if not indeed all of them, have already been discovered by the great political thinkers of the past. On the other hand, other 'laws' or constants which are more numerous and which the social scientist may still hope to discover, depend on the particular circumstances of period and place and on the historical conditions, and the validity of these latter laws is destined to disappear as conditions change.

From these laws the social scientist will construct 'theories' (which in his book *Politics Among Nations* Morgenthau states, in line with a shared notion of theory, must have two characteristics: they must be logically coherent and must not contradict data of known experience).[9] What relationship will there be between such a conception of social science and practical politics? Ruling out a directly applicative solution, social science can help politics above all by warning it against mistaken actions that are caused by contemporary ideological visions (and it must be added that for Morgenthau ideology is similar to, and has more or less the same functions as, the derivations of Pareto and the false conscience of Marx): social science may be useful to politics if it helps it to avoid those actions which go against the social laws which guide human behaviour, and which inevitably end up by provoking unexpected and perverse effects, if not social catastrophes.

The criticism of scientism and of a mistaken conception, in Morgenthau's opinion, both of the nature of the social sciences and of their relationship with practical politics, is necessary to reassess and re-launch – in an era in which political science was still in the middle of a behaviouralist phase – an idea of political science as a practical philosophy (even though Morgenthau does not actually use this expression) which he sees as being embodied in the great theorists of the past, from Plato to Aristotle, from Machiavelli to Hobbes and Burke (to cite an author of whom he is exceptionally fond) and to Tocqueville.

After *Scientific Man* and *Politics Among Nations*, Morgenthau's two most ambitious works of theory, the scholar went on to produce many short essays[10] that developed and illustrated further his vision of political science and international relations. He did so both by directly criticizing political science as it was practised during the 1950s and 1960s in American universities and by analysing the paradoxes and the dilemmas of political action and the problems which those paradoxes created for a political theoretician.

Morgenthau was a harsh critic of the political science of his times. He condemned the fact that, by and large, it amounted to little more than a description of the political reality with no theoretical importance. He also criticized the use of quantitative techniques which, in his opinion, apart from the case of the analyses of elections and little else, were of limited use in increasing our knowledge of politics. He also attacked all the premises of behavioural political science (for example, when he criticized with unnecessary harshness the classic work of the behavioural approach, *Power and Society* by Harold Lasswell and Abraham Kaplan). Against these and other authors who had chosen the same approach, Morgenthau argues that an empirical theory of politics which claims to do without any framework of philosophic reference or inspiring political doctrine is a contradiction in terms. He writes, in direct disagreement with Lasswell and Kaplan and with their claim to draw up a strictly empirical, and not philosophical, theory of politics, that the enduring value of reading Plato, Aristotle, Locke, Rousseau and the authors of *The Federalist* is precisely the fact that, within the framework of a philosophical-political doctrine, each of them gave us the results of their research in the form of propositions for a political science that is much deeper and illuminating than research which claims to be purely empirical could ever be.

Consequently, Morgenthau also criticizes the fact that in the American departments of political science, political theory is considered no more than the history of political thought and political doctrine, and has no link to so-called empirical political science. The resulting divorce between theory and empirical research, in Morgenthau's opinion, renders the latter poorer and largely irrelevant. Morgenthau thus argues that the possibility of political science becoming a genuine science, in the sense that it would be able to investigate politics in the light of theoretical problems and able to make proposals that are both objective and general, is compromised. By 'objective,' he means that the truth of the proposals would not be influenced by the subjective limitations of the observer, while they would be 'general' in the sense that their validity would not be conditioned by the particular circumstances of time and space.

Given that, in Morgenthau's opinion, a split between political science and political theory is senseless, what characteristics must a political theory have? A political theory is always a theory about power and the competition for power. It has a two-fold function, a double aim: explicative and normative. On the one hand, it is a map which permits us to give a rational order to political reality and to understand its essential features. Above all, its task is to divide what is unique and specific to a given historical circumstance from what is general, in that by virtue of the perennial laws of politics, that specific historical circumstance is similar to many others. The validity of a political theory can be measured precisely by this ability to distinguish and separate what is contingent from what is permanent. On the other hand, it is also a guide for political action, a useful tool for identifying the course of action that may be rationally followed under given conditions. In this sense Morgenthau's project may be defined as practical philosophy.

A theory of international relations is, in turn, no more than a theory of politics that has been adapted to the specific circumstances of international society itself: the anarchic condition of the international system, power defined in terms of national interest, the balance of power as an unintentional effect of the competition for power.

The theory of international relations also has a double function, both explicative and normative. The theory of international relations must measure itself against a number of further difficulties compared to other political theories. Because of the lack of a central authority, international politics pushes certain tendencies, that are already present in politics *tout court,* to the very limit. The material on which the theoretician of international politics works is highly inflammable: it is not just that international politics, much more than domestic politics, is very often concerned with violence and war. It is above all the fact that the absence of a central power, as Hobbes had noted long before, means that the opposing moral claims linked to the demands of differing national interests clash in an arena that has no mediator or arbiter.

In Morgenthau's view, one of the specific problems of the field of action in which a theoretician of international politics must reason is that in this context the dilemmas linked to the relationship between ethics and politics can never be neutralized, as may sometimes happen (at least in certain historical periods), within the confines of a single state. This is fundamentally the reason why Morgenthau insists so tirelessly on the relationship between ethics and politics. Surprisingly for those who know him only superficially, he refuses the easy solution of double standards as adopted by the theorists of the reason of state (there is a private morality and a public morality which are different from each other). He believes that the moral dilemmas which political action raises may be cushioned but never resolved. These dilemmas are linked above all to the fact that anyone acting politically must necessarily treat men as a means to the achievement of his ends, a condition that is undoubtedly at odds with the Judaic-Christian moral that, even in its modern and secularized versions, nonetheless influences the western vision of the world.

To sum up, the political theoretician, and to a greater extent the theoretician of international politics, must tackle and master two dilemmas, one of which is intellectual and the other moral: the former is linked to the complexity of the object under study, of the historical and political facts and the difficulty of distinguishing between what is accidental and contingent and what is general and permanent. The second is linked to the moral ambiguity which is a fact of politics. Morgenthau offers no solutions and, indeed, does not believe that solutions exist. However, he thinks that a scholar's understanding of the existence of these dilemmas is an essential precondition to the drawing up of satisfactory political theory.

CONCLUSIONS

Apart from certain unfair criticisms that are the result of a superficial reading of his works, Morgenthau's thinking has been subject to a number of well-founded criticisms. There is no doubt that his way of conceiving power (both as a means and end of political action) and his vision of politics seen exclusively as a struggle for power, leaves him open to legitimate objections. The same is true for his tendency not to give a precise definition of the concepts used: for example, that of the balance of power, which is so central to his theory, and which retains a variety of meanings throughout his works (see Cesa 1987). One could also cite the fact that Morgenthau talks continually of the state without ever clearly defining it, so that at times his theory would seem to be that of a pluralist state (especially when he is talking about American democracy) and at other times, more often in fact, it would seem to come directly from Hegelian political philosophy.

Despite its serious limits, however, Morgenthau's work has certain merits which must be recognised. These merits regard not his position as an exponent of power politics, but rather those he has as the theoretician who, well ahead of his time, identified certain flaws in the behavioural approach to political science (especially, its anti-philosophical radicalism) and attempted to bring political science back to the heart of what he considered the classical tradition. The merits are those of a man who studied the paradoxes and dilemmas of politics and showed just how illusory is the claim of certain political scientists to observe, from a distance, from outside, the same dilemmas and paradoxes. A claim that ends up by annulling, in Morgenthau's opinion, the very aim, the very reason for the existence of political theory. As he loved to repeat (Morgenthau 1970), the aim is to give voice to the truth about power, however unwelcome this truth may be.

NOTES

1. Morgenthau was born in Germany in 1904, emigrated to the United States in 1937 and died in 1980. This essay is devoted purely to the analysis of Morgenthau as a political scientist and theorist of international relations. Before he arrived in America, however, Morgenthau had studied law and had already published some fine works in the field of international law. Moreover, from his time as an undergraduate in Germany he had cultivated his interest in philosophy with passion. According to Frei (2001), the author of a well-documented intellectual biography of Morgenthau, the scholar of the 'American' period is incomprehensible without an understanding of the previous intellectual development that made Morgenthau what he was.
2. Smith (1986) and Rosenthal (1991) have published excellent reviews of the thinking of the American realists.
3. See Watson (1984).
4. See Bonanate (1997) as regards the place of Morgenthau's work in the history of the theory of international relations.
5. Greg Russell (1990) argues the opposite case, i.e. that Morgenthau's work was radically new compared to classic European thinking. More convincingly Sergio Pistone (1973) groups Morgenthau in the German school of thought on state power.
6. *Politics Among Nations* has been edited six times. After its publication in 1948 Morgenthau himself personally edited the following five editions (1954, 1960, 1967, 1973, 1978), updating the text and making corrections or adding explanations as an indirect response to the objections raised by critics of the book. The last edition in 1985 was published by Kenneth Thompson, Morgenthau's disciple, five years after the great scholar's death.
7. Frei (2001) notes that this book was received with much surprise by those who knew Morgenthau's earlier works. *The Purpose of American Politics* is indeed different from his previous publications where political values and ideals are of primary importance. In Frei's opinion, it is necessary to go back to Morgenthau's education in Germany, and his first works as a scholar (in the field of law initially) to discover the origins of an 'idealistic' approach which, to an extent, re-emerges in his book of 1960.
8. On the successive positions taken by Morgenthau regarding different aspects of American foreign policy during the Cold War see Nobel (1995).
9. There is a contradiction between the historicist arguments against applied social science used by Morgenthau in his *pars destruens* and his apparently 'positivist' faith in the existence of laws of human behaviour which may be discovered by the social scientist. Even though Morgenthau would probably reply that he is talking about laws, while bearing in mind those regularities of politics that Thucydides and Machiavelli taught us to look for, the problem remains.
10. The observations which follow refer to some of the collections of Morgenthau's writings (1958; 1962; 1970).

REFERENCES

Aron, R. (1962) *Paix et guerre entre les nations*, Paris: Calmann-Lévy.
Bonanate, L. (1997) 'Introduzione all'edizione italiana', in *Politica tra le nazioni*, Bologna, il Mulino, pp. XIII–XIX.
Cesa, M. (1987) *L'equilibrio di potenza*, Milano: Angeli.
Claude, I. (1962) *Power and International Relations*, New York: Random House.

Dehio, L. (1948) *Gleichgewicht oder Hegemonie*, Krefeld, Scherpe; trad. it. (1988) *Equilibrio o egemonia*, Bologna, il Mulino.

Frei, C. (2001) *Hans Morgenthau*, Baton Rouge: Louisiana State University Press.

Hirschman, A. (1977) *The Passions and the Interests*, Princeton: Princeton University Press; trad. it. (1979) *Le passioni e gli interessi*, Milano, Feltrinelli.

Hoffmann, S. (1977) 'An American Social Science: International Relations', *Daedalus* 1: 41–60.

Kennan, G. (1954) *Realities of American Foreign Policy*, Princeton: Princeton University Press.

Lippmann, W. (1943) *U.S. Foreign Policy: Shields of the Republic*, Boston: Little.

Morgenthau, H. (1950) *In Defence of the National Interest*, Washington D.C.: University Press of America.

(1958) *Dilemmas of Politics*, Chicago: University of Chicago Press.

(1960) *The Purpose of American Politics*, New York: Knopf.

(1962) *Politics in the Twentieth Century*, Chicago: University of Chicago Press, 3 vol.

(1970) *Truth and Power*, New York: Praeger.

(1974) *Scientific Man vs. Power Politics*, 2nd ed., Chicago: University of Chicago Press.

(1985) *Politics Among Nations*, New York: Knopf.

Nobel, J. (1995) 'Morgenthau's Struggle with Power: The Theory of Power Politics and the Cold War', *Review of International Studies* 21: 61–85.

Ornaghi, L. and Cotellessa, S. (2000) *Interesse*, Bologna: il Mulino.

Pistone, S. (ed.) (1973) *Politica di potenza e imperialismo*, Milano: Angeli.

Rosenthal, J. (1991) *Righteous Realists*, Baton Rouge: Louisiana State University Press.

Russell, G. (1990) *Hans J. Morgenthau and the Ethics of American Statecraft*, Baton Rouge: Louisiana State University Press.

Smith, M. (1986) *Realist Thought from Weber to Kissinger*, Baton Rouge: Louisiana State University Press.

von Hayek, F. (1952) *The Counter-Revolution of Science; Studies on the Abuse of reason,* Indianapolis, Liberty Press.

Watson A. (1984) 'Morgenthau's Concept of the National Interest and the New States of the Third World', in K. Thompson and R. Myers (eds.), *Truth and Tragedy; A Tribute to Hans J. Morgenthau*, New Brunswick, N.J., Transaction Books.

index

accountability 53–54, 171
action, political 11–12, 23–24, 233–5
   moral dilemmas and 234–5
action theory 77
Adams, J. 39, 52, 54
Adams, Q. 229
Africa 103
   democratisation of 113, 148
Aldrich, J. H. 39, 47, 53, 60 n.3, 196
Allardt, E. 123
Almassy, E. 188
Almond, G. A. 2, 5, 8 n.2, 14, 19, 26,
   66, 77, 78, 124, 156, 159, 168
   Civic Culture, The 156,
      180–1, 186, 187, 188
      see also under Verba, S.
   political culture, approach to 211
   systems theory of 79, 93
Althusius, J. 24
American Academy of Arts
   and Sciences 63, 208
American Behavioural Scientist 146
*American Journal of Political
   Science* 179, 193
American Political Science Association
   (APSA) 3, 46, 63, 77, 81 n.2, 99,
   141, 179, 182, 183, 189, 196, 208
American Political Science Review
   (APSR) 3, 89, 135 n.1, 179, 196
American Society for Public
   Administration 208
American Sociological Association 141
American Science Review 144
Andersen, K. 181, 182, 200 n.1
Angola 127

Appleby, P. H. 207
Apter, D. E. 211
Aristotle 143, 148, 176, 233
Aron, R. 2, 226
Arrow, K. 39
Austria 147, 148, 191
authoritarianism 20, 133, 185
   Latin America and 125–6, 133
   political participation and 105
   regimes 4, 7, 124, 128–9
      totalitarian, difference with 124, 133
      leadership and 134
   structural pluralism and 26
   transition from 111, 127

Bailey, J. 200 n.1
Bailey, S. 88
   Congress Makes a Law 88
Bardach, E. 210
bargaining, process of 15
Barnes, S. H. 160
Barrett, S. 210
Barry, B. 38, 39, 43, 45, 47, 51
Bartholomew, D. 88
behaviour, political 45, 89, 185
   class and 148
   democratic stability and 187
   religion and 123
   see also civic virtues; voting
Bell, D. 109
Beloff, M. 89
Bendix, R. 142
Berelson, B. 152
Berman, P. 210
Berrington, H. 94

Black, D. 39
Bishop, G. F. 192
Bobbio, N. 1–2, 168, 176 n.2
Bogdanor, V. 96 n.3
Boix, C. 175
Bonanate, L. 236 n.4
Brady, H. 179, 195
Brazil 125
　military dictatorship in 125–6
Brewer, G. D. 81
Brezhnev, L. 108
British Journal of Political Science 179
Brown, C. Jr. 195
Bryce, J. 85
Brzezinski, Z. 108, 109
Buchanan, J. 78
Budge, I. 39, 47, 49, 52, 54, 56, 60 n.6
Bunce, V. 6, 112
Bureau of Applied Social Research 152
bureaucracy 40–1
　see also public administration
Burke, E. 233
Burns, N. 179, 181, 196

Caetano, M. 126
Caiden, N. 209
Calvert, R. 39, 60 n.3
Campbell, A. 191, 192
Canada 158, 193
capitalism
　'crisis' of 110
　relation to democracy 28
Capitalism, Socialism and Democracy 11
Carnesale, A. 113
Cesa, M. 235
Chehabi, H. 121, 131
Chester, N. 89
China 229
　democratisation of 113
church and state, separation of 114
　see also religious belief
civic culture 186–8
　democratic stability and 186–7
　regime support and 187
　values needed for 187
　see also culture, political
civic virtues 27, 29, 30, 187
civic voluntarism 7, 194–5

civil society 130, 153, 186, 194
civilisation(s)
　'clash of' 113–115
　culture and 114
　definition of term 114
　religion and 114
　Western 115–6
　see also under Huntington, S. P.
Clark, J. 205
Claude, I. 226
coalitions 41, 48
　accountability 53–54
　formation of 54
　median parties and 54
Cold War 101, 113, 223, 229, 236 n.8
Coleman, J. 142, 152, 162 n.1
collective bargaining 152
collectivism 212, 213, 214
Collier, D. 176 n.5
colonialism
　decolonisation process 145
　social modernisation and 104
　Western values and 115
Comecon 25
communism 186
　breakdown of 162, 170
community, political 71, 74–5
Comparative Political Studies 6
competence, moral and instrumental 28–9
Comte, A. 29, 231
conflict, political 151–2
Confucian civilisation 113, 115
consensus 23
Constant, B. 25
constitutions
　checks and balances 15–6
　separation of powers and 15
　study of 92
Converse, P. 2, 191, 193
Cooperative Commonwealth
　Federation (CCF) 143
corporatism 125, 153, 212, 214
Cotellessa, S. 226
Coughlin, P. J. 39
Counter-Revolution of Science, The 231
Cox, G. W. 6
Cox, R. 89
Crozier, M. 80

culture, concept of 211
   Wildavsky's theory of 212–13
culture, political 4, 14, 80, 142,
   156–7, 158, 162, 211–18
   civilisation and 114
   democracy and 143, 145, 186
   political support and 80–1
   structural-functionalist approach to 211
   see also civic culture

Daalder, H. 1
Dahl, R. 4, 7, 11–36, 81, 122,
   136 n.11, 152, 213 n.2
   concept of 'polyarchy' 13–15, 17, 24
      conditions for 19–20
   Controlling Nuclear Weapons:
      Democracy versus Guardianship 29
   democratic theory 14, 15,
      18, 24, 28, 30, 31–3
      constitutional structures, role of 21
      maximization and
         description of 18–20
      models of opposition 22–3
      United States and 31–2
   How Democratic is the American
      Constitution? 31
   increments, method of and 23–4
   On Democracy 24, 28
   political equality, problem of 26–7, 33
   Polyarchy: Participation
      and Opposition 26
   Preface to Democratic Theory, A 13, 15
   technocracy and 29–31
   Who Governs? Democracy and
      Power in an American City 22
Dahrendorf, R. 79
Dalton, R. 39
DATA S. A. 135 n.4
Davis, O. A. 40, 209
Dawson, M. 181
d'Azeglio, L. T. 24
de Leon, P. 81
de Madariaga, I. 97 n.3
de Miguel, A. 122, 136 n.8
decadence, political 118
decision-making 17, 209
Dehio, L. 225
democracy 4, 28, 31–3

   as a value 14
   breakdown of 117, 122, 133
   cleavages, political and 156
   consolidation of 4, 122, 133
      Linz's definition 128–9
      Lipset's table and 147
      transition and 122
   definitions of 41
   Eastern European 'new' 183, 186
   legitimacy and 147, 148
   Madisonian concept of
      15–6, 17, 21, 34 n.4
   market economy and 28
   populist theory of 15, 16–7
   social requisites of 144–6
   theories of *see* democratic theory
   underdeveloped regimes and 112–13
   voluntary associations, role
      of in 152–54, 194
   see also under names of
      individual theorists; pluralism;
      polyarchy, democracy and
democratic stability 147, 148, 149, 186–7
   civic culture as central to 186–7
   political conflict and 151
   voluntary sector and 194
democratic theory 7, 37
   evolutionary theory 145–6
   Lipset's basic tenets of 155
   mandate theory 42
   mathematical 37, 39, 40
   'overload', concept of 79
   political support 79–80
   Sartori's 'real' and 'ideal'
      distinction 171
democratisation 100, 110, 111–13,
   130, 128, 145, 162
   democratic transition 125–7,
      128, 134, 136 n.4, 205
      consolidation and 127, 128–32, 147
      modes of 126, 127
   education, effect on 144, 145, 146, 151
   Human Development Index
      (HDI) as indicator of 145
   industrialisation, level of 144, 146, 148
   institutional relation to 131
   market economy and 146
   political leadership, role of 113

political parties, changes in 132–3
socio-economic development
   and 112–13, 145–6
      Lipset and 143, 144–6
      power resource distribution
         (Vanhanen) and 145–6
      social stratification and 148–51
   waves of (Huntington) 100,
      111–13, 117, 145
   Western civilisation and 115
      clash of cultures and 118
   urbanisation, role of 144, 146
   see also democratic stability;
   democratic theory
demos 25
Dennis, J. 74, 76
Deutsch, K. 2
Devitt, J. 162 n.1
Di Palma, G. 188
Diamond, L. 122, 142, 143, 145, 151
dictatorships 19, 125, 144, 154
   military 125
division of powers 15
Dominguez, J. I. 110
Douglas, M. 211, 213
Downs, A. 2, 4, 8 n.2, 11, 37–62, 172, 173
   democratic theory of 37, 42, 53
      mathematical approach
         to 39–40, 52, 57
      reliability, responsibility
         and 43, 48, 51, 53, 54
   Economic Model 38
   Economic Theory of Democracy,
      The 11, 37–54, 56–60, 172
      Sartori's critique of 172
      testable propositions in 56–6
   Inside Bureaucracy 40
   median argument and 46, 54
   party competition 37, 39,
      41, 46–7, 51–2, 53
      multi-party model 48, 55
      unimodal model of two-
         party 44, 46, *47*, 53
   party models
      General Model 45, 46, 56
         assumptions/propositions
            of 57–9
      left/right dimension and 39

   rational choice theory and 37, 39
   spatial and non-spatial models 37,
      38–9, 45, 46, 48, 51, 53, 56–7
      assumptions for 59
      static 51
   Theory of Democracy 37
Duverger, M. 2, 6, 89, 172
   Political Parties 172

Easton, D. 4, 7, 63–83, 224
   'An Approach to the Analysis
      of Political Systems' 63
   Analysis of Political
      Structure, The 72, 77
   Children in the Political System 76
   'Decline of Modern Political
      Theory, The' 64
   Framework for Political Analysis,
      A 62, 64, 65, 77, 79
   general theory of politics 65–6,
      68, 69, 72, 77–8, 79
      for democratic systems 81
   political action, concept of 77–8
   political community,
      concept of 71, 74–5
   political process, model of *70*
   political socialisation 74, *75*, 76, 80
   political structure, concept of 72, 78
   Political System, The 64
   political system, concept and
      theory of 65–7, 69, 79
      'demands' and interests 69–70
         'demand-input overload',
            concept of 79
      objects of 70–3, *75*
         'authorities' 71, 72–3, *75*, 80
         'political community'
            and 71, *75*
         'regime' and 71–2, 74, *75*, 80
         values and norms, use
            of 71–2, 74, 80
      persistence, concept of
         68–9, 74, 76, 79
      'stress'/'support' and
         70–1, 73–4, *75*
         diffuse support 74, *75*, 77
   'Re-Assessment of the Concept
      of Political Support, A' 77

systems analysis and 65–6,
  68, 73, 77, 78, 79–81
*Systems Analysis of Political
  Life, A* 64, 65, 69, 77, 79
Eckstein, H. 211
Economic Development Agency 210
education
  as indicator of democracy 144, 145
  civic attitudes and 188
  political tolerance, role in 159–60
  see also participation, political,
    education, effect of
Eisenhower, D. D. 101
electoral studies 41, 51–2, 192–3
  ideological thinking, role of in 193
  partisanship and 193
  US and 191–3
electoral systems
  median mandate, role of in 54–5
  PR 54, 55
  SMD 55
  see also voting
elites
  democratisation, role of in 112, 167
  military and 101, 102
  pluralist debate and 101
Ellis, J. J. 156, 161, 163 n.9
  Founding Brothers 156
Ellis, R. 205
Elmore, R. 210
Environmental Protection Agency 216
environment protection, public
  policy and 215–8
equality, political 12, 16, 213
  democracy and 26–7, 149
    market economy and 28
  freedom, interaction with 26, 27, 33
  U.S. egalitarianism 159
    Constitutional framework and 33
European Political Science 1, 3
European Union 31
Evans, P. B. 175
  Bringing the State Back in 175
Evans, R. 188

Fabbrini, S. 24
Falter, J. 64
Farlie, D. J. 39, 51, 56, 60

Farneti, P. 92, 97 n.6
  Italian Party System, The 92
fascism 160, 186
federalism 31, 131, 205
  comparative analysis of 122
Federalist, The 34 n.6, 233
Finer, H. 85–6, 88, 92
  *British Civil Service: An
    Introductory Essay* 88
  *Constitutional Government
    and Democracy* 85
  English Local Government 88
  *Governments of Greater
    European Powers* 86
  *Representative Government and
    a Parliament of Industry* 88
  *Study of the German Federal
    Economic Council* 88
  *Theory and Practice in Europe
    and America* 85
  *Theory and Practice of Modern
    Government, The* 85, 88
Finer, S. E. 4, 7, 85–98
  *Adversary Politics and Electoral
    Reform* 92, 97 n.5
  'Almond's Concept of the 'Political
    System'; a textual critique' 93
  *Anonymous Empire; a Study of the
    Lobby in Great Britain* 88
  *Backbench Opinion in the
    House of Commons* 88
  *Changing British Party System
    1945–1979, The* 92
  comparative analysis and
    89, 92–3, 94–5
    search for regularities and 96
  Comparative Government
    87, 89, 92, 93, 94, 95
  Conceptual Prologue, The 87
  Five Constitutions 92, 94, 95
  *Formation of National States
    in Western Europe* 87
  'Generation of Political
    Thought, A.' 97 n.4
  government, study of 94–5
    and politics, distinction between 94
  *History of Government from the
    Earliest Times, The* 87, 90, 94–6

Life and Times of Sir Edwin Chadwick 86, 88, 95
Local Government in England and Wales 88
Man on Horseback, The 86, 93
military
   influences on 86–7, 93, 96 n.2
   political role of 86–1, 103
Pareto: Sociological Writings 88, 95
party systems, research 96
Primer of Public Administration, A 88
Private Industry and Political Power 88
'Perspectives in the World History of Government- a Prolegomenon' 87
Recent Changes in European Party Systems 92
systems theory, critique of 93–4
United Kingdom, political analysis of 92
Fisichella, D. 30
Fondazione della Cassa di Risparmio 8 n.1
Foreign Policy 114
France 92, 193
   democracy in 148
   public policy analysis 215, 216, 217
Francia, P. 196
Franco, F. 18, 125
Freddi, G. 5, 207
freedom 12, 16
   democracy and 26–7, 28, 159
   political order and 106, 107
Freedom House 136 n.7
Frei, C. 236 n.1, n.7
Friedland, E. 205, 209
Friedrich, C. J. 2, 85, 89, 171
Fuchs, D. 72, 80, 81
Fudge, C. 210
Fukuyama, F. 114

GAIL functions 136 n.6
Galli, G. 171, 176 n.7
Gamm, G. 181
Gastill, R. 136 n.7
gender 185, 188, 191, 192
   political participation and 197, 199
German Democratic Republic 147, 229
Germany 32, 79
   civic culture in 187
   democracy in 147, 148
   Left-Right party movement in *50*
   party system 173–4
      Christian Democrats (CDU) 173, 174
      Liberals (FDP) 173–4
      Social Democrats (SPD) 173, 174
   political science in 167
   political system in 79, 92
      multi-party system 49, 50–1
   public policy analysis 215, 216, 217
   National Socialism 79, 133
   Nazism in 134, 154, 186, 230
   socio-economic development of 144–5
   unemployment in 193
   Weimar Republic of 79, 133, 230
Gerring, J. 176 n.5
Giannetti, D. 8 n.2
Gleigewichtoder Hegemonie 225
globalisation 28, 33
Goldfield, M. 162 n.4
Goldwater, B. 192
Gomez-Reino, M. 122
Goodin, R. 7, 136 n.11
Gould, J. 97 n.3
government, use of term 94
Government and Opposition 87, 90
Graham, G. S. 176 n.6
Green, D. P. 81 n.2
Guardian, The 142
Guinée-Bissau 126, 127

Hagopian, F. 6, 110
Hamilton, A. 15, 228
Hargrove, E. 210
Harvard Crimson 179
Harvard Nuclear Study Group 113
Hauser, R. 149
Heckscher, G. 97 n.4
Heclo, H. 208
Hegel, G. W. F. 235
Hirschman, A. O. 109
historicism 64
Hobbes, T. 148, 233, 234
Hochschild, J. 193, 196
Hoffman, S. 2, 223
Hoover Digest 142
Hotelling, H. 39

Howard, M. M. 186
human rights 150
Hume, D. 232
Hungary 147
Huntington, S. P. 4, 5, 7, 99–120, 122, 130
  'clash of civilisations' 4,
    100, 113–16, 117–8
    civilisation, definition of 114
  Clash of Civilisations and the
    Remaking of World Order, The 118
  comparative analysis and 108, 116–7
  democratisation and democratic
    theory 100, 110, 117, 118, 145
    economic development and 151
    'habituation' factor 112
    'overloading' and 110
    US analysis 108–11, 117
    waves of democratisation
      111–13, 145
  military, political role of 100,
    101–3, 105, 113, 116
    civil control, types of 102–3
    garrison state hypothesis and 102
    political order and 105–06
  political development 100,
    103, 106, 117
    social modernisation,
      link with 104, 106
  political order, participation
    and institutionalisation *104*,
    105–7, 109, 110, 111, 117
  Political Order in Changing
    Societies 103, 106, 107, 110
  'Promise of Disharmony, The' 111
  social modernisation and
    political order 103–8, 116
  Soldier and the State, The 101, 103, 105
  Third Wave, The 112, 145
  United States 116–7
    comparative analysis with
      Soviet Union 108
    democracy in 108–11
    policy-making 100
    role of the military 101–2, 103, 108
hyper factualism 64

ICPSR 188
identity 114

Il Corriere della Sera 176
imperialism 115
incrementalism 23–4, 40, 208–16
Index of Power Resources 146
India, political participation
  in 188–89, 191
individualism 158–9, 212–13
  competitive 216, 213
industrialisation 144, 148, 149, 160
Inglehart, R. 159
Institute for Social and Economic
  Research and Policy (ISERP) 142
institutionalisation 104, 107, 117
  Huntington's definition of 107–8
  neo-institutionalisation 175
International Political Science
  Association (IPSA) 89, 142, 167
international relations 205, 224, 225
  realism and 4, 5
  theory of 223, 226
International Society of Political
  Psychology 141
International Typographical
  Union (ITU) 152–3, 154–5
Ionescu, G. 90, 96 n.3, 97 n.7
Islamic civilisations 113, 114, 115, 116
Italy 32, 35 n.25, 188
  democracy in 187, 188
  party system in 172
    Communist Party (PCI) 172
  political science in 167–8, 176
    Centro Studi di Politica
      Comparata 168
    Italian Political Science
      Association 168
  unemployment in 193

Jackson, R. H. 176 n.6
Japan 32, 191, 193, 194
  socio-economic development of 144
Jefferson, T. 229
Jones Finer, C. 87, 90, 93, 95, 97 n.3
Journal of Democracy 142
Journal of Politics 179
Journal of Theoretical Politics 17, 184

Kaase, M. 159
Kaplan, A. 233

Karl, T. 127
Katowski, C. M. 176 n.6
Kavanagh, D. 87, 95, 96
Kennan, G. 224
Kennedy, J. F. 109
Kennedy, R. F. 109
Keohane, R. O. 197, 200 n.1
Keynes, J. M. 87
Kim, J, 194, 191
King, A. 80, 149
King, G. 183, 197
King, M. L. 5
Klingemann, H. D. 1, 80, 136 n.11
Korea 229
Kuhn, T. S. 6–7, 35 n.27

Laakso, M. 173
Lane, J. E. 176 n.6
Lasswell, H. D. 2, 101, 102, 208, 233
Latin America 123, 124, 125, 175
   authoritarian regimes in 125, 144
Laver, M. J. 54
Lazarsfeld, P. F. 8, 142, 143, 152, 162 n.1
leadership, political 113, 118, 144, 160–71
   reciprocal control and 15
   legalism 229
legitimacy 74
   charismatic authority and 160–1
   democratic 33, 144, 147, 148, 161
Lepsius, M. R. 145
Leys, C. 6
liberalism 160
Lijphart, A. 97 n.3, 136 n.11
Lindblom, C. E. 11, 12–13, 15, 23, 24, 30, 209
Linz, J. J. 4, 7, 121–39, 142
   'An Authoritarian Regime: The Case of Spain' 123, 125
   Breakdown of Democratic Regimes, The 122, 126, 128, 129, 134
   comparative analysis of 122–3, 127, 135 n.1
      national and cross-regional 127–8
   'Social Bases of Political Parties in West Germany, The' 123
   political behaviour, analysis of 123
   principles of macro-historical interpretation 132–35
   Problems of Democratic Transition and Consolidation 127
   regime-level analysis 123–25, 125, 126, 133–34
      authoritarian regimes 123, 125, 133, 134
      classification and conceptualisation of 133
      democratic breakdown 122, 126, 128, 129, 133, 134
      democratic transition and consolidation 125m 126–7, 128–31
         causal factors/arenas of 130
         observable conditions of 130–1
         political parties and 132–3
         Spain post-Franco 125, 126–7, 134–5, 135 n.4
   'Within Nation Differences and Comparisons: the Eight Spains' 123
Lippman, W. 224
Lipset, S. M. 4, 5, 7, 44, 51, 122, 123, 126, 136 n.11, 141–65, 207
   'Agrarian Socialism' 142
   American Exceptionalism 142, 157–9
   Class, Status and Power 142
   comparative analysis 141, 143
   Continental Divide 142, 158
   'Decline of Class Ideologies; the End of Political Exceptionalism?, The' 148–9
   democratic theory 143, 155, 162
   democratic stability 143, 147, 148, 151, 162
      cross-cutting cleavages and 151–2, 159
      political moderation and 159–60
   effectiveness, concept of 147–8
   legitimacy and 147, 148, 162 n.3
   intra-organisational democracy, study of 154–5
   social requisites for democracy 147
   socio-economic development and 143, 144–6, 162
      social stratification and 148–51, 160
   structural conditions for 155, 161

voluntary organisations,
    role of 152–4, 157
    U.S. analysis 142, 157–9, 160–1
        political leadership
            and 160–1
        religiosity, role of
            157–8, 163–4 n.6
Encyclopedia of Democracy 142
First New Nation, The 142,
    149, 155–6, 160–1
*It Didn't Happen Here; Why Socialism
    Failed in the United States* 142
methodological approach 143–4
*Party Systems and Voter
    Alignments* 142, 156
Politics of Unreason, The 142
Political Man 123, 142, 144,
    147, 151, 152, 156, 159–60
polities, types of 147
*Social Mobility in Industrial
    Society* 142
social stratification and
    141, 143, 148–51
        class ideology, decline of 148–9
'Social Requisites of Democracy
    Revisited' 162 n.2
*Some Social Requisites of
    Democracy* 144
Union Democracy 142, 152–55, 162 n.1
Littunen, Y. 123
Locke, J. 148, 233
Lorentz, E. 200 n.3
Lowell, A. L. 85
Lowi, T. J. 2
Luhmann, N. 65, 66, 79

McCarthy, J. 180
McDonald, M. 54
McGovern, G. 192
Machiavelli, N. 176, 225,
    226, 233, 236 n.9
McKelvey, R. 39, 47, 60 n.3
Mackenzie, W. J. M. 90
McKinley, W. 229
Macridis, R. C. 89
Madison, J. 15
    concept of democracy 15–6, 17, 34 n.4
Mair, P. 175

Majone, G. 210
majority rule, principle of 16–7
    populist democracy and 17
Mansbridge, J. 196
Marcus, G. E. 193
market economy 28
Marks, G. 141, 142, 143, 151,
    179, 200 n.2, n.4
Masuoka, N. 184
Marx, K. 143
Marxist theory and marxism
    87, 88, 93, 148–9, 170
Mastropaolo, A. 97 n.6
Maud, J. M. R. 88
Mazmanian, D. 210
Mendes, C. 125
Merritt, R. 136 n.5
Merton, R. K. 7, 159
Mexico 174, 187
Michels, R. 13, 14, 143, 154, 167
Miglio, G. 168
military
    control, types of 105
    democracy and 4
    political order and 105–6, 108
    political role of 86–7,
        100, 101–3, 105–6
            Latin America and 103
            'military-industrial complex' 101
            Muslim societies and 116
            US politics and 101–2, 116
Miller, E. F. 79
Miller, W. 39, 179, 191
Mills, C. W. 101–2
mobilisation, social 107, 108,
    117, 126, 127, 154, 169
    Portugal and 127
    student movement (1968) 109, 111
modernisation, socio-economic
    'clash of civilisations' and 115
    democracy, requisite for 144–6, 142
    link with political development
        and 104, 106–7, 108, 117
            technocratic and populist
                models 117
    post-colonial 104
    single parties and 108
Monaco, F. R. 8 n.1

monarchy 24
Montero, J. R. 122
Montesquieu, C. de S. 148
moralism 229
Morgenthau, H. 4, 7, 223–37
　balance of power and 225,
　　227, 228, 235
　In Defense of the National Interest 228
　international relations, theory
　　of 223, 226, 230–1, 234
　political realism, principles of
　　223, 225–6, 227, 230
　Politics Among Nations 224, 225,
　　227–8, 232, 233, 236 n.6
　Purpose of American Politics,
　　The 230, 236 n.7
　political science and theory 230–5
　　critique of 233–4
　political realism, principles of
　　and 223, 225–6, 227
　power politics, analysis of
　　223–4, 225–7, 234, 235
　　states and 223, 226–7
　Scientific Man vs. Power
　　Politics 230, 233
　social science, nature of 231–3
　　relationship to politics 232–3
　U.S. foreign policy critique
　　223–5, 228–30
　　　national interest,
　　　　identification of 228
Morelli, A. 24
Mosca, G. 34 n.7, 124, 167
Mozambique 127
Müller, W. C. 54
Munck, G. L. 1

National Academy for Public
　Policy Analysis 28
NATO 25, 66
Neinaber, J. 209
Nelson, J. M. 117
Netherlands, The
　Left-Right party movements *49*
　multi-party system 49
　participation study 191
New York Times 142
Nie, N. 188, 189–90, 196, 192

Nigeria 191
Nixon, R. M. 109, 111
Nobel, J. 236 n.8
Nordlinger, E. A. 118 n.3
Novak, R. 188

O'Donnell, G. 111, 133
　*Transitions from Authoritarian
　　Rule* 133
oligarchy 19
　'iron law of' 13–4, 154
Olson, M. 45
opposition, political 22
　models of 22–3
Ordeshook, P. C. 39, 47, 60 n.3
Ostrom, E. 2
Orizo, F. A. 122
Ornaghi, L. 226
Orren, G. R. 193

Panebianco, A. 1, 4
paradigm shifts 6–7
Pareto, V. 30, 87–8, 95, 124, 167, 187, 233
parliamentary systems 4, 131, 133, 175
　median position, role of 54, 55
Parry, G. 97 n.3
Parsons, T. 65–6, 71, 94, 136 n.6, 186
participation, political 4, 7, *104*,
　169, 171, 185, 186, 194–5
　'civic voluntarism' and 7, 194
　education, effect on 188, 190, 195, 197
　gender and 197, 199
　institutionalisation, level of and 105
　modes of 188, 189
　'participatory distortion',
　　concept of 196
　political order, relationship
　　with 106, 107
　race and 190, 191, 198
　socio-economic status (SES)
　　and 188, 190, 195
　Verba's participation project
　　188–91, 194–6
parties, political 155–6, 171–75
　historical interpretation of 132
party competition 14, 37, 39,
　41, 51–2, 156, 172
　bipolarism and 172–3

institutionalisation of 155
Sartori's theory of 172–3
two-party 38, 43
party systems 14, 44, 92
class analysis of 175
classification of 173, 174
Downs' models
left/right dimension and
39, 43–44, 48–51
responsibility and reliability
43, 48, 51, 53, 54
spatial and non-spatial models
37, 38, 43–4, 47–8, 51
static model 51
two-party 37, 38–9, 43, 60 n.7
voter information and 45
hegemonic 174
ideological consistency and 54
leap-frogging 49, 51, 59, 60 n.7
median parties 54–5
multi-party 49, 54, 55, 173
opposition parties 42
Sartori's analysis of 172–75
qualitative criterion for
classification 173–74
single-party 108, 174
two-party 38, 43, 173–4
voter distributions in 44
see also voting
Pasquino, G. 1, 2, 118 n.2, n.4, 176 n.1
Pateman, C. 186
Patrick, G. M. 176 n.6
Peele, G. 87
Perlmutter, A. 118 n.3
Perspectives 3
Petrocik, J. 181, 191, 192
Philippines 229
Piereson, J. E. 193
Pistone, S. 236 n.5
Plato 29, 233
pluralism 25–6, 34 n.8, 124
elitism and 101
Poland 174
policy-making 99–100
see also public administration
Policy Studies Association 208
polis 36, 31
political economy 37, 41

Political Oppositions in Western Democracies 20
political order 104–8, 109
freedom and 106, 107
single-party and 108
political realism 223, 225–6, 227
political science and theory 4–6, 233–4
attitudinal data and 13 n.5
behaviouralism 64, 77, 81,
123, 125, 135 n.4, 235
comparative analysis and 21–2, 85, 89,
92–3, 99, 122, 136 n.11, 185, 187
Sartori's critique of 168–9
critique of 5–6
economic approach and
models 11, 41, 52
empirical research, split between 233–4
empiricism 64, 77
ethics, role of 234–5
functional analysis 66
structural-functionalism
93, 124, 211
historicism 64
hyper factualism 64
ideology, use of in 52
knowledge accumulation and 6
paradigm shifts 6–7
neo-Marxism 77
'new institutionalism' 78
'quantification' of 169–70
structuralism 73, 93
systems theory/analysis 65–7,
73, 77, 78, 69–71, 93
Finer's critique 93–4
terminology of (Sartori's critique) 169
see also rational choice theory
political scientists
definition of 'classic' 6–7
definition of 'master' 7, 7–8, 121
U.S. 4, 93, 99, 110, 116, 122, 175
political sociology 142, 167, 168
political system
concept of 93
change, perspectives on 103–104
decadence of 107
development of 105–7
systems theory and 94
Politics, Economics and

Welfare 11, 13, 15, 23
pollution 215–8
Polsby, N. 218, 219 n.2
polyarchy 4, 12–14
　concept of 13, 24
　democracy and 13, 14–5, 18, 24
　preconditions of 14
　role of 13
　see also Dahl, R.
Popper, K. 6, 170
populism 15, 16, 34 n.7, 160
　theory of democracy 16–7
Portugal 125, 126, 136 n.10
　democratic transition in
　　126–7, 129, 130
Positive Political Theory 39
positivism 231
Poulantzas, N. 72
Powell, G. B. Jr. 66, 79, 183, 200 n.1, 211
Powell, J. B. 44, 48
power, politics and 223–4, 225–7
Power and Society 233
Prandi, A. 176 n.7
presidentialism 4, 131, 133, 175
　semi-presidentialism 175
　weakness of 122
Pressman, J. 210
proportional representation (PR) 54
Przeworski, A. 112, 130
public administration 205–8, 210
　historical development of 206–7
　incrementalism and 208–9
　Taylorism 207
　theoretical development of 206–7
　see also under Wildavsky
public finance, budgetary theory 209
Public Interest, The 114
public opinion 171, 179
public policy analysis 4, 7, 210
Putnam, R. 99, 107, 118 n.1, 153, 154, 194
　Bowling Alone 154
　Making Democracy Work 194
Pye, L. 184, 188

race/caste politics 189
rational choice theory 4–5, 8
　n.2, 77–8, 81 n.3, 170
　critique of 6, 52, 127
　democratic theory and 39

development of 37, 77–8
political participation, view of 194
United States and 78, 81 n.2
rationalism 231
rationality 11–2
　maximation of value of 12
　political action and 23
Reagan, R. 109, 111
reciprocity, law of 13
regimes, political
　change of 126, 127, 128
　concept of 80, 125
　functions of 123, 124
　types, definition of 124
　'partial' 129
　see also sultanistic regimes
religious belief 4
　civilisation and 114
　democratisation processes and 113, 151
　political participation and behaviour,
　　role in 123, 189, 191, 195
　separation of church and state 157
　U.S. characteristics of 157–8
representation, concept of 196
republics
　conditions for 15
Riesman, D. 142
Riker, W. 2, 39, 42
*Rivista italiana di scienza
　politica* 2, 3, 168, 169
Robertson, D. 39, 52
Robson, W. A. 89
Rohrschneider, R. 80
Rokkan, S. 2, 44, 51, 136 n.5,
　n.11, 142, 156, 188
Roller, E. 80
Roosevelt, F. D. 198, 229
Rose, R. 80
Rosenberg, M. J. 188
Rosenthal, J. 236 n.2
Rousseau, J.-J. 233
rule of law 130
Russell, G. 236 n.5
Rustow, D. A. 112, 113

Sabatier, P. 210
*Saggio teoretico di diritto
　natural appoggiato* 24

Saint-Simon, C. H. de 29, 231
Salazaar, A. de O. 125, 126–7
Sani, G. 188
Sartori, G. 2, 6, 90, 136 n.11, 167–78
   Comparative Constitutional
      Engineering 175–6
   'Concept Misformation in
      Comparative Politics' 168–9
   democracy, analysis of 170–1
      political parties and 171–5
      'real' and 'ideal' distinction 171
   Democratic Theory 170
   Democrazia; Cosa è 170
   Democrazia e definizioni 170
   Homo Videns 171
   Il Sultanato 176
   'La politica comparata:
      premesse e problemi' 169
   Mala Tempora 176
   Mala Costituzione e Altri Malanni 176
   Parties and Party Systems 172
      party systems, analysis of 171–5
      qualitative criterion for
         classification 173–4
      political theory and
         methodology 168–9, 176
      Committee on Conceptual
         and Terminological
         Analysis (COCTA) 169
      comparative theory, method
         and limits of 168–9, 176
      Italian party system and 176
      quantification and 169–70
   Theory of Democracy
      Revisited, The 171
   'Totalitarianism' 169
Schattschneider, E. E. 171–2, 198
Schlozman, K. 179, 182–3,
   193, 196, 199, 200 n.1
Schmitter, P. C. 126, 127, 129,
   132, 133, 136 n.10
   Portugalization of Brazil?, The 125
   Transitions from Authoritarian
      Rule 133
Schumpeter, J. 41, 55, 143, 171
Schwartz, M. A. 143
scientism 231, 233
Selznick, P. A. 207

Shabad, G. 181, 182, 195, 200 n.1
Shain, Y. 121, 131
Shapiro, I. 81 n.2
Shepsle, K. 183
Simmel, G. 152
Simon, H. 40, 207, 209
Smelser, N. 142
Smith, M. 236 n.2
Smithies, A. 39, 43, 208
Sniderman, P. 184, 185, 187, 199
Snyder, R. 1
social action 11–12
social capital 153, 154
social mobility 143, 149, 151
social movements 143
   disadvantaged groups and 189
   extremists 160
Social Science Citation Index 185
social sciences, explanation in 231–2
Social Science Research
   Council (SSRC) 124
social theory 99
socialisation, political 74, 76–7, 186
socialism 28, 143, 149
Society for Comparative Research 141
Sociologists, Economists
   and Democracy 39
Sola, G. 176 n.4
Sontheimer, K. 89
Soviet Union 92, 154, 229
   Cold War era 113, 229
   collapse of 108, 174
   US relations 108–9, 113, 229
Spain 229
   Centro de Investigaciones
      Sociologicas 135 n.4
   Civil War in 134
   Franco's regime 108,
      123–4, 135 n.2, n.4
   political analysis of 123, 125,
      126, 135–6 n.4, 148
   democratic transition 126,
      134–5, 135 n.2
Stenlund, H. 176 n.6
Stepan, A. 103, 121, 122, 125, 126,
   127–31, 135 n.2, 136 n.9
   Problems of Democratic Transition
      and Consolidation 127

Stern, F. 133
Sternberger, D. 89
Stokes, D. 191
Strange, S. 2
Strøm, K. 54
suffrage, universal 26
Sullivan, J. L. 192–3
sultanistic regimes 4, 122, 131
Sweden 147, 193, 194

Taagepera, R. 173
technocracy 29
Tennenbaum, E. 209
Teune, H. 176 n.6
Thatcher, M. 109
Theory of Democracy 37
Theory of Party Competition, A 39
Thomas, S. 197
Thompson, K. 236 n.6
Thompson, M. 211
Thucydides 225, 236 n.9
Tocqueville, A. de 26–7, 33, 34
  n.15, 143, 154, 159, 217, 233
totalitarianism 20, 154
  Germany's National Socialism 78, 145
  regimes 4, 7, 124, 139
Trilateral 107
Trow, M. 142, 152, 162 n.1
Truman, D. 88, 92, 152
  *The Congressional Party;
  A Case Study* 88
  The Governmental Process 88
  Truman, H. S. 224
Tsebelis, G. 8 n.2
tyranny 15, 18
  prevention of 13, 16, 20

Uhlaner, C. 181
unions, labour 149, 152–3, 195, 215, 217
United Kingdom
  comparative analysis of 110
  constitution 92
  culture, political 187
  democracy in 147
  Labour Party 92
  parliamentary analysis 88
  party competition 39
    Left-Right paths of 52

  Liberals and 174
  party-systems in 92, 173, 174
    classification of 173
  pressure groups 88
  public administration 208
    environment policy 216, 217
  regime change in 74
  Suez debate 1956 92
  unemployment and 193
United Nations 25, 66
USSR *see* Soviet Union
United States
  American Revolution 156, 158, 164 n.7
  chemical contamination, policy
    research 215, 216
  Congress 116
  constitution of 32–3, 161
  civil rights movement 192
  crime and corruption in 159
  culture, political 114–5, 156, 158, 228
    individualism and 158
    citizen role and trust 187
  Democratic Party 44, 47, 49, 50–1
  comparative analysis and
    21–2, 92, 108, 123
  democracy in 4, 32, 108–11, 117,
    146, 147,223, 230, 235
    education and 150, 151
    socio-economic development
      and 148, 149–51
    social mobility, level of 149
    voluntary associations
      and 154, 158, 194
  electoral behaviour 191–3
  equality in 149–50, 151,
    158–9, 194, 198
      impact of activism on 194
      racial 150, 193
  federalism in 31–2
  foreign policy 157, 223–5, 227, 228–9
    Cold War era 229, 236 n.8
    history of 228–9
    Monroe doctrine 229
    national interest, identification
      of 228, 229
  identity, political and cultural 114–5
  military, political role of
    101–2, 108–11, 116, 224

defence strategy 108–11
  see also United States,
    foreign policy
participation analysis 189,
  190, 194–6, 198
  race and 189, 190, 193, 195, 198
  socio-economic status
    (SES) and 190, 195
parties and party systems
  46, 48, 55, 156
  Left-Right movements in 50
party competition, theory/models of 38
  two-party 48–9, 156
presidentialism in 4, 205
public administration 207
  oil and gas policies 209
  environment and pollution
    control 216, 217
religion, role of 157–8, 163–4 n.6
  'utopian moralism' (Lipset) 157
Republican Party 44, 47, 49, 50–1
unemployment in 193, 200 n.5
welfare and 150–1
universalism 115
urbanisation 144, 146, 148

Valenzuela, A. 121, 131
Van Horn, C. 210
Van Meter, D. 210
Van Roozendaal, P. 54
Vanhanen, T. 145–6
Verba, S. 4, 7, 156, 159, 179–203
  American Voter, The 190, 191–2
  *Changing American Voter,
    The* 191, 192, 193
  Civic Culture, The 179, 180, 181,
    186–8, 189, 190, 194, 196, 198
  datasets, collection of 180,
    183, 194, 197–8
  democratic stability 186, 187, 194
    civic culture and 186–7
      values of 187
    civic voluntarism and 194–5
    regime support and 187
    socialisation and 186
  electoral behaviour 191
  equality, analysis of 179–80,
    193–197, 198–9

  impact of activism on 194
  interest groups, dataset 180
  *Modes of Democratic
    Participation, The* 188
  *Participation and Political
    Equality* 191
  Participation in America
    189–91, 196, 198
  political participation project 185,
    186, 188–91, 194, 198–9
    education, role of 188,
      190, 195, 197
    India/US comparison 188–9
    'participatory distortion',
      concept of 196
    socio-economic model,
      use of 190, 191, 195
    typology of participatory
      acts 189–90
    U.S. analysis 188–9,
      191–3, 195, 198
  Private Roots of Public Action, The 196
  *Small Groups and Political Behavior;
    A Study of Leadership* 185
  theory and methodology of
    183, 184–5, 197–8, 199
    comparative analysis
      184, 1186, 189
    factor analysis 188, 189, 191
    qualitative 187, 198
    U.S. analysis 184
  Voice and Equality 195, 196–7, 199
Viet, J. 188
Vietnam War 107, 109, 111, 224
  attitudes towards 188, 192
Vila, D. 122
voluntary associations 152–4, 185, 194
von Hayek, F. 231
von Ranke, L. 225
voting 37, 51
  ideology and 51, 52
  issues and 51, 52
    issue constraint 192–3
  median elector 55
  Michigan model 191
  'paradox of' 6
  reliability and responsibility,
    importance of 43, 48, 51, 53

turnout and 37, 45
see also electoral behaviour;
   participation, political

Waldo, D. 207
Walker, J. L. 22
Wallace, G. 192
Waltz, K. 224
Warren, M. 196
Washington, G. 160, 161, 228
Washington Post 142
Watson, A. 224, 236 n.3
Wattenberg, M. 39
Webber, C. 205
Weber, M. 2, 65, 75, 143, 160–1, 212, 213
   bureaucracy and 212
Wheare, K. 90
Whitten, G. D. 48
Wilcox, C. 197
Wildavsky, A. 4, 5, 7, 205–20
   chemical contamination,
      political analysis of 215–6
   Doing More and Using Less 215
   Implementation 210–1
   incrementalism, analysis of 208–9
   *Leadership in a Small
      Town* 208, 219 n.2
   political culture 211–8
      culture, concept of 211–3
         basic dimensions of 212
         ideal-typical models 212–3
      pollution policy approaches
         to 216–7
   *Politics of the Budgetary
      Process, The* 208, 209
   Presidential Elections 208, 219 n.1
   public administration, analysis
      of 205–08, 209–11
      budgetary and public
         finance theory 209
   public policy research 210–1
      implementation 210
      pollution and, cross-national
         analysis 215–8
   theory and methodology of
      206, 212–3, 215, 218
Williams, R. 97 n.3
Wilson, W. 206, 227, 229, 231

Windhoff-Héritier, A. 81
World Association for Public
   Opinion Research 141
World War II 229
Wright, W. 46

Yugoslavia 191

www.ingramcontent.com/pod-product-compliance
Lightning Source LLC
Chambersburg PA
CBHW071350290426
44108CB00014B/1490